PROSTHESIS

MERIDIAN

Crossing Aesthetics

Werner Hamacher

& David E. Wellbery

Editors

Stanford
University
Press

———

Stanford
California
1995

PROSTHESIS

David Wills

Stanford University Press
Stanford, California

© 1995 by the Board of Trustees of the
Leland Stanford Junior University

Printed in the United States of America

CIP data appear at the end of the book

Stanford University Press publications
are distributed exclusively by
Stanford University Press
within the United States,
Canada, and Mexico; they are
distributed exclusively by
Cambridge University Press
throughout the rest of the world.

for
Norman Williams Wills
and
Frances Ada Wills

Acknowledgments

It would be impossible to provide here an exhaustive account of all those to whom I am indebted for their generous help, in the form of readings and suggestions, during the writing of this book over the last ten or so years: relatives, friends, collaborators, colleagues, students, colloquium participants. I hope they will accept this impersonal but no less sincere expression of my gratitude. Some of them will no doubt recognize their contributions to and in the writing itself.

I am similarly grateful for the financial support provided for the research and writing of this book, namely in the form of summer grants from the Louisiana State University Center for French and Francophone Studies in 1986 and the LSU Council on Research in 1987. Support was also provided by the Elliott Dow Healy Memorial Fellowship in 1990.

Parts or earlier versions of Chapters 5, 6, and 9 have appeared, respectively, in the following publications: Marie-Louise Mallet, ed., *Passage des frontières: Autour du travail de Jacques Derrida* (Paris: Galilée, 1994); *Assemblage* 19 (1992); and E. A. Grosz, Terry Threadgold, David Kelly, Alan Cholodenko, and Edward Colless, eds., *Futur*Fall: Excursions into Post-Modernity* (Sydney: Power Institute of Fine Arts, 1986). Kind permission to reprint from these publications is gratefully acknowledged. An article entitled "Prosthesis: An Introduction to Textual Artifice," which served as the basis for some of what is elaborated in this book, and echoes of which can be heard in Chapter 8, was published in *Southern Review* 17, no. 1 (1984).

A Holiday at Mentone is reproduced with permission from the Art Gallery of South Australia. The extract from Wilson's *Arte of Rhetorique* is reprinted with permission from the Newberry Library.

D.W.

Contents

PROSTHESIS

§ 1   Hamilton, 1970

Shifting from one to the other as though there could be some sort of even transfer or equal distribution, as though beyond it all there was perfect or at least functionally satisfactory balance between the two, and failing to find it, failing to find an end to the discomfort of one and the other position, the one too ready to give way under prolonged exertion, the other too rigidly secure in its own uprightness, and in the interstice no easy middle, no ground for rest or resolution, nothing but more of the same for so long now it seems it is some stubborn automation that keeps bringing things back to this sore and overloaded point where the question is asked as vivid and visceral as the sight of innumerable instruments, where the next fateful step is posed, where the ax is poised and readies for the fall, still, still suspended, waiting for a go or for any other imperceptible but indispensable iota of the informational magma, something to set it off, all of it here and now, to have done, to cross or cut or break the ice, go with whatever flow flows, progressively readied for a command that is an invitation that is a decision, a concentration of diverse modalities at the precise point of their crisis, this point that takes it all in and shunts it through, scoping out the entire field, looking for what it knows already to be the programmed outcome, presuming that there is time for looking, at will or at leisure, for if this were about reflection, rumination, and decision then that would be the tilt on it, rather than another, this one, the idea that anything to come is already in train and not a fact or event of will or design but a repetition, more like another notch or cog or twist through some silicon junction, some slight optic fibrous kink in a long straight line that connects two differences, an event whose precedents can't be seen when it happens from this vantage, the disadvantage at this point where it is about to, where there is shifting, waiting, laborious mechanical buildup, then stirring again, shifting, inclining this way then that, rocking unevenly from side to side under the control of a dislocated fulcrum, as if edging towards a critical terminus, an idiosyncratic master narrative creaking towards breaking, the expectation builds again but it will still manage to come from nowhere, there is no controlling it in spite of finally leaning way out against gravity with all the grace of pure dissent, the candor of a protracted liminal pause that provokes its own interruption, dancing on the fluid edges of an affirmative no return, shifting until it tips, scales and all, flips and suddenly falls, there is no cause or origin for it, it arrives with all the searing intensity of a wild-card ray and razes the field, crossing over with multiple warp atomic swiftness into otherness, cutting through the geometrical cardhouse as if there were nothing there, although the moment seems saturated beyond all logical possibility, so much passing so fast it makes no sense to grasp it, just tap tap tap away with a Pacman impulsive finger as rapid as the tendons allow in the hope of swallowing the odd flying fragment, for the data dam is bursting on this axial pinpoint such that nothing can be said to be present there within the bounds of a confinable space, nothing but phantoms of the present where all is shifting, crossings, functions of relay, except that perhaps, what else to say, across that ghost of a space there comes the change, where once there was only shifting there is suddenly a beast rampant in triumphant otherness, all fluid and gleaming the throes of a cataclysmic future convulsion in which metal fuses with flesh, the cyborg synthetic ecstasy that is the fiction of a science or the science of a fiction and the love of a machine past all fear of rejection, all the way across some still-retreating threshold or barrier—the pain, the language—beyond the familiar landmarks where this writhing takes place, first this way then that in a slow and irregular shuffle that goes nowhere, nowhere in particular and no further than the indifferent here and now, then and there, that is the subject of this, prosthesis.

He would be standing at the kitchen sink, his elbows resting on the edge, his eyes staring vaguely or precisely ahead, one couldn't tell. Ahead was an inlet tap for a hot-water cylinder where a partially dry dishcloth was hanging. It wasn't the cloth for washing dishes but for wiping tables. Behind the tap a wall, obviously an exterior wall. Perhaps he was staring into nothingness or at least the end of sight. There was nowhere to look, he had looked there before and there were no surprises. This was nothing looking could shed light on. He would be half doubled over, an angle of some 135 degrees at the waist, one leg a little tiptoed to enable the other to just swing free. Or, leaning forward on his elbows to displace the weight, he would rock slowly from side to side, sighing an underarticulated groan, breathing deeply to prepare for the next spasm, then contorting his face into his stock wince, the one for all seasons, all varieties of pain and distaste, even before the twitch would come. The next one, for it was never the first, no more than the first of the series. It was something between a phantom pain and a rheumatic or arthritic disorder. Something ethereal, fluid, or mechanical, it mattered little except that it stung like an exposed nerve, like a stump grieving an absent leg. There was nothing to be done for it short of mass consumption of analgesics, so he would wince, sigh and yelp, wait and waver, shift again and again, for the length of a lifetime, then straighten up and get back to washing the dishes.

And back to Virgil. There is a line from Virgil he keeps repeating. It is an incantation pressed into service to preempt the arrival of the spasm, an affirmation of mind over the random mayhem of phantom matter, as if it were already established that pain is matter, that phantom pain is situated in the flesh. It is a chant or conjuration whose sound has some sort of soothing effect, whose rhythm at least sets off what dreams can only be imagined, or simply detracts from the whole gamut of pains he is subject to, the urgent will to closure of tattered nerves that interrupt his sleep and wire his waking hours. It is an incantation or conjuration imported into this occasion from schoolboy memories of foreign tongues; foreign and unspoken tongues. It is a line from a dead language: *quadrupedante putrem sonitu quatit ungula campum*—"the hoof strikes the dusty plain in a four-footed rhythm."[1] As it happens, there is no immediate translation, none rendered explicit, although there is nothing but translation when it comes down to it. To all appearances just the rote repetition to accompany a shifting of the haunches in anticipation of more of the same pain, though it is never the same, for it trades always on the level of the unpredictable, its intensity, its timing, like lightning or an earthquake on the inside of an infirm body.

The line is from Virgil. It contains the maximum number of syllables possible in a classical hexameter, all the feet except the last being dactyls. $|-\smile\smile|-\smile\smile|-\smile\smile|-\smile\smile|-\smile\smile|--|$. It is a chant or conjuration, to exhort or exorcise. It is a piece of narrative extracted by virtue of its excessive poetic effect, a grossly literal application of the Jakobsonian principle, a wholesale syntagmatization by rhythmic effect of the semantic sense.[2] A line about galloping feet the paradigm for a line full of feet, or for feet full of toes, or full of beats, beating hooves, beating feet. But it is the line that gets a one-legged man dancing. Leaning on his elbows shuffling from flesh to metal and back, anticipating the next onslaught of an intimate phantom he is chanting, and before he knows it dancing through the spastic turn that otherwise shifts the weight from one leg to the other at the whim of nervous impulse, dancing through it into a gallop worthy of a classical mounted warrior.

As we hear them through the transliteration of a less inflected English, the Latin words come in well nigh any order. The laws of syntax seem to abdicate their authority, but that authority has simply been displaced from functions of consecution among words to operations of inflection within them. Conversely, the laws of semantics seem to abdicate their authority over the operations of syntax, ceding to the powerful forward impulsion of the sentence's rhythm. In fact the effect of this particular syntagmatic disposition is to reinscribe the semantic sense so that there is continual shifting between linguistic planes. It is quite simply a concentration of what occurs in any utterance, distilled in a form we are used to calling poetry. Still, it amounts to a troubling of order, and of order between orders, a series of questions posed at the points of articulation and about the point of articulation itself.

The Latin is something of a ploy, Virgil a pretext. It isn't as if he spoke it. He quotes it at the kitchen sink bent over with discomfort, shifting from one side to the other, waiting for another stroke to fall, running out of means to parry the blow, trying to second-guess the irregularity of the sequence and opting for the rhythm of the slow shuffle, the back and forth motion that governs much more than dishwashing. And he overlays that with a line from Virgil about four-hooved horses galloping across a dusty plain, doubling the tempo and counterpointing his spondaic two-step with a rapid dactylic waltz, once, twice, three, four, five times, until on the sixth foot he achieves a harmonious resolution, the equilibrium of a perfect self-division, and outruns the spasm that lurks behind every single uttered syllable. Or doesn't, and jerks himself upwards suddenly all out of joint, the body off beat, and thrusts his elbows against his hips and sniffs back the mucus that drips onto the perspiration glistening on his upper lip not the result of the steam rising from the kitchen sink. And straightens up.

He works from right to left. He begins by taking the silverware—not the

2 trombling of order

knives lest he damage the deep beige Bakelite handles—and placing it in one of the smaller saucepans; then he runs the hottest water directly from the cylinder in front of him onto the metal soap dispenser, holding its handle and jiggling to ensure maximum lathering. The soap is homemade, suitable for dish- and clothes-washing only, manufactured by some mysterious process that involves stirring resin and molten fat saved from the Sunday roasts in the copper out in the yard and at some point adding caustic soda. Eventually the mistake will be made of using the newly available aluminum pot, with the result that hydrochloric fumes will blow through the house and almost suffocate an infant. A consensual injunction will thereafter descend on this artisanal soap production, but it is not yet in force at the moment represented here. The saucepan with the silver sits in the corner of the sink that is filled with just enough water to cover a couple of dinner plates at a time, there is more shaking of the soap dispenser, then the washing proper begins, the knives and forks still steaming as they lie in the dishrack waiting to be dried with the white cloth with a tinge of the pink and chemical scent of Goddard's Silver Cleaner, the colored cloth for the rest, they both hang to dry in the cupboard attached to the wall by the back door, at right angles to the window that lets in the sunlight—it was a clever idea, it was his idea to have the tea towels dry there instead of on some overcrowded rack on the back of a door—the window that gives a view straight across the lawn where there used to be a potato patch and now another house, it can all be explained, and perhaps some of it will be but who knows yet how, or in what order.

He works quickly, allowing himself to be interrupted only when the intensity or frequency of the pain cannot be borne standing upright. But even then his body always moves, constantly shuffles, slowly sways. He is forever chiding his children for jigging, as though in repressing the accelerated shaking of their legs he could keep the jerk of his own body at bay. But his is not the jitter he inveighs so automatically against in others; this is more like a rhythmic largo waver in the manner of a martial artist's pose *en garde* against the approach of horses likely to gallop so suddenly roughshod over his body, with Virgil's words the always possible displacement of what hurts like a kick to an open wound returning with all their metonymical precedence so as to almost occupy a relation of cause, or at least an insoluble question about which comes first, Virgil's horses or the wrack of a phantom pain. In one story, or in one recounting of it, what comes first is the Virgil learned in a chalkdusty schoolroom some 35 years previously in a town of often steep sunny hills overlooking white sandy beaches with gentle waves and a name like Tahunanui and all the time in the world to savor for a boy with two good legs and a love of learning and the best memory for Latin verse in the class. Then the horses held no threat or premonition. Learning the line was more like some sort of initiation into adulthood where Virgil replaced the childish ditty heard on his father's knee rocked up and down in accelerating cadence to the rhythm of "this is the way the farmer goes, jig-jog, jig-jog, this is the way the lady goes, trit-trot, trit-trot, etc.," all the way through canter to the huntsman's gallop; there is a whole history of ambulation to be recounted here, from walking to cycling, through hopping and limping, the history of locomotion and propulsion also, starting from the bouncing of a child on a father's knee, bouncing higher with the progression of the verse up and up to the huntsman's gallop that had one launched what seemed like yards into the air to land again on the firm safe ground of a paternal knee. It was part of an oral tradition; his father did it for him and he would do it for his own children, he the father of the child I am closer to talking about from here on, and his artificial leg was no impediment to the movement of the other one when sitting, so there was jig-jogging through infancy for all and galloping to the sound of doggerel as well as Virgil and through it all a mere child was thrust high in the air off his father's knee, with the momentous force of a set of calf muscles developed to do the work of two legs, higher and higher until everything is let go, the universal stays loosened, suspended there for as long as this prose can hold out or hold off the inevitable fall, waiting and hoping that below everything will revert to manageable order, or some suitable or respectable disposition, waiting for the words as well as the legs to be arranged beyond the arbitrariness of Latin verse to receive this descent or catastrophe, the prosodic event that guides me down, this "I" that speaks henceforth out of the caesura of a broken rhythm, punctuating the citation whereby a father fends off his ghosts of pain, thrown into the space above him, the waiting space where I share the anticipation of an unwelcome spasm, it is I who floats in the air inches or miles above him, a rudimentary orbital contraption flying high over a father who could no longer ever jump free of himself and his mechanical attachment but who wants me to come down with all the certainty of a dependable surrogate, the sensation landing where and when he knows how to prepare for it, he tosses me the way the huntsman goes gallopy gallopy gallopy, has me flailing in the air all dactylic and immaterial then coming down again to rest in his lap, my small legs reaching only to his knees, feeling the warmth of the one and learning, me too, to love the cold steel of the other, the prosthesis that was there from the very beginning.

I can relate all this. I am standing there beside him drying the dishes. He is leaning on his elbows trying to decide whether to wait for another spasm, not that he has any choice, for it will come whether he waits or not; it is more a matter of deciding how to deal with it, in which position it would be preferable to receive it, so I am waiting too, pausing in midsentence when he bends over, never sure whether to let his controlled yelp interrupt the flow of my prose, never knowing whether I will still be able to resume along the same lines, indeed in the same language, once the phantom has made its wretched pass. I am left undecided whether to have his ghost materialize, uncertain to what extent to acknowledge the intensity of the pain on his behalf, for that would mean I was collaborating in it, expressing what might for this circumstance be better unsaid, indeed even impossible for me to say, for how many times does he have to speak his pain to remind himself that it is there, and what right have I to impose confession in favor of repression, to adjudicate the precise level of avowal necessary for health or for some other higher good. There I am. I am the age he was when he had his leg amputated. Eighteen years old. I am soon to leave home. He is letting me go, but coming back to me now, stampeding across my consciousness with the chant of a line from Virgil.

My father's Virgil is partly for his own benefit, partly for mine; it is a conjuration against the pains that shoot from his truncated leg and at the same time an exhortation to the junior dishdryer to hurry up and to stop complaining about the overwhelming arduousness of the task. It is not simply consciously one and unconsciously the other; the relation is more one of indifference. It isn't as if he recites it every time he bends over to resist the nervous impulses controlling his body, but it is always there, always within the performative context of the speech his body acts out. As long as I stand next to him I am drawn into the performance. By leaving I can forget his pain, forget his Virgil, until it comes back to me like a chilly haunting, like something one wakes up repeating in the early morning silence of receding dreams. Wanting to recite again what was once imprinted upon my memory like a rhyme from the nursery, wanting again the intimacy of a familiar quotation, I ask him for it. For the sake of academic interest I ask for the reference. He tells me it comes from the

Aeneid, Book 8, line 596. He didn't remember the chapter and verse himself any more and had to call up my old high school. He was surprised to learn that Latin is still being taught there, by a woman now, gone the stern disciplinarian who taught it in my youth, you had to put your cap folded down the back of your shorts to soften the blow from his cane for he was as pedantically meticulous about having the rod fall on exactly the same spot on your arse as he was about our recognizing the fall of the stress as we parsed Virgil. But that is not the Virgil in question here, although the sting of a cane across my backside was the only model with which to make a quantitative comparison between my own suffering and endurance and the spasm that convulsed my father's body. Thus Virgil is always implicated in it, the memory of Latin verse overlaying or overlaid by a burst of phantom pain, such that it is now my way back, a long way back through a way of words, a way with words, to a moment where they are all there is between us, and all he has between the nerve ends flailing like the hairs of some electric anemone threatening to spark on contact.

The Latin is thus something of a ploy; a pretext. It wasn't as if he spoke it, but then he didn't speak any other foreign language, at least not at the time the story was told. He would utter the odd word or phrase in French from time to time, but those phrases were just as much quotations as the Latin. He didn't speak foreign tongues, he quoted them, and the two he quoted were French and Latin. They were the languages one learned, and he had learned them well, or at least had begun to learn them after the citational fashion in which one learned a second European language half a world away from Europe back then. He learned to quote them well enough to earn prizes and distinctions. He would have liked to have learned to speak one properly, but things got in the way—tumors, amputations, prostheses. So he left them with me. In more than one sense I have taken over where he left off in making a habit of a foreign language. My learning of a language replaces what was cut short in his experience by the amputation of a leg. I take it to the academic extreme, make a business out of it, go far out on a limb with it, all in order to come back, to feel again the jolt of a quotation and write the text of a phantom pain, to explore the articulations of one and the other, of one with the other, this first prosthetic relation of a suffering body and a language straining against its classical constrictions, this limping ghost of Virgil and this galloping infirmity of the body standing in for and over against each other in the crowded space of a halting writing.

So the Latin is little more than a quotation now. I can't repeat the performance, just quote the irony of a cripple's repeating a line from Virgil about four-hooved horses galloping across a dusty plain. It was I who would encourage him to repeat it, never, I swear, aware of the irony. Or perhaps repressing it—I'll allow that—such that now it returns, my repressed relation to irony, as an ironic relation to the father, to this writing, to all manner of stepfathers, fathers-in-writing; nevertheless constrained by them, limping along with them in search of a discourse whose rhythms could have an amputee articulate his pain while promoting the cause of quoting, if not writing, texts, rewriting texts, the texts of literature, the texts of life and limb. So here I am, standing beside him, soon to leave with echoes of Virgil for a world of quotations every one of which sounds like a way back to a place next to an amputee father swaying in expectation at the kitchen sink, this way then that, shifting the weight and emphasis from one side to the other, from what he calls his good leg to what I call his prosthetic one, the shifts mine also here and now, alternately, unexpectedly, and indifferently this then that, critical posture and narrative of a father's stance to be adopted whenever a particular impulse kicks in; it is from the same point that I embark upon the doubtful enterprise of this, prosthesis.

Prosthesis begins here, then, or there, now, in a quotation, with a piece of text accompanying the discomfort of an amputee father, and with the difficulty of rigorously separating one from the other. But it only begins to the extent that this writing of it picks up at that particular juncture, seizing upon the fact of a literary reference that triples as a childhood memory and a paternal exorcism to set it in train. Thus the quotation appears, first of all, as excision, in its etymological sense of quota or part belonging to each of many, and hence in its sense of articulation, relation of part to other parts and to a whole, and in the sense of a radical rewriting of that relation in and through the prosthetic. For the writing of prosthesis, as is demonstrated by the triple juncture that serves as its pretext, is inevitably caught in a complex play of displacements; prosthesis being about nothing if not placement, displacement, replacement, standing, dislodging, substituting, setting, amputating, supplementing. It begins in a juncture that is already a displacement from its more obvious focus, with a Virgil and a spasm that are metonymic to a more general written exposition—this book called *Prosthesis*—and a more literal anatomical fact—the prosthesis that my father wears as his left leg.

Prosthesis treats of whatever arises out of that relation, and of the relation itself, of the sense and functioning of articulations between matters of two putatively distinct orders: father/son, flesh/steel, theory/fiction, translation/quotation, literal/figurative, familiar/academic, rhetoric/medicine, rhetoric/cybernetics, French/English, nature/artifice, public/private, straight/limping, and so on. But it is itself similarly divided between "prosthesis" and "*Prosthesis*," a wooden leg and this writing. They are a pair whose difference is the whole matter at stake, and yet whose rigorous differentiation would entail the collapse of this entire critical edifice. It is not simply that their difference is reduced to the extent that whatever there is of a wooden leg comes to be contained within the bounds of this writing, that there is only in fact a *Prosthesis* that happens to be composed, in part, of an account of a father's prosthesis. We can as easily say that the writing of *Prosthesis* is divided within and even against itself not just by virtue of a decision concerning strategy but by the very fact of a father's prosthesis; that is, it is the wooden leg, together with all the returning phantoms that work through it, what can be called a generalized prosthetization, that determines the composition of *Prosthesis*, making it an uneasy combination of different discourses.

The relation between this text and my father's wooden leg should obviously be read as akin to that between a line from Virgil and a phantom pain. Which determines which or what rhetorical relation holds them together is of questionable relevance as long as we cannot know whence a phantom pain derives: to say that a line learned in a dusty schoolroom has been pressed into service by the fear of an approaching phantom pain is perhaps no more logical than to say that the spasm that grieves the loss of a leg is but a symptom of a greater grief for the loss of a language, for an amputation of a life of learning. Virgil, we can but say, is prosthetic to a phantom. Whatever sets itself up as originary in the development of prosthesis—this writing, that wooden leg—has all the consistency of a ghost.

Given, therefore, that prosthesis, *Prosthesis*, begins with a quotation, given that its first uttered pretext is from the literary canon, its conceit would appear to be to undertake an act of criticism or theory that deals with the mechanical in that most humanistic of discourses, the artistic; in order to demonstrate to what extent a supposed natural creation relies on artificial devices of various kinds. But given also that that quotation occurs in a complex articulation—from which it can no longer be extracted—with an amputee father's discomfort, then any single and singular exposition of its conceit would be impossible, divided in its writing by effects of that articulation. *Prosthesis* then becomes a prosthesis. Its act of criticism or theory slips back and forth between an apparent constative and a more obviously performative mode, in and out of fiction and autobiography. This might indeed be a demonstration, but one whose parameters tend to collapse within the experiment itself, whose object has come to problematize its investigative apparatus; like the semantics and syntactics of a line from Virgil.

That would also be what distinguishes it from something like a thematics of the prosthetic in literature. For although it finds an artistic or cultural pre-text for each of its expositions—a line from Virgil, a painting by Conder, a theory by Freud, a film by Greenaway, a text by Derrida, novels by Roussel or Gibson, a sixteenth-century rhetoric, each of which connects thematically or theoretically with the question of prosthesis—it in no way claims to account for the myriad amputees of Western literature. It embarks instead upon the production of its own literary artifact in the form of a fragmentary and episodic story of a father's wooden leg.

Prosthesis—the word will no longer be able to stand alone, confident in its diacritical difference, as the title of a book—is thus the awkward conjunction of two discourses, one with all the institutional legitimacy of the academy, the other haunting and calling from a place that is both more familiar and more foreign, but as insistent as the rhythm of a line from Virgil. And it is similarly the confounding of all sorts of criteria by which those discourses are used to being distinguished, prioritized, grounded, upheld. Such criteria are to some extent suspended, though never simply abandoned, in favor of the fact of conjunction itself, the operations of conjunction by which, obeying some unorganized combination of chance and design, one mode, voice, discourse, or writing is exchanged for another. There is, as I have said, a complicated figure for this, a figure that amounts to a textual configuration: it is the phantom pain that haunts my father's amputated leg, the anticipation of its irregular yet inevitable return, the automated reaction it demands, and the literary quotation that so often accompanies it. When it arrives, the precise shape of all those attendant factors is not easy to unravel, yet it seems to sweep them all away before its implacable surge. All we can say with any certainty is that within the space inhabited by the phantom, we have suddenly switched to another mode. What has occurred above all else is that rapid transfer; a transfer not so much from the artificial, for instance, to the natural, or vice versa, but into the ghostly space of the prosthetic. If, as we are bound to do, we read the pain as the return of some repressed, then it will not be, for me, the body reasserting its primacy over the ratiocinations of everyday existence, calling from some 30 years back to say "you cut me and it still hurts," not that so much as the body in its prosthetic function, in its artificial and contrived articulations, coming like some metallic specter to haunt the well-sewn surface of originary flesh.

The significance and effect of transfer is not something subsequent to a given prosthesis but rather what occurs at its beginning, as its beginning. Prosthesis occurs as a rapid transfer. The extreme form of that transfer is to be developed out of the sense of beginning that this prosthesis finds in a quotation and the necessity of its translation. There may be on the one hand a desire to occlude the fact that it has no idea where else to start. Where would such a thing, a prosthesis, have to start in order to have started? How would it begin? To be made, built, or constructed? To be told or written? On the other hand any occlusion at the beginning is the effect of transfer, the fact of its being already in process. The translation from Latin into English, for instance, is preceded by the imprecise transfer occurring between phantom pain and Virgil, and the phantom pain is an even more unaccountable effect of, or transfer from, an amputation. It is here that we reach the extreme sense of transfer or translation as more precisely ablation, the idea of a transfer across and into nothingness, a carryover that is a carrying off, the event of radical loss or irretrievability. The passage of Virgil's horses galloping through the beginning of this prosthesis thus has the effect of carrying off the very beginning that it might seem to institute, leaving its trace only in the form of a phantom, a chill wind like a sudden violent spasm that renders the surface of things all gooseflesh, the precise cause gone away and awry.

One could posit for it another type of beginning in the conjugational disjunction—the dysfunctional syntagmatic transfer—of a peculiarly irregular Latin verb, *ferre* (to bear; past participle *latum*), doing double duty in a hermeneutic gesture that relates and refers everything back to a series of shifts, bringing discourse back to a fact of being borne, to a point of weight transfer.[3] Whether of a wooden-legged father relaying corporeal mass to run down a nervous spasm, or of galloping horses propelling hooves into the air. Thanks to the same Latin verb, to the idea of trans*fer* as trans*lation*, such a fundamental shift functions as a movement or spacing of and into difference. From earthbound gallop to quadrupedantic flight, from leg of flesh to leg of steel, it is necessarily a transfer into otherness, articulated through the radical alterity of ablation as loss of integrity. And this otherness is mediated through the body, works through the operation of a transitive verb—*movere, ferre*—signifying first of all something carried by the body. In translation, what is carried across or transferred is borne by the body. But it doesn't just carry itself; it carries a self that is divided in its function—walking, carrying. Before it begins to carry anything external to itself it bears that effect of its own internal scission. Thus it is the otherness that the body must carry in order to move that begins—and a first-person adjective is now ready to bear it—this our prosthesis.

To the extent that the paradigm for translation is a transfer through the body, something borne by the body, one can begin to account for something of its structural imprecision or even impossibility. A hexameter of Latin can easily, in spite of its jumbled syntax, pass into another language such as English. We have seen that occur. What does not pass so easily—although a great deal of effort could still be expended in the attempt—is the idiosyncrasy of the rhythmic effect that Virgil was able to create. The galloping horses make only an ungainly stumble into the receiving language; they might be said simply not to translate, not to carry over into English. But this can be brought home much more clearly through the prosthetic relation. There the line from Virgil is already a translation, in the sense of a displacement or transfer of the anticipation of another such—translation, transfer, or displacement—from the body restrained to the body spastic, itself the effect of a transfer from the body whole to the body lacking, and so on. Even if much of what is borne by the word passes, translates, not so readily the horses the body bears, the convulsions that course through it, not without the contrivance of this transferential interface I am calling prosthesis. And that is not to ascribe some authenticity to the body beyond the reach of the word, unless it be the authenticity of some originary mourning, for this is an amputated leg we are talking about here, these are ghosts of pains. The importance of the translation comes to be seen not so much in what does or does not pass through the prosthetic interface as in the operation of transfer itself, especially in the agency of the body in that transfer. Those twitches do translate, however uneconomically, however approximately, however much of them be left unexpressed. We have all felt such convulsions, though not of course these particular ones. So they translate only through the idiosyncrasy of corporeal sensation, yet that implies also the untranslatability of personal pain. The whole gamble here is to translate or render that in this writing, and it is therefore a writing that must fail even as it succeeds, whose sense must be carried away even as it carries over, a writing the imprecision of whose articulations will necessarily approach the impossible.

So we return to the beginning for prosthesis there, in a quotation, with a piece of text accompanying the discomfort of an amputee father or vice versa, in any case with the rapid shift from one to the other, such that we cannot expect to separate one from the other rigorously, prevent the impulse of metonymic transfer. I say "metonymic transfer" in the sense of a bottom-line apposition on the basis of which a whole complicated and imprecise rhetorical apparatus will come into play. There is of course as much of metaphor as metonymy in prosthesis; in fact a powerful will-to-analogy functions through the narrative mode that attaches a wooden leg to a theoretical discussion. But let us not forget that metonymy and metaphor, or syntagmatic and paradigmatic rhetorical operations in general, are transferential modulations whose directional opposition is a contrivance—can we say a prosthesis?—a contrivance that utterance in general, to the extent that it is poetic in Jakobson's sense, is bound to call into question.[4] How much more so this conjunction of a phantom pain and an epic horse, an intermittent story of a father's wooden leg and a series of readings? It is as a result of the transfer, translation, and ablation that is in play from the outset, and as a result of the troubling or suspension of order—the four horses leaving the ground, the pain in the form of a spectral anticipation, the words all back to front, the prosthesis prosthetic to the *Prosthesis*, prosthetic to the prosthesis, or to "prosthesis," and so on—it is as a result of such a suspension that what I called apposition becomes more of an enfolding through which allegory plays but cannot attribute to itself any privilege. At the risk of provoking an abyssal indistinction, I'd like to call every rhetorical form that comes into effect a prosthetic transfer, I'd like prosthesis to be the figure here for differential, and differantial, relations in general. I'd like to ask what it would mean for the term to assume such a universality insofar as reference to it—at least in this instance of which there will be none other, not quite ever—remains connected, in ways that are the whole story here, to my father's wooden leg, and in turn to his reluctant body. How would the particular idiomatic and idiosyncratic pathos of this leg that is like no other, the singular event of my father's prosthesis I am claiming here, how would that remain in and through the inevitable and necessary, imprecise and generalized transfer that occurs the moment this writing begins, and even before? One answer is quite clearly that there never was any such event in its pure singularity: prosthesis is the idea of that. The fact that all this comes down by way of my father is a convenient instantiation of its divisibility; the partial and artificial body that I claim, with dubious authority, as my own, as the basis for at least a part of my text, is a counterfeit countersignature of his suffering and infirmity. Prosthesis is the idea of that and at the same time the insistence on this instance, the singular pathos of this leg. The articulation of one with the other, this leg and that idea, can only be contrived, for instance by means of quotation marks or other diacritical forms, the drawing of distinctions between prosthesis, "prosthesis," and *Prosthesis*, in other words by effects of writing. But all that functions only because of prosthesis, because the whole never was anywhere, neither in the singular nor in the total, because the parts were always already detachable, replaceable, because the transfer effect upon which the general is constructed is there at the very beginning, in the nonintegrality of that beginning, called prosthesis.

A first type of abyssal indistinction occurs, therefore, in prosthesis, between "necessary" contrivance and "willful" artifice. It is impossible to establish to what extent the strategy here represents a form of disingenuousness. Whatever I say on one side or the other cannot but exacerbate the problematic. Since I cannot promise that if I set out to talk about something like the effects of the mechanical in the artistic I will not ultimately or automatically be writing a story of a father's wooden leg, then what better device than to let it come up where and whenever it will; not as if to forestall the effects of the unconscious or memory or the rest, for I warrant there will still be plenty more of all that to go around, but to foreground what exists as contrivance in every utterance. The fiction of a real autobiographical wooden leg will have to be the point of final reference for all that takes place within any prosthesis I choose to write, if only because it has been uttered, because in writing there is no other ontology than that of utterance. Besides, even if it had not been uttered in any of the forms of writing sufficient to constitute an ontology, it would still be difficult to maintain that it had not been uttered, somehow somewhere. Quite simply, it would be difficult to conceive of a writing of prosthesis that did not deal sooner or later with a wooden leg, in some relation or another to a question of paternity. For prosthesis is inevitably about belonging, and paternity an unavoidable model of ownership.

Hence any disingenuousness resides more in the assertion that there are two modes of writing being exploited here, that there are identifiable transfers from one to the other, when the transfer is at its most rapid—its most imperceptible if you will—within each individual utterance; indeed at its most rapid in the idea that there can be no such thing as an utterance that is individual, singular. Any number of appearances might at certain points allow us to determine that one or the other mode is in effect, although one such appearance will always be that which, by tradition and by definition, contrives to give prosthesis the semblance of nature. But, even when we seem to recognize a particular mode, appearances will not of themselves suffice to singularize the utterance in question or to prevent it from entering into a relation with the other mode. It will thus remain impossible to determine rigorously when and where transfer from one mode to the other is supposed to have taken place. The transfer will always be taking place, the ghost hovering even within the utterance that presents itself as the most singular and direct.

A conjunction or enfolding of discourses therefore becomes, in this prosthesis, the pretext for a generalized examination of rhetorical articulations, among others, all constrained by the particular of my father's wooden leg. Or, risking the converse, this would be a story of life with a prosthesis constrained by the strictures of academic discussion. As long as the life in the story cannot be recounted without reference to prosthesis one will not be able to find in this a simple appeal to a naturalness of a leg to preempt a supposed artificiality of the rhetorical or academic. A received idea would have it that the discourse concerning a father, be it fiction, biography, or autobiography, could easily lay claim to deriving from a natural source, from real life. What is at stake in prosthesis, in my father's prosthesis, in this recounting of it—for there can only ever be this or another relating of and to it—is the discovery of an artificiality there where the natural founds its priority. Furthermore, my relating of and to it begins here, in this instance that subscribes to any number of the institutional forms of academic discourse even as it deforms them, from the place and position of something once called and still answering to, somehow, criticism and theory, with respect to which it is a father's wooden leg that has the marks of something unnatural or contrived. Yet, conversely, critical or theoretical discourse has traditionally founded itself as a contrivance, as secondary to and derived from the textual utterance that it takes as its object. What is the status and effect, then, of this leg that is a type of fiction but not a text having regular institutional credentials, being recounted and analyzed within the institutional forms of criticism and theory? The question presumes that we can establish whether the story of a leg occurs within a text of criticism rather than the converse. Thus there is no end to that spiral, not that way, no way back to a single natural origin, yet no way out of the appeals to and of the same.

Quite clearly, the most classically Platonic criteria come into play in valorizing one mode of discourse over another. There is the time-honored notion that the academic is necessarily serious, that fiction, biography, or autobiography—particularly something that can't decide which of those it is nor indeed whether it is one of those as opposed to a work of criticism—has no place upsetting that level of sobriety. As a result a glaring paradox is overlooked. For such a repression of the fictive is a strange disavowal for a criticism that takes fiction as its object, its *sine qua non*, its *raison d'être*. Few would maintain anymore that there is no contamination between criticism and its object, that the former contains no invention, no desire, no narrative, but apart from Derrida's insistence on and exploitation of a double writing there seems only scant investigation of the modes of contamination. It is true that the forms and modes of fiction itself have been exhaustively catalogued, but always by a discourse that tends to repress its own play of invention. And in spite of the fact that a generalized notion of writing has been promoted for some time now as structurally comprehensive of both criticism and its object (without, for all that, conflating the two), one still looks in vain for the experiments with or developments from that.[5]

On the other hand, the converse valorization of fiction as against criticism enjoys widespread institutional and public credence. One hears that it is academic criticism that is frivolous by comparison to supposedly more immediate concerns of life, or to the putative first-level remove of fictional writing; one even hears such things from within academic criticism. So where does that leave the dividing lines, how does that help to locate a center of seriousness, of life, of reality, that would enable us to ward off frivolity or fiction? Is the other to the purely academic, what is so often called life itself, the same other that would be invoked in opposition to fiction? If so, then criticism and its object inhabit the same space or structure, the same "lifelessness." Within those paradoxes there occurs the event of this prosthesis whose hybridity, and hence whose status with respect to fiction, criticism, autobiography, theory—to name but a few contenders—holds open the question, becomes that question itself, or at least an interrogation of it.

The question raised by prosthesis, naively conceived of as artificial appendage to natural member, is particular, or personal, in two obvious ways. Firstly, in that my father wears a wooden leg; secondly, in that I write criticism, or something akin to that. In the traditional rivalry, resting on the Platonic opposition between the prior and the derivative, between so-called creative writing and criticism, the former does not have all the arguments: what it has in terms of logocentric claims, it lacks in terms of at least one type of institutional status—that of the university for instance—or, what amounts to the same thing, in terms of metadiscursive status. Criticism gives itself the advantage of having the last word (although creative writing, by being first, ascribes to itself the ultimate word), whereas creative writing can say it has no need of criticism (although it needs the reading of which criticism is but a formalization). Those are old arguments and old retorts whose paradoxes have been thoroughly de-constructed, and I don't wish to simply repeat them here.[6] But what I hope to have emerge from this particular rehearsal or staging of them is another deconstruction, in the affirmative sense of a displacement of that problem-atic: to have one infringe upon or append itself to the other in an event that can only be called prosthesis; so that there is a rewriting of the relation as prosthesis.

Hence whether it be, as is my guess, that a classic form of analysis is unable to deal rigorously with the complexity of the conjunction I call prosthesis, or simply that I indulge an inclination not to attempt such a rigorously analytic account of it, it comes back to the same thing. In either case it might be said that the facts do not permit it. At least one fact, the fact of my being an interested party. I'm not sure what sort of fact that amounts to. I'm not sure how saying "it is a fact that my father has a wooden leg" proves or changes anything here. Nor in what way saying that would be different from producing a photograph, or a document written by a doctor, or a text, this text, written by me. Prosthesis is the writing of my self as a limit to writing—the relation to or limit of both my father's wooden leg and a series of texts. It is the writing of my relation to a prosthesis, and its writing switches in and out of a classic analytic mode. The reader will, no doubt, similarly switch on and off to it as fancy, or necessity, strikes her.

By saying that this is my father's wooden leg I am talking about—not mine, nor my mother's, but my *father's*, and *my* father's—I do not for all that clearly establish what precise relation thereby obtains between me and any prosthesis. How adjacent to or distant from it do I stand here? What sort of a digression or supplement do I represent in regard to my father's wooden leg? Would the word one might use to describe such a relation necessarily be "prosthesis"? It should be obvious that if I presume to fail at a rigorously objective analysis, it means that whoever presents himself here as a subject cannot have any classically objective status either. The use of the first-person pronoun has consistently served as the excuse for arrogating all sorts of privilege to one's discursive position. As a corrective here, the oft-repeated "I" should always be read as a prosthetic "I," one forced into a combination of natural and unnatural relations, with a father's leg, wooden or otherwise, or with a text; no "I" that is not related to an event of prosthesis, to an event of writing. Only ever therefore a relation, in a number of senses of the word. In the sense, first of all, explained earlier, whereby all re*lations* are articulated through the body, literally "carried back" by or through the body; the body carrying its otherness even as it begins to move. In the second sense of whatever takes me back or attaches me to a memory of, an acquaintance with, a dependence on, a text of my father. In the third sense of a recounting, a retelling, a transfer of textual data to a third party who is a reader, but who, in a strange type of circularity, is in the place of my father to the extent that whatever I write here I write to him. This relation falls thus into the abyss of a relation of a relation: that I or "I" can only relate, that is abundantly clear; that is, it is clear that I can only relate that, and it is clear that I can only relate to that, in many more ways than a seemingly simple play on words would suggest; in all the ways that are all the gamble here.

The current rewriting of prosthesis aims precisely to extend those effects through its doubling and its play on relation as transfer. It always both asks and begs the question of relation as remove. Could we after all measure the exact distance a piece of text or quotation—say one from Virgil representing some prosodic peculiarity—would have to transfer, what rapid transit it would have to effect in order to arrive at the ghostly sensations that are provoked by an articulation between the natural and artificial sections of a paternal limb? Could we know how far we had gone, or when we had gone far enough, before returning to it? How would we know to what extent it could all still relate?

I can find no name for this complex relation that a quotation, to begin with, here puts into play; no name to compete with prosthesis, no more pertinent name, no name for this pertinence, the peculiar appurtenance of the same and the other. So I name it prosthesis, I give a name to the configuration that is too complex and imprecise to have a single name, I let the name generalize out of all bounds, in order to resist or have done with the taxonomical rage or necessity that would presume to account for something that begins as a phantom pain or an ambulatory peculiarity extracted from Virgil. In order to insist that there is no simple name for a discourse that articulates with, rather than issuing from, the body, while at the same time realizing that there is no other discourse—in the sense of no other translation, transfer, or relation—no other conception of it except as a balancing act performed by the body, a shift or transfer between the body and its exteriority. The name for it is the name for the possibility of naming or uttering in general, and thus there is an urgent necessity to name it. To name it with a name that limps into existence; name it, as I do, prosthesis. And then to relate it against the implacable necessity of naming.

Haunting all questions of relation is the notion of proximity, the economy of the family, the *oikos* that is the family as a model for all economies. Prosthesis itself would seem to rely for its definition on such an effect of contiguity. It occurs first of all within the space of a family ritual, a familiar ritual. There the codes are well nigh impossible to render explicit, so subtle are they, so attuned to an intricate and unspoken system of conditioned response. It occurs on the threshold of the familiar, in the liminal suspension between one register or language and another, between the desire for—and its concomitant resistance to—codification, and the necessity of a description whose minutiae can only emerge from the ins and outs of a recounting.

So it is a familiar defamiliarization that occurs: a familiar language is uttered in a foreign tongue, the accents of foreignness spoken with familiarity but never immune from falls into error, like a foreigner who speaks and infringes upon the codes of register operative within the acquired language, for example by confusing familiar and formal address. Every family has its rituals, and every family and every guest their moments of awkwardness when those rituals come without warning into effect; there is some unspoken sign or simply a common expectation that has the ritual operating before its explicit gestures are activated. For example, breakfast is all but over, the Bible is taken from the cupboard, not the one where the tea towels are drying—obviously, this does not take place near the doorway nor any threshold but well and truly in the bosom of the family home—the Bible is opened and a passage is read, picking up from where we left off the previous day, this is the public morning devotional ritual, reading through a book at a time, not from genesis to apocalypse but somewhere in between chosen at random or will or by divine inspiration, and I can't remember how many times the entire Scripture was read through in the space of my lifetime in the family home, but there were very few days when the ritual was not observed during those eighteen years, a few verses were read with little or no commentary, the divine text in this case its own exegesis, perhaps followed by a closing statement, a brief platitude or homily that is less a commentary than the prelude to what happens next, the sign of a shift into a different mode that catches the outsider every time, for the guest sits back and prepares to resume the conversation that was interrupted by the opening of the cupboard door when there is a general shuffling, a scraping of chairs that has the guest thinking she is about to be abandoned at the table, that they are all about to leave, when in fact they are shifting their chairs to kneel on the floor for prayers are said kneeling, or his prayer rather for he is the only one who prays, at least that is the way it was for a long time when it was only very rarely that the house would welcome a guest who was not already privy to the ritual having come from a house where the same codes were observed, but then a general relaxing of the borders came about, the guests became more and more frequent and the kneeling restricted more and more to the one uttering the prayer, he still kneels, one knee only on the ground for you cannot easily kneel on a prosthesis, he kneels on his good knee as he calls it, the wooden one is bent at the knee its foot on the ground, he prays with his wooden leg cocked and unconsciously caresses the steel thigh while he prays, for he is given to caressing his thighs in general, the leg wavering slowly from side to side as he caresses it slowly in rhythm with his prayer, the litany also a form of caress, in obedience to a particularly ritualistic combination of the idiosyncratic and the quoted or repeated, there being of course no written prayers in this fundamentalist code, but his prayer amounted nevertheless to the quiet and protracted version of a line from Virgil, the language perhaps intercessional but there was never anything in it to prevent its being a caress, on the contrary, the regularity with which its terms were invoked could only mean that it served, like any ritual, more within the context of its utterance, where it was accompanied by the strange familiarity of a hand of flesh stroking a leg of steel, more there than in any external space of intercession.

Itself a sort of prayer, the quotation from Virgil works like an oil to soothe his pain, to grease the arthritic joints as well as the articulations of the wooden leg. The Virgil accompanies a first stage articulation, what I might call a human swaying that builds up to a mechanical twitch, whereby the apparent fluidity of movement enacted by the human body is revealed as something more like the jerk of a cog or a piston. The corporeal flips into the mechanical, just as galloping horses become aberrant prosody. In a second stage this articulation of corporeal and mechanical becomes more explicit. It does so on those steep hills in the town of chalkdusty schoolrooms; it is earlier than where we began but after the Latin in the classroom, not much after, just a few years, which is time enough to lose a leg yet not time enough to have a prosthesis fitted. He is out in the mild spring sun, out on his bicycle, the rudimentary single-gear-foot-brake-only 1940 model, pedaling like some Molloy or other fact of fiction with one leg up towards his grandfather's house, easing into a familiarity with his lack, easing into a relation with a bicycle pedal, with the whole mechanism of which he becomes the driving force, still as always a question of control, but the pleasure comes from the cumulative turbine effect, the possibility of producing a movement that exceeds that of the body. This exercise is preparatory to a prosthetic leg, a familiar ride on a familiar bicycle suddenly become a difficult apprenticeship, he is suddenly aware of the rank mechanical otherness of this machine he used to climb on without hesitation, without so much as a second thought, stepping spryly into the saddle, pedaling like second nature through rain and shine, up hill and down dale, but now he feels the apparatus, is conscious of the limitations of his body as though he were required to learn it all over again, the familiar suddenly thrown back into an uncanny warp that is concentrated at the point where his single foot meets the pedal, he watches with bewilderment the other pedal turning free, no leg attached to it, it is no mean feat to pedal a bicycle with one leg, I used to try it now and then in the course of a paper delivery when I had for the first time a bicycle of my own, but only after having begun with my older sister's hand-me-down, the type with no horizontal bar linking seat to handlebars, it made no sense as the signifier of the feminine since the absence of the bar means you don't bruise your gonads every time you slip off the pedal and would be better suited to a male than a female, but there you have it, no doubt it was all about girls not having to raise their legs high enough to bestraddle the bar, in any case I learned about bruised gonads while trying to pedal with one leg doing my paper round on my new three-gear Raleigh Manhattan, which I saved up for with the proceeds of a year-long paper round on a brother's no-gears-footbrake-only hand-me-down, and never mind the gonads I was more concerned for my leg that the dog on the street around the corner would go to take a chunk out of every time I delivered its paper, who knows what part of my anatomy it was aiming for but it was my leg it perforated, still have the scars to prove it but never needed anything more than a temporary Band-Aid prosthesis, and I would soon abandon the experiment in any case, it was only ever a token attempt I made at single-leg cycling, with only one operative leg you have to push with all your strength to get the pedal back up to the apex, pulling from the underside with the arch of the foot, simpler with bare feet of course, and then as it gets out of reach that way, twirl and snatch it with the front of the foot and toes, then as you reach the top twirl again to place the ball of the foot squarely on top and begin the push down once more, and all that from the sitting position makes getting to the top of the hill on a sunny day to see the ocean or one's grandfather a task of no mean proportions, not to mention the risks involved when it comes to the descent for one has only one foot to help position the pedal in order to push backwards and activate the brake, short of which there is the prospect of the real and unsightly crash and fall of a one-legged man from a bicycle, but as long as there is movement, as long as the body is shifting the pedal and turning the wheel he enjoys the illusion of wholeness and with sufficient momentum is as if gliding free of all impediment, wheeling through the air rather dapper in his Fair Isle waistcoat over starched white shirt and pleated charcoal trousers with one leg tucked neatly into the belt, this is locomotion, this is the illusion of sailing self-propelled past corporeal and mechanical alike, the shifting of gears into untrammeled movement, the hopping and limping of monopedantic ambulation forsaken for this gliding, this sliding across blurred asphalt lined with the scent of recent honeysuckle, he pushed, tucked, grabbed, and pulled in a rhythm that outran any risk of cramping, his style all smooth and unbroken, he could pedal for hours with a single leg while waiting for an artificial one, pedal all the way to his rendezvous with that stranger, and still pedal beyond that, three months after it was fitted and he moved to a new job in a new town he took it off, flipped his trouser leg into his belt, positioned his crutch on the handlebars like a lance to ward off oncoming phantoms, and fairly pedaled the twenty kilometers from Foxton to Levin for the hell of it and for the sheer pleasure of self-locomotion, the urgent fantasy of a prosthetic lurch into the full fledge of flight, the switch to other forms of propulsion that is the whole promise of the prosthetic articulation, already there in the chug of leg on pedal, the coupling of leg and pedal whose movement is that of a rod driving a wheel, the transformation from linear to circular movement that is the very principle of locomotion put to the test by this dashing rider in the springtime of his new age.

The first prosthetic phase is linear, confined to the double rigidity of crutch and leg, but once he mounts his bicycle it assumes its mechanical function to unwind upon the whole sunny day of prosthetic possibility. But to say the first phase is to obfuscate; it is to suggest that there is a preprosthetic, a prosthetic, and a postprosthetic when there are only ever the operations of a shifting that is prosthesis. Whichever mode it is in, it is always in a double mode: the one-legged pedaling with its reliance on a cycle of push down, snatch, pull up, reposition, push down, and so on, betokens an interrupted linearity, an irregular binary shift that is reconfigured in the movement that comes into play once two legs are at work, where the linear makes a smoother articulation with the circular, the articulations of hips and knees being occluded by a movement of the legs that appears analogous to the movement of the pedals and of the wheels but still involves the cooperation of two modes. Similarly, what might be called the postmechanical or high-technological mode obeys something more like the irregularity of the one-legged linear shift, for however much its rapid transit through the on/off binary maze of silicon circuits might give the appearance of an uninterrupted fluidity, an information flow, its figure remains the limp or zigzag.

The zigzag is the movement of discourse, the shift involved in the body's articulation with exteriority, but also in its etymological sense (*discurrere*) of running hither and thither. Prosthesis makes the link, as I have said, between at least two discourses, covering the distance that separates two nodes of chatter, as on one familial evening, the adults are in the living room and the children in their bedroom already warned to be quiet and sleep, but as long as the children are conscious of the adults speaking the latter discourse serves as a cover for their own, so they begin again, first in whispers and then in more articulate tones, becoming consistently more animated until the noise is all theirs and their involvement in their own conversing the guarantee that they don't realize an absolute silence has fallen on the adult side, suddenly it is quiet enough to hear a pin drop, the children don't realize until it is too late, until that silence now heavy is broken and they hear the peculiar sound of an angry prosthetic gallop advancing at a remarkable speed given the impediment, running in anger towards the bedroom where the children are at present hoping that discourse could be as empty as sophistry and fall back into silence, taken back as though it had never been instead of an excess generating effects that outrun all it can foresee, they listen to the amplifying iambic beat as he advances with his remarkable sprint, the wooden leg serving as a pivot while the other does all the energetic work, he propels himself rather than runs, always veering slightly off center then correcting just in time, dealing with the sideways as well as the forward momentum, the instinctive compensation that soft flesh makes for the rebound that comes when rigid steel strikes the unyielding ground, it is that opposition of soft and hard that sets the meter, except that it does not quite have the regularity of iambic feet, there is a slight syncopation, a pause between the strong and weak beats as the shift occurs from one to the other, such that the shift itself almost has a beat of its own, shifting the rhythm slightly towards the epic dactylic mode as he bounds towards the bedroom, and if discourse means running zigzag then its feet cannot but be these syncopated iambs, its meter that of a galloping prosthetic falling out of step and overreaching in a double gravitational shift, sideways and forwards, perhaps not structurally different from a natural gait—for remember the simplest prosthesis is designed to reproduce some lost natural faculty—but more pronounced at least, an explicit infraction upon or departure from the straits of linearity.

As I have just suggested, the discourse that can be called prosthetic, characterized by the limp or zigzag and by an iambic rhythm, would be the figure of communication as information transfer, the domain of the high-technological where the linear and circular paradigms of the mechanical are replaced by the binary relays of a computing system. There what is called circuitry is nothing but a proliferation of intersections, iambic switchings, detours and reroutings at a pace to which walking or galloping bears little analogical resemblance. But it is the double movement, the bidirectionality of those ambulations, epitomized by the limp of a prosthetic, that is all there is to prevent the speed of the informational process from seeming to reduce to a pure linearity, when in fact it is the repeated inscription and contradiction of that. What is so easily occluded in that process are the blips of countless relays, the switches between open and closed, on and off options, in terms of which this supposed flow is subject to constant effects of discontinuity.

The wooden leg is not really wooden. Language has already taken leave of reality, the literal taken leave of itself. By the same logic, that of the stand-in or supplement, which is that of language itself, a language that has always already taken leave of itself, by that same logic it is probably not a leg either. In any case it is made of steel, or some alloy. It has a vaguely flesh-colored hue to it, very vague, for there is nothing particularly convincing about it as a simulacrum of a human leg. Near its working parts it looks more frankly metallic, and starts to shine with the burnish of bronze or silver. The shine comes not only from the use of different materials required for optimum functioning but also from the polish and wear of many years of use, from a thumb and two fingers that reach instinctively through the trouser leg to find the lever that needs to be lowered or raised to bend the knee. A small cuboid about an inch long withdraws a pin lock from the hinge or clicks it back into place once the knee is straightened in readiness for walking. This is your basic two-mode prosthesis: straight or bent. It stands perched like some tribute to the triumph of the binary, on the edge of the cybernetic age. It is a far cry from a peg leg on the one hand, but falls far short of a cyborg's computerized and fully automated flesh-covered robotic limbs on the other.

In this way the wooden leg represents the duality of every prosthesis, its search for a way between emulating the human and superseding the human. A particularly supplemental duality once again. The peg leg, it seems easy to say, was conceived simply as a replacement for lost erectile function, with little thought to anything but support; a crutch attached at the hip or knee instead of wedged under the armpit; a unary prosthesis. Whatever articulation was involved was limited to that between animate and inanimate, where wood met flesh. Not that that isn't *the* sense of articulation itself, the adjunction of or relation to radical otherness that conditions the whole prosthetic undertaking. However, the wooden or steel leg takes a big step towards articulation as self-division; it allows for movement at one out of two leg joints, quite understandably opting for the knee over the ankle. Thus it takes a big step towards the reproduction of a functioning more strictly analogous to that of the human leg, but that is also a step towards the more strictly mechanical functions of the human, hence towards the nonhuman. Granted, the wooden or steel leg progresses also in the direction of visual resemblance to the human, with respect to color, shape, and size. But what are demonstrated in the leg's simultaneous advances towards the human and the nonhuman are two competing conceptions of mechanical operations, one based on analogy with the human model and one that opts for the difference of the digital, a digital reduced, however, to the binary. But they are also two competing conceptions of the human model, of difference, of conceptualization itself. For they continue to compete throughout the development of high technology into the domain of robotic operations and into the question of artificial intelligence, and it is hard to know whether the force of analogy has ever abandoned the field in favor of something that might be called the purely mechanical, or the electronic.

The robot, for instance, is conceived of as replacing the tedium of certain repetitive operations performed formerly by humans, supposedly in order to leave humans free to indulge in less mechanical pursuits. But the robot is not only a replacement for but a refinement of the human, a type of superhuman. Though the repetitive tasks it is put to are those to which the human holds itself superior, the robot performs them endlessly, effortlessly, without error. It lifts weights and confronts hazards beyond human capability. Thus the suspicion arises—and the literature is full of it—that the robot might also surpass the human in the area of the nonmechanical, that is, in thinking. The computer is of course conceived of on the basis of such a possibility; it is the brain of the robot. But in terms of thinking, of intelligence, the distinctions between the human and non- or extra-human, the natural and the artificial, simply enfold. The computer is proposed as a model for the human mind, whose surpassability is thus conceived; conversely, the human mind functions as a model for the computer once the latter's potentiality for consciousness begins to be imagined.[7] Thus again, it is no longer clear how or whether the force of analogy remains in effect, or in which direction it functions; whether the computer is being modeled on the mind or according to more recognizably physical principles, or whether the idea of the mind is giving way to the force of the computer metaphor, more and more so as the computers grow in complexity and capability.

The body may seem to have been left out of this equation, but one can still say that its articulations serve as the model for the mechanical; that the mechanical is more readily identifiable in the body than elsewhere in the physical world. Besides, the more mechanical the mind is thought to be, the less viable becomes the distinction between mind and body, the more neurotransmission and *genu*transmission become structurally analogous articulations. From this point of view the whole technological and high-technological departure will come back to the body, back to a bend in the knee, to the turn into the void of an amputation at midthigh, to the subsequent articulation of a phantom pain and a runaway text; an articulation to which I give the name prosthesis.

What is of concern in all this for a relation between prosthesis as artificial leg and prosthesis as writing practice is a particular aspect of computerized writing in the form of word processing; that is to say an aspect of the particular form of prosthesis that finds a human attached to a writing machine. Short of rendering explicit a whole descriptive apparatus to develop that relation into what can only become the most reductive of analogies—something that will nevertheless continue to haunt this and any prosthesis, to the extent that it is, as I have suggested, posited on the very possibility of analogy, as well as on the possibility of the interruption of analogy—I wish to return to one simple function of word processing as textual treatment (*traitement de textes*). I refer to operations of detachability previously referred to as cutting and pasting, the possibility of endless rearranging and grafting of textual material, a possibility that word processing renders more expedient than ever before. It is at this point and through this process that prosthesis is concerned as much with the practice of writing as with the writing of theory. The enfolding of one within the other, their cutting and pasting, simply reinforces the fact that the two are resolutely coextensive. It is their coextensiveness that accounts for any appearance of disorder. What might appear as disorder would be the competing order of a double exigency: on the one hand the necessary same/other concurrence without which prosthesis would not mean anything; on the other hand that concurrence compounded by what prosthesis means for writing in the age of the electronic processing or treatment of texts, namely the radical questioning of order that is the possibility or threat of indefinite reorderings.

To that one might reply that there was never any doubt about the order of the elements constituting the sort of prosthesis that is the paradigm case here; that however double, the wooden leg attached to half a thigh relies on a rigorous subordination of artificial to natural; of machine to human.

Now although that is true within a strict conception of the wooden leg, it is not a truth that holds under scrutiny, not at either end of the prosthetic spectrum. Firstly, no amputation is performed without the forethought of a workable prosthesis; the knife doesn't strike indiscriminately but is guided by the range of prostheses that wait, parasitic, for a suitable host. In this respect the prosthetic possibility determines the shape of the human, the artificial determines the form of the natural. Secondly, the question of order is thrown into doubt by the paradoxical play of analogy, by the fact that the model—wooden leg, robot, computer—well before the advent of any artificial intelligence, can always surpass the original in its functioning, simply do the job better; or rather do all sorts of other jobs the original could not conceive of, like generate this renegade piece of writing.

The wooden leg is detachable, it has a life of its own. Its life is mostly secret, few know of it. It begins at night standing in a corner of the bedroom, holding taut one trouser leg and letting the other fall, while he sleeps, dreaming who knows what dreams of walking straight, he sleeps beside me, I am lying between him and my mother, he has brought me here to sleep with them when I am about the length of his wooden leg and have cried out in fear from my own room on the other side of the house, crying out their names in nightmare panic, again and again until I hear his step, the sound of the rubber foot of his crutch squeaking on the linoleum floor as he turns the corner out of the bedroom across the living room carpet and into my room where no explanation is necessary, I simply make room for him on the edge of my narrow bed and he sits, then lies down next to me and the waiting begins—I watch the minutes tick by doubting his assurances that dozing is worth half as much rest as sleep; I wait for him to fall asleep and don't even know any more if I am fighting to sleep myself or to stay awake, but if he falls asleep and I wake him again he will not repeat the exercise but will issue the invitation I have been waiting for, waking for, the invitation to follow him back to their bed. My only regret here is possibly his greatest, the fact that he cannot carry me when he is relying on his crutch, and so as we retrace steps holding hands across the house I am in a sense carrying him, walking for him, translating his failure to walk right, standing in for the leg he lacks, he robbed of his strength and I of my weakness. Once I am in their bed I make a pact with the leg in the corner—if it will let me sleep as I am letting it sleep, I shall agree to return to it the function I have usurped, and neither of us will say a thing when he emerges from his room dressed the next morning in his suit, and I'll hang off his cane the way we all took turns at doing, and he will don his hat from the closet in the hallway and be gone in his car with the specially fitted knee accelerator so one leg can operate both that and the clutch until stick shift gives way to automatic transmission, at about the time I learn to put myself back to sleep, counting horses galloping across dusty plains, leaving his leg to sleep in peace and dream as only a prosthesis can dream, of uninhibited detachment, of polymorphous substitutability in a metallic thereover that beckons wherever the order of things recognizes its own incontrovertible inversion.

Once the question of order is posed, we no longer know which order of writing encompasses which, and the question is of the order of the theory of writing as much as of the practice of writing. But we would not need prosthesis, not even the slightest notion of it, for that to be so. Quite simply, an act of criticism that does not raise the question of its own operations is not, at this writing, an act of criticism worthy of the name; and that is presuming that an absence of explicit reference amounts to an avoidance of the question. But beyond that first and automatic exigency we can see that the act of writing, criticism or whatever, is a prosthetic act par excellence, the articulation of two heterogeneities. Whether it be a writing that replaces a defective, truncated, or lost memory, the flesh made word, or a function of a body at work with a computer. One cannot simply write *about* prosthesis when one is automatically, just by virtue of writing, writing prosthesis, entering into prosthetic relations, being prosthetic.

Whatever order remains therefore, obeys the double operation of the prosthetic exercise. For the leg functions first from the center, serving as the pivot that all this discussion hinges on, the silent witness within the hallowed precincts of the parental bedroom, the truncated and exiled center, if you will, without which everything could perhaps still be said otherwise, but without speaking of which I would simply be deceiving myself. Conversely, in speaking of it, I cannot but fall into a certain duplicity, the play between what it does and what it does not account for. Thus it functions also from the border, serving as the boundary post, the guardrail, the outside edge of academic propriety, so that its narrative excursions are also incursions, and also so that there is a point, however difficult to assign and even more difficult to defend, beyond which one is no longer speaking of prosthesis. The wooden leg can as easily be read as one as the other: the pretext for all manner of digressions as well as the one solid piece of evidence that keeps all this together. And that is so whether it be a truth or a fiction, for all centers, and all boundaries function just as well as fictions as they do as truths.

Hence the shift as prelude to a wince or suppressed scream, that has been with us from the beginning. It is a matter of continually adjusting the position of the wooden leg, constantly negotiating its vantage point as a hedge against the wholesale reconfiguration of the field that comes with the onslaught of pain. But the whole thing has already been reconfigured; this is not new. Prosthesis is the mark of such a reconfiguration. Look upon it as a switch from control to automatism if you will, from condition to reflex; but as well consider it as a flight from inside to out, a turning inside out, a flight into the inner resources of resistance which is also an expulsion into the unspeakable. At this point the relations enter their most complex configuration. He yelps and I fall silent. I follow through to have him speak it, or forget it, but neither of us can provide the words for speaking or forgetting. And this prosthesis speaks of it at length where he never would, and in doing so fails to speak it, speaks in stolen words, continually forces itself to the point of silence or babble in order to speak it. Its dare is to go as far as possible in assuming a prerogative it can never claim, that of speaking another's pain; it seeks the limits of speaking out of turn, that irreverence or disrespect. The irreverence or disrespect also of claiming that all speaking is out of turn, all writing negotiated through otherness.

There can be no semiotics of pain; pain, like every *ec-stasy*, is the outside limit to any semiotics. Any discourse on it will have to be in the form of a prosthesis, in the most general sense of the term developed so far. Again, this is not to place pain in some natural space beyond the artificiality of discourse, but to insist finally that every discursive operation borrows the structure of the prosthetic, and that pain as discursive limit is simply a paradigm for the prosthetic lot. The cry we have so often read as the paradigm for the inarticulate or prearticulate comes to signify, following the prosthetic model, the postarticulate, an adversion as much as a reversion, an aggression as much as a regression. Pain is already articulated in the shifting, shifting is already at work before the switch becomes twitch, prosthesis as articulation of difference, as differance, is there at the beginning.

At the beginning, accompanied by a Latin citation, transfer and translation the pretexts for this prosthesis; a line from Virgil about galloping horses the refrain an amputee repeats to parry the attack of nervous impulse in a grieving limb. It was in Latin that that grief originated, in some scrawled illegible words, some imprecise doctor's hand, a medical prescription carried home one day that announced a sarcoma, prescribed a treatment that would come too late, and I don't know what language the prescription for a prosthesis is written in, that is my whole problem here, I don't know the precise terms of a letter prescribing an amputation that he carried with him accompanied by his father across the straits of water that separated his hometown from the capital, for it was to the capital that one went for amputation in those days, and one wonders what thoughts filled his head, what inclination to read the letter, to translate the Latin or whatever jargon so concealed its meaning and set in train the hermeneutic desire. One sails down a deep turquoise Queen Charlotte Sound, its waters unrippling, then one heads across the storm-swept straits, a funnel for every wind the Pole can manage to whip up, and even the harbor where Wellington sits offers no respite to it, there is no respite but a solid mooring, and one takes one's prescription to its solemn addressee. There is that anxiety in the transfer of the letter that haunts the prosthetic project, the haunting of all the reserves that accompany and effect such a transfer. I recall the time he declined to take the sea route. We were on holiday back in his home town, and problems with his prosthesis—the constant problem of rejection and accommodation, fitting steel to flesh, that plagues him even now, that makes an updating of a prosthesis almost more bother than it is worth—called him to the capital. He took me along for the ride, or for the comfort of not making the crossing alone, and for assurance of difference we took the airplane one way, it was my maiden flight, and came back by sea. It was probably the first significant trip I took alone with my father, a voyage whose necessity was downplayed in favor of the pleasure he was giving me, attentive to everything that caught my attention, there the profile of the coastline as the plane headed out across the water, there the beach called Tahunanui, there the seagulls and even the occasional dolphin that followed in the wake of the ferry when we returned, the epaulets of the officers, the grades and the chevrons bespeaking the awful responsibility of keeping this ship afloat. We crossed and returned, made the transfer, bore the message to its destination, returned to our days at Tahunanui, a beach where he had strolled full eighteen years old with a close school friend and a war on the horizon, where his friend had announced he would join the air force and my father announced his prescription in Latin that would keep him on the ground, and that would eventually have him limp and hop while his friend flew through night skies illuminated by flare fires until on one mission he just flew out of sight, while my father hobbled into a more secure prosthetic future. There must have been that same foreboding for both of them, the one choosing to take to the air, making the choice that was no choice that was the right choice that was imposed, the other choosing a Latin prescription a prelude to a prosthesis a prevention against being shot down in foreign skies, that same foreboding returning for him whenever there were the alternatives of flight and grounding. The same foreboding that came across the telephone lines late one night, the apparatus ringing its double Commonwealth ring, its spondaic alternance, all fazed through the static of sleep, like any long-distance call, to announce that this time it was his brother who had crashed, a brother who in some strange defiance made it his habit to fly alone and at night now fallen in a field not far from home, the same hometown, his plane broken and straddling telephone lines interrupting who knows what long-distance calls and nighttime electronic rousings. So this is in turn my own foreboding, this fear of what flies at night across telephone lines, the fear of the late-night call—it must come at night, logic makes it so, the logic of time zones and the logic of death—this is the phantom that haunts me, the sound I wait for knowing it will come like a spasm jolting across stratospheric instantaneity and cursing down fiber-optic rush-hour lanes to strike me out of the blue, the cry that will come back at me sleeping confident alone in the darkness and keep up its strident call until I answer, I have no simple conjuration to ward against it, nothing other than this familiar yet foreign body of writing, nothing else now that I have left, now that there is nothing keeping me back drying the dishes next to a swaying prosthetic father, nothing but all the names we have to articulate the past, nothing but nostalgia, memory, desire, and the rest. I leave only to return; it is in such a shift that one can inherit a prosthesis. All of this looks back, back it might easily seem towards the illusion of full recovery, to a recovered fullness, except that the origin is in this case an absence and a double articulation, a displacement of original plenitude into the kinetics of working parts. And if prosthesis occurs as articulation, then this looking back is also a sending forward, this inheritance an endowment, this is the relay for informational transmission, these are the stages Latin horses make in a ride through a phantom network of stumblings, blips, and false starts carrying a father who sways in anticipation of a leap that always heralds a fall, his wrestling with the agony of a mourning body become my agonistic contention between two modes of writing, as we step and fall in and out of the rhythm of our bodies' prose.

§ 2 Mentone, 1888

It is doubtful that he is sunbathing, for his head points in the wrong direction, downhill towards the water. That seems to be a sufficient reason, even if it obeys no convincing logic. He is lying on his left side, prone and dormant in the midday sun. There is no dishevelment in his demeanor; rather his is the disciplined body of an average bourgeois, if anything slightly relaxed by the intensity of a summer antipodean sun. Otherwise he could as likely have been washed up by some freak wave that has retreated without any trace but this inert form, the left arm, in rigid verticality, just touching the line of neap-tide debris, the small shells, wood and algae that follow the uneven furrow some twenty feet from the water's edge. There is nothing desperate about his attitude; he lies there basking, but with arms outstretched, left one high above his head, right one clench-fisted at attention at midthigh, the body as if arrested in some frantic semaphoric gesture. So perhaps this is no accidental piece of jetsam washed up there on the beach, but nevertheless the left leg, as straight and as vertical as all the rest, strangely counterpoints the linearity of his form: it is cut off at or about the knee.

This is not Tahunanui, New Zealand, but Mentone, Australia. This is not my father but a subject in a painting, a man lying on a beach in the center of *A Holiday at Mentone* by Charles Conder, oil on canvas, 1888, Art Gallery of South Australia (see Fig. 1). His leg is nevertheless cut off; a good half of it is missing from the painting. It is cut off by a solid but uneven red rectangle that lies slightly obliquely across both legs, by an object that his right hand holds tenuously in the back corner. He is fully clothed, in three-piece suit and bowler hat. There are no crutches or canes near him; he is

34

abandoned there by the other occupants of the canvas who turn their backs on him, all except a man in dark clothes in the near background, who looks casually in his direction slightly over one shoulder as he repeatedly punctures his own right foot with an upraised cane. Suddenly self-mutilation appears everywhere in this painting. A man in the right foreground gazes out to sea and nonchalantly transfixes his solar plexus or gall bladder with a walking stick. A woman in a white dress and red hat sits on a bench on the pier and similarly impales herself by passing a sharp pointed stick through her body from right to left. Facing her and slightly to the left another woman engaged in conversation has her hand amputated and a crude prosthetic parasol attached to create a peg arm. In the background a woman in black walks towards us as she uses perhaps nothing more than a shadow to scalp a small child. To the right behind her another man sodomizes himself with a cane, while yet another woman in white close to the water's edge is immobilized by a stake protruding from her left thigh. The occupants of the painting are depicted in a struggle against vicious inanimate forces, the paradigm of which is the massive wooden pier that mercilessly divides the scene's perspective as it leads to the enclosed bathing pool in the water in the right middle ground. In fact all four strollers on the pier are either truncated or decapitated by its railing. Our amputee centerpiece has his back crushed by the weight of its solid wooden pillar. The woman in the foreground escapes its influence but even then she keeps one eye on the movements of the right arm of her chair, which has in all likelihood slipped from view in preparation for a surprise assault on her flesh; she remains alert, ready to parry its blow with her newspaper or magazine.

It appears that I am exaggerating, giving myself over to some hyperbolic indulgence in the hope of inserting a theme of amputation and even a prosthetic father into the centerground of a painting of a beach scene by Charles Conder, in the hope of finding him prone there slipping into lunchtime daydreams and catnaps that for a few moments take him outside of his body and its infirmity the way he used to nearly every working day, driving the few miles home from the office to a simple lunch my mother would have ready, then lying down for no more than five or ten minutes on the floor in the middle of the living room, which he always preferred to his bed or a couch, not wanting that added comfort to induce sleep too quickly and so make the waking and the return to the office more difficult than necessary. Of course he wouldn't be wearing his hat but would get up after the appointed time and take it again from the hallway cupboard and be gone. So it appears that I am exaggerating, that my father is a hyperbole in the middle of this painting, and more so the other mutilations I have just described. On the other hand, I am obviously speaking very literally, describing the events according to one version of their phenomenological appearance in the painting. In fact, the more literal one gets, the more the mutilation intensifies. The amputee has truncated with his flat red object not only the left leg but also the right, and very recently at that, for it still lies there where it has been cut off. The seated woman in the foreground similarly sections her left leg with her right leg and grinds the disembodied foot into the sand. The four strollers on the pier walk on their ankles, for the wooden slats have deprived them of feet. And so on. So however much I exaggerate, I cannot be said to be departing from the literal data the painting imparts. Not that this sort of data is any different from that I receive in any perceptual experience.

My point is this: Conder's *Holiday at Mentone*, as I read it, brings into focus an important problematic of perceptual experience as it intersects with visual representation; specifically it is the quandary of what happens to narrative, in the simple sense of what occurs, in a painting on the edge between realism and impressionism. This question was of course already pertinent in the case of realism, but how does one frame the storytelling or hold it in check in a case such as this one, poised at the top of the slope that leads to abstraction? For, from the realist standpoint, the move into abstraction is precisely a move into imprecision of form—the forms of objects, the forms of description—and this imprecision involves as well a fragmentation of the human form. The human form is more and more literally cut up in the refusal of realism, and it would not be an exaggeration, for reasons that will be explained further, to read that refusal and that cutting up as explicitly and literally represented in Conder's painting.

More specifically, as I wish to deal with it here, the question concerns what is left in and what is left out of this and every painting. Now that should not be read as the operation of a subjective versus an objective vision. One does not have to have an amputee father to identify another lying on the sand in a strange position at the center of a painting. And given that one does have such a father, one does not have to view a Conder beach scene as a conflict of prosthetic relations. The question is both more simple and more far-reaching than the parochialism of subjective interpretation. But neither is it simply the debate of perception versus idealism,

Fig. 1. Charles Conder, *A Holiday at Mentone*, 1888. Oil on canvas, 46.2 × 60.8 cm. Art Gallery of South Australia. Reproduced by permission.

or the question of the gestalt, or any other formulation of how the mind logically constructs a total picture on the basis of a necessarily partial vision, however interesting that question may be in and of itself, and however much it may overlap with the present discussion. The question for me arises out of the difficulty, if not the impossibility, of describing any event of painting, from realist to abstract, without the aid of narrative. It is perhaps clearer in the case of the cinematic form, which we may well take to be the paradigm for visual narrative: from the point of view of cinema the question concerns more precisely the difficulty, if not the impossibility, of confining a visual event within the frame it gives itself. The painting, like the cinematic image, comes to be defined in terms of the relation of what occurs within it to what occurs without it, beside it, in the images surrounding it, or off screen, *hors cadre*.

Besides what I have already suggested and will develop further concerning the art-historical significance of this painting, poised on the verge of abstraction, or off the edge of realism, on a particularly pertinent edge of impressionism, there are also the simple evidences of its visual data to confirm the emphasis I have just given to what is without it. There is the quite obvious bisection of the image by the pier and its shadow that gives a line of sight leading to the swimming enclosure and beyond to the open sea; the pointing by the amputee in the same direction, reinforced by the man staring off on the right. In the left foreground the seated woman is absorbed by the otherness of the written word, and it is another written word, "MENT . . . ," that, unknown to her because behind her back, but dominant for the viewer, suspends itself as a fragment within the painted space but presumably leads off to the completion of its syntagm outside the frame but within the canvas's title.

So the prosthetic question is imposed thematically by means of the proliferation of apparatuses carried by characters within the painting, and I find it to be poignantly illustrated by the arresting dormant form at the center. But before and beyond all that, what gives shape to this reading of Conder's image is the structural disposition for which "prosthesis" is as reasonable a name as any other, the disposition that deals with inclusion and exclusion, with the boundaries between what remains and what is discarded, with the facts and functions of the cut-off or fragment. Now, in the absence of any effective means of restraint on the narrative possibilities of the image, and in the absence of any extensive critical readings of the painting in the literature, it may be as well to approach this story of *A Holiday at Mentone* from the point of view of the story of Charles Conder. There the narrative must needs be more restrained, more restrained than that, for example, of a father's wooden leg; there one speaks from outside the painting, although one can also expect something of the story, that of the painter, to find its way in some form onto the surface of the canvas. But in fact, by means of this device or contrivance I hope to show, among other things, that the questions that haunt a painting are merely displaced rather than resolved when the critic turns instead to biography. One never manages to leave the painting that the life of its artist is supposed to have something to do with, and one never of course manages to get inside that life in spite of what popular parlance would have us believe. The Charles

Conder of what follows is not particularly the painter whom we presume to have been seated with his easel on the beach at Mentone one summer's day in 1888. Indeed we are told that he didn't much paint from life but composed from memory, in line with what is called his general resistance to discipline.[1] He is nevertheless that someone or something at the edge of the painting that cannot be separated from it and at times becomes a part of it. The Charles Conder that follows, like *A Holiday at Mentone*, would therefore be more accurately described as a painting of Charles Conder.

Conder, born in England in 1868, was raised in India until his mother died in a subsequent childbirth, whereupon he returned to England. At the age of fifteen he came to Australia to work for an uncle who was a government surveyor. As the emigration was later pricelessly characterized by Julian Ashton, "He was sent out by his people in London to learn under an uncle, a trigonometrical surveyor in the Lands Department, the method of dividing the surface of New South Wales into rods, poles, and perches."[2] Ashton could not have made a more pertinent comment about the relation between biography and art, for in *A Holiday at Mentone* Conder manifestly sets out to divide the space of visual representation into rods, poles, and perches. As a result, the thematics and structure of prosthesis that the painting exploits come to be concentrated in and upon the question of distance. The rods, poles, and perches that appear in his painting, that divide the space of the canvas and also attack the human forms even as they support them, measure the shifting spatial divide that falls between what occurs within the space of the painting and what occurs without it; shifting, for example, among the perspectival emphasis of the pier and bathing pool, the figural interruptions of the written word, that seen and that unseen, and the question called prosthesis that is a question of reading, specifically, if you like, the right to identify the central dormant figure as an amputee of one's acquaintance. The rods, poles, and perches of Conder's officially preartistic experience—never mind that he was shipped off to Australia precisely to thwart his expressed desire not to follow an acceptable profession but to become an artist—those trigonometricized measures applied to the empty colonial space of Australia, have become here the grid for the space of a painting, and also the basis upon which one can begin to talk about the painting as perceptual space, as artificially constructed space, as space confined within strict institutional limits—those of perspective, of the frame, of historical possibility, and so on; as space that continually points to its own outside.

Thus Conder's rods, poles, and perches are both inside and outside *A Holiday at Mentone*: in his life as a surveyor, in the objects on the canvas, in the structural divisions that open up this particular reading of it. Similarly, prosthesis is both inside and outside *A Holiday at Mentone*: in the rods, poles, and perches represented on the canvas; in the question of what appears inside as against what appears outside, or what is left off, or out, and what may be put back in, or simply put in; in the measuring of distance that all that implies. And all of that is before and beyond any designed or random appearance of an amputee in the center of the painting. Prosthesis is about nothing if it is not about measuring distance—that of the necessary separation and unavoidable complication between animate and inanimate form, between natural and artificial; that between types of writing, between memory and art criticism—about the necessity for and impossibility of precision in these relations. It is about close and distant connections of close and distant relatives.

I have no idea why Julian Ashton chose to speak of "rods," "poles," and "perches" when all three terms designate the same measure. Except perhaps to reinforce the point, or to enjoy the sound of the words. A rod, pole, or perch is a standard measure of five and a half yards. Now if I were to give myself over again to a certain literality I would want, after Ashton, to insist on this once again: a rod, pole, or perch is a standard measure of five and a half yards, or sixteen and a half feet. What might be called the protagonists of *A Holiday at Mentone*, those distinct enough to be said to enter into the foreground narrative of the painting, number nine. I refer to the four figures on the pier, the dark couple looking towards the foreground, and the foreground trio. I could say that between them, quite literally, they have sixteen and a half feet; that is if I were to restitute the feet of those on the pier and decline to do so for the missing leg of the amputee and the half-obscured foot of the seated woman. But then I would be really exaggerating, allowing a comment by a sometime art critic and former acquaintance of Conder, published seven years after the latter's death and referring to his occupation before he became a painter, to somehow assume its relevance to a discussion of the painting informed by a reading practice called prosthesis. A rod, pole, or perch or any combination thereof could not stretch far enough, one might say, could not measure the elaborate series of detours necessary to allow that connection. Be that as it may, as long as it does not obscure the fact that the same spacing that allows for the closest relations also allows for the most distant and most obscure. But I would not try to stake a reading of *A Holiday at Mentone* on an implied logical relation between a unit of measurement mentioned by chance, even if also by triple insistence, in a discussion of the artist's early biography and an improbable accounting of the limbs that appear or fail to appear in the foreground and middle ground of the painting. I would however be eager to take advantage of the chance mention of units of measurement representing sixteen and a half feet in order to reinforce the idea of division as amputation, for there is nothing far-fetched in this idea at all. Any unit of measurement is quite precisely an arbitrary division of space, an amputation that removes a spatial integer from what surrounds it and at the same time asserts its codependency with what surrounds it, for the integer removed cannot be defined without reference to something larger or smaller. And that paradox, as I have already insisted, is central to my reading here. What is taken out remains in some sense in. That becomes clearer when one considers that rods, poles, and perches are used to define proprietary boundaries, to measure privately owned space. For what is also at stake in my reading of *A Holiday at Mentone* is the question of private and public space, especially as it concerns the three seemingly unconnected foreground characters in the painting, and the system of boundaries that does or does not allow what I might call a "private," rather than a "subjective," reading of the identity of the central figure.

Returning to the exaggeration of rods, poles, and perches and of the sixteen and a half feet depicted here—to dismiss it might also be to overlook the important question this painting raises about the relations, logical or otherwise, among its sets of characters. It seems to me that the painting establishes two perspectival grids: that of the pier and the triangular one set up by the three foreground characters. One may want to add to the latter configuration the two background pairs of people whose clothing is dominated by dark tones (the woman and child on the left and the man and woman on the right), to make the configuration a chiasmus rather than a triangle. As the two distant points of the chiasmus, and as the only dark figures in a landscape that is otherwise bathed in light and color, these pairs anchor a certain sinister sentiment into the middle ground of the painting and give voice to what would be one way of reading my discovery of mutilation everywhere, namely that the painting's brightness and clarity are undercut by a lurking dark side, that the bourgeois contentment and indifference of the scene is threatened by what it represses, and that there are therefore at least two paintings to be observed in this singularly serene landscape. But, as I shall explain further, I would not want to restrict the sense of otherness to that idea of the dark underbelly of Victorian society.

In any case there is something singularly random, illogical, and unstable about the sets of characters that help focus each perspectival grid. Those on the pier, except perhaps for the man and woman on the left, seem to be on the point of intersecting only in order to separate again, and those in the foreground are striking in their indifferent immobility—providing the "moment" on which the narrative of the painting turns at the same time as they draw in the spectator's gaze only to scatter it in opposing directions. This is therefore a painting that accentuates the random relation, the chance meeting that, while relying upon a simple logic of human activity, empties human relations of their intentional force. The relations that the painting describes are inscribed above all with a sense of distance. Although it may well be that any painting does this even if it be reduced to a series of lines, this one gives a particularly shifting inscription of the distances and directional movement that creates those distances. For instance, it draws the spatial separations between the three foreground characters as absolute: it says there is no connection between these three people who happen to be captured in the instant of their reciprocal indifference. But simultaneously—and hence my insistence and my will to read—it says there *is* something between them, there is a story to be told. They are related, if by nothing else then by the rods, poles, and perches that divide the space of this painting: the man's cane; the pier's pillar that "emits" the tidal marking and forms a barrier that he hesitates to cross; the dormant man's outstretched arm; his legs, which, between the foot and the wound of his amputation, structure the space for the woman's chair, just as his stare sends a line to her back; and so on.

Such an idea of juxtaposition as coincidence is a function of prosthesis. It takes a fact of shared space, the contiguity of two or more differences, and narrates their relation as a coincidental event. But that shared space remains impossible to delimit; for as long as every relation is a relation to difference, what is a close or distant relation cannot be rigorously determined. Am I, for instance, in a closer or more distant relation to my father than his wooden leg is? Are rods, poles, and perches closer to Conder's young adulthood than to his 1888 painting? In other words, such effects cannot be determined, or limited, except by the limits of narrative, logic, and so on; all of which are being stretched here to enable us to cope with the massive coincidental contiguity of flesh and steel.

It is the shifting spatial parameters, the drawing in and sending out, that unsettles this painting, making its rods, poles, and perches both necessary and illusory as precise measures of the relations it describes. And it is that same instability that shifts the painting further into abstraction than its use of color and form would explicitly allow. It makes the question of who relates to whom and who is doing what to whom as indispensable for a reading as it is impossible to answer. Something is missing in the center of the painting—a red object marks the spot—and what is missing is precisely a stable center, something for it all to stand on. If I want to insist upon the idea of amputation to account for that instability, it is on one level to deflect from the obvious, namely that another indispensable reading for this painting concerns castration. The foreground triangular relation reads as an oedipal one: the father erect on the right, parading his cane like a phallus that is also an instrument of censure, contrasts with the mother on the left, who hides her own sexuality with her magazine and left hand; the wounded son looks to the mother for confirmation of what he has seen lacking in her and reaches to the father for approval, while he is struck by the pain of his own capacity to be wounded and deprived of his potency. And so on and so forth. I want to deflect from that obvious reading, but not in order to invalidate it, for the oedipal, as a function of the familial, remains a powerful theory for the structuration of human relations, from the closest to the most distant. Rather I wish to offer the prosthetic as a complement to the oedipal, even if such a complement inevitably contains a hint of parody.

In the first place, the amputation of a paternal limb, the father's carrying of infirmity as a form of lack, serves to some extent to feminize him. The amputated male is not the castrated male, for he is in no way deprived of the law and name of the father; but at the same time the solidity of the name that derives from the indivisibility of the phallus, and of the body as a whole as metonymic signifier of the phallus, is called into question. The structure of prosthesis, Derrida will say, "belongs to intumescence. Nothing stands upright otherwise."[3] If, as the poet via the psychoanalyst states, it is no sin to limp,[4] the failure to walk straight is nevertheless a visible sign of infirmity, a deconstruction of assumed wholeness. After all, according to the accepted etymology, infirmity or "swollen foot" is the name of Oedipus himself.[5] But, for me, the relation to the father and thus to the phallus is articulated through the prosthetic limb, not only through the infirmity but actually through the artificiality of the prosthesis itself. One may be able to go so far as to say that in this case the phallus itself, as arbiter of familial relations, cannot be articulated except by a transfer through the prosthesis, through a series of disjunctions that make the relation with the father also a relation with steel, with a crutch and a cane, with a specific gait, and so on.

By means of prosthesis the relation to the other becomes precisely and necessarily a relation to otherness, the otherness, for example, of artificiality attached to or found within the natural. The relation to the other is denied the reconfirmation of sameness that freezes its differential effect, rigidifies the oedipal structure, and ultimately represses the feminine, the homosexual, and so on. For in spite of the importance of amputation, that relation, once it is a question of prosthesis, cannot be reduced to a matter of presence or absence, of possession or dispossession. It cannot be reduced to a matter of having or not having the prosthesis, for prosthesis is in no way reducible to a wooden leg. Instead, prosthesis of necessity prosthetizes whatever it relates to by automatically inscribing its effect of otherness. Quite plainly, once an artificial limb comes to be attached to a human body, then any second, or rather third body that relates to that divided first one necessarily relates to it as difference, even if it be another divided or prosthetic body.

That radical sense of self-division, of division into otherness, also has the effect of pluralizing the father. Once something is no more single, then it is also no more simply double, as Luce Irigaray has clearly demonstrated for the case of the feminine.[6] Hence the proliferation of fathers and limbs, of rods, poles, and perches, all through this discussion. It's not just that there is no end of them once one begins to look for them. On the one hand prosthesis can as easily do without them; on the other hand the cane or amputee identified, for example, in a painting by Charles Conder is as much an effect of prosthesis as it is an example of it. It is an effect of prosthesis to the extent that the principle of otherness and detachability upon which the identifying of such an image relies, and which it in turn elaborates, allows one to find that amputee "against" a certain logic of the painting and against a certain logic of reading; and also to the extent that the human figure in the center of the painting does not "belong" to that painting, or to Charles Conder, or to this reader, before it "belongs" to the set of differential relations that represent prosthesis. To repeat: according to prosthesis, relations in general are governed by difference as radical otherness, and a given prosthesis such as a father's wooden leg is merely a case of that. Any relation is a relation to difference or otherness, and prosthesis is a name for that. Thus prosthesis prevents the figure in the painting from belonging even as it allows it to belong; even as it attaches it to the space of the Conder beach scene, it detaches it for the benefit of this reading. Prosthesis becomes a staging of the radical recontextualization that, Derrida has insisted, is a possibility for every signifying event.[7] Prosthesis reads this possibility from the following point of view: if an utterance, such as a figure in the center of a painting, can be grafted onto another context, this means that it has no "natural" place, never did have, and that the relations it forms with subsequent contexts inevitably re-inscribe that fall out of naturalness. And prosthesis adds the emphasis that what therefore governs recontextualization are forms of contrivance and principles of artificiality. In this sense a principle such as that of analogy, which means, for instance, that the wooden leg is designed to function as much as possible like the amputated one, can occlude neither the fact that the leg is wooden or steel nor the fact that before the principle of analogy could come into effect, the principles of detachability and artificiality already had to be in play.

The wooden leg detaches—that has been said before. Usually in private, but not so at the beach. There he uses the changing sheds like those to be found in the enclosure off to the right of the painting. He enters the door marked MEN that is not found in the picture even though the word is there in large letters, all that is added to it being the sign of an addition or a chiasmus that leaves the matter of addition and subtraction, of inclusion and exclusion, of convergence and divergence suspended on the edge of the frame, the frame transgressed by its own sign, the letter "T," the rod, pole, or perch that stands precariously on a threshold of this painting, sign of the frame that adds, divides, includes, excludes, and so on, and "T" also the sign of the bracket and of the potence and of support in general; it is the door one enters to take off one's wooden leg, the door behind which lies the place of all the difference in the world, the difference between MEN and ladies, and the difference of what is meant or "MENT" by the words—differences Lacan has underlined and that could well be both reinforced and dismantled here[8]—there he goes into the men's bathing sheds at Mentone or Tahunanui with walking stick and crutch, a son or two trailing him in, not that they will be needed just yet, but when they are young enough they accompany him anyway and busy themselves with undressing as discreetly as possible, not paying particular attention to the other men and boys present or even to my father, whose legless stump is familiar enough, until we are ready to go back outside, and from out of nowhere, from perches away there appears on the scene a boy of about my age, standing utterly agape, transfixed by the spectacle of a man who divests himself of a leg, just takes it off and leans it against the wall with the trousers still on. The kid is astounded and speechless and will not stop staring despite my smile, then my bashful feigned indifference, then rage at his impertinence; and finally his father in turn looks and does a double take then tries to deflect his son's attention from my father's lack, my father who has by this time turned to acknowledge the scene and smiled in turn, awkward smiles all round waiting for someone to break the silence and it is obviously my father's place to do so only this time he likely can't be bothered, but the boy still stares even when his father begins to edge him out the door, he stares and then his open mouth begins to move, I can see it coming even if I don't know what it is, the impudent sonofabitch is going to say something, there was no way to predict where it had come from or how it had found its way to this specific formulation, but he opens his mouth again and asks with the sort of obscenely naive quizzicality that is as aggressive as it is disarming, he asks my father "Has your *mother* got one like it?," italics mine. On the simplest of interpretations he means to ask the question of me, means to ask about my father's wife, using a common childish catachresis. But whether wittingly or not, he has opened up the whole prosthetic network: constructing even as he deconstructs the oedipal relation such that where there is a case of having it or not there is a mother never far away; implying that where there is one prosthesis there must be another never far away; implicating the transferential impulse whereby in addressing my father the boy addresses and so prosthetizes me; and enacting the necessary detachment as a result of which the loose prosthesis comes to rest far from its analogical stays.

   Hence the prosthetic fathers pluralize as they recontextualize. But, still within the context of the oedipal, what I have just explained also means that prosthesis is not a case of a symbol. No cane, amputee, or wooden leg ever signifies prosthesis. The rods, poles, and perches do not stand in for the truth of prosthesis, nor do they revert to a prosthesis, for such a prosthesis is nowhere to be found, not in any one place. For it is variously a memory, fantasy, or fiction of a father's infirmity, an exercise in writing, a set of ideas that explain and allow the latter, and so on. The rods, poles, and perches, for instance, are nowhere in prosthesis before they come to be found in *A Holiday at Mentone*, nor are they in the painting waiting for prosthesis to ferret them out. However much my reading might give that impression or play on that contrivance, that is not what takes place here. It is after all embarrassingly simple as a contrivance; no stick, not even the smallest brushstroke would be immune from it were I really to begin to exaggerate. Instead the rods, poles, and perches are identified in the painting only to divide it and bear off outside of it; they are inserted into it in order to divine its points of resistance and prize open its surface coherence. They form part of the set of prosthetic relations in terms of which this reading attempts to give sense to this painting. In terms of those relations what is is also other than what it is, or is in being other; what is in or on can be taken out or off, or be replaced—but again, not according to a simple principle of presence and absence, or loss and retrieval, but rather according to a complicated principle of *alterability*. Then, further still, what is identified as effect of prosthesis—cane or amputee—is but a stick or baton in a relay of signification (rather than a link in a chain), a stake that signifies the relay as much as it signifies anything in itself, and a relay that involves a passage over the abyss of chance and accident, where contact can only be made as a result of a spacing that each time raises the possibility of no contact, like an amputee who lies bleeding on a beach in Port Phillip Bay and stretches his arm in vain towards the cane of a stranger who turns his back and holds it out of reach, betraying a certain nostalgia as he in turn looks forlornly across the empty space out to the expanses of sea that keep him absent from a beloved father whose memory he tries to retain by adopting a series of affectations such as the port of a cane, the recording of a series of narrative moments that the distance has so shrouded with haze that he could be inventing any part or even the whole of it, perhaps making all this up, listening to the noise of the sea that is the noise of distance, one hears it in the telephone as if it were a seashell held to the ear, the noise of the fog of multiple time-zone separation that is the certain noise of the announcement of death, the noises of death and nostalgia forever confounded with the static of waves, with characteristic lock-kneed gait he stares off out of the frame so much so that he too no longer belongs to it but moves off out of it with his stare while he contemplates the extent of the hemispheric sea passage rendered necessary by the event of a relay called prosthesis.

Charles Conder left his father in India after his mother died there, then moved to Sydney from the United Kingdom, then met Tom Roberts and moved to Melbourne, where he, Roberts, and Arthur Streeton formed what became known as the Heidelberg School, named after the area outside of Melbourne where they set up camp to paint the colony's initiation into impressionism. They also spent time at Mentone and other beaches along Port Phillip Bay and showed together in 1889 in an exhibition entitled "9 × 5 Impression," perhaps Australia's most momentous artistic event. The works of that exhibition were painted on cigar box lids with dimensions of 9″ × 5″. Conder exhibited a number of his own works and also designed the catalogue cover. In fact he contributed $9 \times 5 = 45$[9] cigar box paintings, decorated 45 chambers designed to house instruments of excessive pleasure, and I can't say much more about those boxes at this stage, or about the number of them, not as long as Melbourne 1889 remains separate from Rome 1985; I can't say for instance whether the 45 boxes were painted so as to open frontwards or backwards, only that *A Holiday at Mentone* was not one of those works. That painting measured differently, 17.25″ × 23″, and still does, or at least 46.2 cm × 60.8 cm, according to the details given on the back of the print of it in front of me. That ratio of width to length is in fact untrue, for the print in front of me, on the cover of a greeting card published in Australia by the house of Bodleigh, cuts off almost all of the "т" following the "мен" of the word on the extreme right, whereas the original discloses almost all of that letter. I can confirm this, having seen the original one day in Brisbane in 1988 in the company of a friend who wondered aloud, in spite of his complaints about the noise made by hordes of schoolchildren visiting this bicentennial celebration of Australian art, what the man with one leg might be trying to say in semaphore. I can also confirm the matter of the final "т" in view of a second print of it in front of me on a $5 postage stamp that I received on a parcel in Paris in 1984 while beginning to write this book (see Fig. 2). Although the postage stamp restores the "т" that the greeting card amputates almost entirely, and renders the colors more faithfully, it manages to erase the signature of Chas. Conder in the lower right with the imprint of the word "Australia" in bold capitals, and above that the denomination "$5." It erases the artist's signature but highlights the date of

Charles Conder A Holiday at Mentone 1888   Art Gallery of S A

$5
AUSTRALIA

Fig. 2 Charles Conder's *A Holiday at Mentone* as reproduced on an Australian postage stamp.

the painting's execution, which falls under the arch of the final "A" of "Australia."

Conder's precise place within a postal network of cards and stamps sent between Europe and the antipodes or within the second half of the nineteenth century is not my immediate concern. But it is worth noting here that the history of creative transformation of Conder's paintings begins with the "9 × 5" works since, according to the *Bulletin of the National Gallery of South Australia* (n.p.), a good number of his cigar box paintings were bought by a single collector who stored them in a kitchen cupboard and whose maid cut them up for kindling. The fire still flames at the center of *A Holiday at Mentone*, as the amputee tries with his fingertips to pick up a blazing tinder box that cauterizes the gaping wound of his leg like a pre-1552 amputee victim, to shake it clear of his body, or douse it with sand, or transfer it like some hot potato to the seated woman's hat, then in turn to the ribbons of flame licking down the back of the woman in gray conversing with the man on the pier, and across to the hat of the woman seated on the bench. The object that exposes the danger or destruction at the center of the painting, then blood now fire, sends a gentle vortex of red spiraling up to the left top of the canvas. It will be said that Oedipus has been here again. The seated mother has exposed her sex, which she now turns and conceals; the dormant figure is stricken immobile by the truth of it, the burning or bleeding truth between his legs that he transfers to the women present, who are obliged to wear it in all its visibility to cover their woven tresses and so indulge the fetishistic desire to see what cannot be faced. It is relayed through their accoutrements—the red hats and yellow panamas they were all wearing that year, the ribbons, belts, handbags, parasols—blood or fire with each idiosyncratic brush-stroke or figure matching the incline of the seated woman's head, the angle of the ribbons on the woman on the pier, the imprecise line of the third woman's hat, the splashes on the woman walking off the pier. It will otherwise be said that it is more simply this: a case of imprecision in the brushstroke or the poor draftsmanship that almost every one of Conder's critics is quick to point out; neither blood from an amputee's wound that bleeds from the center like a diagonal gash across one half of the painting, nor the artist's own breakthrough work burning in some bourgeois' fire-place in Melbourne and breaking through the surface of this canvas. Even less, it will be said, the fire built by an amputee from the branches and dead wood he has been pruning from his fruit trees one graying autumn afternoon, spending all day poised precariously atop a ladder while my mother looks on and holds her breath as his prosthetic leg swings loose and he stretches out balanced on one foot to reach the distant limbs; he will keep on doing it in spite of her entreaties, but she can't help fearing what his body would come to if it were really to get into an accident with his leg, how the flesh of his trunk would fare smashed against the familiar steel of the artificial leg if he were to fall, what mangled stump she would have to live with thereafter less tolerable than the one she already knows, knows it well enough to answer her friend who inquires soon after her marriage what it is like to sleep with a man with one leg, to which she replies without hesitation that she wouldn't know since she has never slept with a man with two, in any case he never fell when pruning trees, in fact very seldom fell for a man with one good leg, instead he piles his freshly cut limbs in the front yard and tries to set them alight but fails, for the hibernal damp has already set in, he tries a second and a third time then in frustration takes to splashing some lawnmower fuel on the not quite extinct fire at which point there is a general and sudden conflagration that engulfs him and his eyebrows and sends him reeling backwards with scorched face but much less injury than could have been the case, and it wasn't the injury itself that hurt so much as his utter astonishment at having been such a chump, as if he had been caught playing with fire the way we children were one day and sent to bed in the afternoon, the worst punishment I ever remember enduring, and it was a close family friend we called an aunt whom my mother phoned to come and take care of things, an aunt for all generations and all eventualities who came as always with impeccable Victorian demeanor and abundant warmth of heart to take over and take the heat out of things, to kindle and control the fire with as much aplomb as she would exhibit in putting on a red hat or sitting reading on the veranda of her family's colonial home, puzzling over the crossword that she would bring to him to solve in exchange for quenching his fires.

Even less so that, perhaps. But the "9 × 5 Impression" cigar boxes, chopped and burning or not, remain at the center of *A Holiday at Mentone* to this extent: in those images that, like this one, brought splashes of impressionism like last season's fashions to the far-flung colonies, form was required to compete with color on the surface of the canvas, the hallowed precision of one against the newly discovered vigor of the other, the inherited intellectual realism of one challenged by the emotive realism of the other. As a result there occurs an undeniable rending of the fabric of artistic representation at the site of its central tenets, such that the hand that held a steady drafting instrument begins instead to wield a firebrand that burns its way through fauvism and beyond to abstraction's point of no return. So it is again a kindling of narrative uncertainty, a question about what is happening in the middle of the painting that reaches up and outside of it, about what is happening in the narrative of art history, about what is happening in the narrative of Charles Conder's place in that history, including the question of his right to be considered an important part of it; and also about what is happening when an art object is no longer confined within the frame to which it has been assigned historically—but only since the Renaissance, let us not forget—when, like the top of a cigar box left in a kitchen cupboard, it opens to reveal a clutter of dust, oddments, and mementos, or comes unhinged to disclose the artificial construct that supports it, or cracks, sending fault lines like diagonal striations off the edge of the painted surface.

In 1890 Conder left Australia to return to Europe. He settled for some years in Paris, where he studied at the Atelier Julian and became friends with Louis Anquetin and Toulouse-Lautrec, giving himself over to the bohemian excesses of Montmartre. He ceased being an Australian painter for everyone but the Australians. Whether he ever was, and whether one would know that to look at his paintings, is of course a subject raised by the art historians who treat of him, many of them writing ten years either

side of his death, which occurred in 1909. For Frank Gibson, the time
Conder spent in Australia was "a very impressionable period in a young
man's lifetime, and it is certain that it influenced Conder's colouring."[10]
According to John Rothenstein, "although his work at this time was
generally feeble and unformed, the Australian environment had one lasting effect upon him. From it he learned his love of fruit blossom, which he
was never to tire of expressing. Beyond this, Australia seems to have
affected him little."[11] There is an increasingly explicit tendency to consider
the time spent in Australia more as an accident or aberration after which
he returned to the true center of artistic endeavor. Rothenstein again:
"Only a sojourn in Europe could give [him] . . . the confidence to form a
just estimate of [his] own talents and achievements."[12] Ursula Hoff re-
marks, in terms of an unexplained logic, that Conder left Sydney to go
south to Melbourne "presumably as a first step on his return to Europe."[13]
According to that logic, whichever direction he embarked upon, it could
not but be a return to the artistic homeland or continent. Martin Birnbaum was more peremptory in 1911: "His early years were spent in India
and Australia, and it will always be difficult to understand how his tastes
and sense of color could have been nurtured by, or have survived, a
training for the Government Survey Department. His purely artistic
activity was very brief, for it was not until 1890, when he went to Paris, that
he determined to devote himself entirely to painting."[14] D. S. MacColl
gives this precious insight:

> By an intelligible misunderstanding in the case of an English boy, Conder's
> talents were devoted, at the earliest moment possible, to the trigonometrical
> survey of Australia. Work so elementary, and instruments so inexact for the
> appreciation of landscape, could not, however, content him long. From deserts
> where nothing is to be seen, drunk, or dreamed but cosines, he found his way
> to the garden and embarked upon its more congenial survey.[15]

It is worthwhile reflecting where, in this trajectory from the desert,
where there is nothing but cosines, to the garden, *A Holiday at Mentone* is
supposed to stand; how much of the desert's supposed visual emptiness
and of trigonometrical insensitivity these expanses of sand and water and
blotches of fire and blood still retain; how much from an abandoned past
and how much of a telepathic future converges here.

The fact is that within a few years of arriving in Europe, Conder's art
had completely changed—at least from a standard art-historical perspec-

tive—from that created in his Australian period. His work came to be concentrated more and more in painting on silk, particularly fans and dress panels, and in lithography, in styles reminiscent of Whistler or Beardsley among his own contemporaries, and Watteau or Fragonard among earlier *pompiers*. Though his talent commanded a certain respect, particularly among a coterie that included Beardsley, the Symbolist poet Jacques-Emile Blanche, and Oscar Wilde, and gained a reputation in America, the extent of his genius was doubted by some by the time he died. He had by then returned to England and married, but bad health aggravated or caused by alcoholism plagued him in the last ten years of his life.

He may have ceased being more than an Australian in later life; he may have ceased being an artist at all. The fall from a purer art to a lesser design, from canvas to silk, from creation without purpose to decorative utility, is assumed to be a fall out of painting. It is the outside threat to painting that is a converse to the sculpture that is the outside threat to architectural design. Perhaps the amputee of *A Holiday at Mentone* has fallen from it, fallen into raptures in contemplation of what is offered by the back of the seated woman's dress, of what might be offered by the time spent in her company, painting the panels while the garment was still on her body as Conder reportedly did for Alexandra Thaulow at Dieppe.[16] Nearly a century later he becomes not only a painter of fans but also of postage stamps, and the fall into utility and mercantility is complete. Perrin Joyce could see it coming back in 1925: "The painting of fans is of course a mere avocation; it has no purpose; it does not identify the artist with this or that school of theorists. And so, because the appropriate tag cannot be found, he must go without the label of the artist."[17] For others, the later work is more than just a betrayal of the principles of art; it is also a betrayal of the artist's nature, his talent. Conder's Australian champion, Julian Ashton, finds that he unwisely turned from what he did well—coloring—to what he did much less well—drawing: "It is inexplicable that Conder, the colourist, could ever have been induced to attempt anything requiring draughtsmanship. . . . For colour harmony and a fanciful, if somewhat artificial, sense of design, his taste was unerring; but his vague and capricious dreams had nothing in common with the severity and calculated beauty of form required in the work he attempted."[18] Writing soon after Conder's death, W. H. de B. Nelson is slightly less charitable: "Clever he truly was, great painter he was not. His claim to recognition lies in his easy

mastery of design and the deft manner in which he placed his decorative
fancies upon silk. His predilection for foliage and his choice of silk tend to
show him as a japonisant, but he defies classification. He was just Charles
Conder, whose brain lived in a whirl of Bohemian riot, an apostle of
hedonism."[19] On the other hand Nelson's poison is Birnbaum's meat:

> Conder's paintings are like lyrical poems or inspired melodies. He never
> suffered from the modern disease of realism and the creatures of his delicate
> fancy move about in an engaging world of heroic landscapes and enchanted
> gardens. The pictures are arabesques of sumptuous women basking in their
> own glorious beauty. Nymphs throw back their heads in ecstasy and recline in
> cool dew-drenched arbors of silvery green foliage, or wander thinly clad on the
> shore of a serene sapphire sea. Through a golden haze they are seen flaunting
> themselves in Elysian groves. Sitting among ruined columns under azure skies,
> they listen to playing fountains or to the seductive strains of music wafted by
> perfumed breezes.[20]

Apart from allowing me to round out the story or portrait of Charles
Conder that is the conceit of this essay, those passages continue to raise the
question that still concerns me here, namely what is in a given painting
and what is not, what of an abandoned Australian Conder is to be found in
this or his later work, and what of that later work can already be identified
in potential in a painting such as *A Holiday at Mentone*; not to mention
what narrative input or excess traditionally informs writing on the visual
arts. As might be expected given the tone of the quotations already
provided, those who write on him are concerned to establish some sort of
equation or ratio between a supposedly coherent body of artistic production and the facts of biography, however much mythology and rupture
enter into each side of the ratio. Writing of his Australian pictures Hoff
declares, "there is in them as yet no sign of the fêtes galantes of Watteau,
Fragonard and Monticelli which influenced his later style." Basil Burdett
concurs: "Yet, looking at the pictures he painted in Australia, particularly
at some of the sketches which have survived from . . . the '9 × 5 Impression
Exhibition' of 1889 in Melbourne, one is struck, in many of them, by an
open air quality essentially remote from that of the exotic blooms which
afterwards flowered from Conder's genius in London and Paris."[21] On the
other hand, in a more recent article occasioned by an exhibition held in
Australia in the mid-1980's, and looking at a painting contemporary with

A Holiday at Mentone, Svetlana Lloyd finds that "clearly Whistler and the Japanese were . . . god-parents."[22]

So the question remains as to whether the spectator has to go outside of this painting to know that it represents Australia, or to know that it is painted by Charles Conder; yet the problem is compounded by doubt as to who or what Charles Conder represents, especially in terms of nationality. Undoubtedly he himself subscribed to the idea that he could only become a really *good* painter, as distinct from an internationally recognized painter, by going to Paris. Although he spoke with fond nostalgia of the time spent with Streeton and Roberts in Heidelberg,[23] there seems no reason to assume that he continued to consider himself an Australian once he left that country. But all this is finally by the way and obscures the fact that his itinerary—England, India, England, Australia, France, England—reads as one of alternating exile and return, and therefore that a sense of absence is surely what one would expect to find in his paintings. One needs to interpret in this light the various attempts to identify him nationalistically. For Nelson his work was that of a "man who tempered the dainty Gallicism of a Boucher or Fragonard with an unquestionably Saxon restraint." Similarly Perrin Joyce: "The phrase-makers have called Conder the 'English Watteau'—a meaningless paradox. English is just what Watteau could never have been; and French is certainly something that Conder could never be called." Speaking of Blanche's assessment of Conder, with which he disagrees, Rothenstein writes: "to him Conder, with his enormous stock and other signs of original foppery, seemed the very type of the English eccentric."[24] Yet Blanche's description is in fact more subtle:

> This young Australian was a strange character. He was bizarre and undisciplined right to the end, in spite of his love of work. But in a very English way his eccentricities plead more in his favour than would a normal existence. . . . He is classed among the host of "outlaws" or "outcasts," for whom his compatriots have a most romantic inclination. . . . Whether in Paris or London he was like Verlaine, out of the ordinary, going from inebriation to lucidity as if from sleep to wakening, never working with more inspiration than when he was excited by alcohol.[25]

For him, Conder is variously Australian, English, and—judging from the reference to Verlaine, himself something of an Anglophile and wanderer—

French. As an Australian he is both assimilated to and distinguished from
the English, and it is not clear whether it is his English or his Australian
compatriots who romanticize outlaws. One wonders what makes him "a
young Australian" for Blanche—his having come to Paris from there or his
being susceptible to becoming French, a susceptibility betraying him as
less than totally English. For it is a form of self-recognition by and through
an outsider that Blanche seems to be seeking:

> They [Beardsley, Wilde, Conder] all possessed the cult and intelligence of
> "l'esprit français," and understood our language. . . . They form a small host
> that will be always remembered with gratitude by those of us who so assidu-
> ously frequented England in the last years of the nineteenth century. Our
> literary and musical movements, our painting, in short everything most
> significant and fresh about us, found in them open and receptive minds and
> enthusiastic voices willing to celebrate us.[26]

When it does come to Conder's vision—presumably it is the Elysian scenes
of his later work that Blanche has in mind—Blanche again identifies it as
Australian, although in this case the Australian gets assimilated to the
Indian in terms of their both being colonial:

> His kind dark blue eyes seen through the haze of cigarette smoke, would gaze
> vaguely off into the distance, as if lost in a dream, probably one of those Indian
> or Australian, or at least *colonial,* settings that were the habitual decor of his
> hallucinations. Intoxicated by the enchanted palaces, dancing maidens, foun-
> tains and black slaves that he remembered from the childhood he spent there,
> he felt that they were close at hand, there, just the other side of the bridge,
> although far across the ocean.[27]

One can only imagine how Blanche may have been privy to the subjects of
Conder's hallucinations. Yet such clairvoyance is a talent shared by Rothenstein, who objects, "when Conder day-dreamed (and he day-dreamed
often), it was neither of Australia nor of the Indies, but of orchards and
wooded hills and green fields in Normandy, or small French villages that
he loved: Vetheuil, La Roche-Guyon, Chantemesle." Elsewhere he states:
"His vision was in essence neither local nor objective; and therefore
neither Australian nor Impressionist. His chosen country was Arcadia."[28]
   It is clear, however, that what is going on in these characterizations—or
indeed these hallucinations in which the imaginer seeks more the reflection of his own desire than anything else—is a form of reading "towards

the center" that is presumed to apply indiscriminately to both painter and work. As a result, not only do painter and work become interchangeable, but the painting itself becomes a hallucination, whose decor is alternately Australian, Indian, or French, whose occupants are alternately slaves (black and in any case colonial), swaying dancers, and wood nymphs. In such descriptions the vision never changes; it remains resolutely European, no doubt as much so for Conder as for Blanche and Rothenstein. One simply places in the frame whatever one already sees.

In spite of appearances, none of this is beside the point. In perfectly natural tones—those one comes to expect of a certain critical discourse that manages, in spite of itself or through its very naïveté, to highlight a question of immense proportions—those who write on Conder pose and occlude the undecidability that is not just a function of a particular artist with a varied geographical itinerary and an artistic output that changed dramatically but indeed and inevitably a function of art criticism and reading in general. It is clearly the case in *A Holiday at Mentone*, whether or not one takes to heart my rods, poles, and perches, my amputations and mutilations. It is clearly the case that the otherworldliness, or just plain otherness, that the critics wrestled with in approaching the idiosyncrasies of Conder's later art is very much a part of this painting. For all its being undeniably Australian, or "antipodean"—a study of the use of color and light could presumably confirm that, for at least those emphases form the basis of a certain ideology and mythology of Australian impressionism[29]— it is singular, as I see it, in its centrifugal lines of force: the man on the right gazing off across the ocean, dreaming of Arcadian wood nymphs or dancing maidens, black slaves or smoke-filled Montmartre bars, the woman on the left absorbed in her reading, her back turned to the water, and the amputee fallen into a torpor that sends back the spectator's gaze, while the pillar behind him takes it up and then deflects it simultaneously off to the left and the right along the pier, which itself already competes with the horizon of the coastline for perspective prominence.

Clearly, then, the painting is one of dislocation; the foreground half of the canvas is full of it. And that dislocation sets in train a movement of signification, in the sense of a suspension of signification, that no effort of restitution can bring to an end. Restitution is, once again, the figure Derrida uses as something of a paradigm for discourse on the art object.[30] The effort of restitution occurs "outside" the painting, in the identification of a nationality, of a style, a type of talent, to better effect a stabilization of the elements within the painting. And conversely, dislocation observed in the painting finds its confirmation in questions about the painter's history. My desire here is not to belabor those obvious points that informed criticism and theoretical writing have been analyzing for a long time now, whether with respect to the plastic or the literary arts. On the other hand, my own process of identification—of mutilation, of an amputee—with all its disingenuous exaggeration, appears to fall within that same framework of questions, and once again I would want it to be read as something other than just parody.

Firstly, starting from something like parody or hyperbole, it reinforces the dislocation that is already obvious in this painting but that, as I have suggested, may necessarily be waiting to be read in any painting, at least any painting that inherits the realist tradition; namely, what I referred to previously as the question concerning narrative, the impossibility of discourse on painting without recourse to narrative. That question arises simply because a painting consists in a spatial arrangement, or consecution, of form and color, and consecution implies narrative. With the move to abstraction traditional forms of narrative, namely realist ones, are challenged. The question of narrative becomes more urgent as its form seems to become less certain. It is that effect of dislocation that my process of identification seeks to reinforce, extending the question of narrative to the edges of the painting and beyond. This is in line with the idea, also made explicit in Derrida,[31] that whatever occurs within the frame can only be contained there by a series of framings, physical, institutional, and discursive, that are held to reside outside it. By seeming to impose an entirely "foreign" narrative upon *A Holiday at Mentone*, my reading in fact underlines the discussion of home and foreignness, of space and distance—from self, from tradition, from history—that seems to inform the totality of writing on the work of Charles Conder. Yes, on the one hand that discussion is merely stating the obvious in the facts of his biography and his art. But on the other hand, to read those critics, the facts they record—that Conder traveled and lived in a number of places and that he painted both real and utopian landscapes—are by no means articulated in terms of foreignness; on the contrary they amount to an attempt to put him each time at home there, in the middle of whatever object he creates. My putting "him," someone else, far from home, there, amputated, bleeding and on fire, is a resistance to and undercutting of such attempts.

Secondly, and this has nothing to do with hyperbole or parody any more, the whole exercise of prosthesis, of which the "identification" of an amputee in the middle of *A Holiday at Mentone* is a part and an example, seeks to extend—or rather have rebound—not only the forms of discourse on art for which traditional writing on Conder provides a paradigm but also more recent efforts to displace that paradigm. If that traditional paradigm can be summed up in terms of putting the artist at home in and with the painting—presuming her to control its execution and its sense— then more recent analyses have insisted upon the artist's role as represent- ing various configurations of absence and, conversely, the spectator as being implicated in the viewing process in an avowedly active manner. The work of Derrida once again provides the context for extending such analyses, and in his discussion of literary as well as plastic art objects, and indeed of philosophy, he has developed the notion of the creator as signatory.[32] Nowhere is this more explicit than in the case of a painting, for instance this one here, signed "Chas. Conder—1888," unless one looks at it on a $5 postage stamp, in which case it is Australia that signs. The artist signs, thereby attesting to the authenticity of the piece, but by the same token the proper name becomes a part of the design, no more than form and color on the canvas; and also it becomes open to manipulation and forgery. What is gained by the signing is lost in the same movement, as much by an institution like the post office as by any past, present, or future counterfeiter. Furthermore, as important for Derrida as the initial signing by the artist is the countersignature of the spectator, the institutions of history, the museum, and so on.[33] It is by means of this countersignature that the painting is recognized as such, as an authentic work of art, signed, for example, by Chas. Conder. The emphasis of prosthesis is to reinforce and radicalize this sense of the countersignature of the spectator or reader; to inscribe it as both recognition and misrecognition. In reading or analyzing the work of art one recognizes the work of the author; but in the same movement, one inevitably requires that that author stand aside, that she yield some space for the discourse of the spectator. How much space, and in what form it should be yielded, are, of course important and, I would argue, ultimately unanswerable questions that necessarily become part of the critic's analysis. A reading informed by prosthesis might be seen to take liberties in this regard, but one object of my exercise is to test the limits of such liberty. At the same time, the countersignature of prosthesis, that which occurs, for instance, through an identification of an amputee in the center foreground of this painting, also participates no less explicitly than the signature in the form and color of the painting. If it could not recognize itself in the painting it would have no meaning with respect to the painting; but, in running counter to it, it must also inscribe its difference. Prosthesis, as autobiographical interruption within the space of criticism, or as incursion of such a divided criticism within the space of its object, here a painting by Charles Conder, seeks to assure that such a countersignature takes place; that the reader takes place, albeit in a contrived or prosthetic form, within the discourse of criticism and within the art object. In this taking place however, no simple identification or substitution occurs, rather a kind of palimpsestic tracing of the forms and configurations that the object already deploys. Both an authentication of the artist's hand, and thus of the signature, and a forgery or misuse of it; both a dislocating of the forms within the painting and a recognition of them. Thus the "signs" of prosthesis—canes, amputees—are effects of a prosthesis that, in being a reading, signs, and, in being a signature, countersigns, and in countersigning, signs *counter* to what it signs.

In effect, something of a duel has taken place between painter and spectator. As a result they, or someone or something related to them, lie wounded or dying on the painted surface of *A Holiday at Mentone*. The painter does not simply die by means of the signature, but his name does bleed into the canvas. And similarly, the spectator cannot pretend that the work will fall into place around his reading; he needs to struggle and force the issue, putting his name and perhaps his reputation at risk, in order to effect the analysis. Thus it is not simply a case of identifying an amputee in the center of the painting. It never was, for we have seen his identity shift, now bleeding, then on fire; now a sleeping father, then Oedipus; and finally there is this duel to divide the identity between a dying author and a wounded spectator. But whichever configuration is adopted, the foreground narrative of the painting remains, if not one of a duel—though the possibility of such a reading is surely provided—then one of a struggle, between recognition and disassociation, between reaching and separation, between prosthetic and integral versions of self, between the *heimlich* and the *unheimlich*, and so on. And that struggle is merely an effect of the struggle between what is confined within the frame of the painting and what bears in on it from the outside.

Something of a duel took place in Conder's life in Paris. A writer, Edouard Dujardin, seems to have won the heart of Conder's mistress, Germaine (history doesn't record the color of her hat), who had become disaffected with Conder's dissoluteness. Dujardin insulted Conder publicly and weapons were discussed, but the thing was resolved without a fight.[34] So Conder wasn't dead until 1909, 21 years after his *Holiday at Mentone.* There and then, I suppose, the narrative comes to a close of sorts. The painting begins a different itinerary, into a different kind of otherness, coming to rest variously in a museum in Adelaide, in a touring exhibition on the occasion of a national bicentennial, on the front of a greeting card that trims the painting's edges, on a postage stamp signed "Australia" and framed by the semicircular tears of its perforations, in the particular prosthetic disposition of the present discussion.

It is time therefore, perhaps, for a certain play of hyperbole to come to a close, time to recognize the man in the center foreground as a catnapper or daydreamer, lying with one leg tucked underneath the other, falling asleep as he lets drop his reading matter. It is a book, this end of the narrative will say, or at least something to be read. It is a book, or a magazine, or a newspaper in one of those replaceable bindings with a stick down the spine, those reading prostheses that one can still find in certain quaint cafés or old-worldly hotels and libraries. The seated woman is reading the same thing, for one can discern the red cover of hers also. We shouldn't pay too much attention to the red cover, for in this closing narrative the painting is an impressionist work in which the strength of particular hues is indulged for its own sake, according to a heightened perception of the dominance of certain primary colors as revealed by the effects of sunlight. The red cover would be somewhat clearer to us if Conder had been a better draftsman, but there is no such thing as absolute precision—one wouldn't expect it to extend to the title of the book or the words on the page the woman is reading—and as has been insisted here, the moment the precision falters, which is necessarily always, the narrative begins all over again. So we shall be content with something red to be read held tenuously by a supine man on the beach at Mentone.

Too large for a postcard, perhaps a letter. Not the letter "T" both included and excluded from various reproductions of the painting, although it is worth remembering that nothing leads us more explicitly outside the frame than this fragment of a word that may not in fact be completed as transparently as one, or "ONE," might presume, it all depends on the language one is using, but I shall hold that in reserve, rather the sort of letters that start to be published after the death of an artist, as for instance in R. H. Croll's *Smike to Bulldog*, where it is recounted that the Heidelberg trio addressed each other with nicknames, and although Streeton's "Smike" and Robert's "Bulldog" had some rational explanation, that used for Conder, which, incidentally, he took with him to Paris, where it may or may not have undergone phonetic transformation, "remains obscure."[35] It was "K" or "Kay," the name of a letter, a name that is a letter, but it doesn't seem to be the letter "K" that the supine man is holding on the beach, although that letter could also be a sign for an open book on a lectern or reading stand, yet there seems no reason why it should be, why the painter should be signing his own nickname in the center of his painting when he has well and truly signed in the lower right corner, even if the country that may or may not have defined his nationality and his painting style has been known to usurp that place and that signature in exchange for the restoration of a letter and as a pretext for a tax of A\$5 on volumes of a certain weight and import, and even if every painting is in fact signed not so much by this or that written name as by an X, the sign of the chiasmus that defines the uneven distribution of forces competing for the definition and sense of the work,[36] such as that I have already identified crossing precisely through the body of the amputee in the center of *A Holiday at Mentone*, extending backwards to the two black couples, and forward to the man and woman and beyond, outside to where painter and spectator elbow each other for the best perspective on this scene, and even if as a result that supine body can be read as a "K" of sorts, a line drawn across the center point of half a chiasmus, two of them in fact, one facing forwards and another facing backwards, such that it is a divided body that lies there, and a painting that divides vertically right down the middle and creates its own abyssal effect of Ʞ and K, a mirror down the middle producing a real and a virtual painting on the same canvas, the whole thing divided by a rod, pole, or perch and reverting to a complicated play of 45-degree and 90-degree angles, so whether it be divided by the intersection of perspectival lines or by the intersection of competing narratives or discourses, it amounts to the same thing, a divided body and a divided sign, tenuously holding something red that remains to be read, a piece of writing, a letter, a sign, or an ensign perhaps,

perhaps this is a semaphoric gesture he is making that has caught the attention of one person only, the black male figure on the right who cocks his head slightly to better observe what is obscured by the pillar of the pier, but if it be semaphoric signs that he is in the process of sending, if he is flailing some desperate message as he lies beached there, then there are two letters that present themselves as better candidates than any others, namely the K formed with a vertical left arm above the head and the right arm at 45 degrees to the shoulder, which he could well have been signaling when he fell asleep or was stricken by whatever it is that ails him, or the D which is formed by a vertical right arm above the head and the left arm crossing the body, and he seems then to have got it back to front, but that would be one way for my name, or a letter for my name to find its surreptitious way into the painting, to compete for a place with a name of the artist, to allow me as reader to sign the painting in a backhanded fashion, to countersign it, to finally unload what is no more just a competition of narratives, but rather a whole pile of images that find themselves deposited in the middle of this painting, a whole pyre of images composed of tidbits pruned from this or that memory and heaped ready for a future conflagration, this is no longer Conder's *Holiday at Mentone* without also being my holiday at Wood Bay, where I went to stay with my uncle and family the first time I ever stayed away from home, he was tall and upright and two-legged and nothing like the father I had left, we could look for an image of him in this painting if we had the time, but that would start the narratives all over again, he would work all day in the city and come back to the beach house at an hour that was inconceivably late for me, we would eat dinner as the summer sun went down and then he would want to go for a walk, only what he called a walk was for a boy raised in the company of an amputee a major expedition to the ends of the earth, namely it meant following the road around the bay to where, when one looked from the veranda of their house, it seemed there was a pine tree growing out of a chimney of the house on the promontory, and although it was an optical illusion brought about by a particular trick of perspective just like the mutilations revealed here, it was an image that remained with me and remains with me now, for it was an image that occurred at the other end of the earth where it was too far and inconceivable for me to walk, it was countless rods, poles, and perches away, one just didn't walk that far, and certainly not that late at night and certainly not the first night one spent away from home when the whole world was folding in with a crush of nostalgia, so they went, all of them except my cousin, of about my age, she kept me company and we watched from the balcony and when they reached their terminus point they waved to us from the other end of the earth, making counterfeit semaphore signs or fake trigonometrical signalings that I took anyway to be signs of my name, the recognition of my prosthetically induced frailty, my inability to walk both acknowledged and parodied as I fought with the fatigue taking over my body, wanting to sleep and opting for bed rather than waiting for their return in spite of the shame of going to bed before the cousin who was my junior, we looked at picture books together until I nodded off, but it wasn't really a child's book it was an adult's, and it wasn't really a picture book but a book of images, a book of paintings from something called the school of impressionism, which I wanted nothing of, it was all entirely foreign to me and nothing like the books we looked at at home where we ate before dark and never walked far, the forms were as indistinct as trees growing from chimneys and men not having all their parts about them but there was an eerie fascination that called me and seemed to make a sign of my name through the accumulating layers of fatigue and disorientation, so much so that I spent many hours over the next few days poring over the book and by the end of my stay although I still had not walked to where the tree grew out of the chimney at the other end of the world I wanted to take the book home with me but was uneasy about how well it would sit with a man with one leg who didn't walk far although we had been known to run together up the driveway, and now I sit at the other end of the world with an image of an amputee that makes something of a sign of my name and however much I try to respond and put off the inevitable it still happens that I want above all to fall asleep flipping through the pages of a book, like him in the picture, having one image fall upon another, in his place, close to him.

If it is a letter he is holding and if he falls asleep, the letter risks blowing away, like the umbrella on the left. The umbrella is the one thing I have all along left out of this discussion. But I haven't forgotten it. Someone has; someone has forgotten the upturned red umbrella, or rather parasol, in the left foreground. It has been lying there all through this, belonging to who knows whom—the amputee, the seated woman, or someone outside the frame of the painting, like so much else. It is all spikes, spokes, and pointed handle, too hot to handle, a late medieval rack or some miniature satellite dish transmitting across centuries and continents further than even the most exaggerated reading could hope to venture. It seems the wind has blown it there, will soon pick it up and deposit it again closer and closer to the edge and finally outside of the field of vision altogether.

I think it best to leave it forgotten there.

§ 3 Africa, 21st Century

When it comes the sensation must be immediate, arriving with the flick of a switch, not some gradual stimulation that progressively appropriates the functions of the body but a sudden and complete immersion. Like diving. The waters divide and he is among them, floating through them, buoyed along by them, fully supported within them. He casts the crutch and cane aside—a boy will take them back to the dry sand, as if a grim reaper wading dancing through the surf—while he floats free in buffeting waves and smooth calm alike. He has no need even of vision, can as well negotiate the waters with eyes open or closed, there is no simple visual measure of this immensity to take, no urgent need to direct his labors linear towards a vanishing point. His body is indiscriminately whole and lacking. Enclosed within the fluid casing his single leg is utterly appropriate, assuming an amphibious complicity in the company of the creatures of the sea. He pushes against liquid walls, rolls streamlining through folds of molten silk, flips into a free fall where down becomes round and back over, at will and at leisure. The leg is in the bathing shed, the boy is a phantom figure on the sand holding at arm's length the habitual forms of prosthetic constraint, and he is swimming free. This is the oceanic feeling, the postprosthetic future of his dreams, the apocalyptic uncovering, the promised transformation, the unwinding of a defective mortal coil into the limpidity of ever-expanding watery reaches. But it is not as he imagined. He was never more in it than now, never so, to use the two words that constitute a whole paragraph and a whole conceptual apparatus in a novel by William Gibson,

jacked in.[1]

66

Gibson calls his sea "cyberspace," or "the matrix." "The matrix is an abstract representation of the relationships between data systems."[2] It is composed to a great extent of ice, "*ice* from ICE, Intrusion Counter-measures Electronics" (*Burning Chrome*, 169), which protects cores of sensitive information. In the so-called near or "extrapolative"[3] future of Gibson's science fictions, protagonist cowboys or hackers make their living by breaking the ice to steal corporate data. What is conceptually revolutionary about Gibson's description[4] of the matrix is the transformation of data representations from the print medium to that of representational graphics, and along with that the use of sensors or dermatrodes attached to the head to relay brain signals or mental representations directly into the computing system, again bypassing traditional language systems. The keyboard, computer, and modem have been superseded by the derma-trodes and a "cyberspace deck" that, by means of its monitor and controls, provides access to the type of virtual reality that is the matrix.[5] The data systems are thus represented in forms analogous to the images, visions, hallucinations, and fantasies of the mind. Cowboys have learned to exploit the visual representations of their mental reaches through a familiarity with experiences that are indistinguishable from those of drug-induced hallucinations, or dreaming. By jacking in they are able, thanks to their skill in differentiating the constantly mutating mass of forms composed of sensitive information and the defense programs designed to protect that information, to negotiate the intricate maze of data systems and obtain the particular items whose commerce becomes their livelihood.

Though this very distinction between hard information and defense systems, between the ice and whatever it contains, remains the telos of the cowboy's art, or *métier*, in Gibson's novels it is a goal that is situated at the vanishing point of the activity's perspective, and is so for a number of reasons. Firstly, the defense systems themselves are as valuable as the information they protect, capable of being sold for use elsewhere, modified, and so on. Icebreaker programs succeed to the extent that they are able to resemble either the ice or the hard data. Secondly, although cyberspace is "just a tailored hallucination we all agreed to have,"[6] and thus a form of language constituted by convention and presumably relying on principles of difference, the level of individual invention exploited in its regard far exceeds that acceptable within a traditional language system. In other words the cowboy's success in breaking ice relies on his capacity to invent something akin to a private language, using his mental resources to outwit the conceptual apparatus of the matrix through some unexpected maneuver or by inputting some new construct. Conversely, "ice, all the really hard stuff, the walls around every major store of data in the matrix, is always the produce [*sic*] of an AI, an artificial intelligence. Nothing else is fast enough to weave good ice and constantly alter and upgrade it" (*Count Zero*, 78). As a result certain forms of ice, so-called "black ice," are able to feed back and burn the unsuspecting cowboy's brain ("Ice that kills. . . . Some kind of neural-feedback weapon, and you connect with it only once. Like some hideous Word that eats the mind from the inside out. Like an epileptic spasm that goes on and on until there's nothing left at all," *Burning Chrome*, 182). This sort of bad trip can be avoided by performing a superior defensive maneuver or more simply by jacking out before the damage turns fatal (although death may not be immediate and may ensue instead from a slow viral decay initiated by the black ice). Thus the functions of the matrix, and those of the cowboy that become indistinguishable within it, can be said to be constituted by the possibility of contravention of their own norms and of the norms allowing for what we might call the transcendental distinction between ice and hard data.

There is a third way in which, in describing the act of double-crossing, object of theft, or similar thwarting of corporate systems that is the narrative impulse of Gibson's novels, his conceptual apparatus comes up against its own impasse. This occurs as a result of the shift in representational systems from a print base to forms of visual conceptualization not based on a traditional hierarchical distinction among real image, dream, hallucination, construct, and so on. In the three novels known as the matrix or Sprawl trilogy[7] that will be my focus here—*Neuromancer*, *Count Zero*, and *Mona Lisa Overdrive*—the probe into "deeper" or outer cyberspace ultimately functions as a move through abstraction to another, presumedly higher plane of realism, one that falls into the flatness of the real itself.

As *Neuromancer* begins, the nervous system of Case the cowboy is destroyed by the criminal employers he has double-crossed, then repaired by a new employer who requires his expertise. Before jacking in again after his operation, Case accesses a documentary on cyberspace:

> The matrix has its roots in primitive arcade games . . . in early graphics programs and military experimentation with cranial jacks. . . . Cyberspace. A consensual hallucination experienced daily by millions of legitimate operators, in every nation, by children being taught mathematical concepts. ... A graphic representation of data abstracted from the banks of every computer in the

human system. Unthinkable complexity. Lines of light ranged in the nonspace of the mind, clusters and constellations of data. Like city lights, receding. (51)

Then he accesses the matrix: "And flowed, flowered for him, fluid neon origami trick, the unfolding of his distanceless home, his country, transparent 3D chessboard extending to infinity. Inner eye opening to the stepped scarlet pyramid of the Eastern Seaboard Fission Authority burning beyond the green cubes of Mitsubishi Bank of America, and high and very far away he saw the spiral arms of military systems, forever beyond his reach" (52). This cross between a stylized, colorized night flight through a labyrinth of abstracted obstacles and a kaleidoscopic free fall through a dream landscape is what, at the outset, characterizes descriptions of being jacked in. But the climax to *Neuromancer*, which has Case breaking into the far reaches of cyberspace to meet with the artificial intelligence that will be the key to the infiltration of the Tessier-Ashpool central terminal, takes the form of an encounter with a boy on a beach, dancing at the edges of the surf (242–44). Similarly, in *Count Zero*, Bobby Newmark's confrontation with Virek is represented as a stroll through a park, albeit, perhaps, Virek's construct of Barcelona's Güell Park (230–33). In these moves into the far reaches, perhaps into the "beyond" of cyberspace, after all the virtuoso mindspins and bodyspins through the matrix of "black-mirrored shark thing[s]" (*Neuromancer*, 227) and "neon hotcores" (*Count Zero*, 165), there occurs a warp back into a form of representation where the real is indistinguishable from the dreamed or constructed, for it is all mediated by the same sort of visual flatness.

Now, according to the discourse of postmodernism that is so readily evoked in discussion of Gibson,[8] the constructed realities of the beach and Barcelona would be examples of the simulacral hyperrealities that the novels deal in. But the neon hotcores are no less simulacral hyperrealities within the logic of cyberspace. Jacking in by definition provides entry to the hyperreal, to constructions that cannot be distinguished according to a hierarchy based on the presumption of a familiar or first-order real. Yet as long as Gibson's descriptive apparatus operates in terms of a progression through the abstractions of the hotcores to the hyperreal of the beach, cyberspace risks falling back on the presumption it is supposed to deconstruct.[9]

In *Mona Lisa Overdrive* the logic of this mechanism becomes apparent. In that novel Bobby (the Count) Newmark arrives on the scene addicted to the construct of cyberspace he has acquired for his own exclusive use, a gray slab like an intraneuronal dripfeed permanently attached to his decaying body. If, as it seems, the new biosoft technology that was the subject of the action in *Count Zero* has allowed for this sort of portable, private, and eminently prosthetic matrix, then a step beyond the terms of reference of the first two novels has indeed occurred. Thus when the visionary Gentry finally persuades the naïf Slick Henry to jack into Bobby's gray slab, it no longer requires passage through anything like the "primitive ice belonging to the New York Public Library" (*Neuromancer,* 56) or through "a 'pirate's paradise,' on the jumbled border of a low-security academic grid. . . . The kind of graffiti student operators some-times left at the junctions of grid lines, faint glyphs of colored light that shimmered against the confused outlines of a dozen arts faculties" (81), but involves direct access to the hyperrealist mode:

> Jacked in.
> His boots crunched gravel.
> Opened his eyes and looked down; the gravel drive smooth in the dawn, cleaner than anything in Dog Solitude. He looked up and saw where it curved away, and beyond green and spreading trees the pitched slate roof of a house half the size of Factory. There were statues near him in the long wet grass. A deer made of iron, and a broken figure of a man's body carved from white stone, no head or arms or legs. Birds were singing and that was the only sound. (*Mona Lisa Overdrive,* 148)

This is the only mode of cyberspatial experience in *Mona Lisa Overdrive,* which ends with the principal "intelligences" of the novel, seeming to survive their own deaths as constructs within the matrix, answering a "final question" inside a car that has drawn up on the gravel drive (258–59).

To recapitulate: the experience of the matrix in the first novel, *Neuro-mancer,* and to some extent the second, *Count Zero,* is especially character-ized by what I described as nightflights or dreamscapes, although there is a narrative progression towards constructs that could be described as hyper-realist. By contrast, in *Mona Lisa Overdrive,* only the hyperrealist cyberspa-tial mode is represented.[10] This is not inconsistent with Gibson's own admission that he stepped back from the open-endedness of cyberspace,[11] but I want now to read this step beyond that is also a step back in terms of something other than the progression leading to its own impasse that the narrative seems to have put in place. Rather than supposing the descriptive apparatus to have "regressed" from abstraction to realism, or "fallen" into a naive and contradictory form of transcendent vision, I would hold that what has in fact occurred is an abyssal enfolding of the variety of forms of visual representation that cyberspace allows or exploits. If the whole progression towards abstraction is presumed to take place within the mimetic space opened by realism and the possibility of its distortion, then Bobby's house can be seen to open a window or a mirror within that progression, on the basis of which the process can repeat itself *ad infinitum*:

> "That's it?" he [Slick] asked Gentry. "What you've always been looking for?"
> "No. I told you. This is just a node, a macroform. A model . . . ."
> "He's got this house in there, like a castle, and grass and trees and sky . . . ."
> "He's got a lot more than that. He's got a universe more than that. That was just a construct worked up from a commercial stim. What he's got is an *abstract* of the sum total of data constituting cyberspace." (174–75, Gibson's italics)

When Bobby's macroform is in turn jacked back into the matrix on his advice towards the end of the novel, the abyssal effect of his personal version of cyberspace comes into play at the level of cyberspace itself; one "universe" invaginates another. Hence the finale just referred to brings together a series of other cyberspatial "totalities" to create an infinite *pro*gress or *in*gress of representational forms within coordinates that are no longer identifiable as belonging to either the macroform slab or the matrix itself. Against the logic of the narrative, according to which the characters of the novel have died and are about to go to cyberspatial heaven, I read them as folding in upon their "cyberspatial" or prosthetic selves, experiencing the differences that they were always constructed of.

This enfolding or abyssal effect would therefore be the prosthetic deconstruction of difference that is already familiar to this discussion. According to its logic there never was any idea of the human constituted without reference to prosthetic articulations, relations to supposed external othernesses; what seem to be the possibilities of subsequent prosthetic attachments—principles of nonintegrality, detachability, and replacement—are in fact the constituting principles of the human mechanism. On the one hand a prosthesis as advanced as Bobby's slab of biosoft, supplementing or replacing his mind, is an instance of a type of difference that is as undeniable as a wooden leg, but on the other hand the matrix that his slab "contains" offers an explicitation of such a difference deconstructed, by means of the "leveling" just described. In the matrix what appears as the real can have no claim to priority over what appears as a distortion of that real, an abstraction from it, or construct of it. But, we might say, this is so not because an artificial slab has come to be accidentally or by design attached to Bobby's real head but because the body was only ever being constructed in its relations to difference and otherness, only ever in prosthesis, jacked in.

Although we can only surmise on the basis of the scant information given in the novels, it seems that the progression from silicon chip to biosoft itself represents a sort of paradigm shift into a new type of prosthetic body. The name "biosoft" suggests that it is a form of circuitry and information storage modeled on the human brain. But on the other hand, once we see its effect on Angie's brain, it seems to function on the basis of a more symbiotic relation with the brain that "accesses" it, as if it weren't constrained by the spatial limits of a constructed entity like the silicon chip but had the capacity for such limitless growth as we imagine the human memory to have, perhaps even the capacity to form its own consciousness, and conversely to determine the growth, or control the unconscious, of the mind it works in conjunction with. Perhaps the shift here is simply from the prosthesis of the body to a prosthesis of the mind, but the point is precisely that once *soft-ware* becomes *bio*logical, it can no longer simply be worn; it has become the same sort of commodity as the body, or else the mind itself has become such a commodity, in any case the distinctions among software, body, and mind can no longer be maintained by means of criteria of naturality and artificiality. Similarly it is no longer relevant to ask whether information systems or artificial intelligences do in fact function like the human brain. They become prosthetized to the brain, at least in terms of this reading of a science fiction, in such a way as to insist that the brain is always already designed or destined for them, not just functioning like them but infected by them, always already an intelligence determined by the sense of the artificial, the detachable, the replaceable; always already the site of the prosthetic deconstruction of difference that it contains or produces and that inhabits or infects it.

Thus both the teleology of the cyberspatial experience—breaking through the ice to steal the hard data—and its eschatology—breaking through the abstractions to an apocalypse of some hyperrealist revelation of truth—that are inscribed by the narratives of the three matrix novels are undercut by the logical extensions of the conceptual framework that they put in place. The distinctions they rely on are deconstructed by the fact of cyberspace itself, by its explicitation of the constructedness of realities in general and of the prosthetization of the human subject, the generalization of being jacked in. However, the matter does not rest there. The narrative itself finally comes to participate in this deconstruction of the conceptual premises of cyberspace by means of a particular event whose consequences structure all three novels of the trilogy, the event that is the substance of the "final question" of *Mona Lisa Overdrive*. As a result of the marriage of artificial (and natural) intelligences that takes place at the end of *Neuromancer* there occurs a fundamental mutation of cyberspace that throws its whole definition into doubt and its functioning awry. In the subsequent novels this moment of mutation is referred to in historico-mythological terms as "When It Changed." As a result of "its" having changed, Gibson's fictions attain a level of narrative complexity, metaphysical reflection, ideological naïveté, and what might be called deconstructive propensity that is highly reminiscent of Pynchon. Its having changed means "nobody ever really understood what happened up there, when Case rode that Chinese icebreaker through their [Tessier-Ashpool's] core ice" (*Mona Lisa Overdrive*, 138). As a result of its having changed, obsolete 30-year-old cowboys trade stories and theories over drinks in The Gentleman Loser, the inhabitants of the orbiting archipelago suffer various and rampant mixtures of madness and creativity, and a voodoo cargo cult is loose in the matrix and grafted into Angela Mitchell's head.[12]

Explanations for the Change abound, alternating among what might be called the rational, the moral, and the metaphysical, although none of these exists in isolation from the others. The variants of these explanations given in each novel may be susceptible to and worthy of detailed analysis, but that is not my concern here.[13] Simply put, there is a view that holds cyberspace to have been infected as a result of the activities of some inspired and/or deranged operators; another view that traces that "infection" back to some megalomaniacal plan perpetrated by Lady 3Jane, with or without the collusion of voodoo influences; and a third that sees the Change as a necessary, inevitable, and catastrophic mutation into another form of intelligence or being. Hence Molly recounts her version of the *Neuromancer* story in this form:

> Had a lot of money we got for the run. . . . Tessier-Ashpool's AI paid it through a Swiss bank. It erased every trace we'd ever been up the well. . . . Case checked it all out when we were back in Tokyo, wormed his way into all kinds of data; it was like none of it ever happened. . . . He had this idea it was gone, sort of; not

gone gone, but gone *into* everything, the whole matrix. Like it wasn't *in* cyberspace anymore, it just *was.*   (*Mona Lisa Overdrive*, 138, Gibson's italics)

At the other end of the scale there is the data feedout given to Angie by Continuity, her company Sense/Net's AI:

"What would you like to know, Angie?"
" 'When It Changed' . . ."
"The mythform is usually encountered in one of two modes. One mode assumes that cyberspace is inhabited, or perhaps visited, by entities whose characteristics correspond with the primary mythform of a 'hidden people.' The other involves assumptions of omniscience, omnipotence, and incomprehensibility on the part of the matrix itself."
"That the matrix is God?"
"In a manner of speaking, although it would be more accurate, in terms of the mythform, to say that the matrix *has* a God, since this being's omniscience and omnipotence are assumed to be limited to the matrix."
"If it has limits, it isn't omnipotent."
"Exactly. Notice that the mythform doesn't credit the being with immortality, as would ordinarily be the case in belief systems positing a supreme being, at least in terms of your particular culture. Cyberspace exists, insofar as it can be said to exist, by virtue of human agency."
"Like you."
"Yes." . . .
"If there were such a being," she said, "You'd be part of it, wouldn't you?"
"Yes."
"Would you know?"
"Not necessarily."
"*Do* you know?"
"No."
"Do you rule out the possibility?"
"No." . . .
"How do stories . . . about things in the matrix, how do they fit into this supreme-being idea?"
"They don't. Both are variants of 'When it Changed.' Both are of very recent origin."
"How recent?"
"Approximately fifteen years."   (107–8)

Thus *Mona Lisa Overdrive*'s final answer to the final question can only repeat what is already known, that the matrix came to know itself, and in so doing came to know that there was an other, except that the novel ends with the protagonists about to reach that other, "in a New York minute, no shit" (260). One can only wait for that future transmutation, in an outside to the novel and to the trilogy, whether or not it becomes the basis for a sequel. But what remains of interest in the Change around which Gibson's novels come, in a more and more concentrated manner, to be organized is precisely its differential effect. The Change becomes a case of the play and catastrophe of difference at work within the matrix, within the space of informational birth and becoming, and the novels subsequently fall prey to an abyssal collapsing among descriptive and explanatory forms, as narrative falls into metaphor, as voodoo dreams cross into artificial-intelligence construct and vice versa, as the matrix invaginates into modes of being. Within such a catastrophe of difference a shorthand device like an acronym might easily become the variable figure for an act of reading. It might all be bound up in some cathexis called ICE.

Ice floes. Ice flows. The enfolding of conceptual oppositions that Gibson's novels both depend on and call into question can also be tracked via an unresolved tension between, on the one hand, a representation of the matrix as information flow, molten lava, movement of light, neon hot-cores, the whole tendency to fluid abstraction already referred to and, on the other hand, solid forms, walls of ice, nodes of resistance. The cowboy icebreaker operators are involved in breaking through and breaking down; their telos, the narrative conceit of the novels, and the Change itself involve a disintegration into the matricial fluidity.[14] But again, in Gibson's narratives there can be no pure flow, not if institutions—not the least being the institutions of property and ownership—are to function. Hence the role of ice in solidifying cores of information belonging to this or that corporation and in preventing the matrix from dissolving into the un-differentiated flow of information, the anarchy if you like, that the cowboy encourages in order to effect his theft but that, were it to come about, would deprive hacking of any profit or sense. The tension just referred to can therefore be read as the necessary impasse of any imagined future conceived of within the perspective of the machine—and it would be difficult to conceive of any other future—namely the impossibility, as well as the necessity, of describing the machinal in terms of purely liquid rather than solid form. Perhaps the strength of Gibson's science fictions resides precisely in this impasse, which means that there can never be a pure future fluidity, only ever a movement between the mechanics of solid

forms and a physics that overreaches itself in accounting for the fluidity of
constant change.[15] Still, the future becoming of ice is, from here, only ever
water. If the machine, if the whole "technic" venture has, since Prometheus, been represented by fire, by the theft of fire, then it is water that
waits as its future other, waiting, like some inversion of an apocalyptic
promise, waiting, in the form of ice we might say, in and for a mode of
being, or at least of functioning, that is or seems to be beyond articulation,
the mechanized body gone swimming in pure information flow. It is a
utopia or a catastrophe on the edge of a dream, "there by the edge of the
sea" (*Neuromancer*, 243). It is a boy called Neuromancer dancing on the
edge of the surf, waiting for a meeting with his Wintermute other, waiting
for that moment When it Will Have Changed, a boy who is the future and
who is "the dead, and their land." A boy who is an artificial intelligence,
chunks of ice, "cracking. The ice is breaking up" (244); a boy who does
"handstand[s] in the surf, laughing. He walked on his hands, then flipped
out of the water" (243); a boy who has need of neither crutches nor legs,
will have no truck or commerce with them, not in this future imagined
form, who can turn somersaults and turn the tables on the past and make
the future the present and lead the adult now down to the water's edge and
take away, fairly snatch away his forms of support, throw his crutches
aside, launch them into some orbital thereafter, announce a strangely
inverted aquarian tomorrow and have him swimming, have the science
fiction of his unencumbered body all fluid and undifferentiated, a postarticulate amputee careering through waves in frictionless abandon, a single
foot for a rudder, the trunk all constant curvature itself a wave rolling
forward across vast oceans to come and shatter in turmoil and silent
glistening upon the welcoming sands. This then will have been the
change, if I can dance I will have it so, this promise and practice of
prosthetic meltdown will have been its moment. But it only comes of
being jacked in; this is but water on the brain.

Gibson's novels offer the dream of a fully developed prosthetic future.
Hold your breath and begin *Count Zero*:

> They set a slamhound on Turner's tail in New Delhi, slotted it to his phero-
> mones and the color of his hair. It caught up with him on a street called
> Chandni Chauk and came scrambling for his rented BMW through a forest of
> bare brown legs and pedicab tires. Its core was a kilogram of recrystallized
> hexogene and flaked TNT.

He didn't see it coming. The last he saw of India was the pink stucco façade of a place called the Khush-Oil Hotel.

Because he had a good agent, he had a good contract. Because he had a good contract, he was in Singapore an hour after the explosion. Most of him, anyway. The Dutch surgeon liked to joke about that, how an unspecified percentage of Turner hadn't made it out of Palam International on that first flight and had to spend the night there in a shed, in a support vat.

It took the Dutchman and his team three months to put Turner together again. They cloned a square meter of skin for him, grew it on slabs of collagen and shark-cartilage polysaccharides. They bought eyes and genitals on the open market. The eyes were green. (1)

Molly has her inset mirrored glasses, Case his neurone blockers to cure him of a drug habit, Angie has biosoft *vévés* in her head, Bobby a whole matrix attached to his. Everyone has nodal jack sockets behind the ears. But there is one prosthetic combination that only remains implicit in Gibson, well buried beneath the high-tech bravado, entirely forgotten. It is foreign to the worlds described here, a version of the foreignness that from time to time inserts itself, like some anomalous remnant woven into the fabric of the future. We can call it the past, or history, and its relation to the twenty-first century of these cyberspatial fictions makes for a tension and a set of impasses similar to those just identified between the mechanical and the fluid. History is a more solid and weighty otherness than the ice floes within the information flow; it is like the sand in the machine, returning it to inert metallic obsolescence.

The past, in the form of recent history, has already inserted a strange anachrony into Gibson's work and would threaten to do so for any such science-fiction construct. For the future cannot but be described from the point of view of this present, and its past. And this present, at the time of Gibson's writing, was a world divided between two superpowers, such that the war that serves as the background point of reference for the events of these novels was conceived of as one of short duration between the Western powers and a country called the Soviet Union. But there are potentially other historical blind spots: an assumption of continued population growth in the eastern United States to form the Boston-Atlanta Metropolitan Axis, the BAMA Sprawl; a presumption of the continued techno-industrial strength of the Japanese and German economies, in the face of a decline of the American economy and the widespread museumification of Europe. But these are academic musings given the fact

that a near future such as Gibson imagines is required to retain a semblance of the known present; it succeeds precisely as *Unheimlichkeit* by
virtue of its combination of the familiar—and here Gibson's range of
cultural references, from Duchamp to Howard Hughes, is comprehensive—and the unfamiliar: a science fiction such as this thus becomes an
extrapolation or a projection rather than a prediction.

History, in the form of geopolitical configurations, is something of an
impediment to the fluid relations of capital that structure this imagined
near future. Perhaps the most fascinating projection of Gibson's, apart
from the evocation of postindustrial decay, with its conjunctions of alienation and criminality, centered—it is no accident—in the information and
prosthesis markets and surgeries of Chiba (e.g., *Neuromancer*, 3–25), is his
representation of the transnational corporate conglomerates and their
mirror images provided by the organized crime networks. This is a world
where nationhood has little remaining sense, at least in the First World;
where the Third World of Asia seems to have been incorporated into the
Japanese sphere of influence and that of Latin America remains as a tourist
resort, only that of Africa playing any important role in the narrative.[16]
Africa is, after all, where voodoo would issue from; it is where the weirdness might have begun that brought about When it Changed. I shall argue
that Africa, as the repository of history, is what comes back to infect the
utopian fluidity of the matrix.

Africa enters the picture through the Finn's narrative of Wigan Ludgate's
part in the Change in *Count Zero*:

> The Wig, in his first heat of youth and glory, had stormed off on an extended
> pass through the rather sparsely occupied sectors of the matrix representing
> those geographical areas which had once been known as the Third World.
>   Silicon doesn't wear out; microchips were effectively immortal. The Wig
> took notice of the fact. Like every other child of his age, however, he knew that
> silicon became obsolete, which was worse than wearing out. . . . The Wig
> reasoned that all that obsolete silicon had to be going somewhere. Where it
> was going, he learned, was into any number of very poor places struggling
> along with nascent industrial bases. Nations so benighted that the concept of
> nation was still taken seriously. The Wig punched himself through a couple of
> African backwaters and felt like a shark cruising a swimming pool thick with
> caviar. Not that any one of those tasty tiny eggs amounted to much, but you
> could just open wide and *scoop*, and it was easy and filling and it added up. The
> Wig worked the Africans for a week, incidentally bringing about the collapse

of at least three governments and causing untold human suffering. At the end of this week, fat with the cream of several million laughably tiny bank accounts, he retired. As he was going out, the locusts were coming in; other people had gotten the African idea.

The Wig sat on the beach at Cannes for two years, ingesting only the most expensive designer drugs and periodically flicking on a tiny Hosaka television to study the bloated bodies of dead Africans with a strange and curiously innocent intensity. At some point, no one could quite say where or when or why, it began to be noted that the Wig had gone over the edge. Specifically, the Finn said, the Wig had become convinced that God lived in cyberspace, or perhaps that cyberspace *was* God. . . . In due course the Wig ran out of money. . . . Sank without a trace.

"But then he turned up one day," the Finn said, "crazy as a shithouse rat. He was a pale little fucker anyway, but now he wore all this African shit, beads and bones and everything." (120–22)

The Wig ends up in the abandoned Tessier-Ashpool mainframe cores of the orbiting archipelago trading in the Joseph Cornell–type boxes sculpted by a robot and in the software, eventually biosoftware, presumably supplied to him by Lady 3Jane.

The Wig's Africa is, to begin with, the cowboy's cyberspatial paradise. The Robin Hood renegade of the First World's corporate incest and murder turns his attention to a continent of sand, a continent too hot for the ice to form. Africa becomes again the undiscovered frontier, retarded by an outmoded technological base, ripe for plunder. This is the future as indifferently past and present, the stasis of economic exploitation and subjection. Africa is the dark dry continent made fluid for the profit of the Western imagination, a desert turned pool, thick with caviar. The Wig dives into it, a shark swimming free for a week. He gets fat on caviar chilled on a bed of crushed African ice. He opens wide and the combined funds of individuals and governments simply flow into his pool; for a week he lives on a diet of fluid caviar, then retires to Cannes to swim some more.

In Gibson, in terms that need no longer surprise us as being particularly futuristic, money, and commodities in general, have been superseded by information flow. New yen exist but are illegal and used only on the black market; there is an active art futures market, but the works remain unseen in crates in some warehouse (*Count Zero*, 102–4); transactions take place by means of credit chips. No more restrained by the anal retention of the gold standard, the ingot turd, or even by the semiliquidity of cash, economic exchange is but a series of functions within the complexity of informational operations constituting the matrix; part of a more general and more expansive flow. And not only the individual or renegade but also the corporate effort seems to be concomitantly motivated by something other than the accumulation of commodities, namely by the concentration of power over information systems.[17] It is the faucets of cyberspace that are opened by cowboys and corporations alike to keep endless credit lines flowing into the right bank accounts, much more liquid than cumbersome wads of cash.

Within this perspective, the Wig's bloated African bodies appear as a troubling anachronism. Lying on a beach, his own caviar-swelled body regards them with "a strange and curiously innocent intensity." They are parched and sunbaked, the fluid in their bodies become all solid protuberance. Their mechanisms are blocked by a reliance on obsolete technology, their limbs listless from trying too hard to swim upstream in the matrix. In the rush towards the postprosthetic fluidity of a cash-free economy, Africa's bloated dead bodies represent the technological inelegance of poor streamlining. How can they be expected to swim in the flow when, in a prosthetic throwback, it is their very bodies that carry whatever water they deal in? From the Chiba clinics of Gibson's near future, with bodies fabricated of sleek metallic implants and vat-grown organs, we are thrown back to the insurmountably proximate past, present, and likely future of the Chiga tribal peoples of Kenya. Here a mother rouses her four children just after sunrise and sends two young girls up the mountain a kilometer to the nearest safe water source, where they will fill their small pans and carry them back on their heads. After breakfast she sets out herself to return with an 18-kilogram load (some carry pans weighing up to 40 kilograms), then realizes once she begins cooking for the noontime meal that another load will be required. The children will each make two trips back to the source after school. About six woman- and child-hours are spent each day for this purpose (in some cases it is socially acceptable for a man to carry water, but normally not on his head or back). Daily use per capita is in the 12-liter range. The woman will expend just under 4 kilocalories per hour for each trip, which adds up to 15 percent of her daytime energy, a figure one can compare with the 8–10 percent of income spent by a city dweller (Nairobi) on water purchased from a carrier, a figure one can compare in turn with the 0.57 percent of income spent on water by an average family in urban America, where the daily per capita use runs anywhere from 100 to 600 liters.[18]

The woman has no need to balance the pan on her head; it is as if attached, like Bobby's biosoft slab. She is in turn attached to it; it may have been a wedding gift from her parents.[19] This woman is among the 70 percent of the human race who are water carriers and are likely to remain so in the future. The future has become stagnant here, stillwater ponds of the past proving to be intractable obstacles to the desire for and progress towards universal flow. Long past is the voluntarist future of 1980, when the United Nations General Assembly declared an International Drinking Water Supply and Sanitation Decade after the 1977 Mar del Plata Conference had set the goal of a safe rural water supply to be universally reached in 1990. The present that the Wig observes on his screen at Cannes is this past and also that future. It is populated by bloated African bodies, by two thirds of the race, or at least its women and children, doing their own grim yet graceful dance as they set and balance their pans atop their heads beside some stream or pond, sliding into prosthetic mode for an hour or two a day, then lying down to die with distended bellies, without a good contract or a good agent, far from the overflowing vats of Singapore or Chiba. As the artificial-intelligence constructs dance in the surf and prepare to marry and produce the Change, it is quite clear—and it seems to become so to the Wig—what this voodoo madness is that suddenly infects the matrix. It is the madness of African death, an aquarian viral strain seething through the channels of cyberspace, fogging the brains of Angie and the rest. The name for it would be dry ice.

The postmodern economic simulacrum, the system of exchange that seems to be posited on purer and purer flow, an always more fluid abstraction from the solidity of the commodity, simply occludes its own reliance on a play between solid and fluid forms. The futures and futuristic simulacrum of a commodity, for being part of a metasystemic abstraction of the principles of exchange, nonetheless require the structure of the solid entity in order to function. As we have seen with the functions of the matrix, there can be no move into pure abstraction or pure fluidity, only an occluding or repressing of the versions of the real and the solid that the system depends on. Once we understand that there were only ever representations of the real, then we can also understand that any level of abstraction of those representations still deals with the mechanism of representation, with the forms of difference that constitute it. So it is with the abstraction of metanational information flow, with the waters of the matrix; they depend on forms of ice, on an Africa of sand steaming like dry ice. The artificially intelligent boy dancing in the surf is on the edge of the sand. The waters so tempting to dive and swim in flow over infinite expanses of sand. The dead African bodies of the Wig's rape and plunder come back like handfuls of sand thrown into the matrix, reimposing the mechanical grinding that its functioning always depended on, infiltrating the whole system with the rhythmic incantations of voodoo subversion. This is all about still being jacked in, about forms plugged into their own otherness.[20]

The dry ice of a thirsty Africa with its rudimentary prosthetic form of the female water carrier can only come into effect as a result of a reading that stretches and interweaves a series of narrative, thematic, and conceptual strands from Gibson's novels. There is neither dry ice nor African water carrier in these novels. Yet there is an Africa with poor quality and malfunctional ice, and an Africa blocked within the past of antiquated information systems, an Africa that is a throwback, trapped in its reliance on obsolete silicon, outmoded sand, as though mired in any version of the past—poor people's silicon, the industrial, the preindustrial—constrained by some version of the mechanical form as it tries to swim with the school into what is represented as the fast fluid future. Yet the prosthetic is common to all these modes; it means again that there is no future beyond mechanical functions, no water without ice, white, black, or dry, no Wig swimming like a shark imbibing caviar without the bloated body of a water carrier, no Bobby with a slab of microsoft on his head without an underfed African woman balancing a pan of unsanitary water.

This is the sense of a wooden leg standing as an outmoded token for prosthetic operations in general, nevertheless generating a universe of information and narrative effects, folding into and enfolding the space of the prosthetic construct that is this writing. On the one hand the story of a father with a wooden leg has more in common with the pathos of an African water carrier; more like dry ice, a consistent otherness that the fiction of a free-flowing critical discourse normally leaves unspoken; on the other hand it is the point of entry into a network of information like some miniature construct of cyberspace, the pretext for jacking in to modes of writing that are alternately mechanical and fluid, cases of picking through the ice of textual systems as well as experiences of free flow; but never one without the other. The wooden leg is always both a step towards the water, the hope and promise of a postprosthetic immersion—the boy dancing in the surf with the father's divested appendages, the father swimming free—and a limp backwards into the realization that there is no such fluid oblivion beyond the articulations of difference, that for all the streamlining of relations between the human and the machine, we can never move further than the sense of an originary structural, rather than accidental, prosthesis; that any future end can only be another version of that divided beginning. The father can take off the leg and dive into the water, the son can run in the surf spinning words like some crude prototype artificial intelligence gone autonomous, dancing with borrowed limbs, throwing them out of reach up on the sand, but they have nevertheless both always been jacked in.

The form of prosthetic constraint that is the cowboy jacked into cyberspace itself provides, of course, a model of reading, of reading that is necessarily also writing.[21] In the absence or near absence of print media in Gibson's science fictions, there are two principal activities that involve some combination of the visual sense with manual and mental functions. I refer to simstim and jacking in. Simstim has the feel of a sensitized and privatized cinema. Its stars, Tally Isham and later Angie, package and transmit their fantasies for mass consumption. As explained in "Burning Chrome," the story that is something of a conceptual prototype for the three novels of the matrix trilogy, "artists . . . are able to break the surface tension, dive down deep, down and out, into Jung's sea, and bring back—well, dreams. . . . Neuroelectronics lets us access the experience . . . package it, sell it" (*Burning Chrome*, 123). Although "Burning Chrome" provides for a scenario whereby characters jack into each other, thus bypassing the packaged commodity that is simstim, the latter is not conceived of as an interactive medium. Besides, such interpersonal interaction would also negate the status of simstim as art object: "The stuff we get out to the consumer, you see, has been structured, balanced, turned into art" (123). It is a commodity produced at great expense, functioning according to the same principles of advanced capitalism as cinema, with the same star system and sexual economy, similarly designed for passive consumption. On the other hand, the cowboy who jacks in—and he is almost exclusively male[22]—is involved to varying degrees in producing the cyberspace he negotiates. Thus Case, the cowboy hero of *Neuromancer*, disdainfully refers to simstim as "a meat toy" (55). Later he will disdain travel in the same terms (77). Simstim is body, cyberspace mind: "He knew that the trodes he used and the little plastic tiara dangling from the simstim deck were basically the same, and that the cyberspace matrix was actually a drastic simplification of the human sensorium, at least in terms of presentation, but simstim itself struck him as a gratuitous multiplication of flesh input" (55). Case seems to know and repeat, as does Gibson's fiction in general, the contradictions inherent in such a reductionist representation of difference. It is the same logic that produces the very ordinary sexism of these novels, the metallicized and violent female bodies, the *vaginae dentatae* of adventure fiction in general. Molly embodies this sort of "macho" female, with her death-dealing prosthetized body, assertive sexuality, emotionless aggressivity. She is a rough-and-tumble cowboy in the old style, a "meat" cowboy, copied from the rugged swaggering individualism of a whole history of fiction, traditionally performed by a male hero, a male body; and she is at the same time the ageless repetition of the female as vampire. In the person of Case, Gibson simply gives us a transposition from a swaggering body of a cowboy to a swaggering mind of a cowboy, leaving the female lead to pick up the former role (although as Turner in *Count Zero* demonstrates, there is still room for male versions of the same). The same rugged individualism obtains, the same reductive conception of the human subject. What has escaped Gibson's attention is the extent to which the prosthesis that is the cowboy jacked in has called into question the status of the individual subject, the extent to which it has rendered the nonintegrality of that subject explicit.

In *Neuromancer* Case has a cyberspace deck custom made to enable him to switch between the matrix, where he is busy working to break through the Tessier-Ashpool ice, and the one-way simstim that allows him to follow Molly's progress as she does the "physical" work of breaking and entering corporate premises or the Villa Straylight:

> The new switch was patched into his Sendai with a thin ribbon of fiberoptics.
> And one and two and—
> Cyberspace slid into existence from the cardinal points. Smooth he thought, but not smooth enough. Have to work on it. ...
> Then he keyed the new switch.
> The abrupt jolt into another flesh. Matrix gone, a wave of sound and color. ... She was moving through a crowded street, past stalls vending discount software, prices feltpenned on sheets of plastic, fragments of music from countless speakers. Smells of urine, free monomers, perfume, patties of

frying krill. For a few frightened seconds he fought helplessly to control her body. Then he willed himself into passivity, became the passenger behind her eyes. (55–56)

By means of this flip-flop an opposition is drawn between the narrative that Molly impels and the reflection, description, or thematic development that occurs by means of Case's access to cyberspace. But of course these are merely two types of narrative, and, as things progress, they enfold in the same way that we saw versions of realism and abstraction enfold within descriptions of the matrix. Molly's meat and Case's mental machine were always already enfolded, and long before we arrived at cyberspace. A "reader" as astute as Case should have realized that.

Jacked in simultaneously to simstim and the matrix, Case is a futurized version of Oedipa Maas trying out as a sensitive on John Nefastis's Maxwell's Demon machine in Pynchon's *The Crying of Lot 49*. The demon relates the thermodynamic idea of entropy to the idea of entropy obtaining in information flow, using the information gathered on the molecules in a closed system to separate the hot from the cold, effect an exchange, and produce energy.[23] The sensitive in turn connects with the demon to set the process in motion. In Pynchon's model the process requires some sort of leap of faith between the literal and metaphoric senses of entropy. In Gibson's the switching has been resolved by technological fiat. It provides the illusion of two mutually exclusive modes, occludes the fact that the criteria for differentiation—mind/body, ideas/narrative, representation/reality, metaphor/literality, and so on—rely on false oppositions. The African water carrier has been repressed again. The work of the body has been occluded, unrefrigerated bodies allowed to bloat and fry in the desert sun, the meat left to rot.

Jacked in, prosthetized, there is no structural distinction between body and machine, indeed between the mechanics of the switching and the fluidity of immersion in one or the other mode. Yes, there is a switch, everything depends on it; no, the switching doesn't take you to an opposite mode, not opposite in the binary sense that the on/off, in/out function of the switch would seem to presume. Yes, the leg is off, he dives in, the waves smother his infirm body while the boy dances at the water's edge; no, this is no less prosthetic than the morning's wakening, shuffling to the side of the bed, easing the stump into the leg and clamping the buckle of the harness, like settling a waterpan on one's head and setting off up the hill; no less jacked in, in one or the other mode.

Yes, this is criticism, the lure of a well-wrought mesh between text and theoretical reflection, but when it switches to the partially simulacral simstim of an autobiographical narrative it is but another enfolding of the same scriptural possibilities; feeling like an immersion in the flow of the poetic or lyrical but as much a jacking in to the pretense of automation that is word processing, released from one set of constraints, on a random course in search mode through the compilations of memory and cultural reference, allowing the connections to be made as if unconcerned by the codes of a euclidean rhetoric, logic, even aesthetics, but working nevertheless through another configuration of the same. There is no free un-programmed flow, no water without ice, no poetry without logic or vice versa, the plod of a wooden leg is there to remind us of that. But by the same token one is at a loss to know, for the appearances can be deceiving, on which side the greater logic or lyricism resides, where more theory and where the greater force of narrative. Though the switch is thrown in the most binary of terms, there is something working to scramble the codes, something outside the scope of either description or narrative, something to which prosthesis pertains only in the mode of increasing uncertainty, some African voodoo biosoft mutation such that in being jacked in there will have been change, and the desired rendezvous with a boy dancing on the sand will have been an embracing of pitch black ice: " 'Neuromancer,' the boy said, slitting long grey eyes against the rising sun. 'The lane to the land of the dead. Where you are, my friend. . . . Neuro from the nerves, the silver paths. Romancer. Necromancer. I call up the dead. But no, my friend,' and the boy did a little dance, brown feet printing the sand, 'I *am* the dead, and their land' " (*Neuromancer*, 243–44). Case's epiphany or salvation occurs in the context of this meeting. He learns not to so despise "the meat, the flesh the cowboys mocked"; he connects with the vastness of the thing "beyond knowing, a sea of information coded in spiral and pheromone, infinite intricacy that only the body, in its strong blind way, could ever read" (239). He finds the meat in the mind, the sensuality at the extreme end of the machine, the intelligence of the artificial, the otherness that deconstructs his version of a cyberspace where jacking in means switching out the prosthetic basis of his connection. But in learning about the body, to the extent that we can still presume to talk about the body, he is learning about death. The boy in the surf who calls himself the dead is an artificial intelligence that wants to be joined to its own other, Winter-mute, the silent ice. According to the narrative, especially as it is recounted in later versions, they will get together and everything will have changed. The level of their intelligence, their ability to replicate and mutate, the havoc they will create, the inability of the system to identify them clearly as exogenous or endogenous, everything points to a failure of information and a cause of death for which the word is "virus." Cyberspace catches a case of viral entropy. We are back to another word that links two worlds, the word "virus" as a crossover between information processing and immunology,[24] where an opposition between literal and metaphoric won't do, for it comes undone in a dance on the edge of the salty wastes of death.

It happens without warning, comes faster than any cowboy can deal with, repeating and at the same time mutating, it comes together in this indistinction of a wave that breaks and dissolves around the ankles of a boy of doubtful progeny. It is here that they will meet, he and the other one; this is the point where it will come together and perform its routine or its service, from where it will go off into its hauntingly familiar delirium, here on the beach where the paternal paraphernalia are transferred and abandoned, the stark crutch and stick left to attract and repel an impressionable son and generate myriad mutant narrative digressions, the father gone diving into the foam, this is where we meet, where we impress our skipping feet upon moistened common ground and watch the forms we produce dissolve into a limitless expanse, the water washing over the traces, there we will be, you and I playing intelligences of our own making for the first time, you who have come from close by and far away to this meeting, dancing on the sand, and you would dance far off even after that first encounter, it was the early seventies and we met in the guise of learning to speak French, our tutor had us talking drugs, and we found our forms of complicity and of opposition, remember, of course you remember even if you can no longer speak of it, can no longer speak at all, the teacher brought her haunting tales of mongoloid children and warned us not to fuck with biology and we laughed a laugh of innocence, eighteen or nineteen years old, we laughed for a long time after that, even up to six months ago, for she exaggerated the dangers of cannabis, we danced at her expense and biology took care of itself, I'll speak of it for you and for us both now that you no longer speak, now that you lie like some Count Zero with a drip in your arm and a tumorous slab on your brain growing all exponential and your name suddenly Wintermute as I struggle to have you and me dancing together in and out of fading airwaves, now that your only voice is an intermittent wheeze over the silicon shards of international telephony that your friend tells me is you reacting to what I say, he thinks you heard me trying to speak, and I presume I heard you trying to tell me as you had only days before how ditzy you were, it's my mind you said, as if the distinction counted anymore, as if an immunoblastic lymphoma of the brain could allow for a distinction to be maintained between mind and body, as if the virus were not such a scrambling of the codes, as if your body could still dance as it had from the start, dancing far off after that first meeting, I could never keep up even though I made my own departures, and our paths crossed in the various continents you danced in, tripping the light fantastic it has to be said, all of this has to be said, although I am not sure whom I am talking to, whether I am talking to you who talked so much and now can't talk back, I am trying to tell you one last time how exceptional you were to me, what laughter you spread, what flair, saying thanks and love and goodbye my friend, but there was ice in my mouth and sand in your ears, your brain and body almost dead, you who do your dance of death sashaying into this story of a father, at the precise moment in the writing of this when I begin once again, in grim determination, to shape my schema for bringing together in prosthetic articulation the various strands of the discussion, searching around for the most econom-ical device that will link water, Africa, and jacking in, like some green cowboy I hack my way through mountains of ice in search of the LF, say it over and over and it will become the aleph that contains the whole shebang, I crash my way through the possibilities not knowing that it will come down to a matter of a virus until it hits me that there is only one virus that stands for them all, you are standing there on the beach at the end of it all to tell me so, at that precise moment you call to say you will soon be dead, you give me the gift of your death as the most obvious motor of everything deployed here, you do the obvious thing that we have waited these last few years for, for eight years we wait with you the long-term survivor, we wait and see you alive enough to believe you will outlive the statistical mandate, but suddenly you begin to die with astonishing rapid-ity, while I am picking at the edge of a glacial truth the icebreaker virus that is death is flipping through its infinite permutations and chipping inexorably away at your defense codes until it comes up with a winner with which to infect your brain, and so to infect this my story of a father, you my oldest friend whose death I experience like a dress rehearsal for his death, the same late night telephonic static and time delay, the same voices that speak over each other as the message cranks through its satellite transfer, the same hollow echo of one's own utterances, the whole massive *nachträglich* nightmare, you who danced away from fathers all, shining in utter flamboyance, a renewable fire in diverse climes, burning like a brief star across scented skies, remember, I'll tell you these things though you will only wheeze back through the intercontinental fog and likely die before I reach an end of telling, you will be dead at 40 and I decidedly middle-aged, you will be gone into some version of the matrix, born into some novel womb or scattered into the circuits of memory and forgetting, you become the biosoft of these my recollections inscribed like some fateful *vévé* in my head while in yours the tumors grow and press the linguistic modes completely out of service, I shall store them for read-only access for there will be no adding to them, there will be no more dancing together, no more strutting down equinoctial windswept streets a gaudy paper flower the size of a lampshade in your lapel, no more birthday parties where you dress as Marilyn and have a confused magician saw you in half, you just had your last birthday, I spoke to you from sixteen hours away ten days ago as the hairdresser inspected your highlights and you laughed in its face and said your 40 years had been full ones, and I could only marvel at your courage, as I did again a few days after that while you struggled against your ditziness thinking I had been there for the party, your last, but I was half a world away and you about to die having lived half a life to the full, strutting your stuff through a whirl of times and places where we would sometimes find each other again, all in leather wielding a hammer in the London underground we waved through the speeding windows and you went off with another friend, he's had a sex change now you say, sells himself and drinks gin, or when we shared a bed in Paris our bodies all knees enough to laugh over for years and half a lifetime to come, or your welcome my first time in New York of an all-night freebasing binge, you led me like a blur through every Village bar and then through every 24-hour corner store looking for pumpkin puree for Thanksgiving, you had to do it right and had to do it big, like the friend you introduced me to there, I took her with me and never left, long after you had gone back home to deal with your diagnosis, to learn to live with the virus, leaving at about the time you should have been witnessing our union, and we are still here alternating now the nightly calls, she from New York, I from New Orleans, to you in New Zealand, such multiple new versions of old worlds, old enough to die at 40, we alternate the calls and call and cling to each other and sob over the phone while we wait for you who brought us together to go and die, we wait until now, now the news has come, a new version of old news, your death that news, it was tightly programmed to occur in the middle of this writing, it happened as I left for work, the news came some seven hours later, and even now I am still waiting for the historic moment to arrive local time as out of order as a declaration of war, never mind the biology, it is the physics that is all fucked up here, the intersection of time and space that not even death seems capable of configuring, you lay there in your mother's arms as the jasmine bloomed full-perfumed, I wrote this in air-conditioned mustiness and somewhere sometime in it your death occurred, there will be daffodils to wave you goodbye we will see to that, and we will greet the charred half of you that will come back to rest here, now that we know, now that the moment has come and passed in its own peculiar phasing too alien to grasp, you have died and the moment is buried even in the present of this writing, doubly so in the machine age of multiple edits, the order of the event can only appear as contrived, your death becomes a truly prosthetic happening, its precise coordinates irretrievable, it is simply gone like a voodoo haunting into the matrix I am negotiating here, a blip of informa-tion consigned to a silicon grave, one final addition to the memories I am banking, it will all register in some form, your red hair, your poses whether outside the Bus Stop Café after frugal breakfast in the gathering fall, or in extreme parodic drag falling all over Hudson Street parking meters, or the botanical gardens some Auckland winter, or your pastiche of the Rubaiyat lingering at an *abribus* on the Rue Gay Lussac, the emotion, the tears we saved for now and so few for you were never given to them, the embraces, the changes, all converted to the microbytes of this frantic input such that some slight incandescent flicker around the edge of a cyberspace hotcore will be forever you, flickering again whenever the chip dust combusts in the heat of an occasional access, as I burn my way back to some recollec-tion of you, you my rock of solid laughter gone crumbling now in forlorn cascade into the electronic reaches, this then is the matrix, the only jacking in is to death and it comes long before the black ice is let loose in your direction, it is there from the beginning, the death in the machine of course, the technological *gris-gris*, but more than that, the massive consol-idation of memory, the exponential compounding of the past, of course, but still more the transit to a foreign place that trades in overwhelming loss, connecting to a landscape that is all mutation, shifting into the otherness of pure invention whose paradigm is death, this is the inevitable and consistent curse they call the change, the fall into the viral flow, the virus and the flow, a systemic dysfunction out of Africa, it is from there that the virus is said to come, we are presented with the whole mythology all over again of a monkey on a hot continent coming to afflict the homosexuals, hemophiliacs, and Haitians of this world, like a voodoo curse let loose in our matrix, and it is in a neglected Africa once again that an obsolete technology means dead bodies by the thousands, the threat of millions that would likely have me as dead as you were I one of them, for some strange reason they just keep on dying there in wholesale quantities of causes as old as bad water and as new as AIDS, while the First World disingenuously searches for the software glitch that must be causing it all, so Africa comes back to hang on our necks, the weight and movement of it has you dizzy, it is Africa that you balance on your head, its dry ice the tumors searing their way through your brain, the tendency to zero flow that has you dead, your body burned by now, your brain burned and all this burning back, the information turning lethal as black ice, all death and forgetting, the whole system gone seropositive apeshit, the science of it forsaken, compounded by a virus that can no longer distinguish its physics from its biology, its solidity from its fluidity, this code that fixes itself to flow like poison, that parasites yet replicates the encodings of life itself, the tumors that grow indiscriminately on your 40-year-old brain and on my father's thigh at 18, dancing like us on the beach watching the war clouds gather, waiting for death but dancing oblivious still, then diving unencumbered into the waves, at his age we picked up where he left off, where he took off and left for me to handle his crutch and cane, they lie there and I dance around them with you until now, now in this instant and without the slightest warning you are gone in the middle of our dance, in midlife falling abruptly backwards into the water all on fire your body an inferno that evaporates oceans, you rise with them like ether and vanish, and me, scarcely the time to turn around, I am left here on deserts of dry sand with a father's ambulatory apparatus and he beached on a shoal far out towards the retreating horizon calls to me and I will go balancing arms full of equipment to hobble back with him whatever the distance, back home bearing the news that you are gone into the limitless pattern of the universe and the well is dry.

§ 4   Berchtesgaden, 1929

To hear Ernest Jones tell it:

The huge prosthesis, a sort of magnified denture or obturator, designed to shut off the mouth from the nasal cavity, was a horror; it was labeled "the monster." In the first place it was very difficult to take out or replace because it was impossible for him to open his mouth at all widely. On one occasion, for instance, the combined efforts of Freud and his daughter failed to insert it after struggling for half an hour, and the surgeon had to be fetched for the purpose. Then for the instrument to fulfill its purpose of shutting off the yawning cavity above, and so make speaking and eating possible, it had to fit fairly tightly. This, however, produced constant irritation and sore places until its presence was unbearable. But if it were left out for more than a few hours the tissues would shrink, and the denture could no longer be replaced without being altered.[1]

By all reports Freud was more fortunate than Louis XIV, who lost large chunks of the roof of his mouth through bad dentistry and expelled as much food through his nose as he swallowed in the last years of his life. "We are astonished to learn of the objectionable smell which emanated from the *Roi Soleil*," Freud wrote.[2] He was lucky to have the advantage of a prosthesis, even if it had to be replaced many times after the diagnosis of and first major surgery for throat cancer in 1923, about the time of *The Ego and the Id* (*SE* xix). He returned to Berlin for yet another replacement in 1929, after finishing *Civilization and Its Discontents*. That text was completed at Schneewinkl, near Berchtesgaden, on July 28, 1929, as Freud recounted to Lou Andreas-Salomé:

You will with your usual acuteness have guessed why I have been so long in answering your letter. Anna has already told you that I am writing something, and today I have written the last sentence, which—so far as it is possible here without a library—finishes the work. It deals with civilization, consciousness of guilt, happiness and similar lofty matters, and it strikes me, without doubt rightly so, as very superfluous, in contradistinction from earlier works, in which there was always a creative impulse. But what else should I do? I can't spend the whole day in smoking and playing cards, I can no longer walk far, and the most of what there is to read does not interest me any more. So I wrote, and the time passed that way quite pleasantly. In writing this work I have discovered afresh the most banal truths.[3]

In that book, presented here as something of a work of dotage, of the psychoanalyst turned dilettante, Freud nevertheless presents ideas very dear to his heart concerning the superego, the death drive, and their relations to religious belief. One might well wonder, therefore, to what extent the superfluity of *Civilization and Its Discontents* reaches back to affect or infect *The Future of an Illusion* (*SE* xxi), published shortly before and in a similar vein, and indeed back through all the works of that decade, especially *The Ego and the Id* and *Beyond the Pleasure Principle* (*SE* xviii). To what extent are those works banal, less than creative, and presumably less valued by their author than those preceding them? Granted, Freud does not specify what earlier works he considers to be in contradistinction to *Civilization and Its Discontents*, and he may in fact be referring to the important modifications his theory underwent with those two essays of the earlier part of the 1920's. On the other hand, if we follow the logic of what I have just said, then the question that continues to be posed even as far back as *Beyond the Pleasure Principle* cannot be seen to stop there, given the pivotal nature of that work with respect to everything that preceded it, and indeed with respect to the whole armature of Freudian theory.[4] If there is a hypothesis to be advanced at this juncture, it would be that the armature put in place in the works of 1919–29, has something of the prosthetic about it, something precisely of the monster that became an unavoidable part of Freud's body and existence. But this is no psychobiocriticism I am advancing, and the hypothesis no more relies on the fitting of a prosthesis in 1923 than does the death drive on the death of Sophie in 1920. It is quite the opposite of psychobiocriticism. It is rather the figure for certain aspects of Freudian theory, and perhaps for a certain type of theorizing in general, which lends something of an inevitability to

Freud's affliction, as if a theory informed by prosthesis and all that it involves could not but find some sort of fulfillment of its own prophecy in its author's health problems beyond a simple relation of cause and effect. For what Freudian theory brings about more than anything else—and we will likely be still dealing with its consequences for a long time to come—is an upsetting of the order of supposedly straightforward relations, those of time and consecution, of cause and effect, and so on.

There is on the one hand a very straightforward and logical idea at work here, namely that theorizing—Freudian theory in particular—and perhaps knowledge in general advances by means of successive accommodations, molding itself to a better and better fit with the data it is placed over. That seems very obviously to be the story of Freudian theory, Freud's prosthesis, and prostheses in general. On the other hand, a contrary logic threatens at the same time to ruin everything straightforward and obvious about that. It finds that the major tenets of Freudian theory, from childhood sexuality to the uncanny and the death drive, turn the obvious on its head, set things back to front, and finally do the same for those tenets that bring about the very operation of reversal. It is such effects that will go, here also, by the name of prosthesis.

My hypothesis is developed in the space between the pro*positions* that constitute Freudian theory and an ill-defined series of pro*jections* that can easily be seen to grow out of it, indeed that still identify themselves as belonging to it. It is the space of a prosthetic supplement, falling between or upon what is posed in the quiet confidence of the apposite, the here and now of the current state of research, and what shocks as the banal and commonplace within the rarefaction of scientific inquiry; or, on the other hand, between the apposite and what is thrown up as that inquiry's outer possibility; in either case continually broaching and breaching the threshold of the opposite or of contradiction. It is those latter tendencies that seem to characterize more and more the works of the 1920's. By his own avowals, the author values as little more than conjecture what he propounds in works ranging from *Beyond the Pleasure Principle*—"What follows is speculation, often far-fetched speculation. . . . It is further an attempt to follow out an idea consistently, out of curiosity to see where it will lead" (*SE* xviii: 24)—to *Civilization and Its Discontents*—"In none of my previous writings have I had so strong a feeling as now that what I am describing is common knowledge and that I am using up paper and ink and, in due course, the compositor's and printer's work and material in order to expound things which are, in fact, self-evident" (*SE* xxi: 117).

However, the importance for science and for theory of such speculation or conjecture, or of such everyday musing, was something psychoanalysis made explicit from the very beginning, once it set out to elaborate a theory that could not but draw the scorn of official science. Analysts, Freud wrote in 1921 in a piece that he declined to publish (about which more later), "cannot repudiate their descent from exact science," but "they are ready, for the sake of attaining some fragment of objective certainty, to sacrifice everything. . . . They are content with fragmentary pieces of knowledge and with basic hypotheses lacking preciseness and ever open to revision" ("Psycho-analysis and Telepathy," *SE* xviii: 178–79).

Freudian theory will therefore have more than a little of the *bricolé* or ad hoc about it. It will be constantly adjusting itself to accommodate whatever its musings and speculations bring to bear upon it. It will be prepared when necessary to throw out the whole apparatus of its tenets and replace it with another that better fits, one that can be more easily swallowed, sticks less in the throat. It will be determined to make do as best it can, to prop itself up by whatever means are at hand. For example: "Of all the slowly developed parts of analytic theory, the theory of the instincts is the one that has felt its way the most painfully forward. And yet the theory was so indispensable to the whole structure that something had to be put in its place" (*SE* xxi: 117). Given that, one cannot help but ask to what extent the theory thereby distinguishes itself from superstition on the one hand and philosophy or pure science on the other. Such a question lies beyond the scope of the present discussion even though it is automatically posed by it. That is to say the answer to such a question can only, in the present context and perhaps anywhere, take the form of speculations of our own. But whence and on what basis does psychoanalysis derive its exact dose of rigor—indeed how can we measure the exact dose—and why the recourse to scientific principle at the same time as a suspicion of official science? How precisely does its skepticism articulate with its scientificity? Because of, and indeed in spite of, such questions Freudian theory, with its musing and propositions, projections and conjectures, will attach to itself a series of differences that, while perhaps molding themselves to its fit, nevertheless distinguish themselves as irrevocably other, as opposite in nature, as opposite as is the artificial or prosthetic to nature itself.

"Projection" is of course a psychoanalytic term. As Freud reminds us in *Beyond the Pleasure Principle*: "a particular way is adopted of dealing with any internal excitations which produce too great an increase of unpleasure: there is a tendency to treat them as though they were acting, not from the inside, but from the outside. . . . This is the origin of *projection*" (*SE*XVIII: 29). It is not that precise mechanism that I am imputing to Freudian theory in general, but there is one aspect of it made explicit here that I wish to reinforce, namely the fact of a change in direction, the psychic fact of looking in the wrong direction. When things don't fit they are felt to be back to front, inside out. The idea of a change in direction, an adestination on the part of the psyche, presented in the guise of a decision of convenience, can be seen to underscore the whole of the Freudian opus. It is there from the beginning, in the line from Virgil's *Aeneid* that *The Interpretation of Dreams* takes as its epigraph: *Flectere si nequeo superos, Acheronta movebo*— "If I cannot bend the higher powers, I will move to infernal regions" (*SE*IV: ix). Changes in direction, or reversals, occur time and time again, with narcissism, with masochism, with projection, with the instincts or drives. The unconscious, and psychoanalysis, might be said to be defined more by the possibility of directional change or teleological contradiction than by anything else. By virtue of being internally excited, in a state of change, reexamination, revision, speculation, and so on, psychoanalysis permanently projects. How far out its projections reach, to what extent they lie beyond the reach of recovery, in what precise direction they might be seen to be leading, these are some of the questions that underlie this discussion.

However, what I have just described as the prosthetic structure of Freudian thinking is, as I have also suggested, not necessarily specific to his theory as distinct from theory in general. Nor is it absent from this set of musings and speculations on the basis of that theory; and by no means is it reducible to a relation between a theory and a Freud suffering from throat cancer. Rather, what I am calling here the figure of prosthesis appears, in striking profile, through a discussion of some of Freudian theory's liminal relations, through examination of what it approaches when it acknowledges—and it does so particularly explicitly—its own fringe.

Take for instance—what will develop for me as *the* instance—the not infrequent reference to the occult as it relates to the wider question of religious belief in general. Given the possible objections to such belief, one might reasonably expect it to display a prosthetic structure parallel to that just described for Freudian theory: a sort of overreaching and compensat-

ing attempts at accommodation, a structural crisis and a contrived solution. Instead of speculation, a suspension of rational standards of examination in favor of faith; instead of scientific rigor, a certain doctrinal
consistency that tends in many cases to be applied in the extreme; but the
two currents coexisting and producing their own tensions and contradictions. Now, on one level the two types of belief—religion and the occult—
are, for Freud, distinct, the latter being characterized by a particularly
superstitious form of credulity and the former more by its propensity to
moral and behavioral injunction, how it regulates relations between the
individual and society. In his view, religion is less a question of ideas than
of behavior; it is a function of and a question of civilization, occurring at
the interface between psyche and *socius*. The occult is regarded as more of
an individual psychic phenomenon, reduced finally to the questions of
telepathy and thought transference.

But from another point of view it is clear that the occult connects with a
"general tendency of mankind to credulity and a belief in the miraculous."
Given that "a resistance stirs within us against the relentlessness and
monotony of the laws of thought and against the demands of reality-
testing," one must accept that "the interest in occultism is in fact a
religious one" ("Dreams and Occultism," *SE* XXII: 33, 34). And religion,
occultism, and psychoanalysis alike give rise to similar objections: "It does
not follow as a matter of course that an intensified interest in occultism
must involve a danger to psychoanalysis. We should, on the contrary, be
prepared to find reciprocal sympathy between them. They have both
experienced the same contemptuous and arrogant treatment by official
science. To this day psychoanalysis is regarded as savouring of mysticism"
(*SE* XVIII: 178). Thus when Freud talks about his growing interest in
telepathy it becomes, however tongue in cheek, both a conversion and a
fall into sin: "When anyone adduces my fall into sin, just answer him
calmly that conversion to telepathy is my private affair like my Jewishness,
my passion for smoking and many other things."[5] It is doubtful, therefore,
that one can talk about the occult outside the context of religious belief in
general, and it is just as doubtful that one can talk about psychoanalysis
outside the same. When the discussion begins, when it comes to the
interpretation of dreams, it has to be acknowledged that some of the best-
known examples in the literature are the prophetic dreams of the Jewish
tradition, such as the hand writing its portentous *mene mene tekel upharsin*
upon the walls of Babylon. Freud doesn't refer to that famous case but

quotes the Greek tradition of two types of dream, those that refer to the past and those that foresee the future (see *SE* IV: 3).

The question of religion becomes most explicit in the two texts of the late 1920's, *The Future of an Illusion* (1927) and *Civilization and Its Discontents* (1930). The fact of their being, by the author's own admission, banal, saying "nothing which other and better men have not said before me in a much more complete, forcible and impressive manner" (*SE* XXI: 35), perhaps obscures a greater failing, namely that they are singularly unprophetic in their positioning with respect to an approaching catastrophe. In a final sentence added to *Civilization and Its Discontents* in 1931, added to a paragraph that raises the specter of the "current unrest," "unhappiness," and "mood of anxiety" and the hope of a resurgence of Eros to counteract the instincts of aggression and self-destruction, the question is asked: "But who can foresee with what success and with what result?" (*SE* XXI: 145). However, we may be reading precipitately if we do not find anything prophetic about Freud in these or other texts. For the gist of my whole argument is that Freudian theory projects more than it knows, even to the point of contradiction. But to read in that sense of prophecy a vision of the apocalypse (is there any other sense of prophecy?), we will have to read even more in opposition to what seems to be the impetus and direction of the theory itself.

In *Civilization and Its Discontents* religion is posited first of all in terms of the reconciliation it offers between psyche and *socius*, as the experience of the "oceanic feeling." But that reconciliation, the coming together of what has been held apart, is also read as a reversion to an ideal prior state, before the emergence of the ego; or at least the sign of the persistence, or survival, of a "primary ego-feeling" (*SE* XXI: 68). From that basis Freud goes on to trace the relations between the ego and the threats presented by the external world, the antagonism between the desires of the individual and those of the community, or more generally of civilization.[6] By means of the "oceanic feeling" the religious experience comes closest to whatever might be represented in vague or specific circumstances by the occult. Yet Freud devotes only his first chapter to the idea, conceding that it exists in many people, but reducing it to "something like the restoration of limitless narcissism" traceable "back to an early phase of ego-feeling" (72). In subsequent chapters the discussion follows through the matter of the quest for happiness, the extent to which civilization stands in the path of that happiness, the sacrifices it demands of the sexual and aggressive-destructive drives, and the imposition of the superego.

Now, an important question can be raised with respect to the idea of religion as regression to an early phase of ego-feeling. In terms of the developmental progression from the subject's failure to differentiate between itself and the world to the varying positions of compromise it adopts between the principles of pleasure and reality, there is no binding logical obligation to read the oceanic feeling as a regression rather than a progression. There may be good ideological reasons for that, a resistance to idealism and so on, but the idea of reconciliation is in fact held out as a *future* promise for the psychic system when it comes to the schism between the libido and the death drive. That is certainly how I read the final words of *Civilization and Its Discontents,* where it is "expected" that Eros "will make an effort to assert himself in the struggle with his equally immortal adversary" (145), Thanatos. Again, it is no oceanic reconciliation that is promised, although in hindsight the prophecy seems fraught with its own version of quietism. Why then would a similarly *pro*spective reconciliation be refused for the ego and treated instead as reversion? Why this change in direction? Does the theory know its back from its front?

In fact, my desire here is not to decide between the progressive or regressive psychic status of the oceanic feeling but again to point to something that disturbs the logic of Freudian theory, a problem of accommodation. The analogy Freud uses to explain the principle of regression is instructive in this regard, for he draws an example from Roman archaeological and architectural history. He will end up by dismissing it as "an idle game" and conclude that his analogy "has only one justification. It shows us how far we are from mastering the characteristics of mental life by representing them in pictorial terms" (71). But the well-known analogy of Roman ruins deserves a closer look. In order to illustrate his contention that "in mental life nothing that has once been formed can perish" (69), he asks the reader to imagine all the strata of Roman architectural history as being simultaneously perceptible: "On the piazza of the Pantheon we should not only find the Pantheon of today, as it was bequeathed to us by Hadrian, but, on the same site, the original edifice erected by Agrippa; indeed, the same piece of ground would be supporting the church of Santa Maria sopra Minerva and the ancient temple over which it was built" (70). That is the Rome Freud asks us to imagine, the Rome he imagined as he stood on the Piazza della Rotonda on September 5, 1901, with his daughter, Anna, on his first visit there at the age of 45, looking backwards. He asks us to defy, as his theory constantly did, the space-time coordinates of an architectural and archaeological chronology in favor of the impossibility of a historical simultaneity. It is the same idea that was imagined by means of the magic writing-pad, the idea of successive imprints upon the unconscious "surface" that do not obscure each other but remain accessible and legible. And because what he asks us to imagine defies logic, he will remain dissatisfied, as he is here, with a topographical representation of mental activity.[7] But it needs to be emphasized that it is the temporal representation that defies logic here as much as the spatial or topographical one. It defies logic simply because we cannot imagine all those buildings occupying the same site at the same time. There is therefore nowhere to go with the analogy from there. But it also defies another type of logic, namely that according to which we might ask why the series of projections of monuments comes to a halt at some ideal present moment. Given that such a moment cannot be defined even within the constraints of chronological time, and given that the constant in all the cases that Freud evokes up to and including the present Pantheon is the fact of ruins, why does he dwell on the example of past ruins and fail to foresee the future ruins? Why indeed does the extraordinary revelation of Freudian theory singularly avoid mention of the apocalyptic? True, there is a certain logic that resists it: the unconscious is rigorously constructed as the repository of memory, as a receptor of stimuli in the past. On the other hand, as I have suggested, and as I hope to show in more detail, any number of examples from Freudian theory make that logic more problematic than it would at first glance seem to be. Suffice it to say at this point that if one is capable of envisaging a reconstruction of Roman architectural history one is equally capable of projecting an architectural future, one that, like the past, will above all be strewn with ruins, with buildings and bodies in all sorts of dysfunctional stress and indeed just plain dead. He might have foreseen as much standing in the Piazza della Rotonda one torrid night in September 1901, smoking his pipe, the first cells mutating under prolonged radiation, the canker at work at the top end of the ingestive trail, the smoke eating at his mouth and moving his bowels, with his daughter Anna for traveling companion throwing desire all awry; Rome might have taught him that if he had looked under it all to see not just a structural decrepitude but a constant will-to-cataclysm.

In the successive palimpsestic replacements or prosthetic constructions of Roman monumental architecture that lead us, for example, from a temple to a church to Agrippa's and then Hadrian's Pantheon, each building replaces what was destroyed and at the same time departs from it. Underneath all four constructions is a desire for shelter, for accommodation, a space where humankind can reside with its gods. Civilization is described by Freud as a progressive appropriation by humankind of godlike characteristics—omnipotence and omniscience—and in the famous passage in chapter three of *Civilization and Its Discontents*, we are told:

> Man has, as it were, become a kind of prosthetic God. When he puts on all his auxiliary organs he is truly magnificent; but those organs have not grown on to him and they still give him trouble at times. . . . Future ages will bring with them new and probably unimaginably great advances in this field of civilization and will increase man's likeness to God still more. But in the interests of our investigations, we will not forget that present-day man does not feel happy in his Godlike character. (91–92)

Freud's progressively prosthetic god is very much a future projection. The past and present are represented in terms of problems of adaptation or accommodation quite unlike the sort of psychic determinism that marks instances of regression such as the oceanic feeling. Whereas there man was something of a prisoner of his psychological past, here he seems assured of a promising cybernetic future. Granted, present-day man is not happy, but future ages will increase his likeness to God and presumably improve his adaptation to the prosthetic state. Of course the rest of the discussion in *Civilization and Its Discontents* does concentrate on the level of unhappiness of present-day man and his inability to resolve the differences that constitute his psyche. But what is nevertheless given in this description, as I read it, is a prosthetic construction oriented towards a future possibility that is a counterpoint to the future in ruins that was never stated although it was there for the reading in the analogy that went the Roman way.

Civilization, as Freud describes it in these pages, is a prosthetic conglomeration of the technological (fire, ships, spectacles), of the esthetic/cultural/intellectual (beauty, cleanliness, order, religion, philosophy), and of the social (relations between the individual and the community). It is a set of devices that, as they are acquired, progressively if imperfectly give humankind the status of the gods. But once Freud turns his discussion to trace the parallels between "the process of civilization and the libidinal development of the individual" (97), then the same set of multiform devices that are said to make the human into a prosthetic assemblage simulating God becomes, as it were, compressed into one overarching form of restraint: the conscience as superego: "Civilization, therefore, obtains mastery over the individual's dangerous desire for aggression by weakening and disarming it and by setting up an agency within him to watch over it" (123–24). Of course the explicit figure of prosthesis has dropped out; it was, in any case, but a brief mention in passing in an early part of the discussion. But the structure that, by accident or by design, it has become the name for, is now firmly in place. Something foreign has been implanted. The structure of the superego is marked by a problematic of accommodation brought about by the imposition of a harsh remedy, and, more specifically from here on, by a calling into question of the limits between what is externally and what is internally imposed, by a mechanism that amounts to an ingrown outgrowth:

> What happens in him [the individual] to render his desire for aggression innocuous? Something very remarkable, which we should never have guessed and which is nevertheless quite obvious. His aggressiveness is introjected, internalized; it is, in point of fact, sent back to where it came from—that is, directed towards his own ego. There it is taken over by a portion of the ego, which sets itself over against the rest of the ego as super-ego, and which now, in the form of "conscience," is ready to put into action against the ego the same harsh aggressiveness that the ego would have liked to satisfy upon other, extraneous individuals. (123)

Conscience for Freud still derives from a natural origin, that of the destructive instinct, but it has passed through a detour as a result of which what was directed outside is turned inwards. It is that diversion or perversion of original purpose that defines the prosthetic structure of the superego. The mechanics of the impulse are natural enough, but the directions are wrong. It fits by going back to front, and so doesn't fit comfortably. It fits well enough, for it has, as it were, grown naturally into the space it fills, but in turning against itself it takes on characteristics of the monstrous.

Freud gives a second explanation for the same mechanism, this time returning to the idea of the father as model for the superego. But the operating principle still involves what I just referred to as a calling into question of the limits between internal and external. The father exists as the outer limit of relations to otherness learned by the child.[8] He, or more precisely the law he represents, acts as the pivot in the redirecting of the aggressive instinct, for he is the authority that does in fact give vent to that instinct in repressing forbidden behavior. Thus the external is doubly internalized: the aggressive instinct directed towards others is instead directed towards the ego, and the real external threat of paternal disapprobation is internalized to become the sense of guilt managed by the superego: "We have also learned how the severity of the super-ego—the demands of conscience—is to be understood. It is simply a continuation of the severity of the external authority, to which it has succeeded and which it has in part replaced" (127). In having allowed that replacement to take place we are said to have traded the threat of loss of love, or the punishment imposed by external authority, for the economy of a permanent internal unhappiness, namely the sense of guilt. It is an economy that in the first place operates through expenditure of psychic energy; that is the primary sense of Freudian theory in general, a theory of psychic economy. But if we read the exposition of that theory here, then its economy has also to be evaluated, as etymology dictates, in spatial or even architectural terms, as a loss or gain of comfort, of room; as a question of accommodation, of what fits in the space provided; a question, need I repeat, that is intimately tied to prostheses, oral, ambulatory, or otherwise; a matter of dealing with the monster within, the part that refuses to adapt. That could not but be so once contradictory forces were discovered inhabiting the same psychic space—conscious and unconscious, libido and death drive. But much as in *Beyond the Pleasure Principle* with its steps forward that go nowhere,[9] in *Civilization and Its Discontents*, the text that is nothing but commonplaces, that discovers "nothing that is not universally known" (*SE* XXI: 96), it is finally the discussion itself that is spatially embarrassed and not just theoretical elements within it: "I suspect that the reader has the impression that our discussions on the sense of guilt disrupt the framework of this essay: that they take up too much space, so that the rest of its subject-matter, with which they are not always closely connected, is pushed to one side" (134). I would suggest therefore that this embarrassment results from more than just the normal process of sorting, rearranging, and displacing that is bound to be a factor in the organization of a discourse. It is no doubt that on one level, and a function of the fact that a discourse can never avoid disclosing its operational principles, whether it choose to or not. As I have already made clear, the tone of and explicit

statements within *Civilization and Its Discontents* demonstrate that it is a
text-in-process, a text of banal musings, one whose informalities are sure
to appear in its organization. There is thus an admitted ungainliness about
it. Where *Beyond the Pleasure Principle* limped along, this text both gathers
up and trails its various and cumbersome appendages as it moves from one
idea to the next, pulling in different strands of the theoretical concepts its
author has already developed. On the other hand, however, we are back in
the Piazza della Rotonda, with a set of ideas operating like the psychic data
of the memory processes, coexisting in spite of the restraints of space. And
we are perhaps at a pivotal point in Freudian theory, or at the other end of
a pivotal point that began ten years earlier, with the theoretical armature
undergoing an important shift, being turned around within the confines
of its own limits, feeling as if the available space were shrinking while the
future rushes on at its inexorable pace.

In his discussion of religion Freud pays little attention to one aspect of it
that might have the most to gain from psychoanalysis, namely the phenomenon and psychology of the sect. Nor is this an emphasis of his *Group
Psychology and the Analysis of the Ego* (*SE* XVIII). Religion is viewed as a
system that activates or acts in conjunction with a whole range of psychic
functions as they relate to cultural formations, but there is no attempt to
do for the psychology of the sect what Max Weber had done for its
sociology.[10] Clearly, what would be of interest to me about the sect would
be its relation to the matter of space, the fact of its having been modeled, in
recent religious history, on the cloister, although its mechanics would be
that of any minority group formed and maintained as a defense against
real or perceived outside hostility. Thus obvious questions could be asked
concerning the history of the psychoanalytic movement, especially from
the time of the formation of the committee of six—Freud, Rank, Jones,
Ferenczi, Abraham, Sachs—coming into being as it did in response to the
threats to the integrity of the movement posed by Jung's increasing
independence, and given its progressive shrinkage with the later defections
of Rank and Ferenczi. As in any such case what was involved was the
preservation of the integrity of a body of doctrine, the drawing of the line
between acceptable diversity of opinion and heresy—the question of libido
for Jung, a theory of birth trauma in the case of Rank, and seduction
fantasies and clinical practice in the case of Ferenczi. Though the mechanisms displayed are particularly telling—Freud's cultivation of Jung as his
successor, the Gentile who would evangelize the world with the gospel of

psychoanalysis; the character assassinations under the guise of analytic judgment (Abraham's assertion of Rank's "unmistakable regression into the anal sadistic")[11]—we should not be so naive as to think there is anything exceptional about the political configurations and machinations of this group or school over a period of 30-odd years as compared with any other. But one would be hard-pressed to decide finally whether the Freudian psychoanalytic movement amounted to a political organization or to something more akin to a religion, or whether, in the terms being developed here, that distinction is valid. On the one hand there would be the formation of the committee in 1912–13 and the internationalization of the movement; on the other hand the question of methods of induction and parallels between analysis and confession, and in between the weighty matters of dogma and doctrine, rigor and justice. Freud's role as either benign guardian of the truth or jealous warrior for purity would of course be central to any such examination of psychoanalytic history, but neither could such a study neglect the familial and political relations among his followers, the question of inheritance that, Derrida has shown (in "To Speculate—on 'Freud'"), permeates much more than historical developments around psychoanalysis, being a constituting function of the theory itself.

If Freud was ready finally to "convert" to telepathy, he took some time to come around to that opinion. He left the vanguard to Jung, who was from the beginning too enthusiastic for his own good about all things mystical. In 1911 Freud wrote to Ferenczi: "Jung writes to me that we must conquer the field of occultism and asks for my agreeing to his leading a crusade into the field of mysticism. I can see that you two are not to be held back. At least go forward in collaboration with each other; it is a dangerous expedition and I cannot accompany you."[12] But it was not to be so. Ferenczi seemed at that point and for a while longer to be dangerously close to following Jung in defecting, but in the end held true. He maintained his interest in the occult and continued to discuss it with Freud until the latter made his position clear some fifteen years later, in 1926: "Moreover my own experiences through tests I made with Ferenczi and my daughter won such a convincing force for me that the diplomatic considerations on the other side had to give way. I was once more faced with a case where on a reduced scale I had to repeat the great experiment of my life: namely to proclaim a conviction without taking into account any echo from the outer world."[13] This is not a projection but the proclamation of a conviction; it is moreover a resistance to a superego expressing itself in the form of an interdiction coming from outside. It is the force of truth itself, that of a conversion to telepathy, the psychic and psychoanalytic turning quite back to front.

But if Freud converted to telepathy, he made no mention of reincarnation. Jung had long since run off with a monopoly on Eastern religions. So it is doubtful that when Freud died in London in 1939, the morphine flowing through his veins one last euphoric time, his prosthesis a moot point, taken out finally in defiance of the impending atrophy, that it had anything to do with a young man that this has everything to do with, the prosthetic paradigm case that sets a staggering course though my investigations here, the case of a young man about to reach his eighteenth birthday at the other end of the earth, about to be diagnosed with an operable sarcoma requiring amputation of the left leg and the placement of a prosthesis with perhaps fewer problems of attachment but as much discomfort of accommodation and adaptation, and as long a list of side effects. For Freud there was defective speech, difficulty in eating, and impaired hearing on the right side that required him to reverse the positions of his analytic couch and chair, reversing thereby the whole analytic process.[14] For my father there was limited cycling, renouncement of ambulatory sports in general, constant intermittent pain with attendant migraines, and the refitting of his car with a knee accelerator.

Don't ask me or tell me why I am recounting all this, in which direction I am setting out, before or behind the theory, with this story of the day after the death of Freud, with this telepathic transfer of prostheses, with the fact, for instance, that the prosthesis did nothing, it seems, to impede my father's insertion into social and professional life. He had, after all, the unimpeachable alibi that was the Second World War. But he also had the protection of membership within a sect that he inherited from his father and his father's father before him, and then assumed by conviction. Its members were inspired by a man named John Nelson Darby, who left the law profession for the cloth then split with the Anglican Church while serving in Ireland and drew the faithful around him in Plymouth in the 1830's. His group made a further split in 1845 over the question of the formal organization of worship, with Darby opting for that to be left to the Holy Spirit and forming a Central Meeting over which he presided in suitably autocratic fashion to preserve the integrity of the sect and its doctrine; and so was formed what came to be known as the "exclusive" branch of the Plymouth Brethren. Darby wrote over 30 volumes of devotional texts in concatenated sentences with frequent recourse to parenthesis that many found difficult to read, and also retranslated the Bible into French (the Pau version), German (the Elberfeld version), and English, producing in the latter a version that supposedly "is based on a sound critical appraisal of the evidence. . . . The version, however, falls short in regard to English style—which would surprise no one acquainted with Darby's voluminous prose writings."[15] How that also amounts to a translation in which "the literary was made to give place to the literal" and which is thus "characterized by a certain abruptness of style"[16] is anyone's guess, but all that is literary criticism. There it was, however, the Darby version that became ours, and one wonders how the style translates into French and German, and whether there are still remnants of the sect sitting in houses or small halls in the Pyrenees after a Sunday lunch of foie gras or cassoulet, digesting the intricacies of Christian doctrine. Darby added copious exegetical notes that naturally made for much discussion whenever the spirit so moved. By the middle of the twentieth century they had none of the evangelical fervor that their spiritual relatives developed in America, although they established themselves with small but solid numbers in various corners of the New World. They practiced a version of Protestantism that involved strict adherence to the Pauline admonitions and prescriptions to the new Christians. The women kept their hair long, keeping it covered also in public and during any form of worship, improvising with a linen serviette if breakfast prayers caught them unprepared; they also abjured makeup and masculine attire like trousers; the men for the most part took jobs with others of their persuasion, the families renounced all "worldly entertainment," which proscription kept radios, television, dancing, and movies on the Index all through my childhood. The same went for most secular books and music but the distinctions and the logic of admissibility were sometimes blurred in those cases, the lines of defense between heaven and earth sometimes softened for high art, subtly and silently, silence was something I learned about early three times each Sunday during the services of worship—the "morning meeting," the "reading," and the "gospel"—which involved all ages and sexes sitting for one and a half hours on end with long periods of silence while the men gave themselves over to quiet devotion to be interrupted now and then by a spontaneous short Scripture reading and discussion, we sat there learning in spite of ourselves the dynamics of an

undisclosed hierarchical group structure and the mechanics of the hermeneutic hurdy-gurdy, the codes of its drive to exegetical refinement with an
inevitably concomitant progression towards interpretative dissent, this
was my first sense of reading, this sitting still in reverence in the outer rows
of a circular configuration, out there with the women, watching as long as
the attention span permitted, alternately in awe and impatience, while
fathers, uncles, grandfathers, and others pored over the textual minutiae,
made constant reference to the Greek and to the notes that were signaled
on the delicate rice paper by tiny lowercase letters, dreaming somewhere in
the unconscious reaches of one day being able to insert such discreet and
elegant appurtenances in my own text, of being able to diacriticize at
length on the basis of a small modification in pitch and spacing, desiring
also to have done with the reverence, to break out of the confines of such a
rigid code of respect, that was how reading developed in the middle of a
Sunday afternoon with the weight of roast lamb and vegetables and too
much dessert tempering the fascination with effects of fatigue to bring me
to this pass, in contrast to my brother, who through the same experience
found the call to medicine in resisting the need to urinate, he sat there and
imagined an apparatus that would allow him to quietly pee without
disturbing the assembly, a urodome or cannula worthy of an Ambroise
Paré, we sat through long *explications de texte* followed by prayers that
could themselves last up to 30 minutes, a sort of devotional filibuster to
stave off the decision to close and return to a hostile world, or we waited
for the announcement of what we hoped would be one final hymn, one
that, like all the others, would be sung without musical accompaniment
and depending on whoever had taken the initiative to lead the congrega-
tion in such song the tune might or might not be begun on the right pitch,
which might or might not have vocal chords straining to reach the high
notes at the end of the second line, so much so that it sometimes simply
petered out, the attempt was abandoned and the melody begun again in a
lower key, and my father attained a certain respect among the 60 or 70
souls who so met each Sunday in my hometown for his ability to redress
the wayward chorusing with a perfectly pitched second attempt, and he
gained a certain respect for his biblical exegesis no doubt reinforced by his
love of Latin and dilettantish interest in the Greek, and a certain respect
for his four children sitting well-groomed in a line with their mother in
one of the rows behind the menfolk, and definitely a certain respect for his
acceptance of his infirmity and his integrity and leadership within the fold,

but none of that counted when it came to his supporting a particular interpretation of the Epistle to the Galatians 6:1 that says, in Darby's translation, "Brethren"—and the Word always seemed to be addressed directly to their denomination—"if even a man be taken in some fault, ye who are spiritual restore[i] [i as 'mending.' Matt. 4.21: see Note, 1 Cor. 1.10] such a one in a spirit of meekness, considering thyself lest *thou* also be tempted," it is a verse all about accommodation and adaptation, the whole prosthetic caboodle, about those whose actions reach out beyond what can be permitted and foreseen but who are still able to be brought back within the fold, and the Greek verb translated as "restore," as in "mending," *katartizo*, means also "to complete thoroughly, i.e. repair or adjust—fit, frame, mend, (make) perfect (by joining together), prepare," and the epistle as a whole concerns what needs to be kept on and what can be dispensed with, for it is Paul's response to those who advocated continued adherence to Judaic practices—metonymized throughout by that precise form of ablation that is circumcision—in opposition to his advocacy of a new order where the law would be superseded by a more individual faith, it was a point of view that would be repeated by the reformists and so on down the line to the point in question, but this slightly progressive interpretation was taken by some of the Australian branch to be an endorsement of the practice of absolution and hence a return to the apostate past of the Catholic Church, even though it was intended to allow for peers to heal their own disputes and to encourage a spirit of admission of fault and mutual reconciliation, this was definitely a hermeneutic abyss that yawned in the middle of the text and of the assembly, and so the reading was deemed inappropriate by the Australians, and then for all the respect they showed him his limping was heard loud and clear echoing through the sanctity of the cloister, it had just seemed like a commonsense reading of the Scripture in question at the time, not particularly *recherché* in its understanding of the principle involved, this was no arcane piece of sophistry nor indeed any deconstructionist practice at work, just a clash of literalities but suddenly there he was left carrying a clunker, the weight of a conviction that he had no problems declaring to be his own, that he would wear with a certain embarrassed awkwardness but would never consider disavowing even when they characterized it as some kind of perversion or monstrosity once it was time for expulsions and recriminations and soon thereafter a wholesale purging, not to suggest he initiated all that, although he should have thought through the question of disagreement to its logical conclusion, he above all should have understood the limits of accommodation of difference, about tolerance and expulsion, containment and amputation, and he quite possibly did and so had sought to position the limit a little more liberally than the norm, but the purging he was nevertheless caught up in would last for years and come to be like a cultural revolution in miniature, without the corpses but nevertheless sufficient to decimate the ranks of the faithful with reports reaching into the popular press of families torn apart and livelihoods ruined, there are examples on both sides of my own family, my mother losing contact with her brothers at least one of whom wouldn't come to his own father's funeral, my father tracking down his brother in Nelson only to be repeatedly snubbed, my paternal grandfather separated from my grandmother during meetings for a time, he in the back forbidden participation, she a few rows forward still within the fold though behind the participating males, it went on until her youngest and somewhat wayward son the pilot fell out of the sky and the telephone rang through the night and I heard my father limp on his crutch up the hallway to answer it and limp more slowly back, they tried to insist that she not attend her son's funeral but she declared enough already, all this turned on more and more frivolous interpretations of this or that biblical prescription that tended to depend more and more on the caprice of those who held the power on the American side of a sect that supposedly had no formal power structure, more and more foreign interference, more and more repression from the center, but all that was later and we were long gone, but not completely, my father held on tenuously for a few years after his ejection during which time he joined the four children sitting with their mother now in the very back seat of the assembled throng, the whole family something of an ungainly appendage sitting there on the fringes of the fold and on the threshold of the available space, all of us now forbidden participation but still singing, if not commencing, the hymns and perhaps adding an amen to this or that prayer, it was called "sitting back" and he did it with chastened pride and a certain dignity even though it meant being ignored by those who used to be friends, and even by relatives close or distant who declined now to say even as much as a hello, we sat back the six of us and we hung back around the edges of groups of the brethren who congregated outside after the service, waiting for I can't remember what, perhaps for one or two brave and independent souls to deign to speak to us, we sat back and endured being ignored for two or three years three times each Sunday, for morning meeting, reading, and gospel, we skipped the Assembly and Care meetings they held during the week to make executive decisions, the former coming to be called with more and more regularity as the purge accelerated for that was where the expulsions were ratified, so we weren't invited, not that we were especially welcome at all, but we came back every Sunday and also for holiday weekends, when they had what were called "three-day meetings" that took up God alone knows how many hours, the only compensation being that they ordered in food to keep those assembled sustained, it was like a mini-convention and my mother took it upon herself to decide that we had paid sufficient dues to partake of the food one long weekend in a hired cinema, the same one in which a few years later I would be hopelessly enchanted by my first motion-picture experience, it was *The Sound of Music* and even the credits thrilled me as I remember, particularly the credits, perhaps it was my memory of readings at work, in any case we didn't have the credit my mother had assumed and our eating of their three-day-meeting food became the subject of an Assembly meeting soon after, while we continued to sit back, it seemed to be the only choice after three generations of our families had been cloistered within the framework of the sect and every-thing outside it was still just as wicked and apostate, we sat there, remain-ing intact as a family, and he sat in limbo there on the edge waiting for forgiveness, or reconciliation, or amends, reparation or adjustment, not yet understanding whether there was room for him dissent and all or not, with his leg doing its characteristic waver from side to side and its occasional twitch, perhaps trying to reconcile himself slowly to a painful and absolute separation that seemed more and more inevitable, perhaps trying simply to work through the logic of the situation and of his conviction which meant that his beliefs had been rejected as wrong by those whose beliefs, he had always assumed, were right against the world, he sat there stroking what he always called his good leg while his prosthetic one oscillated and he wondered why this peculiar combination of differ-ences become opposites and the questions of accommodation seemed so strangely familiar, he sat back until it made no sense any more and until the defections grew not only numerous enough for him to feel vindicated but also enough to form a breakaway groupuscule, they amounted to about fifteen in number in that small city, that is to say three or four families, but it was enough for us to meet, still two or three times each Sunday but for perhaps closer to an hour and a quarter at a time, for this was true reform, in the living room of our home, where we even baptized

my sister, and for a time we kept up the ritual of the evening gospel service
that was strange enough when practiced by the original number given the
lack of their evangelical outreach, preaching to the converted being a gross
understatement, but how much stranger among fifteen heretical and
slightly bewildered souls of whom a good percentage were children, but
they did it all the same, repeating the same rituals in microsimulacrum,
only now he could be relied upon to start the hymn on the right pitch
every time even if the volume didn't come to much with the few voices
available, and to offer prayers that didn't ramble too much and to make
exegetical comments on verses of Scripture that displayed a certain intelligence in spite of their dogmatism, and to make frequent use of his
encyclopedic knowledge of holy writ, but subtly so as not to show up the
others by always correcting them, for the other men were few and far
between, about three of them in all, and it was with eager anticipation that
they therefore looked to the young boys who would pick up the mantle
and assume the inheritance, I was mostly too young to know what was
going on but whatever it was I saw it through the experience of my father
who was a key player, the whole thing lasted from about my fourth to my
twelfth year, and I saw it as a form of grief that he suffered like the pain that
wracked his severed limb, it was the pain of prosthesis all over again, the
pain of excision, the long and painful period of accommodation and
adaptation to a new situation, the slow but inevitable grafting onto a new
and foreign form of religious life, I saw it like some primal event, too
young to register but learning in spite of myself how hard it is to make a
job of letting go, and in the parlance of the day the whole experience
reduced to two words that we children heard time and time again in the
adults' everyday conversations, for every friend and relative was described
as being either "in" or "out," as still belonging to the original sect or not,
this revolving door controlled everything they said like some electronic
binary adjudication, although in reality it was more complicated than that,
there were those, of course, who were out but still in to the extent that they
were sitting back, there were those who were in only because of familial or
professional pressure but consorted with those who were out, there were
those who were out then back in, and so on and so forth, the liminal
possibilities were extensive and the directions, as always, ready to change
when you least expected it, the whole question of belonging and of
exteriority open to redefinition, he sat back and gently rocked his leg from
side to side, the leg that he trusted would find its reconciled double in

some future resurrection, he kept hoping for a while then backed off slowly and reluctantly, and eventually turned on his heel, put his best prosthetic foot forward, and limped off to a different religious life.

One can point to "The Uncanny" (*SE* xvii) as the point where Freudian doctrine came unstuck. There the other is found residing within the same in the most unspecific yet undeniable terms. There the question of spatial *coincidence* takes on, as in the example of Rome, overtones of the temporal and hence of the prophetic. The text is contemporaneous with *Beyond the Pleasure Principle* and already foresees the death drive, but it also announces the splitting off of what will soon become the superego, the instrument of prosthetic oversight. The idea comes out of the notion of the *Doppelgänger* that is given extensive treatment in "The Uncanny": "A special agency is slowly formed there, which is able to stand over against the rest of the ego, which has the function of observing and criticizing the self and of exercising a censorship within the mind" (*SE* xvii: 235). With the uncanny it is as if the unconscious as double is discovered all over again, and with a vengeance, so that henceforth there has to be something destructive inhabiting even the familiarity of a well-developed theoretical construct, something working against what presents itself as the logic in force. When it comes to examples, and the choice is Hoffmann's sandman, Freud wants to generalize the effect beyond the framework developed by Jentsch, for whom "one of the most successful devices for easily creating uncanny effects is to leave the reader in uncertainty whether a particular figure in the story is a human being or an automaton" (quoted in *SE* xvii: 227). For Freud "the feeling of something uncanny is directly attached to the figure of the Sand-Man, that is, to the idea of being robbed of one's eyes." For him it comes down to a matter of castration; on the other hand "uncertainty whether an object is living or inanimate, which admittedly applied to the doll Olympia, is quite irrelevant in connection with this other, more striking instance of uncanniness" (230).

First, Freud protests rather too much in downplaying the importance of the inanimate as source of the uncanny. As Sarah Kofman points out, in Hoffmann's tale the eyes need to be read in the context of the question of mimesis, of good and bad mimesis, such that when they are related to Nathanael's inability to have Klara see things as he presents them in his writings, and to his obsession with Olympia that is from the beginning articulated through Coppola's prosthetic instruments, the eyes become "the principle of an artificial life."[17] Similarly, the Hoffmann story has a singularly prophetic ring to it, Nathanael's childhood fears mingling with his dreams to create a premonition concerning Coppelius, and his poem foretelling the climax in which the eyes, said to be his, are flung at his breast.

From these points of view the matters of inanimateness and castration can be seen to have more in common than Freud states here. The uncanny evoked by fear of the automaton and that evoked by fear of castration coincide if the fear of castration is projected so that rather than referring to a fear of amputation it refers to a fear of prosthetic replacement of the penis. If one projects the idea of substitution that is necessary for Freud to maintain that the eyes symbolize the penis, and if one reads the structure of detachability as necessarily implying that of replacement, then the fear of castration becomes in fact the fear of an inanimate otherness performing a human function. If one were to accept the hypothesis of such a projection then the castration complex would be undercut by its own uncanniness; it would represent not so much a founding structure of the human psyche, a sort of static determinism, as a dynamic that set in train the always future possibility of a switchover into radical otherness. The fear of castration would be the fear of prosthesis as a future projection rather than a past event that the child is supposed to have observed as "actual" in the female. The logic, little Hans's for instance, would instead read thus: if she can lose hers then I can lose mine, and if it can be lost then it can be *replaced.* As I suggested, none of that contradicts the logic of the castration complex; it simply projects it. In fact, the idea of eyes being replaced rather than just lost comes through Freud's text as well. When he concludes by admitting that source material for discussion of the uncanny comes most easily from literature because of the narrational devices by means of which an author creates a world, he puts it in these terms, referring again to Hoffmann:

> It is true that the writer creates a kind of uncertainty in us in the beginning by not letting us know, no doubt purposely, whether he is taking us into the real world or into a purely fantastic one of his own creation.[18] . . . But this uncertainty disappears in the course of Hoffmann's story, and we perceive that he intends to make us, too, *look through the demon optician's spectacles or spyglass.* (230, my italics)

According to that formulation, a writer first creates the uncanniness of the animate/inanimate uncertainty by having us look through his eyes and by thus keeping us in doubt as to whether we are looking at the real world or a fantastic one. But then, in the case of Hoffmann, that uncanniness disappears in favor of that of the castration threat, although we are all the time being made to look through the demon optician's prosthetic eyes. In other words the prosthetic effect, the animate/inanimate uncanniness, has merely been displaced from the author's eyes to those of the demon optician; one set of eyes has been replaced by another. The sandman, after all, is the threat that comes when the eyes are closed, when sleep-prone children discover that in abjuring sight, just as if they had lost their eyes, they do not however cease to *see*; the eyes they see with when their lids are open are simply replaced by the demon prosthetic eyes their fears force them to look through when their lids are closed.

The idea of the castration complex as prosthesis complex is thus a projection from Freudian theory, an attachment to its logic that may well to some extent undercut that logic. But it is permitted, as it were, by the uncanny itself, by the idea that a logic carries its own double within it. It is also—it goes without saying—the idea of Derridean deconstruction.[19] What I wish to point to here is an uncanny that runs against the grain of Freudian theory in the specific sense of being opposite *in direction* to it. Such an uncanny pretends—for here I am making a projection that cannot be verified and that amounts to something of a contrivance—to consist in what Freudian theory cannot predict or foresee about itself, what lies on the future edge of its reasoning. But it is something that, as I have already tried to show, nevertheless continues to haunt that reasoning, to haunt it not as a psychic relic but as a future possibility. This uncanny reveals itself most explicitly in terms of Freud's interest in the occult and in telepathy.

But it is already there in other forms, for example in the concept of wish fulfillment that was the basis of *The Interpretation of Dreams*. That text ends with the following: "Nevertheless the ancient belief that dreams foretell the future is not wholly devoid of truth. By picturing our wishes as fulfilled, dreams are after all leading us into the future. But this future, which the dreamer pictures as the present, has been moulded by his indestructible wish into a perfect likeness of the past" (*SE* v: 621). At first reading this presents nothing particularly paradoxical about the dream: past events and memories merged with, or motivated by, a desire or wish are projected into the present of the sleeping imagination. But there are some difficulties with that idea, not the least being the doubtful status of the temporality of a dream, the fact that its temporality, and thus any notion of wish fulfillment, has to be imposed upon it from the outside. To call a dream "what the dreamer pictures as the present" is to ignore the fact that it knows no time, that its "consecutionality" can make a mockery of temporal logic, for example of the laws of cause and effect. It only becomes a present with respect to the past of its unconscious "origin" once it is reconstituted by dreamer and analyst. Furthermore, the concept of wish fulfillment again only emerges through the logic that is imposed upon the dream, in spite of itself, by analysis. The dream might be better described as a future projection than a wish fulfillment, for as long as a desire has the status of a hallucination, it continues to pose itself in terms of a hypothesis that I find difficult to conceive of without the stamp of the future: it refers by definition to something that has not (yet) occurred. Or else, referring back to the dynamic model of castration just described, we might read the dream as an intermediate fulfillment of a wish that nevertheless continues to project itself towards the conscious recognition that only analysis, or another type of satisfaction, can provide. In other words the temporality of dreaming, both internal (how time functions within it) and external (its description as a "logical" psychic mechanism), runs into the same sorts of complications that plague the topography of the unconscious, complications that Freud came progressively to acknowledge in the course of his research.

A similarly problematic temporal mechanism seems to operate in *The Psychopathology of Everyday Life (SE* vi), in cases of lapsus and parapraxes in general. There we have the present phenomenon before us in much more explicit forms—in the slips of tongue or pen, or in forgetting—but by the same token the directional impulse of the unconscious can be said to be futuristic, and, more importantly, the unconscious can here be said to have an effect upon the present, to "alter" a present perceived of as a future with respect to the unconscious desire. Now on the one hand what is going on is nothing but the obvious logic of a causal relation—the past bringing about the present and the future—such that we understand anything consequential to be also consecutional, and therefore unidirectional, projected towards the future. It is the logic of time itself. In this sense the causal chain established by the conscious is interrupted by a competing one issuing from the unconscious. On the other hand, it is not a simple causal relation that is involved. Freud often insisted on the opportunistic nature of unconscious wishes, and what we must imagine therefore is an unconscious waiting for its future chance to reveal or impose itself *in spite of* the logic of causal relations, but running into competition with a conscious that presumes it can control its own actions. This is not a simple matter of competing causes: what I am calling the unconscious causal chain does not exist in parallel to the conscious but simply waits for the opportunity to act parasitically upon an event of the conscious; the causal relation thus comes to be divided by its uncanny other. The "logical" future—or future wish become present—falls prey to a more arbitrary projection of desire oriented towards the future.

By the time of *Beyond the Pleasure Principle*—the title is particularly telling in its sense of projection—the idea of the wish or desire itself as a unitary impulse has become irredeemably problematized. But much of what occurs henceforth is, as has already been suggested, "speculation, often far-fetched speculation . . . an attempt to follow out an idea consistently, out of curiosity to see where it will lead" (*SE* XVIII: 24). It is therefore a projection that cannot foresee its own future, that may well act opportunistically in terms of that future, as it follows the path of least logical resistance. It is less a theory of desire than a theory of the projection of desire, or of the desire of projection; desire as inexorably futuristic, but running backwards however fast it runs forward, or running towards death as fast as it runs to embrace life.

I shall enlarge upon that. The restatement of the position of psychoanalysis—that favoring a causal logic—is expressed in the opening words: "In the theory of psychoanalysis we have no hesitation in assuming that the course taken by mental events is automatically regulated by the pleasure principle. We believe, that is to say, that the course of those events is invariably set in motion by an unpleasurable tension, and that it takes a direction such that its final outcome coincides with a lowering of that tension" (*SE* XVIII: 7). But this position is soon complicated by the compulsion to repeat. However, Freud will refuse to define the repetition compulsion as simply a revisiting of past trauma or of past experiences prompted by memory; it is instead another impulse projecting forward from the unconscious. This is not, as Freud's experience with little Ernst's willfulness will teach him, a case of dragging a train behind one on a string, but rather of throwing it out as a projection. The idea that repetition is not the same as regression, or more generally that there can be no simple repetition but only a series of returns with an eternity of differences, or *progressive* accumulations, dangles there to be toyed with. To take that step would be child's play.

Yet, once the compulsion to repeat reveals the death drive, it is clear that Freud wants to read the movement involved as a movement into the past. The conservative nature of the death drive is a sign of its retroactivity; in Freud's terms it signifies a desire to return to a past state:

> Moreover it is possible to specify this final goal of all organic striving. It would be in contradiction to the conservative nature of the instincts if the goal of life were a state of things that had never yet been attained. On the contrary, it must be an *old* state of things, an initial state from which the living entity has at one time or other departed and to which it is striving to return. . . . We shall be compelled to say that "*the aim of all life is death*" and, looking backwards, that "*inanimate things existed before living ones.*"   (*SE* xviii: 38, Freud's italics)

Now, there is already enough contradiction in the idea that different drives, the sexual and the death drives for instance, should act in different directions, the former prospectively, the latter retroactively. But that is complicated by the fact that Freud cannot but continue to refer to the death drive in prospective terms, as a drive that goes "forward" towards its aim, even if that involves returning to a prior state. When he discounts the so-called instinct towards perfection as a result of repression, what seems to go forward is said to reach backward, whereas the real instinct that leads inexorably forward is one that leads to destruction. This is presented on page 42 in terms that make it well-nigh impossible to distinguish one direction from the other:

> No substitutive or reactive formations and no sublimations will suffice to remove the repressed instinct's persisting tension; and it is the difference in amount between the pleasure of satisfaction which is *demanded* and that which is actually *achieved* that provides the driving factor which will permit of no halting at any position attained, but, in the poet's words, "*ungebändigt immer vorwärts dringt.*" The backward path [*Der Weg nach rückwärts*],[20] that leads to complete satisfaction is as a rule obstructed by the resistances which maintain the repressions. So there is no alternative but to advance in the direction in which growth is still free.

Clearly there is more than a breakdown in language here. The death drive, which becomes more and more difficult to distinguish from the sexual drive, which comes to be more and more prior such that by the end "the pleasure principle seems actually to serve the death instincts" (63), is based on a contradiction. What seems more and more to be the basic life principle seeks to restore an earlier state of things, namely death. It drives, or advances, backwards. But why should this new drive, which contradicts the others, be read as confirming what defines them, namely the desire for conservation? Why should it not also contradict that definition? Death works both ways, exists at both ends of life. What Freud seems to want to see as a return to the presumed inanimate origin can as easily be viewed as a progression to a mortal end. The reluctance, if that is what it is, to see the movement as anything but a return when the logic continually points in the opposite direction is perhaps what prevents the death instinct from becoming the suicide instinct. Such a reluctance might betray the fear of revealing an apocalyptic side to this theoretical speculation or the fear of giving up life to an unknown prosthetic future, to the uncanny of a prosthetic inanimation. Whichever way one looks at it, though, it cannot be denied that the limits to life appear on all sides. It is because Freudian theory takes those limits as its object, and in the process constantly comes up against its own limits, that it is constantly in the process of adapting, being forced to change what does not fit; and more specifically here, changing direction, starting out on a different course, always supposing that a new course remains to be charted, even if in order to do so one becomes crippled and prosthetized, alternately Icarus and Hephaestus. Freud's well-known conclusion is as follows: "We must be ready, too, to abandon a path . . . if it seems to be leading to no good end. . . . In the words of the poet: *What we cannot reach flying we must reach limping*" (64).

By the time of *Beyond the Pleasure Principle*, then, the theory of the drives has infected the drive of the theory. Forward is back and back is forward. It goes both ways. Conservation cohabits, not with regression, but with the forward impulse of speculation, for "it is impossible to pursue an idea of this kind except by repeatedly combining factual material with what is purely speculative" (59). And even though there is always a possibility, at times even a necessity, to go further out than ever in charting a different course, "thus diverging widely from empirical observation" (ibid.), there remains the assumption of a factual base. For instance: "I do not think a large part is played by what is called 'intuition' in work of this kind" (ibid.). The "intuition" Freud refers to here is a conviction based on "a kind of intellectual impartiality" (ibid.). It seems not to be the same as those words it can come so dangerously close to: instinct at one end of the scale and premonition at the other end. As I have been describing it, however, Freudian theory has through all this been continually projecting towards its counterdirectional other—one of whose forms must be telepathy—even and more so as it "retreats" into the contradiction of the drives.

So what then of telepathy, and particularly of its prophetic outside beyond the bounds of the thought transference that Freud had no problems allowing for from the beginning? Jones claimed to have observed in him "an exquisite oscillation between scepticism and credulity," and although he reports in full everything relevant to Freud's "conversion," he masks poorly his surprise at the attention the father of psychoanalysis gave to the matter:

> And yet only two years later [1921] there was a pronounced swing once more in the opposite direction, and we find Freud again more than hovering on the brink of reinstating his occult beliefs. Perhaps this curious reversion may be correlated with the remarkable release of his imagination, or phantasy, that led him to propound hypotheses on the deepest problems of mankind: the nature of death and the conflicts between love and hate, between the constructive and the destructive tendencies in life.[21]

The significant texts on telepathy are four in number. The first—"first" in the sense that it was conceived in the context of *The Interpretation of Dreams*—is a section of the 1925 text "Some Additional Notes on Dream-Interpretation as a Whole" (*SE* xix: 135–38) entitled "The Occult Significance of Dreams," where "veridical prophetic dreams" are rejected but not so "telepathic dreams." The second, "Psycho-analysis and Telepathy" (*SE* xviii: 173–93), is the address prepared in 1921 but only ever given to the committee of six—Freud agreeing with Jones's and Eitingon's advice and not wanting to encourage publicly the link between psychoanalysis and mysticism—and only published posthumously. In it he recounts two possible cases of telepathy and leaves the details of a third at home ("visible proof of the fact that I discuss the subject of occultism under the pressure of the greatest resistance," *SE* xviii: 190). There, thought transference has this description: "an extraordinarily powerful wish harboured by one person and standing in a special relation to his consciousness has succeeded, with the help of a second person, in finding conscious expression in a slightly disguised form" (*SE* xviii: 184–85). The following year he writes "Dreams and Telepathy" (*SE* xviii: 195–220), whose publication details call it a "Lecture given before the Vienna Psycho-Analytical Society" although it was never given there. In it Freud begins with an account of two of his own seemingly prophetic dreams and concludes that they were unfulfilled and indeed that "during some twenty-seven years of work as an analyst I have never been in a position to observe a truly telepathic dream in any of my patients" (199). He continues some pages later: "Telepathy has nothing to do with dreams. . . . The essential nature of dreams consists in the peculiar process of 'dream-work' which, with the help of an unconscious wish, carries the preconscious thoughts (day's residues) over into the manifest content of the dream. The problem of telepathy concerns dreams as little as does anxiety" (207). The material from "Psycho-analysis and Telepathy" is reworked in more detail in the fourth text, "Dreams and Occultism," published in the *New Introductory Lectures* in 1933 (*SE* xxii: 31–56). While raising objections to the occult in general, including the objection that interest in it is "religious," he repeats that "there remains a strong balance of probability in favour of thought-transference as a fact" (43) and offers this modulated conclusion:

> I am sure you will not feel very well satisfied with my attitude to this problem—with my not being entirely convinced but prepared to be convinced. . . . No doubt you would like me to hold fast to a moderate theism and show myself relentless in my rejection of everything occult. But I am incapable of currying favour and I must urge you to have kindlier thoughts on the objective possibility of thought-transference and at the same time of telepathy as well. (54)

However, in spite of the conversion of 1926 and the multiple returns to the topic, and in spite of statements as "open-minded" as that just quoted, it seems that the line remains drawn on this side of telepathy *as premonition*. The unconscious, Freud finally seems to say, cannot project outwards towards the future. Yet, as he reminds us in "Dreams and Telepathy," the unconscious does not obey conventional logic: "the language of [dream] symbolism knows no grammar; it is an extreme case of a language of infinitives, and even the active and passive are represented by one and the same image" (*SE* xviii: 212). What holds here for grammatical voice should also hold for tense: if the dream's lack of grammar implies a lack of distinction between active and passive voices, the same must also be said for past and present tenses. One should not be able to determine, therefore, that a dream points backwards any more than that it points forward. Freud's objection to such an argument is, of course, that there is a distinction to be maintained between the lack of grammar obtaining within the dream and what I am suggesting to be an agrammaticality or temporal illogicality in the relation between that dream and an event in the world, such as would allow the dream to be called a premonition of that event. A dream, Freud will say, comes from within and is a product of mental life, whereas "the very conception of the purely 'telepathic dream' lies in its being a perception of something external" (208). But such an objection ignores the psychopathology of everyday life, which insists on the intrusion of the unconscious upon the subject's relations with the external world.

Freud thus backs into a defense of last resort: he has recourse to a determinate sense of "inside" as opposed to "outside" for mental life when the whole sense of psychoanalysis has been to undo the series of such oppositions that were supposed to structure the human psyche—unconscious/conscious, perceived/unperceived, familiar/uncanny, backwards/forward, empiricism/speculation, and so on. But the inside/outside question is, as we learned from projection, a question of direction, and also the very problem of accommodation, in its specific sense of adapting and fitting, and in its acquired sense of putting up (with), of providing room and shelter for, of accepting something as belonging to a given space. It is clear that telepathy is beyond psychoanalysis, just as it is beyond science, logic, rationality. There is no possibility of proving it to be true, for if it were proven to be true, then that would disprove all the criteria by which the categories of the true and proven are currently decided. Freud seems to recognize that in his repeated references to the "reciprocal sympathy" (*SE* XVIII: 178) between psychoanalysis and the occult, and to their hostile reception by official science. But it is nevertheless the voice of science that draws the line: "The notion that there is any mental power, apart from acute calculation, which can foresee future events in detail is on the one hand too much in contradiction to all the expectations and presumptions of science and on the other hand corresponds too closely to certain ancient and familiar desires which criticism must reject as unjustifiable pretensions" (*SE* XIX: 136). It takes Derrida's deconstruction of the economy of externality, from the treatment of writing in *Of Grammatology* to the question of the frame in *The Truth in Painting*, to lay bare the mechanism at work in Freud's work on telepathy. And he turns his attention precisely to those texts by Freud in a piece excised from the "Envois" of *The Post Card*, a piece left at home, like Freud's third example in "Psycho-analysis and Telepathy," when the manuscript went to press and published elsewhere somewhat later.[22] For Derrida, the kernel of truth Freud wants to seal off from the inroads of telepathy is quite clearly the theory of dreams. Here is Derrida parodying Freud—let us not forget the complicated system of senders and receivers at work in "Envois"—as he does throughout "Telepathy":

> Above all, don't speak of anything else, it's that, our theory of the dream, which must be protected at any price. . . . What a strategy, don't you admire it? I neutralize all the risks in advance. Even if the existence of telepathy . . . were to be proven one day . . . there would be no need to change anything in my theory of the dream and my dream would be safe. I am not saying whether I believe it or not but I leave the field open to every eventuality (just about), I appropriate it in advance as it were. My theory of the dream, ours (the first, the second, it matters little), would be able to *accommodate* it and even still control it. ("Telepathy," 23, my italics)

Indeed it doesn't take much irony to read Freud's sensitivity, both positive and negative, to the question of telepathy as a symptom of an anxiety about something that threatens psychoanalysis. Thus when he advises Jones to tell those who inquire that it is "my private affair" he is, as it were, announcing the symptom ("back off, I won't be exposed to this") and at the same time inviting us to analyze it ("it is a mental affair"), to treat what is external—a matter for addresses (although he never gave them), papers, debate—as internal, a private affair; as an internal psychopathological fact of everyday external life.

I say that it takes Derrida to lay bare this mechanism, for it is his notion of the letter with its defining sense of adestination that removes from Freudian theory the comfort of a kernel of truth, namely the idea that a message can reside and belong in a particular place, and that it can return home to where it belongs and be accommodated there. For Derrida, the message as we ordinarily conceive of it, operating through a closed circuit of sender to addressee, is divided by its always possible adestination. That is the whole thrust of his debate with Lacan in "Le Facteur de la vérité" (The purveyor of truth). Derrida will find in telepathy what he calls his "final paradox," the final twist to the idea of adestination, according to whose logic the idea that a letter can *not arrive* becomes the idea that a letter *cannot arrive*. That is to say that adestination is built into the structure constituting the letter to the extent that arrival cannot be determined by the letter considered as an event of sending. With telepathy a so-called message—say a premonition—arrives from "nowhere" to form part of its receiver's conscious or unconscious. It is therefore constituted by the event of its arrival rather than by a point of origin, for that "origin," presumably the future event it predicts, cannot be conceived of as an origin since it works backwards. Telepathy is an event of adestination both in terms of sending—it comes from nowhere identifiable, or from the future, is therefore forward backwards—and in terms of its arrival—its message waits in a kind of limbo until an event comes along that it can attach itself to, so that when it arrives it is utterly unexpected. The final paradox Derrida refers to is therefore that "it is because there may be telepathy that a postcard cannot arrive at its destination" ("Telepathy," 16).

Thus whether it originates or resides in the conscious or unconscious the message departs never to return; it is by definition a diversion. The question of directionality is raised for every event of communication, and especially for Freudian theory inasmuch as it identifies certain mechanisms by which the very untrustworthiness of naive conceptions of communication is revealed. Again, somewhat speaking for Freud, Derrida advances the hypothesis of what might be called a generalized telepathy:

> I am not putting forward the hypothesis of a letter which would be the external occasion, in some sense, of an encounter between two identifiable subjects—and who would already be determined. No, but of a letter which after the event seems to have been launched towards some unknown addressee at the moment of its writing, an addressee unknown to himself or herself if one can say that, and who is determined . . . on receipt of the letter; this is then quite another thing than the transfer of a message. Its content and its end no longer precede it.   (5)

He concludes that the idea of telepathy, rather than being the outside of psychoanalysis that it threatens to be for Freud, should be considered as concomitant with the theory of the unconscious itself (14).

The "outside" that psychoanalysis wants to retreat from when it appears in the form of telepathy seems to be a specific function of distance. In other words the forms of spacing that psychoanalysis finds operating in psychic processes, such as the paradoxical, contradictory, or illogical communications between conscious and unconscious, provide structures similar to those operating in the case of telepathy, except that the latter fall in an outside that Freudian theory cannot comprehend. But there is something more precise still that is betrayed by the analogies Freud draws: "it [telepathy] is a kind of psychical counterpart to wireless telegraphy" (*SE*

XXII: 36); "the analogy with other transformations such as occur in speaking and hearing by telephone, would then be unmistakable" (55). Once telepathy is related to telephony and to telegraphy, the outside it represents becomes that of the *technē*: the distance traversed becomes a crossing into mechanical otherness. What has occurred is a fall into the structure of the inanimate, the structure of lifeless machines, forms of the automatic. We might say that telepathy appears again as a form of the uncanny that *prosthetizes* psychoanalysis. The threat posed by telepathy is that it will install a form of otherness that is other than human. This is the same threat that was posed by man as prosthetic god with the appendages of civilization: "If there had been no railway to conquer distances, my child would never have left his native town and I should need no telephone to hear his voice; if travelling across the ocean by ship had not been introduced, my friend would not have embarked on his sea-voyage and I should not need a cable to relieve my anxiety about him" (*SE* XXI: 88). Trains are fine as long as they are dragged along behind a playing child; as long as our relation to them is a relation to the past, the effects can be controlled. But once we take to throwing them out with a whoop of satisfaction into an unknown future, then the whole edifice trembles, something threatens to undermine the theory at its very base; a whole different drive is set in train.

The phenomenon should by now be familiar to us: whichever part of the theory it comes down to—the drives, the wishes—they seem to be capable of acting in a direction opposite to that which the theory has set for them; something is out of control, more than the theory bargains for. In the last article he produces on the subject, Freud attempts one last time to put telepathy in the past. Writing "Dreams and Occultism" in 1932 he draws a comparison between telepathy and the way insects communicate; it might therefore be "the original, archaic method of communication between individuals." But no sooner is telepathy situated in that archaic past than it returns to an ominously fascist present that will give rise to an unspeakable future, for it is noted that it might still be able "to put itself into effect under certain conditions—for instance, in passionately excited mobs" (*SE* XXII: 55).

In "Dreams and Occultism," the case that Freud's "resistance" caused him to leave at home and leave out of his first paper, the paper he was dissuaded from delivering except to the assembled faithful, finally reaches the light of day. It is a complicated account of a visit paid to Freud by an

English Dr. Forsyth, a patient who, by Freud's account, unconsciously exploits his own name to express his discontent. Thanks to this, Freud is able to evoke a saga of a similar name by John Galsworthy, and to give himself over to free-associating among every *foresee*able possibility imaginable. Reading Freud's account leaves no doubt in my mind concerning who is inviting the analysis. Freud and his patient have changed places; the analysis has changed direction. What is up for analysis here is precisely the idea of foresight or foreboding, of whatever would make telepathy a matter of premonition. It haunts the whole story in the most uncanny fashion. Even Jones, recounting it all like a faithful dog, cannot help, in spite of himself, pointing out Freud's continuing resistance in wanting to put it further in the past than it is, or at least in failing to recognize the importance of the temporal sequence: "One minor error I can myself correct. Freud said I had been in Vienna a month before Forsyth's visit. In fact it was the same week, for I dined with Forsyth in Zurich when I was returning from Vienna and he on his way there."[23] That was back in 1921. But by the time Freud gets around to talking about it in the early 1930's the future has all but arrived. So it was no minor error. It is what propels us towards the apocalypse.

It will go very fast from here on. There is no holding it back, the pressure forward is relentless. There can never be enough room to get it all in. We are suddenly in some white hotel, interpreting our worst nightmares. But not so suddenly, for we have all been there, all along. All along, as I said from the beginning, there was a problem with accommodation. But not the sort I thought. I don't always look in the right direction. It isn't a problem of what fits inside, of how to adjust to what is enclosed, like a monster over the roof of the mouth, or a room the lovers never leave, nor is it the problem of a character called Anna in a novel by D. M. Thomas, a problem with how much of Freud's son she can fit inside of her—"he took my hand and slid my fingers up beside him there, our other friend the plump corsetière slid hers in too, it was incredible, so much in me, yet still I was not full"[24]—no, the real problem all along is outside, outside the window where the flood waters are rising and the whole place is going up in flames, the trees turning red and hanging with charred bodies, the people falling past the window, the outside as if falling inside. When Frau Anna G. comes to Freud in the year beyond the pleasure principle that is 1919, with symptoms of pain in her pelvic region and breast, he will correctly look back to the history of the mother's adultery, to the burning hotel where she died inseparable in the arms of Anna's uncle, and read the white hotel as the mother's body we are all homesick to return to; he will adapt his analysis to the information she gives him and as she slowly admits to her childhood memories and early sexual experiences and her husband's anti-Semitism, it will all fall into place. He will write to her in 1931, the year he adds the final disquieting sentence to *Civilization and Its Discontents*, and will complain of his prosthesis and speak of Ferenczi and telepathy like a convert ("your gift is entirely unconscious. There is nothing you can do about it").[25] Then they will lose contact and he will wait out all the signs and refuse to admit that the worst is happening, up until and even after the horrors of the Anschluss, then he will take a final train flight to London with his own Anna, and take a final dose of morphine a day after the invasion of Poland. It will all fall into place. But that is all a fiction of the past. It will all fall into place but it will never fit, for the place and time will suddenly be projected elsewhere; the place to look in respect of Frau Anna's symptoms is in fact forward to a future where her only protection will be a prayer her nurse has taught her, something that will come back with force across the waves of time and memory, like a line from a hymn, "when sorrows like sea-billows roll, whatever my lot Thou has taught me to say it is well, it is well with my soul," a song from *Hymns and Spiritual Songs for the Little Flock*[26] that we sang with a haunting melody begun by a man with an excellent sense of pitch, a song about the pitching and rolling of the oceanic feeling whose rhythm he drew his relief from like the rhythm of his swaying leg, a song I remember most from funerals and can foresee the singing of it at his funeral and will carry the tune of it towards my own as an incantation against future time and tide, something like an insurance policy he never took, he said we should leave the material things like cars and houses to His care, they were not that which is Caesar's, I could never understand the logic but he stuck with it even when one day we were holidaying and he turned the car around outside the gate of an air-force base and took too wide a berth and collided with a short pole that was hidden on the left side denting and scratching two doors, it seems so trivial now and even though he argued at length by letter with the authorities he got no satisfaction as far as I know and had to pay for the damage from his pocket, but we got a repainted car finally, it was nothing, just an amputee colliding with a short metal pole but I remember when we got out to inspect the damage there was the sound of ocean waves I felt sure would overwhelm us, my sturdy father suddenly gone all frail and I carry with me still the fear of the sea whenever I am driving near it at night and it is thoroughly confused with a nostalgia for the sound that is the sound of childhood, the oceanic sound of a child's relation to his father, the homesickness for the mother's body washed over with a desire for the father's prosthesis, that is to say that the longing for the security of the parental arms is articulated, other than by means of a simple regression, through a sense of the inanimate and of infirmity that announces the future and a future death, so it is a nostalgia that is also a mourning, prosthesis is nothing if not that, coming to terms with loss, learning to accommodate a lack, talking forward towards a cure that is also the acknowledgment of death, the one that will come with the oceanic static time-lag emptiness of international telephonic communications, the sort Freud regretted in *Civilization and Its Discontents* in 1929, blind to what he was saying, remaining blind to the future in spite of his references, such as that to a city with a less checkered past than Rome, like London spared the visitations of an enemy (*SE*xxi: 71), or a Jew awaiting a pogrom (89), or even "the idea of setting up the use of soap as an actual yardstick of civilization" (93), he was already thinking the unthinkable Blitz and Holocaust of a very near future, where a viciously adestinational usage of bars of soap would indeed become the yardstick for a civilization rushing precipitately towards backwards, where even the supposedly self-evident consequential logic of prosthesis would be turned on its head once human skins came to be used for lightshades, the inanimate calling for, as if giving rise to, the animate, it will always be shown to go the other way when you least expect it, to change direction without warning, Freud was already thinking in that direction but couldn't see the destruction for the ruins, getting it backwards, but then Rome will be far away and Ferenczi will already be dead by the time his former fictitious patient Anna will take the invitation to move to Kiev and remarry, she will be there with a future, the future that is Stalin's dekulakization purges that claim her new husband, the future of a meager existence in the Podol ghetto and finally a new morning waking with her adopted son for a train ride to the promised land that will take her nowhere but to the street seething with a press of thousands filling it to overflowing and pushing slowly but massively forward towards the realization of the unimaginable that waits for thirty thousand at the cliff face of Babi Yar. Then and there in the pit with no roof there is room and accommodation only for death, the suffocation of being buried alive, the unadaptability of a breast crushed by a jackboot, the inadmissibility of a bayonet thrusting repeatedly into her vagina:

> The thirty thousand became a quarter of a million. A quarter of a million white hotels in Babi Yar. . . . The bottom layers became compressed into a solid mass. When the Germans wished to bury their massacres the bulldozers did not find it easy to separate the bodies. . . . The bottom layers had to be dynamited, and sometimes axes had to be used. These lower strata were, with some exceptions, naked; but further up they were in their underwear, and higher still they were fully dressed. . . . The Jews were at the bottom, then came Ukrainians, gypsies, Russians, etc.[27]

Against such a future she has for protection a fragment of a prayer from an adopted religion from a repressed childhood. While the billowing flood-waters of blood roll and well up about her there is that ripple of an oceanic feeling. She whispers "You who are Saviour" in the face of a world that is a "world of little children being hurled over a wall like sacks of grain,"[28] a world where the feeling is of oceans breaking up, of egos finding nowhere to regress but to naked fear, of the complexes that form when sex organs are exposed to firearms, of the elemental pileup of blood and shit and death that is always at the other end of the psychoanalytic inquiry, for it is a theory of how the unthinkable comes to be thought and points at some point to the future interpretation that is a massacre, an event whose analysis is interminable and for which there are many names and no name, whose interpretation is the uncovering of its names, Trebizond, Babi Yar, Deir Yasin, Shatila, names that can turn up anywhere, names whose perpetrators come from anywhere and everywhere, whose receivers too easily become senders, and always back and beyond of what will be known of it the certainty of its repetition, the name that cannot yet be named but will be named, the always future unforeseen but inevitable name of the next and so-far-unheard-of killing field, the compulsion to kill and die that waits beyond the reach of knowing and saying so atrociously familiar.

§ 5   Paris, 1976

On a dit alors que la prothèse s'écrit au moins deux fois, et de plusieurs façons. Cette fois, ici et là, au milieu, en deux formes, en plus d'une langue. On a dit qu'on n'écrit jamais dans une seule langue, plus précisément qu' "on n'écrit jamais ni dans sa propre langue ni dans une langue étrangère." Derrida écrit la phrase dans "Survivre," l'ayant d'abord publié en anglais. Et l'ordre ou peut-être la recette est donné par la suite: "On n'écrit jamais ni dans sa propre langue ni dans une langue étrangère. En tirer toutes les conséquences: elles concernent chaque élément, chaque terme de la phrase précédente."[1] Derrida l'a écrit d'abord dans une langue étrangère, ou plus précisément on l'a d'abord publié et moi je l'ai lu pour la première fois dans une langue étrangère. C'est-à-dire en anglais, ce qui n'est pas bien sûr une langue étrangère pour moi pour peu qu'on possède sa propre langue. J'écris en brouillant ainsi la langue, comme j'écris en deux langues, incertain d'être dans l'une ou dans l'autre, parce qu'on ne peut pas savoir dans quelle langue et dans quelle étrangeté et étrangéité précises on écrit. Quand on dit "langue étrangère" en écrivant dans une langue étrangère, qu'est-ce que cela donne comme renvoi dans un abîme de sens? Est-ce que moi, en écrivant, saurai mieux que vous, en lisant, dans quelle langue, en premier ou en second lieu, dans quelle langue ceci s'écrit? Pourrions-nous dire, ensemble ou séparément, quel texte est original et quel texte est la ou une traduction de quel autre? De ces questions que ne cesse de poser la réflexion de Derrida je tire donc certaines conséquences, de certains éléments et de certains termes, me concentrant sur celles qui concernent la prothèse, un peu au hasard, mais pour me frayer un chemin qui obéira à la logique de ce qui est mis en marche avec elle.

§ 5 Paris, 1976

It has been said: prosthesis is written at least twice, and in a number of ways. This time, here and there, down the middle, in two forms, in more than one language. It has been said that one never writes in only one language, more precisely that "one never writes either in one's own language or in a foreign language." Derrida says as much in "Living On." In English first of all, then somewhat later in French. An order, or perhaps a recipe, follows: "One never writes either in one's own language or in a foreign language. Derive all the consequences of this: they involve each element, each term of the preceding sentence."[1] Derrida's formulation was written, or at least published first of all, in a foreign language. In any case that is the language I read it in, namely English, which is not of course a foreign language for me, although what is foreign to whom remains as uncertain as does the extent to which one can be said to possess one's own tongue. So I write mixing the languages, in two languages, uncertain which is of the first order of alienation, given that one cannot know precisely what language or what sort of foreignness one writes in. What does it mean to say "foreign language" while writing in a foreign language, or in one's own language that one doesn't possess; how far down do the echoes sound within such an abyss of sense? Do I, in writing, know better than you, reading, what language this is written in, in the first or second, or any other place? Could we tell, together or separately, which is the original text and which is a translation of some other? Such are the questions that Derrida's work continues to pose, encouraging me to derive certain consequences from certain elements and terms, concentrating on those that concern a prosthesis, somewhat randomly, but in an attempt to force a passage through the workings of its logic.

Or, ce n'est pas l'étrangeté qui est censée exister entre deux langues, ou à l'intérieur d'une même langue qui m'intéresse le plus ici. Il faut préciser encore: la phrase de Derrida que je viens de citer ne vient pas en fait du texte même de "Living On," ni de "Survivre" mais plutôt de leur sous-texte, la note continue qui forme un article à part, en bas de page, en parallèle avec le texte "principal," espèce de commentaire sur sa rédaction et sur sa traduction. Il s'appelle en français "journal de bord," "border lines" dira le traducteur américain, ce qui donne le coup de génie en anglais du titre "Living On / Border Lines" (survivre/vivre sur la frontière, sur les bords, sur le bord [de l'abîme]). Je vais donc retraduire tout cela à ma guise, dans la perspective de la prothèse et en brouillant un peu la survie, le journal, et le bord, dans ce but: écrire sur le vif. Afin de poser la question de ce qu'est écrire sur le vif d'une prothèse. Quels effets d'étrangeté se créent entre le mot et le corps quand il s'agit d'écrire une prothèse?

La prothèse s'écrit donc au moins deux fois, de plusieurs façons, en plus d'une langue. Par exemple, on écrit "prosthèse" et "prothèse" pour distinguer la philologie de l'orthopédie, pour différencier l'adjonction d'un élément non étymologique à l'initiale d'un mot d'un appareil servant à remplacer un membre amputé. Cette distinction-là, avec l'histoire de ce mot qui subit ainsi, en français au moins, sa propre opération d'ablation au cours de son développement, sera à reprendre, dans une autre langue. Je la laisse en suspens ou entre parenthèses ici. Deuxième exemple, plus propre à la question: comme je l'ai déjà constaté, la prothèse peut bien n'être que le dispositif, elle n'en implique pas moins, et en toute rigueur, l'idee de l'amputation—ou celle d'un manque ou d'un mal—qui l'aurait précédée. La prothèse renvoie forcément à deux opérations contradictoires bien que complémentaires: enlèvement et addition; et puis, bien sûr, animal et minéral, vivant ou naturel et artificiel, et ainsi de suite. Aucune simplicité, aucune singularité prothétique; aucune intégralité originaire. Troisième exemple, le paradigme dont je traite et que je traite ici: la prothèse comprend la sienne et la mienne, la jambe de bois de mon père et cette prothèse de texte. Je ne dis pas ce texte qui s'appelle prothèse, même si l'on insiste. Un texte, n'a-t-il pas du moins la possibilité d'être une prosthèse, à savoir un morceau d'écriture comprenant, soit au début, soit au milieu, soit à la fin,[2] des éléments impropres ou étrangers à son sens authentique, à son *etumon*? Et puis, n'a-t-il pas après tout la possibilité d'être une prothèse, l'*usage* et non seulement la *mention* de la chose, dans la mesure où il

In fact it is not the foreignness that might exist between two languages, or within a single language, that interests me the most here. Let me add a further detail: the sentence just cited doesn't in fact come from either "Living On" or "Survivre" but instead from their subtext, the continuous note that forms a separate article running along the foot of the page, parallel to the "main" text, as a kind of commentary on the writing and translation of it. In French it is called "journal de bord," which is like a ship's log, but this is brilliantly translated as "borderlines" to give the title "Living On / Border Lines," with all its senses of brinkmanship as well as a tracing of the frontier between inside and out. It gets retranslated here, after a fashion and in the prospect of prosthesis, and with a little mixing of life, writing, and edges, as follows: writing in the quick of things. In order to ask the question of what it is to write in the quick of prosthesis, to write about it as a live (t)issue. What effects of foreignness are created between word and body once it comes down to writing a prosthesis?

So "prosthesis" is written at least twice, in a number of ways, in more than one language. For example, it is written in both philology and orthopedics, referring to a non-etymological element that comes to be attached to the beginning of a word as well as an apparatus designed to replace an amputated member. In French, the spellings *prosthèse* and *prothèse* distinguish the two senses such that the word undergoes its own literal ablation in the course of its development, losing an *s* in the middle before it can refer to amputated limbs, but that story can be told another time, in another language. My second example is more closely related to the question: however much "prosthesis" refers to an apparatus alone, it cannot fail to imply the idea of the amputation—or of a lack or deficiency —that would have preceded it. "Prosthesis" necessarily refers to two con-tradictory but complementary operations: amputation and addition; and then, of course, the animal and mineral, living or natural and artificial, and so on. There is nothing that is simply or singularly prosthetic; it has no originary integrity. Third example, the paradigm being treated and treated of here: "prosthesis" includes his and mine, my father's wooden leg and this prosthesis of a text. I do not say "this text called prosthesis," even if one objects. After all, is it not possible for a text to *be* a prosthesis in the first sense, namely a piece of writing including at its beginning, middle, or end[2] elements foreign to its authentic sense, its *etumon*? And isn't it also possible for a text to be a prosthesis in the second sense, a *use* and not simply a *mention* of the thing, to the extent that even as traditionally

consiste en une adjonction de choses soi-disant naturelles et artificielles, humaines et non-humaines, de deux ordres, et cela même dans une conception traditionnelle du langage qui se réfère à un dehors réel, à un auteur et aux mots qu'il produit? De ce point de vue ce texte-ci a toute l'apparence d'un appareil servant à remplacer un membre amputé, il fonctionne afin de désigner une absence quelconque, celle de la vérité ou de la réalité si vous voulez, de la jambe de bois de mon père ou de tout autre chose. Or, comme je l'ai déjà suggéré, à l'examiner de près une prothèse n'est plus simplement un appareil, elle ne fait pas que remplacer, et ce qu'elle remplace—si on arrive à déterminer qu'elle remplace quelque chose—ne pourrait en aucune manière se réduire à l'idée d'un membre amputé. De façon évidente alors, dans la mesure où la prothèse cherche à remettre en question les termes de sa propre définition et le système de priorités qui assure une telle définition, elle fait allusion à la logique derridienne de la différance, du supplément et de la signature divisée, avec pour résultat que ce que je viens d'appeler une possibilité—la possibilité qu'a un texte d'*être* une prosthèse ou bien une prothèse—est plutôt une condition nécessaire pour qu'un texte quelconque se constitue. Le texte est structuralement prothétique, comme toute écriture forcément inscrite à sa propre dérive et dans un certain artificiel. Dans la mesure où il résonne, le texte rend un son métallique.[3]

Revenons donc à la question: qu'est-ce qu'écrire sur le vif de la prothèse? Dans quelle substance pénètre-t-on en l'écrivant, sur quel support pose-t-on son instrument ou vers quel subjectile applique-t-on la matière de son dire? Question qu'il faudrait reposer de la façon suivante: par quel biais se permet-on de définir le rapport qu'entretient le mot avec le corps? Comment une chose se pose-t-elle par rapport à l'autre? Vieille et naïve question qu'a relevée et refoulée toute l'interrogation du signe en s'appuyant sur la relation du mot avec la chose. Car la chose, dans la perspective prothétique ne peut être autre que le corps. C'est l'hypothèse de tout ce qui est tenté ici, ainsi que son engagement thématique. Ce dont on parle, ce à quoi la langue se réfère en nommant l'autre, ici et peut-être en général, c'est le corps. La relation linguistique comme relais de l'altérité, comme espèce de traduction, ou plutôt de *translation*, s'articulerait par le corps, mon propre corps, celui de l'autre, de ma mère, de mon père, et ainsi de suite, par l'expérience du corps comme expérience de l'autre. Or, le corps, comme articulation de cette relation linguistique, et toujours dans la prospective prothétique, sera nécessairement un corps infirme, ou

conceived of a text refers to a real outside or to a living author who produces words; it consists of some sort of mixing of the so-called natural and the so-called artificial, of the human and nonhuman? From that point of view this text has all the appearances of an apparatus designed to replace an amputated member, or some sort of absence, that of truth, or of the real if you wish, my father's wooden leg or something else. But as I have suggested, a prosthesis is shown under close examination not to be simply an apparatus, nor to be something that simply replaces, and what it replaces—presuming it could be determined that it did replace something—cannot in any way be reduced to the idea of an amputated limb. Thus, to the extent that prosthesis seeks to call into question the terms of its own definition and the system of priorities that underwrites that definition, it of course alludes to the Derridean logic of differance, of the supplement and of the divided signature, with the result that what I have just called a possibility—the possibility that a text might *be* a prosthesis— must be considered a necessary condition for the constitution of any text whatsoever. The text is structurally prosthetic, like any writing necessarily inscribed within its own drift and within a certain artificiality. To the extent that a text resonates it has a decidedly metallic ring to it.[3]

Let us return to the question: what does it mean to write in the quick of prosthesis? What sort of matter does one enter into in writing about it, what is the basis it all rests upon, what does one draw on in beginning to talk about it? In other words from what perspective may we define the relation between the word and the body? How does the one position itself with respect to the other? It is an old and naive question, one that has been both raised and repressed by the whole contemporary inquiry into the sign as articulation between word and thing. From a prosthetic perspective, the thing in question can only be the body. That is in any case the hypothesis as well as the thematic undertaking of everything elaborated here. What one talks about here and in general, what language refers to when it names the other, is the body. The linguistic relation, as a form of translation, is articulated through the body as relay for alterity, my own body, that of my mother, of my father, and so on; it is articulated through the experience of the body as experience of the other. Now, still within the perspective of prosthesis, the body, as articulation of this linguistic relation, will neces-

bien manquant, à la demande d'un autre. En-deçà de toute physiologie et au-delà de toute psychopathologie, le corps qui arrive sur la scène de la prothèse ne se suffit pas à lui-même, n'est pas entier, ne l'a jamais été. Alors, dans la mesure où la relation que j'appelle prothétique règle l'opération du sens en général, et dans la mesure où le corps y sert de référence en premier et en dernier ressort, dans les termes que je suis sur le point de développer, le modèle de la prothèse ne serait pas un cas exceptionnel mais le paradigme du corps. Si vous voulez c'est par la prothèse que je cherche à insister sur le statut non-originaire du corps, sur la non-intégralité de son origine, pour résister à l'idée que la dissémination originaire du sens soit infirmée par la supposition d'une singularité corporelle, supposition qui subsume le concept du sujet individuel et la loi du nom propre. Je répondrai plutôt que c'est précisément dans la désarticulation du corps que la dissémination du sens puise toute sa force. Mon hypothèse est donc la suivante: la référence première de la langue est faite à un corps, corps non-originaire, corps divisé.

Faisons un pas de plus: dans le cas d'un texte qui parle de la prothèse, d'une prothèse qui est à la fois texte et jambe de bois, usage et mention, texte divisé, mise en service et panne fondamentale de toutes les tendances allégorisantes, texte prothétique à une jambe de bois réelle, quand il s'agit d'écrire sur le vif de la prothèse, le rapport référentiel entre mot et chose-corps s'abîme assez sérieusement. Ainsi, en dépit de ce que je viens de dire, ce n'est plus une simple relation de référence qu'entretiennent corps et mot, c'est un jeu d'adjonction, un effet de prothèse. Dans ses relations avec le corps il me semble que le mot perd sa pertinence référentielle en faveur d'une série de poses qui ne sauraient s'appeler autrement que prothétique.

On peut identifier au moins quatre poses, certes non exhaustives, par lesquelles se noue la parenté du corps avec le mot. Celle, toute naïve et essentialiste, par laquelle le mot sort de la bouche pour se faire corps une première fois. Venant remplacer le corps à corps du toucher et du geste, il entre dans l'altérité irrémédiable de ce qu'on appelle le langage. C'est le paradoxe, ou l'irrémédiable et l'abyssal de cette différence que déjà on nomme écriture. Il y aurait dorénavant entre corps et langage le tout et le rien de l'abîme; le tout qu'il y a à refaire dans les diverses relations qui peuvent se développer une fois qu'on a reconnu que rien n'y est donné— pas de recours sûr, mais nécessité de parler et faire parler; et le rien menaçant que représente la rupture absolue.

sarily be infirm, or lacking, in need of the other. Before any physiology and beyond any psychopathology, the body to be found at the scene of prosthesis is deficient, less than whole, and has always been so. Thus, to the extent that the relation called the prosthetic regulates the operations of sense in general, and to the extent that the body functions in that relation as the reference of first and last resort in the terms that I am about to describe, then the prosthetic body will not be an exception but the paradigm for the body itself. If you will, it is by means of prosthesis that I wish to insist on the non-originary status of the body, on the nonintegrality of its origin, in order to resist the idea that the originary dissemination of sense might be weakened by the presumption of a corporeal entity (a supposition that subsumes the concept of the individual and the law of the proper name). I would hold on the contrary that it is precisely from the disarticulation of the body that the idea of dissemination derives its force. My hypothesis is thus as follows: language's first reference is made to a body, a non-originary and divided body.

Let me take things a step further: in the case of a text that speaks of prosthesis, of a prosthesis that is at the same time a text and a wooden leg, use and mention, divided text, putting into service and fundamental breakdown of allegoric functions in general, a text that is prosthetic to a real wooden leg, when it comes to writing in the quick of such a prosthesis, then the referential relation between word and thing-body is thrown awry. Thus, in spite of what I have just said, what takes place between word and body is no more a simple relation of reference but rather a play of adjunction, an effect of prosthesis. It seems to me that in its relations with the body the word loses its referential pertinence in favor of a series of poses that can only be called prosthetic.

It is possible to identify at least four poses by means of which the body relates to the word, and the list is by no means exhaustive. There is the naive and essentialist idea that in coming out of the mouth the word has ascribed to it a certain corporeal materiality. Replacing body contact or the language of gesture, the word enters into the irremediable otherness called language. It is the paradox, or the irremediable and abyssal nature of that difference, that has, by now already, been called writing. Between body and language there is henceforth the all or nothing of the abyss; all that has to be renegotiated once it is recognized that nothing is given—no sure recourse but an insistent need to speak and have speak; and the threat of the void that would open upon an absolute rupture between the terms.

Deuxième pose: le mot nomme le corps, n'en sort jamais pour ainsi dire, instaure la relation référentielle. Nouveau paradoxe: en nommant le corps le mot se trouve obligé de se nommer en même temps, obligé en fin de compte de se nommer "corps" car la nomination ne peut s'opérer que depuis une position d'extériorité et c'est le corps même qui sera appelé à définir les termes de l'extériorité en général. Jamais de simple mouvement d'extériorité une fois qu'il s'agit d'énoncer quoi que ce soit concernant le corps, a fortiori un corps reconduit dans sa fonction nécessairement prothétique.

Le paradoxe pourrait également s'expliquer de la façon suivante: c'est par la nomination, ou plus précisément par le nom propre, que le mouvement constitutif du langage vient résider à jamais dans le corps. C'est ainsi que le déchirement qu'est le langage s'occulte en se corporalisant, pour ne pas dire se concrétisant ou se monumentalisant, en loi, en solidité patronymique et patriarcale, en même temps qu'il se fend—cette solidité, ces pères—en différence, en filiation bâtarde, en disputes d'héritages et ainsi de suite. Et c'est pourquoi le langage ne sort jamais du corps, que le corps qu'il se donne est prothétique, celui du nom, morcelé.

Troisième pose: le mot retourne au corps, se fait surface et profondeur corporelles, et cela par le jeu du langage familier. Ce n'est pas que la distance est abolie, cet écart sans lequel—on l'a bien répété—le langage tout simplement n'aurait pas lieu. D'abord parce que ce retour n'est pas l'annulation régressive, le mouvement en arrière, d'une "progression" qui part de la langue concrète pour aboutir à l'abstraite ou à la figurée—progression qui d'ailleurs se contredit dans le fait que le familier se situe précisément dans l'espace du figuré—car c'est un retour qui fait figure d'un retors, un dédoublement qui s'opère à même le mot dit simple. Le familier s'attire tout discours sur le corps, sur les fonctions corporelles ainsi que sur la physicalité du mot—tout ce qui est phatique ou poétique. Et c'est par le discours sur le corps que la langue se diffère le plus, empruntant en même temps le ton de tout ce qui est propre et proche, de tout ce qu'on ne peut dire que dans l'intimité d'une présence pleine et spontanée; et également celui de l'outrance, de l'*ob-scène*, de tout ce qui s'exclut du cercle et du circuit familiaux, de la décence.

On pourrait donc identifier une quatrième pose, celle par laquelle le mot se fait corps, non pas dans le sens d'une nomination, mais comme le fait d'agir selon des modèles de corporalité. Les exemples en sont multiples: Carroll, Joyce, Leiris, Desnos, l'Homme aux loups, etc.[4] Retour à la

In the second pose the word names the body but, as it were, never leaves it. It installs the referential relation. But there is a new paradox here: in naming the body the word is obliged to name itself in the same movement; it is obliged in the final analysis to name itself "body" since nomination relies on an idea of exteriority and the body offers the model for exteriority in general. There can never be a simple movement of exteriority once it comes to naming anything whatsoever to do with the body, all the more so once the body is brought back to its necessarily prosthetic function.

The paradox could also be explained in the following way: it is by means of nomination, or more precisely by means of the proper name, that the constitutive movement of language comes to reside permanently in the body. It is thus that the rending that is language is occluded by a corporealization, if not a concretization or monumentalization, in the form of law, patronymic, and patriarchal solidity, at the same time as it comes undone; the solidity, the fathers fall into difference, produce bastard sons, dispute the inheritance, and so on. Thus language can never be said to leave the body, and thus the body it assumes is that of the name, become piecemeal.

In the third pose the word comes back to the body, becomes corporeal surface and depth through the play of the familiar. That doesn't mean that distance is abolished, for as has been oft repeated, without an idea of spacing language would simply not take place. This return to the body is not to be considered as a retrogressive canceling, or reversal, of a movement that would have begun with the concrete and progressed towards the abstract or figurative (such a progression would in any case be annulled by the fact that the familiar is itself situated in the space of the figurative), for this re*turn* has more the appearance of a twist, a doubling that occurs at the simplest level of the word. The familiar attracts all discourses on the body, concerning bodily functions as well as the physicality of the word, its phatic and poetic effects. And it is by means of the discourse on the body that the word demonstrates the extent of its difference, borrowing on the one hand the tone of everything proper and present, everything that can be said within the intimacy of full and spontaneous presence, and on the other hand the outrageous, the *ob-scene*, all that is excluded from the family circle, the familiar circuit of decency.

Hence a fourth pose for the word, that of the word become body, not through nomination but through subscription to models of corporality. The examples are numerous: Carroll, Joyce, Leiris, Desnos, the Wolfman, and so on.[4] Back to square one, it might be said, and in fact what is

case départ tout de même, et effectivement tout ce qui marque cette pose avait déjà fait son effet lors du premier mouvement de corporalisation ou de vocalisation. Comme je viens de le dire, ce n'est qu'en se divisant, en se morcelant, que le corps se fait langage, que le langage est né. Or, ceci serait tout de même à considérer en sens inverse, que ce n'est qu'en se faisant corps, corps malléable, que le mot devient apte à la division, à l'amputation, que s'inaugure le processus que j'appelle prothétique. La chute dans la matérialité, la corporalisation effective du mot, est également le signe de sa partition. Et évidemment cela ne commence pas par le mot. Il n'y a aucun corps intègre, dès qu'il s'agit du mot, car le mot en tant que corps n'arrive jamais à assurer son intégrité; mais selon la même logique qui se dessine dans tout ce que nous disons ici, ce n'est que grâce au mot, que le corps se nomme, et ce n'est que grâce au corps que le mot prend forme. Nous voilà donc aux prises avec une réciprocité du corps et du mot qui se réduit difficilement à la référence, qui n'assure aucune unité, qui installe plutôt la divisibilité comme principe au sein d'une énonciation quelconque. Aucun corps alors qui ne s'articule, aucune articulation qui n'implique la divisibilité radicale. En disant "prothèse," on dit d'abord articulation, divisibilité, et inversement, dérive du processus additionnel, chaîne prothétique, indifféremment contagion et promiscuité. C'est tout cela qu'il s'agit de faire marcher par l'opération nommée prothèse.

C'est donc un effet de chiasme, celui du corps avec le mot—ou de "chasme," cet abîme où tombent en corps à corps les mots de la prothèse— qui règle, ou au moins surveille, les mots qui se donnent dans la suite, comme pour marquer le temps de la condition prothétique. Je dis bien "condition" même s'il donne par moments l'impression d'une consécution conséquentielle, puisque l'effet de chiasme, je l'ai bien dit, affecte, infecte, ou infirme l'idée de l'ordre comme tout le reste. L'ordre des mots, par exemple, cela veut dire non seulement la manière dont on les place l'un après l'autre, mais celle dont on les force dans leurs rapports étymologiques, comment on les traque et les détraque dans leur syntagmatique intérieure, comment on repose les questions de priorité parmi les opérations linguistiques, sémantiques, et rhétoriques. Dans une telle déconstruction de l'ordre, là où d'autres ne verront sûrement que le désarroi et l'obscurantisme, mon but serait en revanche de ne négliger aucune ressource possible, de jouer toute carte sur table dans la recherche d'une articulation quelconque de la problématique présente, d'insister sur le fait d'urgence, car c'est toujours la mort qui nous traque dans un quelconque

characteristic about this pose was already evident in the first instance of corporealization or vocalization. As I have said, it is only through self-division, by coming apart, that the body can become language, that the word can be born. Yet that idea could be taken in the converse sense, in the idea that it is only once it becomes a malleable or divisible body, ready for amputation, that the word can inaugurate the prosthetic process. The fall into materiality, the corporealization of the word, is also the sign of its partition—and of course the process doesn't begin with the word. There is no integral body once it is a matter of the word, for the word as body can never assure its own integrity. But according to the same logic that underwrites everything developed here, the body can only be named thanks to the word, and the word can only take form thanks to the idea of the body. The struggle here is therefore with a reciprocity of body and word that cannot be reduced to reference, that continues beyond any hope of unity, and that on the contrary installs divisibility as the principle of any enunciation whatsoever. There is no body that is not also an articulation, and no articulation that does not imply a radical notion of divisibility. In writing prosthesis, one enunciates first of all such ideas of articulation and divisibility, and, conversely, a drift along the process of adjunction, a prosthetic chain, indiscriminately contagion and promiscuity. That is the shifting ground the operation known as prosthesis stands on.

It is therefore the figure of a chiasmus, that between body and word—or indeed a chasm, that into which the words of prosthesis fall locked in a corporal embrace—that structures or at least regulates the words that follow, marking the time of the prosthetic condition. I say "condition" even if it seems at times that a consequential sequence is involved, for, as I have insisted, the chiastic effect affects and infects, indeed weakens the idea of order as much as anything else. The order of the words, for example, refers not only to how they are situated one with respect to the other but also to how their etymological relations become forced, how their internal syntagmatic order is rearranged and deranged, how the priority among linguistic, semantic, and rhetorical operations is called into question. Some will surely see nothing but disarray and obscurantism in such a deconstruction of order, but my aim throughout is to exploit every possible resource, to put every card on the table in the search for a suitable articulation of the problematic at hand, doing everything possible to get

cas de prothèse, de tout faire, quoi, pour qu'en fin de compte je puisse faire
marcher mon truc.

Reste la question donc d'une moralité ou d'une éthique du mot, ana-
logue à celle du corps. Dès qu'il s'agit de jouer avec l'intégralité d'un corps,
d'un corpus, la question éthique, la question du respect si vous voulez, ne
sera pas loin. La même question se pose aussi bien au niveau des interventions génétiques et des mères porteuses que dans le cas du néologisme.
Comment donc respecter une prothèse? Ou plutôt comment faire respecter cette prothèse? Par quels moyens modérer le niveau des interventions?
Etant donné la violabilité, voire la violence ou violation originaire du mot,
y aurait-il des actes illicites à son égard? Comment situer la limite du jeu
des artifices? Etant donné la réciprocité du mot et du corps dans la
prothèse, comment juger les exigences éthiques quant au mot par rapport
aux celles qui traitent du corps? Ou bien, quelle éthique serait servie par
l'exploitation de cet enchevêtrement du mot et du corps que j'encourage
ici, en faveur de qui ou de quoi se déroule cette série de retors chias-
matiques?

Il faut supposer qu'à la limite une telle éthique réponde à la mort. Facile
à dire que mon père serait mort sans la jambe de bois, c'est-à-dire sans
l'amputation qui l'a rendue possible, ou nécessaire. Je ne sais même pas si
on appelle cela une décision éthique, car ce serait aussi bien le comble des
convenances, une espèce d'opportunisme heureux, le chemin de la moindre résistance, comme on dit. Or, la question éthique est loin de se
résoudre dans le cas-limite de la mort; elle ne fait que se compliquer
davantage. Et cela parce que la prothétisation du corps s'intensifie à
l'approche de la mort. Je ne parle pas seulement de la médecine contempo-
raine où les décisions qui concernent la mort ne sont pas forcément prises
en faveur de la vie, où la vie peut être une mort vivante et la mort une
forme de vie artificielle, bien que la question y prenne des formes nouvelles
et spécifiques; je parle également des pratiques et des discours, soit scien-
tifiques soit culturels, qui ont en tout temps essayé de récupérer le corps
mourant ou mort, de le conserver comme intégralité. Je tiens à suggérer
que c'est précisément ce que j'appelle la prothétisation du corps, sa non-
intégralité originaire et finale, qui produit la problématique éthique de la
mort, ainsi que de la vie, et qui veut dire qu'une solution ou réponse de
type classique devient impensable. La convenance (le recours à l'artifice) et
l'éthique (la supposition de l'intégralité) n'offrent plus de résistance à un
effondrement en abîme dont l'issue—si c'est le mot qui convient—n'aurait
même plus la forme classique d'une question.[5]

the thing to run, insisting that matters are urgent, for it is always death that one finds lurking behind a case of prosthesis.

A question remaining to be addressed concerns the morality or ethics of the word, based on that, or those, applied to the body. As soon as one plays with the integrity of the body or any sort of corpus, the question of ethics, of respect if you wish, arises. It is the same question that is raised in the context of genetic intervention, surrogate motherhood, and neologism. How does one respect a prosthesis, or rather how does one have it respected? By what means can one control the level of intervention? Given the violability or indeed the originary violence or violation of the word, are there some interventions that should be regarded as illicit? How can one place a limit on the play of artifice? Given the reciprocity between word and body that prosthesis assumes, how is one to judge the ethical demands upon the word as compared to those dealing with the body? Or else, what ethical interests are served by the exploitation of an entanglement between word and body such as I am encouraging here? In favor of whom and what does this series of chiastic twists turn?

One should presume that at the outside such an ethics turns on the matter of death. It can be easily stated that without his wooden leg, that is to say without the amputation that made it possible, my father would be dead. But I don't know whether that means that an ethical decision was made any more than one of extreme convenience, a kind of fortunate opportunism, a following of the path of least resistance. For the question of ethics is in no way resolved by the outside case that death represents; it only becomes more complicated. In saying that I am not simply referring to contemporary medicine where decisions concerning death are not necessarily made in favor of life, where life might be little more than a living death or death a form of artificial life, even though the question undoubtedly takes on quite new and specific forms in those cases; I am also referring to those scientific and cultural practices and discourses that have always sought to co-opt the dead or dying body, to preserve it as a form of integrality. I would suggest that it is precisely what I call the prosthetization of the body, its originary and final nonintegrality, that produces the ethical problematic surrounding death, as well as that of life, as a result of which a classical response or solution to the question becomes inconceivable. Ethics (the presumption of integrality) and convenience (the recourse to artifice) collapse into the same sort of chiastic embrace as the body and the word, and if indeed some way out can be found it will no longer have the classic form of a question.[5]

Il n'empêche que cette prothèse représente une pratique éthique: celle
de la confession, du deuil, de la colère, de la soumission, et puis également
celle, à venir peut-être, de la perte, de la détachabilité, de l'artificialité, de
l'étrangéité, et ainsi de suite; ainsi qu'une pratique politique ou socio-
logique: démystification, information, résistance, affranchissement. Mais
c'est peut-être du point de vue éthique qu'elle démontre mieux qu'ailleurs
que son explication ne se développe jamais qu'à partir de sa démonstra-
tion, de sa mise en marche. L'éthique de la prothèse reste donc à lire, dans
la prothèse.

Il faut que ça marche. C'est dans une telle optique que ça a commencé.
Que cela fonctionne comme une mise en marche. Ce n'est pas pour rien
que le fonctionnement mécanique s'exprime ainsi à la mesure animale,
sinon humaine, du moins dans cette langue que j'écris ici.[6] Car il n'existe
pas de marcher originaire, une fois que la condition s'entame, c'est-à-dire,
dès le début. C'est-à-dire aucun marcher humain ou animal qui ne soit
atteint par le mécanique, et aucune machine qui ne soit atteinte par la
structure de la panne; aucune condition pré-prothétique. Au début, au
pied de la lettre, ceux-là se sont déjà scindés; et le début et le pied. Son début, c'est une dé-marche qui se démarre sous la forme d'une panne. Le
nécessaire, si vous voulez, ne se trouve pas là dès le début, il faut l'inventer,
il faut faire marcher. Entre l'automatisme d'un faut-que-ça-marche et le
mécanisme du faire marcher, il n'y a qu'une chose qui s'explicite, c'est
l'articulation, c'est donc la prothèse.

Nous voici reconduit au début d'une démarche, là où ça bute contre les
effets de différence entre deux langues, dans les points chauds de la
traduction, de la translation ou du transfert. Ça se passe dans les coulisses,
dans le couloir où claquent les portes pour faire passer ou plutôt caser
l'idiome sorti d'un côté et réadmis de l'autre. Là où soufflent les courants
d'air dans des trous de serrure béants, où les paroles sont en suspens, aux
limbes, comme tout ici, dans un lieu de passage où la rencontre se fait avec
l'autre, comme dans n'importe quel couloir, voire celui où marchent sur
place un père prothétique et un fils venu le joindre dans la grande ville où
ce dernier fait des études, car celui-là est venu changer de jambes dans un
organisme d'état qui s'appelle Artificial Limb Factory, usine aux prothèses,
mais également espèce d'ombilic des limbes artificielles, le père vient
s'accaparer d'une nouvelle prothèse et le fils le rejoint là pour qu'ils passent
un bout de temps ensemble dans une période où les visites à la maison se
font de plus en plus rares, question de différences de styles de vie, de

That is not to say that this prosthesis lacks ethical content—that of its recognizable confession, mourning, anger, submission, as well as that which remains to be formulated, perhaps, of loss, detachability, artificiality, foreignness, and so on—nor is it to say that it lacks political or sociological content—demystification, information, resistance, enfranchisement. But it is perhaps in terms of its ethics that prosthesis demonstrates most clearly that its explanation can only be elaborated on the basis of its demonstration, in the way it works. The ethics of prosthesis therefore remains to be read, in prosthesis.

Firstly then, as easy as it might be to say it, the thing has to be made to run. It was, after all, from such a perspective that it began. It must be mechanically sound enough to run. It is not for nothing that mechanical functioning is expressed in terms borrowed from animal, if not human, activity, namely running, at least in the language I am writing in here.[6] There is no form of ambulation that is exempt from the sense of the mechanical, and no sense of the mechanical that is exempt from the idea of a malfunction; no preprosthetic condition. This is a running start that gets going on the basis of a breakdown, that of the start itself. What is necessary is missing from the beginning, it has to be invented, somehow or other it has to be made to run. Between the automatism of having it run and the mechanics of taking a walk there is one thing that comes up time and time again, namely the question of articulation, that is to say prosthesis.

All this brings us back to the beginnings of the whole operation, there where it catches on the differences between two languages, in the hot spots of translation, transplantation, and transfer. It happens behind drawn curtains, or in the corridor where doors open and slam shut to admit, or perhaps commit, an idiom come from one side into the other. There where drafts blow through gaping keyholes while the words are held in suspense, in limbo, like everything here, along a passage the site of an encounter with otherness, as in any corridor, for instance that in the city where a father cools his heels and marks time with his son come to join him during a break in his studies, he has come to the state institution called the Artificial Limb Factory, both a prosthesis plant and an artificial limbo center where the father has come to change legs, to take possession of a new prosthesis, and his son has joined him there so that they might spend some time together during a period when his visits home are rather few and far between owing to differences of lifestyle, belief, behavior,

croyances, de comportement, de politique, de morale, de tout quoi, ces différences qu'on arrive facilement à taire dans le couloir de l'ombilic des limbes artificielles où on attend surtout, on attend qu'on vous échange la jambe, on marche sur place allais-je dire, ce n'est pas vrai du tout, on s'asseoit gentiment sur des bancs bien durs qui longent le couloir car comment voulez-vous qu'on reste debout sur une seule jambe pour ne pas dire marcher sur place, on est là en mal de jambe, planté là à ne rien foutre car l'organisme d'état compétent en matière de prothèses dérive précisément sa compétence d'une économie de pièces, ce qui veut dire qu'on ne vous donne pas la nouvelle jambe avant de vous enlever l'ancienne, c'est comme si on devait la passer par le guichet avant de clopiner grâce à une béquille d'un guichet à l'autre à la recherche de la remplaçante, guichet commande, guichet dossier du patient, guichet retouches et ajustements, et ainsi de suite, on attend surtout, d'une nouvelle jambe la pose est longtemps suspendue, comme la conversation du père avec le fils, il n'y a plus grand'chose à dire tant qu'il est question du transfert de la prothèse, c'est là que tout se passe et rien ne se passe, ça court tout seul de l'autre côté du guichet mais rien ne marche du tout entre temps et moi je suis là encore une fois à me demander comment je peux lui servir de prothèse provisoire si c'est cela qu'il veut, si c'est cela dont il a besoin, comment soutenir ou même supporter un père en mal de prothèse en attente dans l'ombilic des limbes artificielles.

En fait je ne sais pas combien de jambes on possède, use et remplace dans une vie prothétique. Je sais tout simplement—information que je tiens des toutes dernières nouvelles—que l'adaptation à la neuve devient de plus en plus difficile, les hanches vieillissantes de moins en moins prêtes à accepter de faire le dressage ou le rôdage nécessaire, qu'on arrive à un point où on commence à parler de la dernière dont on aura besoin, comme la dernière voiture ou n'importe quelle autre machine ou quel harnachement qu'on achète ayant bien pris la mesure d'une vie, on fait de même dans le cas d'une prothèse, vous pouvez vous assurer que cette information s'inscrit quelque part dans un dossier quelconque à la Artificial Limb Factory bien que ce ne soit pas une information qui passe par le guichet, mais elle arrive tout de même dans le couloir où tout se passe, des idées aussi insolites que l'approche de la mort c'est sans doute tout ce qui s'y passe dès qu'on enlève une jambe, de toute façon on est là dans ces limbes où on s'asseoit gentiment avec une jambe manquante et un fils provisoirement

politics, morality, everything in fact, but one can easily avoid those differences in the artificial limbo factory where above all one waits, waiting for
them to change your leg, one marks time I said but it isn't true, one sits
down quietly on the hard benches that line the corridor for how do you
expect someone to stand on one leg let alone mark time, he is there semi-
legless and feeling like an arsehole, for this government department that is
qualified in the matter of prosthesis derives its competence precisely from
its ability to economize on parts, as a result of which you never get your
new leg until you hand over the old one and they determine that it
definitely needs replacing, although I don't mean that they treat a prosthetic badly and as far as I know he got a new one if he needed it or got the
old one repaired and got a sympathetic ear when he told of the difficulties
or pain it was causing him, but in any case the image I have is of passing
one through the window, then hobbling on a crutch from one window to
the next in search of the new one, one window for ordering, another for
researching one's file, a third for measurements and adjustments, and so
on, all the time waiting, above all waiting, having a new leg fitted involves
an interminable suspension it seems, like the conversation between father
and son, for there is little left to say once it comes down to a transfer of
prostheses, there everything and nothing comes to pass, it all runs by itself
on the other side of the window but nothing walks in the passage in the
meantime and I am once more forced to ask myself how I can serve as a
temporary prosthesis if that is what he wants, if that is what he needs, how
to support or tolerate a father hurting for a prosthesis waiting in the
artificial limbo factory.

In fact I can't tell you how many different legs one possesses in a lifetime.
I only know—because I have recently been told—that adapting to a new
one becomes more and more difficult, one's aging hips less and less
inclined to break or run it in, such that one reaches a point where one
begins to speak of the last one that will be needed, like the last car or any
other machine or accoutrement one buys, one is able to measure a lifetime
in wooden legs, you can be sure that that particular piece of information is
written somewhere in a file in the Artificial Limb Factory or in some
Department of Health office even though you wouldn't be able to locate
the window across which the statistic might pass, it never gets out into the
corridor where all this comes to pass, ideas as bizarre as the approach of
death are no doubt all that ever comes to pass here where one sits down
quietly with a missing leg and a briefly found son while things gear up in

retrouvé pendant que ça chauffe côté différence, côté indifféremment traduction, translation, et transfert, passage et relais, et comme je l'ai dit je me trouve là au milieu, espèce d'agencement également en suspension, prothétisé à mon tour, ça passe par moi, je laisse passer ceci et cela, des mots par exemple qui passent entre nous, père et fils, vous et moi, entre nos corps partiels, amputés, ou en réparation, supplémentaires et complémentaires, passent des mots qui servent de membres, des mots qui soutiennent un corps ou deux, qui les relaient d'un côté ou de l'autre d'un passage d'un réseau où se fait et se refait une prothèse tout le long d'une vie.

Je hasarderai trois mots pour marquer le temps d'une condition de prothèse; trois mots qui correspondent tant bien que mal aux moments diagnostique, anesthésique, et orthopédique de l'affaire, pour lui donner une espèce de répertoire sémiologique ou une banque de données sommaire. Ces mots sont *trancher, subir*, et *marcher*. La tranche concerne bien sûr la décision, ce qui met fin à la suspension. Elle est loin d'être étrangère à la prothèse, lui servant d'initiative et représentant tout ce qui l'entame. L'origine de la prothèse a beau être le fait accompli du manque ou de la panne, le dédoublement d'une articulation toujours déjà à l'oeuvre qui veut dire qu'il n'y a jamais eu de moment pré-prothétique et qui implique une suspension de la décision quant à l'origine, mais il n'empêche que son opération dépend de la décision même. Ce qu'on dit être vrai pour l'indécidabilité en général compte également pour la structure prothétique: la suspension n'empêche en aucune manière la décision, au contraire:

> Une décision ne peut advenir qu'au-delà du programme calculable qui détruirait toute responsabilité en la transformant en effet programmable de causes déterminées. Il n'y a pas de responsabilité morale ou politique sans cette épreuve et ce passage par l'indécidable. Même si une décision semble ne prendre qu'une seconde et n'être précédée par aucune délibération, elle est structurée par cette expérience de l'indécidable.[7]

Or, dans le cas de la prothèse, la décision se marque de façon particulièrement nette, et non pas une seule fois. Bien qu'il n'y ait pas de moment décisif qui inaugure la prothèse—c'est-à-dire son idée et sa structure—une prothèse particulière sera marquée tout de même par la décision de trancher, par la tranche diagnostique qui prépare la tranche chirurgicale. Par le trancher le mot passera dans le corps, par l'agencement d'un couteau

the difference department, in the department that is indiscriminately translation, transplantation, and transfer, passage and relay, and as I was saying I find myself in the middle, similarly a kind of agency held in suspension, prosthetized in turn, it passes through me also, I let this and that pass, for example the words passing between us, father and son, you and me, between our fragmented, amputated bodies, those under repair, the supplementary and complementary bodies, there words pass that stand in for members, words that hold up a body or two, relaying them from one side to the other of a passage in a network where a prosthesis gets made and remade for the measured length of a lifetime.

There are three words or expressions that can be used to situate a prosthesis, three simple expressions that correspond more or less to its diagnostic, anesthetic, and orthopedic phases. Those expressions are *to come down*, *to undergo*, and *to run*. "Coming down" concerns first of all the decision, having the force of a legal judgment, the bringing to a close of suspension, and the irredeemable effect of such a decision. It is far from foreign to a prosthesis, being its initiative and representing whatever it both breaches and broaches. The origin of prosthesis may well be the *fait accompli* of a lack or a dysfunction, the doubling through articulation that is always already in operation and which means that there is no pre-prosthetic moment and that the decision concerning the origin remains in suspense, but its functioning still depends on a decision. What is true for undecidability in general is also a fact of prosthesis; suspension in no way preempts decision, on the contrary:

> A decision can only come into being in a space that exceeds the calculable program that would destroy all responsibility by transforming it into a pro-grammable effect of determinate causes. There can be no moral or political responsibility without this trial and this passage by way of the undecidable. Even if a decision seems to take only a second and not to be preceded by any deliberation, it is structured by this *experience and experiment of the undecid-able.*[7]

In fact, in the case of prosthesis decision comes down in a particularly explicit manner, and more than one time. To repeat, although there is no decisive moment that inaugurates prosthesis—that is to say that inaugu-rates its idea and its structure—any given prosthesis will all the same be marked by the coming down of a decision, the diagnostic sentence a prelude to the surgical falling of the ax. Whatever word comes down passes

ou d'un bistouri le trancher-parler cédera le pas au trancher-inciser. Car par un beau jour d'hiver doux dans la ville la plus ensoleillée du pays arrive un médecin spécialiste qui annonce qu'il faut trancher, et là, dans le vif, à la mi-hauteur d'une cuisse âgée de dix-huit ans, il faut isoler au maximum le sarcome dont le poison circule déjà périlleusement dans les artères, plus aucun apaisement possible, je dis cela car à l'autre bout du monde on vient de sortir du pastis munichois, c'est la guerre déjà et dix-huit ans c'est l'âge reconnu bon pour faire la guerre, bien que ce ne soit pas possible dans son cas, celui de mon père, qui, comme toute la famille par principe ne fait jamais la guerre, ce qui ne les a pas empêchés d'embarquer son père à lui vingt-quatre ans plus tôt quand lui avait dix-huit ans et deux belles jambes, on l'a embarqué en Europe pour faire la guerre style non-combattant comme tous les pacifistes à l'époque où il s'agissait de protéger l'empire britannique en France surtout, les colons reliés par je ne sais quel rapport prothétique à la vieille Europe, et même si mon grand'père n'était pas parmi les plus francs ou militants des pacifistes, d'autres si, on l'a embarqué tout de même en France, mais gentiment, tandis que les autres on les liait franchement à des poteaux sur le front bien combattant côté Somme ou Verdun, sans doute très près de Damvillers, là où en 1552 Ambroise Paré a fait sa tranche si célèbre, et je ne sais pas s'il faut trouver là l'idée qu'on ne fait jamais que la même guerre depuis des siècles et que c'est une guerre sur l'amputation et la question de la prothèse, je ne sais pas non plus s'il existe quelque rapport entre une résistance de principe à la guerre qui vient d'éclater en 1939, et la croissance nocive d'un sarcome, je ne sais pas si se faire amputer la jambe a quelque rapport avec se tirer au pied pour éviter la guerre car le risque était loin d'être moindre, il était à deux doigts de cuisse de la mort, le chirurgien ayant à choisir parmi trois possibilités: trancher trop bas et la mort aurait été certaine, trancher trop haut et cela aurait été le fauteuil roulant à vie, ou bien trouver le juste milieu, ce qu'il a fait tout en se méfiant, s'attendant à une fatalité prochaine tout de même, enfin, reste que mon père sera toujours bien civil dans son amputation même si les noms géographiques où tout ceci se passe appellent des guerriers et des

into the body; through the manipulation of a scalpel the word come down gives way to the fall of the knife. One fine mild winter's day in the sunniest town in the country a specialist arrives to announce his decision, let the chips fall where they may that leg has to come off right there, cut through the quick halfway up an eighteen-year-old thigh, for we have to isolate the sarcoma as much as possible and as soon as possible since its poison is already circulating perilously through the arteries, no time for appeasement, I say that only because at the other end of the earth they have just come through the Chamberlain business, the decision has come down and war has broken out and eighteen is well recognized as the age for going off to war, although that is not possible in his case, I'm talking about my father, who, like all the rest of his family, never goes to war, it is a matter of principle, although of course that never stopped them in the case of his father 24 years earlier when he was eighteen and had two good legs good enough for them to pack him off to Europe to make war as a noncombatant as they did with all the pacifists at that time, after all it was a matter of saving the Empire, in France especially, and the colonies were linked by the strangest of prosthetic relations to the mother country, and even if my grandfather wasn't the most outspoken of pacifists others were, and they still packed him off to France, but considerately, whereas others were quite frankly tied to posts at the most combatant front possible in some scenic spot in the Somme or Verdun, no doubt close to Damvillers, where in 1552 Ambroise Paré performed his famous amputation, and I don't know whether one can read in that the idea that it is only ever the same war that has been waged all these centuries and that it is a war over amputation and the question of prosthesis, I don't know if there is something to be said connecting conscientious objection to a war that has just broken out with the growth of a malignant sarcoma, I don't even know if having one's leg amputated can be related to shooting oneself in the foot to avoid going to war, for the risk was far from reduced that way, he came within a few inches of thigh of dying and the surgeon had to choose between three possibilities: coming down too low and having him die, coming down too high and condemning him to a wheelchair for life, or the perfect middle way that he found while all along thinking it wouldn't work anyway, expecting him to die, in short, in spite of a coincidence of dates my father's wooden leg has all the marks of civility and nothing combatant about it, even if the geographical context where this all goes on is overcrowded with warriors and amputees of every denomination most of them concerning

amputés de toute sorte et concernent des relations belliqueuses, par exemple franco-anglaises, la ville se nomme Nelson où le médecin tranche à présent et diagnostiquement, l'autre s'appellera Wellington où le chirurgien tranchera pour de bon et dans le vif âgé de dix-huit ans, on passe de l'une dans l'autre à travers le détroit de mer tempétueux où nous avons déjà rencontré le père en la compagnie de son fils, un bras de mer tel un couloir liminal, toute la région infestée de manchots, de décisions, de déclarations de guerre, de champs de batailles gagnées et perdues, tout cela dépendant bien sûr de quel côté on se trouve, de quelle langue on parle, n'empêche qu'à dix-huit ans on voyage de Nelson à Wellington pour, pour ainsi dire, "rencontrer son Waterloo," la décision par laquelle tout le corps va se défaire dans le trancher que suppose la prothèse.

La tranche est par définition une coupure multiple. En tranchant, à suivre également au moins un des leurres étymologiques, le latin *trinicare*, on coupe en trois. Ce par quoi la tranche se distingue de la *bi*section, ce par quoi trancher n'est ni *é*cart*er* ni es*quin*ter; ce par quoi on coupe dans le numéro et dans la structure d'un éternel retors. La tournure critique qu'est le trancher diagnostique et chirurgical de la prothèse ne fait que répéter, en se multipliant, la structure d'articulation qui la marque toujours: en premier lieu, articulation du mot et du corps, en deuxième lieu, articulation de l'instrument chirurgical et du corps. Or, en troisième lieu ça tranche plus généralement et aussi évidemment du côté mécanique; dans la prothèse ça tranche à chaque pas, dans l'agencement régulier de la machine avec de la matière humaine—question plus spécifiquement orthopédique peut-être mais la tranche n'est pas importante entre ces rayons-là—c'est ce qui met les nerfs à vif, les vrais et les fantomatiques, pour qu'en fin de compte ça vienne à trancher automatiquement dans le spasme incontrôlable qui décide tout, comme et quand il veut, le spasme-fantôme qui met un terme à tout ce qu'il fait, vaisselle ou récitation de tel vers de Virgile, le spasme qui monte par la cuisse coupée et envahit le corps entier sans aucun préavis, tranchant ainsi dans les moments de calme aussi bien que les plus animés comme un rappel à l'ordre arbitraire et autoritaire par lequel la prothèse impose son propre rythme douloureux.

La tranche fait donc tellement mal que l'opération de la prothèse dépend toujours de l'insensibilisation anesthésique, ce sera le deuxième temps que je veux marquer ici. Bien avant tout apport narcotique, l'anesthésie prend la forme d'une capote qui protège le moignon dans son

bellicose Anglo-French relations, the city the specialist came to to come down on the side of prosthesis is called Nelson, making his diagnostic decision to amputate there, and the other city is called Wellington, where the surgeon lets the knife fall for good into the quick aged eighteen years, one passes from one city to the other through the stormy strait where we have already encountered a father in the company of his son, it is a stretch of sea that is like a limbic corridor, the whole region infested with missing limbs, decisions, declarations of war, fields of battles that were lost or won depending on which side you fall, which language you speak, such that it is true that at the age of eighteen you go from Nelson to Wellington to meet your Waterloo, to wait for it to come down on your body broken open by the event of prosthesis.

In French there is a simple verb to sum up these senses of cutting and decision. *Trancher* has an antiquated English equivalent, *to trench*, whence "trenchant" to mean sharp and decisive. Whether it be derived from the Latin *trinicare*, to cut in three, or from *truncare*, to truncate, the action is obviously a multiple one; the ax falls repeatedly. The diagnostic and surgical decision that, as I have said, far from inaugurates prosthesis, simply repeats, by multiplying it, the structure of articulation that has always been its hallmark: in the first place there is the articulation of word and body, in the second place that of surgical instrument and body. But now we also need to mention the extent to which it comes down, in the mechanical sense, up and down with each step, in the regular articulation between machine and human flesh—a more specifically orthopedic question perhaps but there is no need to come down in favor of one department over another here—it is what reaches into the quick of the nerves, both real and phantom, such that in the end there is a trenchancy that automatically activates the uncontrollable spasm that decides everything, how and when it wishes, brings to a close whatever he is involved in, dishwashing or recitation of Virgil, it is a spasm that rises from the sectioned thigh to invade the whole body without warning, coming down upon the moments of calm as well as the moments of greatest animation like a stroke of the gavel or the doctor's reflex mallet to impose the very painful and particular rhythm of a prosthesis.

To be quite plain, prosthesis hurts so much that its operation requires the insensitivity only analgesia or anesthesia can provide; the anesthetic is the second prosthetic moment to be considered here. Well before narcotic relief, such provision involves a form of protection for the flesh where it

articulation avec le fer. Ça s'appelle une chaussette de moignon—*stump-sock*—et j'ajouterai entre parenthèses qu'il serait toujours pertinent de savoir quelle compétence est requise pour s'occuper du rayon "néologisme" en matière de prothèse comme en matière d'invention en général, comment s'articule l'invention du mot avec l'invention du corps artificiel. Ces chaussettes de cuisses coupées on les change aussi souvent qu'un slip, on les lave aussi normalement avec le reste du linge, et on les suspend sur une corde à l'aide d'une pince tel un vers de Ponge et tout cela ne représente rien d'extraordinaire pour quiconque a fait l'expérience d'une prothèse bien que les voisins regardent ces capotes d'un oeil toujours un peu étonné, elles ressemblent à des chapeaux cloches un peu allongés, l'effet étant on ne peut plus an-*esthétique*, car il y a une certaine suspension de l'esthétique en prothèse, les capotes en laine la démontrent, elles sont toutes faites sur mesure mais ne sont pas signées, on les tient de la Artificial Limb Factory qui mesure leur vie avec le même souci d'économie que pour une jambe de bois et à les voir suspendues sur la corde-à-linge on voit également les cicatrices d'usure et les marques du reprisage appris par ma mère sur les chaussettes de ses frères en temps de guerre, en tout cas les capotes suspendues de la prothèse diront tout ce qui va sans dire et ce qu'on passe sous silence, tout ce qu'on anesthésie à son égard. Le mot qui cherche à dire tout cela, le mot de l'anesthésie sera *subir*.

Subir dit d'abord la passivité et la patience, la sujétion de la prothèse. Mais il faut demander tout de suite dans quelle mesure on peut distinguer entre le sujet *de* la prothèse et tout ce qui est sujet *à* la prothèse. Ou plutôt, dans quelle mesure la prothèse fonctionne-t-elle comme une machine à assujetir, ses parties sujettes à l'hégémonie de toute la chose; ou bien est-ce que cette prothèse-ci, tellement bavarde, véritable machine à mots, ne fait que passer sous silence tout en prétendant les faire parler la jambe de bois et mon père qui la porte? Il est vrai que cette prothèse se marque par la pluralité de ses sujets—père, fils, jambe, texte—et par l'incertitude quant à leur ordre, voire leur priorité. Or le "passage sous . . ." qui est tout le sens du verbe "subir," l'opération qui se fait sous le couvert de la nuit anesthésique, permet la traversée d'un sujet à l'autre, la mise en articulation de l'un avec l'autre qui définit la prothèse en général et la fait généraliser hors des limites classiques d'un sujet simple. Cela ne dépend pas d'un jeu de mots non plus, celui par lequel le sujet ou le concept de la prothèse se confond avec le sujet humain ou les sujets humains qui sont ainsi impliqués; un tel

joins with steel. This is called a *stumpsock*—and as an aside I would raise the question of what qualifications are necessary to indulge in neologism in the matter of prosthesis, as with invention in general; how does the invention of a word articulate with the invention of an artificial body? Stumpsocks are changed as often as underwear, washed just as normally with the rest of the laundry, and hung out to dry on a line with a peg like a line from Ponge which is far from extraordinary for those experienced in prosthetic matters although neighbors or visitors might be a little surprised by the sight of these woolen analgesic prophylactics, looking like slightly elongated cloche hats, and the effect is somewhat an-*esthetic*, something that is true for prosthesis in general, the question of esthetics being suspended somewhat there, stumpsocks demonstrate that, they are made to measure but there are no designer brands, just the generic Artificial Limb Factory variety, their life measured with the same attention to economy as that befitting a wooden leg and as they hang out to dry they show the scars of wear and from the darning my mother learned from practicing on her brother's socks in time of war, in any case the suspended stumpsocks express everything that is taken for granted, goes without saying, and so retreats into the silent underground of the prosthetic experience. The verb for all that here is *to undergo*.

The word, according to the principles of prosthesis, articulates to the point of reversibility: one can as well say *to go under* as *to undergo*. It expresses the passivity and the patience, the subjection that is prosthesis. A question arises: can a distinction be made between the subject *of* prosthesis and something or someone subject *to* prosthesis; in other words, to what extent does prosthesis act as a machine of subjection, its parts subject to the hegemonic appropriation of the whole; or conversely, does this prosthesis, a veritable word machine, not reduce to silence a wooden leg and a father who bears it, even as it claims to have them speak? It is true that prosthesis is marked by the plurality of its subjects—father, son, leg, text—and by an uncertainty regarding their order and priority. Going under, general anesthesia, the knife, undergoing an operation, whatever is done under cover of the anesthetic night, is precisely what permits the crossing from one state or subject to another, the putting-into-articulation of one with another that defines prosthesis in general and has it generalize beyond the classic limits of a single simple subject. None of that depends on the various wordplays that might come into effect, for instance that by which the subject or concept of prosthesis, what it deals with, is confused

jeu de mots est plutôt un effet de la prothèse, ou de la prothétisation, d'une part spécifique, d'autre part généralisable, selon laquelle les articulations se réinventent à chaque pas, ainsi que les ordres, les dispositions, les vieilles habitudes. Grâce à l'anesthésie on s'endort patient ou sujet et on se réveille prothétique, si vous voulez on s'endort humain et on se réveille chose—machine, mécanique, mécanisé, ou du moins tout prêt à l'être. On subit ainsi rien moins que le bouleversement de tout, du tout.

De ce point de vue le passage qu'emprunte le subir de la prothèse, le "passage sous . . . ," devient manifestement un passage souterrain, ce que, dans ma langue étrangère j'appelle un *underpass*, pour dire l'espèce de mise en oeuvre clandestine de l'articulation qui s'y opère. Et puis, toujours de ce point de vue et ramenant la question plus près de son coeur, le modèle de la prothèse, plutôt que la jambe de bois, devient le *bypass*. Tel mot n'est pas la recommandation officielle, celle de l'Académie ou tout autre surveillant de la pureté linguistique. Il existe tellement de mots tout à fait appropriés en français: pontage, dérivation, déviation, contournement, évitement, voire bipasse. Mais ils n'ont encore une fois rien compris ces académiciens. J'écris cela dans une langue étrangère pour forcer un peu la chose, pour dire avec plus de force qu'on se passe de quelque chose en passant à l'autre. A commencer par son intégralité, sa totalité, sa constitution totalisante. Pour dire aussi que ce n'est pas simplement une déviation, comme un leurre rhétorique la vague divagation par laquelle un texte profite de sa propre indiscipline pour brouiller les choses ou pour *canuler* à son gré—car c'est précisément d'une canule qu'on se sert pour faire un bypass—mais pour appuyer de nouveau sur le fait que le passage est également une liaison nécessaire, une connexion obligatoire parmi tout ce qui se déploie au nom de la prothèse pour représenter parmi d'autres choses ce qu'une critique ou lecture dite normale serait en passe de refouler, que ce soit les cicatrices de greffes d'implantations mammaires ou péniennes, les artifices grâce auxquels elle se gonfle ou bande, ou bien les stimulateurs cardiaques qui donnent le coup de pied nécessaire dès que la logique ne coule plus, ma nuit anesthésique avec tout son passage sous silence et sous une certaine passivité et ma jambe de bois grinçante étant tout cela et en même temps le contraire de leur bruyante assurance sur leur sujet ou objet de savoir.

Alors, on s'endort, on subit la sujétion, et on se réveille prothétisé, muni d'un bypass quelconque. Dans le cas de mon père ce n'était pas le coeur qui crevait à l'âge de dix-huit ans, mais l'abcès d'une jambe. Il s'est réveillé donc avec une jambe de moins—en attente d'une prothèse bien que déjà

with the human subject or subjects that are implied in it. On the contrary, such a play on words is an effect of prosthesis, or of prosthetization, both specific and generalizable; it is rendered possible by it, by its step by step reinvention of articulations, orders, habits. Thanks to anesthetics one goes to sleep a patient or subject and wakes up prosthetic, or if you wish one goes to sleep human and wakes up thing—machine, mechanical, mechanized, or at least on the point of being so. One therefore undergoes nothing less than the overturning of the whole applecart, the whole thing, everything.

From this point of view the passage taken by whoever undergoes prosthesis, the effect of its passing under, becomes quite manifestly an underground one, what I might refer to as an underpass in order to express the clandestine movement to otherness that so occurs. Furthermore, still from the same point of view but bringing it closer to the heart of the matter, the model for prosthesis would then become not the wooden leg but the bypass. I don't wish to valorize some more advanced technological form of prosthesis, for the bypass in fact has little of that about it. However much it might rely on advanced surgical procedures it is a rather crude device. Nor is the important sense here so much that of an artificial deviation, like a rhetorical ploy scant justification for the serendipitous digressions that a text makes from itself by operations of stealth or plain wantonness. The bypass reinforces rather the idea of a necessary departure, that of every sense from itself in constituting itself that prosthesis attempts to reinforce in reaction to a mode or model of criticism that in practice leaves the same unsaid, presuming to present itself as intact, hiding its scars and grafts, who knows, silicon breasts or a penile implant to make a bigger or more rigorous show, or else whole computerized pacemaker contraptions that kick in when the flow of the logic slows down, my anesthetic night and passage into silence and a form of passivity, and my creaking old wooden leg being all that and at the same time the contrary of the loud assurance criticism normally presumes to possess over its subject or object of inquiry.

Thus one goes to sleep, one goes under or undergoes, and wakes up prosthetized, furnished with some sort of bypass, some digressive device or implanted otherness. In my father's case it wasn't of course his heart that was giving out at the age of eighteen but his leg. He woke up with one leg less, in the expectation of a prosthesis although already prosthetized by his

en état de prothèse car muni de pansements de toute sorte et de béquilles— et puis plus tard avec une jambe de plus. L'amputation à mi-hauteur d'une cuisse ne permet pas de marcher sans l'aide d'une prothèse double, la jambe de bois plus une canne. Ça ne va donc qu'en se multipliant, en se pliant à de multiples exigences, à maints endroits, s'articulant à son aise. Le bypass pertinent pour son cas sera cette canne, la chose qui relie le déséquilibre de la jambe de bois à la solidité de la terre, qui relaie par raccourci la marque visible de la prothèse à l'infirmité en général. La canne servait également de moyen de contact à un enfant se tenant légèrement hors de portée d'un père, maillon de la chaîne prothétique, indicateur muet de tout le silence qui entourait ces choses-là. Elle est le signe de tous les égards qu'il fallait avoir à son sujet, de toute la patience dont il fallait faire preuve.

La canne avait bien sa place, suspendue par son crochet à la barre d'un porte-serviette attaché au bout du comptoir de la cuisine, à moins qu'elle ne se soit égarée, oubliée dans un endroit où la nécessité l'avait transportée et que mon père avait quitté de façon plus autonome, en s'appuyant sur certaine autre paraprothèse, meuble, mur, enfant. La canne ne se donne pas, ne dépend pas d'un organisme d'état, car elle est aussi supplémentaire qu'une baguette de Rousseau[8] avec tout ce que cela implique côté dérivation d'intention possible et nécessaire, chute dans l'ornement pur, plaisir extra-prothétique, affectation et dandysme, et je ne sais pas non plus combien de cannes il se donne par vie mais il me semble que c'était une seule noire dont la peinture abîmée mesurait la longévité de ma propre cohabitation prothétique et plus, et il est vrai qu'on a fêté sa retraite en lui en offrant comme cadeau une magnifique neuve travaillée à la maorie en kahikatea ou rewarewa ou rimu ou autre bois aussi beau à regarder que son nom est agréable à entendre, cadeau de retraite que lui offrirent les collègues et qu'il réserve pour les occasions les plus cérémonielles comme celles par exemple où lui aussi prononce quelques paroles bien pesées mais tout à fait correctes en maori comme plus tard il le fera en japonais en représentant la ville à sa jumelle nippone, abandonnant son vieux latin et se donnant au plaisir de bipasser dans d'autres langues tout en sachant que ses trébuchements lui seront permis grâce à la canne.

La vie prothétique était souvent ponctuée par l'angoisse de la canne égarée lorsqu'il s'agissait de marcher de nouveau, et le reproche s'adressait toujours aux enfants, reproche non sérieux car que ferait un enfant avec la canne de son père et pourquoi nourrirait-il l'idée de la cacher quelque part;

bandages and crutches, and then finally with one leg more. An amputation at midthigh doesn't permit you to walk without the aid of a double prosthesis, the wooden leg plus a walking stick. It only runs with all its parts, articulating at will, and to go with it means complying with its multiple demands. The bypass in his case is therefore this stick or cane, the thing that grounds the instability induced by the wooden leg, and also what marks this particular prosthesis with the shortcut sign of infirmity in general. But it is as well the means by which a child can be held in contact even if out of reach of a father, a link in the chain of prosthetic relay, and it is finally the mute witness to the silence surrounding it all. It is the sign of whatever allowances have to be made, whatever patience to be suffered.

His stick had its place, hanging on the towel bar at the end of the counter where the kitchen became the breakfast room, always found there except when it was misplaced somewhere, discarded in a place necessity had taken it but which my father had left without its help as he often did, leaning on some other paraprosthesis, piece of furniture, wall, child. The walking stick is not provided by a government department for it is a supplement to a prosthesis as much as Rousseau's wand,[8] with all that that implies in terms of possible and necessary supplanting of purpose, fall into pure ornament, extraprosthetic pleasure, affectation, and dandyism, and again I don't really know how many canes one goes through in a lifetime but it seems to me that it was the same black one with well-worn paint that measured the whole period of my own prosthetic cohabitation and longer, and it is true that his retirement was celebrated by the gift of a magnificent new hand-carved Maori one made of kahikatea or rewarewa or rimu or some other native wood as beautiful to look at as to hear its name pronounced, it was a retirement gift from his coworkers at the furniture store where he was secretary-accountant for 30 years or so and he keeps it for the most auspicious occasions like those when he himself proffers some well-chosen and absolutely correct words in Maori or in Japanese when representing his hometown in its Nippon sister-city, abandoning his old Latin in favor of the pleasure of deviating further into the foreignness of language while knowing all along that if he trips over his tongue his cane will be there to give him some supplementary leeway and support.

The life of prosthesis was often punctuated by the anguish of not being able to find his walking stick when he needed to walk again, and it was usually the children who got the blame, not seriously for why would a child take it into his head to hide his crippled father's cane, but the

or, le reproche servait aussi à renforcer l'interdit, le passage sous l'interdit total du canular par le moyen de la canne car celle-ci représentait une tentation terrible quand on jouait au chat avec un frère ou une soeur en courant autour du comptoir, la tentation était énorme de profiter de la portée supplémentaire que cela offrait. Mon père avait des droits de possession absolus sur cet instrument, interdiction formelle de jouer avec, et à lui de lever de temps à autre cette interdiction mais uniquement pour de tout petits enfants qu'il invitait à se balancer sur la canne tandis qu'il la tenait droit et haut, on se balançait les bras étendus les pieds cognant contre ses jambes, la bonne et l'artificielle, la douce et la dure, les deux jambes d'un père gentil mais autoritaire. La canne était interdite également comme instrument de punition bien qu'à un certain moment il s'est décidé à avoir recours à une petite verge en bambou, ça n'a pas duré longtemps, peut-être un mois ou deux, il s'en est servi une seule fois avant que ma mère ne la jette sans souffler mot, si je m'en souviens bien, et là, suspendu à la canne, je grimpais, je faisais des culbutes manquées et réussies grâce à elle quand j'étais encore tout petit, et puis plus tard, plus grand, trop grand peut-être, après l'avoir accompagné en l'aidant à sortir les ordures, transportant la poubelle le long de l'allée graveleuse qu'on appelle toujours le droit de passage pour la déposer au bord de la route, j'étais trop petit pour porter la poubelle tout seul mais assez grand pour courir plus rapidement qu'un père prothétique dès qu'il s'agissait de rentrer à la hâte à la maison, j'accélérais à toutes jambes en écoutant le crépitement syncopé de son pas derrière moi, pas toujours certain de pouvoir le distancer et sachant qu'il se servirait volontiers de sa canne pour supplémenter l'étendue de son bras et pour complémenter ce qu'il manquait côté jambes, je sentais le léger coup d'aiguillon dans le dos, le toucher d'un fil communicateur ininterrompu tel un rayon de force sciencefictive dès que je commençais à le devancer, une ligne de force qui tremblait néanmoins en réaction avec le roulis décentré d'un prothétique qui s'exprime à pleine vitesse, c'était donc sa façon de m'éperonner tout en me tenant à sa portée et, qui sait à quel point il cherchait aussi à m'encourager à le dépasser, et à dépasser l'interdiction de la canne et de pas mal d'autres choses, en tout cas je courais et je le sentais derrière en passe de me toucher, jusqu'au jour où il ne le put plus et où je partis, abandonnant la canne et la sensation de son embout en caoutchouc dans le dos mais trimballant

reproach also served to reinforce the taboo, the absolute interdiction against playing with it for it held out a terrible temptation when one was playing tag with a brother or a sister around the counter, toying with the overwhelming desire to take it and use it for the extended arm's length and sizable advantage one gained thereby. My father had absolute rights of possession over his cane and in spite of the interdiction against playing with it he also had the right to lift that interdiction from time to time but only for very small children whom he would invite to swing from the stick as he held it tight and high enough for their legs to leave the ground, one swung there legs crashing against his, the good one and the bad one, the hard and the soft, the two legs of a kind and authoritarian father. His stick was also forbidden as an instrument of chastisement although at one time he decided he would use a small bamboo cane like the ones at school, but it didn't last long, perhaps a month or two, my mother saw to it that he only used it on us once before she spirited it away and disposed of it without a word if I remember correctly, but I was never thinking of that when I hung there and climbed horizontally up his thighs to perform many a failed somersault and some successful ones thanks to the stick while I was very small, and then when I grew somewhat, perhaps too much, after accompanying him to put out the garbage, carrying the bin down the gravel driveway to place it for collection on the side of the road, I was too small to carry it by myself but big enough to run faster than a prosthetic father when we would hurry back to the house, I would accelerate and hear the crunching of gravel and his syncopated step behind me, unsure whether I could outlast him and knowing that he would use his cane if needs be to extend the length of his arm and compensate what he lacked in legs, I would feel the gentle prod in the small of my back, the touch of an uninterrupted line of communication like some science-fictional ray or force as soon as I began to outpace him, a line of force that teetered nevertheless in response to the shifting gait of a full-speed limping prosthetic, full tilt and listing, it was his way of spurring me on while at the same time keeping me within reach and who knows now to what extent he was also encouraging me to go faster and leave him behind, him and his infirmity, leaving behind the interdiction his stick represented, as well as many other things, in any case I ran and felt him behind close enough to touch me until the day when he could touch me no longer and I was gone, abandoning the stick with the feel of its rubber stopper on the end in my back but traipsing everywhere and always in my own way with my own

partout et toujours et à ma façon mon espèce de prothèse, car le risque terrible est couru dans la phase anesthésique que le passage soit fait à l'oubli, hors de rappel, que le passage souterrain soit passage à l'irrémédiable, passage à l'impasse où rien ne se tient plus, ce pourquoi je fais glisser la chose, je fais greffer les mots, les mots aux corps, et les mots à d'autres mots greffés comme des corps, comme si tout bypass convenable était tout de suite valable, je fais cela sans arrêt car ce serait bien un arrêt de mort, la mort qui guette au tournant du passage anesthésique, il faut donc que ça passe chaque fois et que ça passe sans arrêt, il faut que ça marche toujours.

Je dis "marcher" et je le dis pour la prothèse dans sa perspective ortho*pédique*, même si ce qu'on redresse dans le sens de ce mot-ci n'est pas le pied mais l'enfant, le *paidos* et non pas le *podos*. Du pied, il n'y en a plus, mais l'enfant reste à redresser. Or je ne parle pas de la correction corporelle à laquelle je viens de faire allusion mais d'un certain retour à l'ordre dont dépend la prothèse—encore des égards à avoir—et qui implique par la suite tout l'entourage familial dans le but de faire marcher. Marcher se présente ainsi comme une action collective. Du support que donne un enfant lorsque la canne s'est égarée ou bien quand il s'agit de se baigner, jusqu'à la complicité de silence avec laquelle toute la famille autour de la table accueille les grimaces et les jurons qu'il mâche avec son dîner chaque fois que le spasme lui mord les nerfs écorchés, comme si de rien n'était, tout cela fonctionne grâce à une certaine solidarité, selon un rythme coopératif de l'acquiescement et de la rectitude qui empruntent sans doute leur pose aux habitudes pieuses en général, et moi aussi je me tais en enfant sage et correct et j'écris ma prothèse, un peu aussi la sienne. C'est comme cela que ça a toujours marché.

Mais la collectivité de la phase orthopédique se rapporte plus précisément à un certain embarras spatial, un surcroît de membres qui à la longue entravera la marche même. Ça ne marche évidemment qu'en boitant.[9] Pour tout ce qui ne marche pas bien, il y a tout naturellement un pied bot derrière: clocher, clopiner, claudiquer, il y va toujours du pied dès qu'il s'agit de caractériser de façon péjorative une démarche défectueuse. Le mal est oedipien, qu'il s'agisse du corps ou de l'esprit, de la marche ou du raisonnement, ça cloche à tous les coups. Ce qui se révèle ainsi par le biais orthopédique c'est bien la conception mécaniste, pour ne pas dire prothétique, et du corps et de l'esprit. C'est que la difformité de nature, la

prosthesis, for there is an awful risk in the anesthetic state that one will go under all the way to oblivion, beyond recall, that the underpass will be a passage to the irremediable, to the impasse where nothing holds together any more, which is why I keep it moving, why I graft words to this body, and like bodies graft them each to the other, as if every convenient bypass were valid and for the taking, I do it without stopping trying not to end the sentence for fear of a sentence of death, death that lies in wait around every corner of the anesthetic passage, that is why it has to get through, and why I try anything to stop the arrest, to have it get going out from under and run again.

To run properly is what prosthesis requires from its orthopedic perspective. A running that makes for walking. The word "orthopedic" seems to say as much, but in fact it is a child (*paidos*) that it brought in to line in the Greek, not a foot (*podos*). It is the child that needs to be kept straight in the absence of a foot. I refer not to the corporal punishment just mentioned but more to the ordering or self-discipline, the extra allowances to be made in living with a prosthesis if it and its entourage are to work at all. Running of course assumes a certain collectivity, even at the level of the rapid and multiple articulation of a single prosthetic unit. More simply, it requires the cooperation of more than one leg. From the support provided by a child when the walking stick has been misplaced or when he takes a swim, all the way to the complicity of silence with which the whole family greets his grimaces of discomfort and the suppressed oaths he bites on along with dinner when the spasm flays another nerve, as if nothing had happened, that can only function thanks to an unspoken code of solidarity, according to a cooperative rhythm of acquiescence and rectitude no doubt learned as a function of piety in general, so I also keep quiet like a good child and write my prosthesis, and a little of his at the same time.

But the collectivity of the orthopedic phase refers more specifically to a certain overcrowding, a surfeit of members that sooner or later will prevent the smooth running of things. Quite obviously, it always runs with a limp.[9] To put a good face on it, and to use a homonym that goes better for both corporal and mechanical modes, we can call it "skipping." Generally speaking when an engine isn't running well there is always an irregular footing in there somewhere, a lightness of step that creeps in, or of course a corresponding heaviness that upsets the balance, introduces a syncopation. It begins to dance instead of run, missing and at the same time skipping a beat, whether it be the gait or the logic that is defective,

monstruosité ou mutation toujours possible, se traduit rapidement en mauvaise articulation: le pied bot donne un raisonnement boiteux. Mais ce qui s'articule de façon oedipienne dans l'orthopédie, c'est avant tout, comme je l'ai déjà dit, l'effet familial. Tout ce qui boite dans la prothèse bute contre l'effet familial, contre le seuil de la maison de famille, contre le seuil du familier. C'est la raison de l'embarras rhétorique, si c'est bien cela, où se trouve mon texte, incertain de son registre, importuné constamment par des anecdotes et des idées venues d'un ailleurs qui m'est tout proche, butant de façon permanente contre la chose qui ne s'oublie pas et qui me reste incessamment familière.

De quelque façon qu'on le tranche, le triangle familial est là, dans la marche même. Celle de mon père se transfère à la longue sur celle de ma mère—je l'ai vu de mes propres yeux, et mon équilibre à moi se déglingue un peu dès que je recommence à marcher à côté d'eux—sa démarche à elle devenant légèrement titubante à force de l'accompagner si longtemps à l'allure exagérément lente d'un prothétique, elle chancèle suffisamment pour se frayer un chemin plus large que la normale, aussi large que celui dont mon père aura besoin avec la canne et la jambe de bois qui d'ailleurs ne s'articule pas à chaque pas, pas au genou en tout cas, et dont le pied arque un peu en marchant, je les ai regardés partir ainsi dans le hall d'aéroports regrettablement internationaux après les adieux, un véritable couple prothétique et moi derrière terriblement attaché et conscient de la moindre anomalie qui puisse me concerner, ce n'est donc pas par esprit de contradiction que je fabrique la chose prothétique, j'inventorie plutôt ma propre boîte à prothèse pour dessiner la claudication congénitale de toute dé-marche, le fait de dépendre d'un support orthopédique ou artificiel quelconque.

Il faut faire remarquer cette chose évidente qu'est la facticité de la prothèse. L'artificiel implique d'une part la *tekhnē* et le *constructum*, tout ce qui se fabrique et qui se doit ainsi à la main humaine plutôt qu'à celle des dieux. Or, cette première opposition se divise et se retourne en plusieurs sens: pour donner en premier lieu le factice comme perversion de la capacité humaine en faveur de la tromperie, ce qui est également une espèce de surhumanité ou la prétention surnaturelle de l'invention pure; pour donner en deuxième lieu le contraire de l'humain dans le sens du machinal, l'automatisme de ce qui fonctionne sans l'humain; et puis en dernier lieu pour signifier l'objet cultuel doué de sens extra-humain,

skipping to its own rhythm when he runs up the driveway behind me or into the bedroom where we are playing instead of sleeping, he fairly skips as he runs, dancing his idiomatic shuffle at whatever speed desire has set on the dial.

The father of all limpers is Oedipus, and it is also in collective or familial terms that one has to deal with the matter of gait. Whatever limps or skips in prosthesis stumbles, as I have already explained, against the familial effect, against the family threshold, the threshold of the familiar. That is the reason for the rhetorical bind—if that is what it is—that my text finds itself in, uncertain as to its register, constantly importuned by anecdotes and ideas appearing from an elsewhere that is close by, always stumbling against what can't be forgotten and what remains incessantly familiar.

Whichever way you slice it, the familial triangle is there, in the way it walks, limps, skips, or runs. My father's gait is transferred to my mother—I have seen it with my own eyes and even felt my own balance pulled a little off center when walking with them—she staggers just noticeably as a result of walking for so long in accompaniment with the exaggeratedly deliberate pace of a prosthetic, wavering just enough to clear a wider path than normal as she moves, as wide as that my father needs for his cane and the leg that doesn't bend with each step, the foot swings out a little as he walks, I have watched them walk away that way, sauntering together across the gigantic spaces of all too international airports after saying goodbye, a veritable prosthetic couple and me remaining behind but terribly attached and conscious of the smallest anomaly in my own workings, it is not contrariness that has me concocting the prosthetic object, I simply inventory my own prosthetic repertoire to outline the congenital limp or skip that keeps everything running, its dependence on some sort of orthopedic or artificial support.

The obvious needs to be stated: the prosthesis is an artifice, a contrivance, a fabrication. To begin with, the artificial implies whatever derives from the *technē* and the *constructum*, everything that depends on the human rather than the divine hand. But that first opposition self-divides and comes back with a number of other differences: firstly the artificial contrivance is read as a perversion of human capability in favor of the counterfeit, or trickery, but also as a type of superhumanity or the supernatural presumption of pure invention; secondly, the artificial comes to refer to the contrary of the human in the sense of the mechanical, the automatism of what threatens to function without human control; and

toujours dépendant du *facticius* et du *factum*, qu'est le fétiche. Je n'ai pas à raconter ici tous les rapports possibles ou nécessaires de la jambe de bois avec un objet de culte, ni avec un remplaçant de l'organe sexuel; cela se raconte tout seul, en d'autres façons et dans d'autres lieux. Je tiens simplement à souligner à quel point l'idée de l'artificiel se déconstruit au niveau du mot, dès que le mot est appelé à parler du corps, dans quel sens le corps est toujours déjà l'autre. Même si on peut très bien parler d'une jambe sans qu'elle soit artificielle, on ne peut pas à la longue empêcher l'évocation de son usage mécanique à partir duquel toute la dérive prothétique entre en jeu. Le traitement du corps, du corpus, et de l'incorporation du mot se révèle particulièrement fécond pour la démontrer.

La dé-marche qu'est la prothèse du point de vue orthopédique concerne en fin de compte la pose autant que le pas. Pour y insister une dernière fois, c'est le mot même qui le dit. La thèse, c'est la pose; la prothèse la pro*pose*, la proposition. "Spéculer—sur 'Freud'" le dit en détail, et comment par l'athèse/pas de thèse le texte de Freud fait avancer son argument selon une logique on ne peut plus prothétique.[10] Nous n'avons pas à nous traîner dans les préfixes prépositionnels, ni à faire grand cas de la distinction entre la *pro*thèse et la *post*iche, pour apprendre que la prothèse, tout en remplaçant par un artifice, se met en avant; elle implique sa propre démarche. Pour reprendre les termes de Derrida, elle démontre donc parfaitement dans quelle mesure la pose se relie à la poste, comment l'espacement qui ouvre le sens en général se précise ici comme espacement postal et transférentiel, inaugurant une économie spéculative qui se base sur la suspension de la destination:

> Dès la première intuition, dès son seuil, tous les transferts spéculatifs sont de la partie. Je regroupe à dessein tous les mouvements en *trans-* sous ce mot de *transfert*, qu'il s'agisse de traduction vers le langage descriptif ou théorique, de transposition d'une science à l'autre, de transposition métaphorique dans le langage, etc. Le mot de transfert rappelle à l'unité de son réseau métaphorique, précisément, la métaphore et le transfert (*Ubertragung*), réseau de correspondances, de connexions, d'aiguillages, d'un trafic et d'un tri sémantique, postal, ferroviaire sans lesquels aucune destination transférentielle ne serait possible.[11]

Proposer est toujours un geste speculatif, une espèce de sollicitation. Ce n'est donc pas par la seule étymologie que la prothèse se rapproche en fin de compte, et la mienne la première, de la prostitution. Non seulement que je me pose en proxénète, bénéficiant d'un corps infirme tout en faisant

lastly, still through the *facticius* and *factum*, it comes to signify the cult object that represents and displaces the divine, or the unmentionable, namely the fetish. I have no need to recount all the possible and necessary relations between the wooden leg and a cult object or a substitute for the sexual organ; such yarns spin all by themselves, in other ways and other places. I simply want to emphasize the extent to which the idea of the artificial comes undone at the level of the word, once the word is called upon to speak of the body, in what sense the body always already expresses otherness. Even if one can easily speak of a leg without its being artificial, one cannot for very long prevent reference to its mechanical usage on the basis of which the whole prosthetic drift comes into play. The treatment of the body, of the corpus, and of the incorporation of the word is particularly apt at demonstrating that.

Finally, the orthopedic side of prosthesis concerns the pose as much as ambulation. For the last time the word itself says so. A thesis is what is posed; prosthesis proposes. For discussion of it one can return to Derrida's "To Speculate—on 'Freud,'" as well as for analysis of how the athetical in Freud's *Beyond the Pleasure Principle* advances his argument in a way that couldn't be more prosthetic.[10] It is worth noting also that prosthesis, in replacing with an artifice, literally puts itself forward; it displays its own artificiality. To take it further along the lines of Derrida's argument, it might be repeated that prosthesis shows clearly in what way the pose is tied to the postal, how the spacing that opens the possibility of sense in general is made more precise in terms of a postal distancing, that is to say a transferential spacing which in turn allows for the whole speculative economy based on the idea of destination, or rather adestination:

> From the first intuition, from its threshold, all the speculative transferences are involved. I am purposely regrouping all the movements in *trans-* under the word *transference*, whether it is a matter of translation toward descriptive or theoretical language, transposition from one science to another, or metaphoric transposition within language, etc. The word transference reminds one of the unity of its metaphoric network, which is precisely metaphor and transference (*Ubertragung*), a network of correspondences, connections, switch points, traffic, and a semantic, postal, railway sorting without which no transferential destination would be possible.[11]

Putting something forward is always a speculative gesture, a type of solicitation. It is thus not only through etymology that prosthesis refers in

mine de payer des dettes; c'est plus sérieusement que je profite de tout le réseau postal particulier et général que sont les diverses articulations et démarches employées ici, et de leur promiscuité, pour faire des correspondances express à tout moment, laissant dériver mon discours vers le plus offrant des liaisons, de sorte qu'on n'aurait pas tort de croire qu'en dernière analyse la pose de la prothèse se dérègle en une espèce d'*ana*thèse.

Or, je dirais en revanche que ma prothèse n'est ni plus ni moins que *le texte de ce qui m'arrive* que je suis en train de lire; texte dont l'analyse est soutenue par l'armature d'une autre prothèse, la jambe de bois. Ni simple jeu, de mots ou de corps, ni obscurantisme volontaire. S'il est vrai qu'un tel texte, le texte de ce qui vous arrive, a visiblement sa place et son genre—histoire, autobiographie, ou fiction—j'insisterai que dès qu'il s'agit de la prothèse, dès qu'il traite de tout le réseau signifiant que j'ai cherché à développer jusqu'ici—dédoublement, substitution, transfert, articulation, facticité, boitement—il ne saura plus se présenter sous l'uniformité d'un genre, et cela bien avant toute complication qu'y apporte une histoire personnelle et paternelle d'une jambe de bois. Alors ce n'est qu'en raison de la difficulté, à la rigueur de l'impossibilité, qu'on a à distinguer, ici et partout ailleurs, entre texte autobiographique, texte fictif, texte critique, et texte théorique, en raison par exemple des effets narratifs qui les subsument tous, que je laisse les genres se brouiller, que je me laisse partir à la dérive du récit anamnésique, mais non sans poser comme support de lecture la constance qui est la jambe de bois, avec, bien sûr, tout le protocole plus ou moins explicite—styles, tons, discours—qui l'accompagne. Or, puisque cela a pour résultat une indifférence abyssale des niveaux de lecture historique, littérale, parodique, allégorique, et paragrammatique, on est toujours en droit de poser la question de la compétence ou de la rigueur:

> Que se passe-t-il quand des actes ou des performances (discours ou écriture, analyse ou description, etc.) font partie des objets qu'ils désignent? Quand ils peuvent se donner en exemple de cela même dont ils parlent ou écrivent? On n'y gagne certainement pas une transparence auto-réflexive, au contraire. Le compte n'est plus possible, ni le compte rendu, et les bords de l'ensemble ne sont alors ni fermés ni ouverts. Leur trait se divise et des entrelacs ne se défont plus. . . . Sa démarche est l'un de ses objets, d'où l'allure, et c'est pourquoi ça ne peut pas aller très bien ni marcher tout seul. . . . Alors ça boite et ça ferme mal.[12]

the final analysis to prostitution. Not simply that I pose as a pimp, profiting from an infirm body while claiming to pay my debts; more seriously it is my taking advantage of the whole particular and general postal networks that are implied by diverse articulations and their promiscuity, their wholesale promotion of commingling, making for sudden route changes at any given moment, allowing my discourse to switch from one bidder to the next, going anywhere for the asking, such that in the end the posture of prosthesis may be said to slouch into a kind of *ana*thesis.

To counter that, it might be argued that my prosthesis is no more or less than a reading of the text of whatever occurs to me, an analysis held together by the armature of another prosthesis, namely the wooden leg. Neither a mere game, a play of bodies or words, nor willful obfuscation. If it is true that such a text, the text of whatever occurs to you, has its place and its genre—as history, autobiography, or fiction—I would insist that when it comes down to prosthesis, once it begins to deal with the signifying network that I have been endeavoring to follow through here—doubling, substitution, transfer, articulation, contrivance, disorder—then it can no longer preserve the uniformity of a genre. That is so well before we begin to deal with complications brought about by a personal or paternal story of a wooden leg. Hence it is only because of the difficulty—the impossibility finally—of distinguishing, here or anywhere else, among autobiographical text, fictive text, critical text, and theoretical text, that I allow the genres to mix, but not without offering the stable basis for reading that the wooden leg offers, along with the more or less explicit protocol that attends it in terms of style, tone, and discourse. Since that mixing brings about what I might call an abyssal indistinction among levels of reading—historic, literal, parodic, allegorical, paragrammatic, and so on—one has every right to raise the question of competence and rigor:

> What happens when acts or performances (discourse or writing, analysis or description, etc.) are part of the objects they designate? When they can be given as examples of precisely that of which they speak or write? Certainly, one does not achieve an auto-reflective transparency, on the contrary. A reckoning is no longer possible, nor is an account, and the borders of the set are then neither closed nor open. Their trait is divided, and the interlacings can no longer be undone. . . . Its procedure [*démarche*] is one of its objects, whence its pace [*allure*], and this is why it does not advance [*aller*] very well, or work [*marcher*] by itself. . . . Thus it limps [*boite*] and is hard to close.[12]

Je n'ai qu'à répéter que c'est là que je cherche à réduire la confusion, en
donnant comme point de repère constant et en dernier ressort la jambe de
bois, même si sa con*stance* se tient de guingois. Car je peux dire tout
franchement que prétendre préciser le niveau exact où intervient une
jambe de bois paternelle ou autre ou tout autre chose dans un texte
quelconque, ou prétendre préserver l'unité d'une seule lecture ou d'un seul
niveau de lecture—genre historique, allégorique ou parodique—préten-
tions faites par quiconque écrit en général, serait à mon avis plus obscuran-
tiste que ce que je tente ici. Du point de vue de la prothèse prétendre
l'unicité ou l'uniformité d'un discours ou d'une écriture serait une fabrication plus extravagante que les digressions parenthétiques de ma jambe de
bois, ou de la sienne (car, je le répète également, je ne sais pas laquelle
contient l'autre, ni comment).

Si donc la prothèse ne se pose simplement pas, si sa thèse, comme son
assise, est bancale, elle ne cesse pas pour autant de proposer; parathèse ou
prothèse, ce qu'elle donne, elle le donne en penchant, elle le tend plutôt,
toujours un peu de biais, par le biais de la jambe de bois. Ça va rester
suspendu ou ça va tomber, ça va courir ou se casser la gueule; ça va
trancher, ou endormir, mais ça va tout de même (faire) marcher. Il le faut
bien, car c'est par la performance même que sa démarche sera à juger. En
voilà une pour finir, histoire à deux temps ou en deux langues, comme tout
ici, revenons au point de départ, dans la capitale, car, je l'ai bien dit, on
vient toujours dans une capitale ou une autre pour faire sa prothèse car dès
qu'il s'agit de la jambe la tête n'est jamais très loin et ce qui menace
l'intégrité du corps menace essentiellement la chose capitale. Alors, je
viens à Paris et je prends le métro, c'est une chose difficile mais non pas
impossible pour un prothétique, mon père en a fait souvent l'expérience, il
a pris son métro à Paris, à New York, à Tokyo, s'asseyant dans les places
réservées en priorité où les enfants amputés de guerre la disputent aux
femmes enceintes de moins de quatre ans, il a bien fait ses correspondances, empruntant les passages souterrains, négociant les marches des
escaliers stables et roulants, il l'a fait comme moi je le fais, moi je le fais
maintenant de façon régulière, prenant toutes les habitudes qui vont avec,
m'y mettant au train-train intégral, y compris la vue d'un certain amputé,
pas du tout assis dans sa place reservée en priorité, mais debout dans la
station Denfert-Rochereau pour être précis, il se pose là où le couloir et la
foule se divisent entre la direction Nation et le RER, il se pose dans
l'endroit qui lui est réservé même si la chose n'est pas écrite, d'autres choses

To repeat, my aim here is precisely to reduce the confusion, offering the constant point of reference provided by the wooden leg, even if its con*stancy* is a little askew. For I can say with all honesty that to claim to be able to determine the exact level at which a paternal or any other sort of wooden leg, or anything else that one may care to specify, intervenes in a given text, or to claim to be able to preserve the unity of a single reading or of a single level of reading—historic, allegoric, parodic, and so on—claims which are made either implicitly or explicitly by readers and writers in general, would in my opinion be a far more egregious case of obfuscation than what I am practicing here. From the point of view of prosthesis, to claim the unicity or uniformity of a discourse or a writing would amount to a much more extravagant contrivance than the parenthetical digressions of my wooden leg, or of his (for, repeating myself yet again, who knows which contains which, and how?).

If, therefore, prosthesis does not simply pose, if its thesis, like its footing, is lopsided, it still continues to propose; parathesis or prosthesis, whatever it proffers it tends obliquely, according to the bias of a wooden leg. Either it will remain suspended or it will fall; come down, go under, or run rings around. It has no other choice, for its performance will be the sole measure of how well it runs. Here then is one to finish, a story told twice, in two parts or in two languages, like everything here, let us return to the point of departure, to the capital, for, as I have said, it is to one capital or another that one goes to get a prosthesis. So I come to Paris and I take the Métro, something that is difficult but not impossible for a prosthetic, he has often managed it, in Paris, New York, and Tokyo, sitting in the reserved seats, where amputated war children have to fight it out with pregnant women aged four years or younger according to the strict order of priority printed for all to read, he has made the necessary train changes, taken any number of underpasses, negotiated stairs and escalators, just like me, as I do it now regularly, adopting all the habits that go with it, the whole daily routine grind that is involved, including the sight of a certain amputee, by no means sitting in the seat reserved by state-decreed priority but standing in the Denfert-Rochereau station to be precise, he stands there where the corridors and the crowd divide between the Nation line and the RER, he stands there and he holds out his alms tin like a mug of Second World War vintage, the war that is declared first at the other end of the earth if only thanks to the advanced time zone, all of which has little importance for an eighteen-year-old close to an amputation, the amputee tends his tin and

si, je vous le dirai tout de suite, il tend sa boîte à aumône genre gobelet
militaire époque deuxième guerre mondiale, celle qu'on déclare en premier aux antipodes même si ce n'est que grâce au décalage horaire mais
tout cela n'avait pas beaucoup d'importance pour un gars de dix-huit ans la
veille d'une amputation, l'amputé dont il s'agit tend sa boîte en l'agitant,
heureusement qu'il n'est pas dans le métro en train d'essayer de s'asseoir
car il n'aurait pas énormément de priorité n'étant qu'invalide civil, même
s'il est aveugle avec, amputé mendiant aveugle je laisse à l'Académie de
disputer de l'ordre de la chose et de distinguer les parties du discours, elle
saura sans doute trancher comme on l'a fait dans son cas, je ne parle pas de
la jambe, vous voyez bien que je ne parle pas toujours de la jambe, je parle
du petit écriteau suspendu à son cou qui décrit son cas en termes précis et
académiques, invalide civil n'ayant pas droit à la Sécu, etc. Il est toujours là
au même endroit, enfin pas toujours mais je parie qu'il y met ses huit
heures, sa quarantaine pour la semaine, ne parlant pas, n'écrivant pas son
histoire à l'aide d'une craie sur le trottoir, comme d'autres le font, les mots
écrits et raturés par des pieds pressés et piétinants, marchants, courants,
boitants, par des chevaux partis au grand galop, n'importe quoi qui les
emporte mais en principe ils le font tout seuls, les mots obéissent à leur
propre logique de la différence et de la digression dès qu'il s'agit de la
prothèse, lui par contre il se tient là, il emprunte les passages pour se passer
sous silence, pour se réduire au bourdonnement anonyme des passagers, il
se pose là à l'aide de deux béquilles car il n'est pas muni d'une jambe de
bois, chose que l'ecriteau n'explique pas comme pas mal d'autres choses
d'ailleurs, et je prends l'habitude dans mon train-train quotidien de le
croiser toujours au même endroit, toujours sauf un beau jour qui a dû
être—c'est du moins ma supposition—la journée nationale et pourquoi pas
internationale puisque j'y etais aussi, la journée internationale des handi-
capés tous genres confondus avec trente-six invalides, paraplégiques, vic-
times de la poliomyélite, amputés, tous jeunes et bien portants, je parle
relativement car ils étaient assis ce jour-là dans de super-beaux fauteuils
roulants extra avec touche électronique et contrôle téléguidé informatisé
hyperhitech qu'ils manipulaient avec une dextérité incroyable, roulant en
avant, en arrière, tournant sur place, se déplaçant avec une rapidité
épatante pour franchement intercepter les usagers du métro pour leur
demander la contribution qu'on n'osait pas refuser tellement on était
étonné par les progrès faits en matière prothétique, et j'ai beau chercher
mon vieil amputé dans son coin habituel car il n'y était pas ce jour-là et je

shakes it, and it is fortunate that he is not in the Métro trying to sit down for he wouldn't have a great deal of priority being nothing more than an invalid of civilian causes, even if he is blind to boot, a blind amputee beggar such as would need the Académie Française to decide on the priority of the adjectives, the order of the thing and of the parts of speech and of the discourse, no doubt somehow they would come down in favor of this or that, blindness or amputation, as has been done in his case, but I don't want to talk about his leg, I don't only talk about legs, what interests me rather is the small sign he has hung about his neck, which describes his case in the most correct and academic of terms, how he is civilian and invalid and lacking in Social Security and so on. He is always there, in the same spot, well almost always but I am sure that he puts in his 40 hours at least, never speaking for all I know, not writing his story with chalk on the ground as others do, words written and erased by hurriedly treading feet, walking, running, limping, skipping, herds of galloping horses, anything can take them away but most of all they are carried away of their own accord, the words creating their own logic of difference and digression once one begins with a prosthesis, he on the other hand just stands there silently at the intersection of two passages within the anonymous hum of passersby, he poses there with the help of two crutches for he has no wooden leg which is something his sign doesn't explain, and I make a habit of passing him by in the course of changing my train in the course of a daily grind, every day I pass him there except this fine day in question, a day that if my supposition is correct must be the national and even international day of the handicapped, for the whole station is overrun by invalids of every description, paraplegics, polio victims, amputees, all of them young and healthy, relatively speaking of course, all sitting in their extra-modern wheelchairs with super high-tech electronic and comput- erized controls, showing how adept they are at using them as they whirl and turn, forwards and reverse with amazing dexterity, they fairly intercept the passersby to request a contribution that one cannot in any way refuse so astonished we all are by the progress that has been made in matters prosthetic, and I look in vain for my old amputee that day wanting to know whether he had been warned in advance and so knew not to come or if he had indeed arrived only to find his place and pose preempted, or whether he knew the date of international handicapped persons day and so saved a little of his earnings to compensate for his expected losses, I have no idea and didn't ask, I never spoke to him for he seemed to hide behind

veux toujours savoir si c'était parce que on l'avait prévenu d'avance ou s'il était arrivé comme d'habitude pour trouver sa place et sa pose dépassées et assumées par d'autres, ou s'il savait par coeur la date de ladite maudite journée internationale et économisait sur les autres jours pour combler le déficit que cette révolution technologique allait évidemment lui léguer, je n'en sais rien en fait et je ne lui ai pas demandé, je ne lui ai jamais adressé la parole, il paraissait s'enfuir derrière ses lunettes noires, et heureusement, car en le passant et en passant par chez lui deux possibilités aussi monstrueuses l'une que l'autre ont tendance à se présenter: ou bien il enlève ses lunettes et il porte les yeux de mon père, qui n'a jamais rien mendié de sa vie, grâce peut-être à la Sécu et à la prothétisation familiale, communautaire et autre; ou bien il n'enlève pas ses lunettes car il ne peut pas, elles sont implantées et informatisées comme dans un roman de science fiction et que derrière elles il est en train de négocier la matrice *cyberspatiale* des passants multiples, nous projetant tous dans un avenir prothétique où un père à la jambe de bois ne sera plus reconnaissable, enfin c'est un peu ce dilemme-là que je rencontre, que j'aborde et que j'ignore au cours de mon train-train, de mon train-*train*, là où il faut décider quel train prendre, quelle langue parler ou écrire, il se tend, tout prothétisé, il tend tout et il se divise en tendant, comme ceci et cela, même si la décision est prise je reste prêt à emprunter le couloir le plus proche l'heure venue pour le rejoindre, muni de mon billet aller-retors, il se divise et je me divise, je le rencontre et je le quitte, j'arrive en face et je pars derrière, je prends mon contre-pied pour m'enfuir jusqu'aux antipodes, j'arrive *da* je pars *fort*, je tire mes effets de père derrière, un peu pêle-mêle faut-il dire, mais au lieu de jeter pardessus bord je tire derrière et il me rattrape, ils me rattrapent tous, trains et pères et langues, ils me suivent et me devancent tout le long d'un trajet où le corps entraîne les mots, ou les mots les corps, dans au moins deux sens, s'entraînant en corps à corps avec l'autre à marcher et à parler prothèse.

his dark glasses and fortunately so, for in passing him by two equally monstrous possibilities occur to me: either he will take off his glasses and he will be wearing the eyes of my father, who never begged for anything, thanks perhaps to Social Security and to family and community prosthetization; or else he won't take them off because he cannot for they are implanted as in a science-fiction novel and from behind them he is negotiating the cyberspatial matrix of the passersby, projecting all of us into a prosthetic future in which a father with a wooden leg will no longer be recognizable, such is the dilemma I encounter there, that I come across and ignore amid the noise of a badly oiled daily grind, deciding which passage and which train to take, what language to speak or write in, and in the middle of it all he holds out his can and holds out for a decision, fully prosthetized, he holds out everything and divides what he proffers, like this and that, and even if the decision is made I am ready to switch at the last minute, to take another corridor that will bring me across him again, knowing the ticket is good until journey's end, any number of changes as long as the trains are in service, he stands there and divides and so do I, I meet him there and leave him again, I arrive from the front and leave by the back, I arrive *da* and leave *fort*, I pull it all behind me, granted somewhat pell-mell, but it catches up with me all the same, they all catch up with me, fathers, trains, languages, they follow me and get ahead all the way through a train of thought where the words draw the bodies, or the bodies the words, into the fray, in at least two senses or directions, pulling, straining, and always in training to speak a more fluent and better-running prosthesis at the end of the day.

§ 6 Rome, 1985

Ventimiglia, twenty miles from who knows where. Menton perhaps. Border towns, however insignificant, assume such an importance. The name is irrepressibly marked in a particular language. Or so it seems before you strike the transpositions and transliterations—Nice/Nizza, Mont Blanc/Monte Bianco, Brenner/Brennero, Trst/Trieste. But there remains from time to time the sound of a name that has no other, in the idiosyncrasy we call experience, or by means of the idiosyncratic imposition of history; one that represents the passage into the other. "Ventimiglia" sounds like such a name. It too has a French counterpart that you missed because you never crossed over by that route. You say it, *Vintimille,* and it just doesn't have the same effect. For there is already the desire, it seems, perhaps nothing more than some Rousseauist nostalgia, to pass into the register of the final vowel, in spite of the linguistic suspension, in spite of the gape of a word such a sound produces in your own tongue. *Ventimiglia,* pronounce it and you have crossed unmistakably into Italian. And into the belly of the Western world, or into its sex; into a confounding of the two. Into Liguria for example, where the dish of predilection is known by the tool(s) that produce it—*al pesto*—done in the way of the mortar and pestle of unlimited suggestiveness. Cross into Italy and you cross into a confounding of digestive disorder and fecundation, or in the version I know, digestive disorder and penetration. I have no reason for it, it might just be the traveling. It might just be the sitting for hours on end on a train en route to the expectation of hot white nights, any season, hot nights of slow sex in a patient exploration of a whole body eroticized from toe to forehead, clean and fresh but sweating nevertheless, nothing but the simplest ingredients, ripe tomatoes or fruit eaten with or without the skin, something fresh and moist, peeled and consumed in a combination of your choosing, like *fichi e prosciutto*, gently invert the order, the season, the language, the gender, engender the whole disarray of the digestive system that that entails, eating when you should be sleeping, making love when you should be eating, sleeping only when there is no more love to make or nothing else to eat, doing all three at once is enough to close down the metabolism or have the stomach and bowels explode. There is no constipation without vomiting and diarrhea, no traveling without some alternation of both, no possibility of Rome without each in close association with close repetitions of the sexual act, in turn, in congruence, or in competition with the sight of monuments in varying stages of decay.

It is in Rome that this will finally take place. Ventimiglia, once pronounced, serves little purpose here. It has nothing to do with numbers, or distance, it turns out, but is rather derived from a family, the Vento, who established their fief over the county of Menton in the middle of the thirteenth century.[1] Back then, and ever since, and not only around a town, a name, or an image, like Menton, the borders are constantly shifting. Ventimiglia simply serves to signify a crossover, an idiosyncratic assertion—that of the Italian language, that of a personal travelogue—which is also a confounding, of languages, of places, of bodily parts; the whole parergonal gambit that I wish to implement here. So if I have no particular explanation for it, I have a sort of pleonastic reconfirmation of it in a film by Peter Greenaway. *The Belly of an Architect* (1987) begins with a train crossing from France to Italy, through Ventimiglia, its countryside, its cemetery, its station. It begins with a conjunction of sex and (in)digestion, a concurrence of growth and decay, of expansion and constipation such as will structure the whole film. Stourley Kracklite, architect, and his wife, Louisa, are making love—she conceiving, it turns out—in a train passing through Ventimiglia en route to Rome, where he will attempt to organize—and be thwarted at it—an exhibition honoring the eighteenth-century French visionary architect Etienne-Louis Boullée. Kracklite will fall to his death from the Vittorio Emanuele II monument, provoking Louisa to give birth (or provoked by her giving birth) in the company of the Italian organizers of the exhibition, Io and Caspasian Speckler—her father's countrymen—who have seduced her. And so the film will end. For the time being.

The film consists of a progression of events from Ventimiglia through

scenes organized around a series of Roman monuments that inspired
Boullée, except in the last case, which might be said to have been inspired
by him. The progression or procession leads through the Mausoleum of
Augustus, Pantheon, Colosseum, Baths of the Villa Adriana, St. Peter's, the
Forum, Piazza Navona, and EUR Building, to the fatal conclusion of
Kracklite's fall.

The role played by those constructions is less explicit than the sorts of
contrivances that structure much of Greenaway's other work—the drawings in *The Draughtsman's Contract* (1982); various things, outlined elsewhere,[2] in *A Zed and Two Noughts* (1985); the numbers and drownings in
Drowning by Numbers (1988); the colors in *The Cook, the Thief, His Wife,
Her Lover* (1990). If there is a major contrivance in this film it is more
simply a narrative one, that which impels the events through the count-
down to the date of the exhibition, set for nine months from the beginning
of the film, defining, of course, the period of a gestation. Constant among
the films, however—yet this is as far as one might want to go in establishing some sort of thematic progression in Greenaway's films—is the attention given to "unnatural" relations with the body: drawing the body
(*Draughtsman*), reconstructing the body (*Zed*), photocopying the body
(*Belly*), killing the body (*Drowning*), and finally eating the body (*The
Cook, the Thief, His Wife, Her Lover*).[3]

Similarly, what can be identified as being repeated with some consistency in at least *Zed, Belly,* and *Cook* is a fairly familiar moral schema that
contrasts and probably valorizes an idea of natural creativity, or creation—
that of Louisa's baby desired by both husband and wife but a long time in
coming—over against the constipated creativity of Kracklite, who, like
Boullée, rarely manages to see his projects to fruition, has very few
buildings to his credit, and has it all rot inside to produce what seems in
the end to be stomach cancer. Through that same schema another opposition might also be drawn, thrown up with almost predictable regularity,
that between practice and theory, one fruitful, the other barren, one
responsive to the demands of the market place, the other collapsing under
its own visionary (over)weight.

But in spite of all that we are not in the film, we cannot pretend that
contrivance. We are at best in some writing of it. Never more nor less than
that. We can have recourse, for instance, to the book of it,[4] wherein
Greenaway reproduces a series of 124 postcards sent by Kracklite to Boullée
during the course of the film. Some of those appear in the film, many more

of them in the book. It is a strangely prosthetic conjunction, this film with the book of it, with its appended postcards. Especially since "it is hoped shortly to present this postcard correspondence as a short film called *Dear Boullée* which will complement *The Belly of an Architect*" (*Belly*, 115), and since that film seems not to have arrived, unless it be here and now, among other places, leaving us with only the idea, support, constipation, and decay of it.

The book of the film, any book marked in some way by a film—this film, any film, this book, any book—will necessarily be a curious text. Offered as a supplement, it can afford to reveal something of its ad hoc status, but without for all that uncovering the complete overturning of priorities and orders that it institutes. Which, indeed, comes first? Answer that question in terms of production, and the answer will likely be wrong in terms of consumption. Sooner or later one would have to fall back on a presumption, the presumption that production necessarily precedes consumption, in spite of a generation of arguments to the effect that there never can be one without the other, in spite of an exhaustive calling into question of the priority of one over the other. Either that or one must give in to the structural aporia of the supplement.

This one, signed by Peter Greenaway, is a scenario rather than a novelization, but it still betrays at least one sign of the indecent haste presumed to attend such publications or reeditions in the wake or expectation of a film's release. The casualty here seems to be the "series of reflections by Peter Greenaway on the making of the film" promised by the back cover blurb, unless the one-page introduction be the fulfillment of that promise, in which case it is a promise poorly fulfilled. Necessarily inscribed within the junk consumption of its genre, this is a text that nevertheless addresses a serious reader. So it lapses into bad editing on the one hand and offers the textual abundance of the appended postcards on the other. But I repeat only for argument's sake the litany of hierarchical assumptions just recited: high over popular art, proper over derived text, specialized over curious reader, complete over partial form, and so on. The effect of this book of this film, this film of this book, this text of this text, this itself, is to be itself ad hoc, little more than a series of supplementary incidents, or accidents, a series of reflections lost, a few score postcards gained.

Besides the whole set of discrepancies between scenario and final cut, some of which will be referred to in the course of this discussion, the written text also provides a discursive framework that is absent from the film. And that framework, whether it be signed by Greenaway or by an editor, front or back matter, reinforces what I called above the familiar moral schema. In Greenaway's one-page introduction, he mentions the "architectural heritage of two and a half thousand years" that puts "Kracklite's nine-month predicament into perspective," underlining "the ephemerality of one foreign individual striving for significance in an eternal city" (*Belly*, vii). Similarly, the blurb argues, "architecture is the least perishable of the arts and the most public. Architects (perhaps like film-makers) are supposed to be accountable to art, to finance, to the specialist critic, to the man in the street and perhaps to posterity." Kracklite, then, has ignored the weight of the past by presuming his importance in the present, but he has also ignored the accountability of the present and responsibility for the future. Instead he acts, or rather reflects, in some ideal timeless realm called art. This anti-aestheticist slant, working in and around a film whose aesthetic sense and aestheticist contrivances are highly developed, barely conceals an appeal to a prior and recoverable nature: natural pleasure, natural creativity, natural architecture. What follows returns to that, and against it, in much detail.

Kracklite sends his postcards to Boullée's last known or imagined Paris address, to the Quai d'Anise on the Rue Réaumur, the last of his buildings still standing in that city. In a moment missing from the film, part of the final climactic scene, that of Kracklite's real and final fall, it will be revealed that those same cards are reaching a destination that prevents their destination, that *adestines* them, for it is the ex-wife of Io Speckler who inhabits that building in Paris and who sends them back to the Roman conspirators, enabling them to read them as a further sign of Kracklite's decline.

Boullée never went to Rome. His whole visionary experience of the classical moment was conceived without perceiving either the front side or the back side of that city; without regarding its cracks and ruins. His was an idealized experience, leading to a proto-fascist architecture, entirely conceived in Paris. In 1990, the passage to Rome begins there also; the Ventimiglian pause, its whole epochal and pivotal importance refers back to the Parisian apex as some sort of simulacrum, a virtual image of Rome; and this turning and perverting, paean to ruination and blind decadence, is something of a deflection from Paris as other origin for whatever is exposed here. Greenaway's Boullée's Kracklite's eight Roman architectural inspirations might therefore have their contemporary complement in the seven grand Parisian projects of the 1980's: Grande Arche de la Défense,

Grand Louvre, Ministère des Finances, Institut du Monde Arabe, Musée d'Orsay, Opéra de la Bastille, La Villette. A public building spree unmatched since the days of Haussmann and the Universal Expositions, as the pamphlets and the president proclaim—"We will have achieved nothing if in the next ten years we have not created the basis for an urban civilization"[5]—and one surmises that of all the lofty promises made by the Socialists at that time the grand architectural projects will remain as those that have come to fruition, perhaps at the expense of social reforms.

The question raised, as much by Roman monuments as by contemporary Parisian ones, is whether any state-instituted building program can be benign and user-friendly, whether it can signify something more than the aggrandizement of its instigator, the self-congratulatory nationalism of its hosts; whether there isn't necessarily a desire of and for monumental proportions linking a Hadrian to a Speer to a Mitterrand. A question as thorny as it is specious, since on the one hand there is nothing less political about the private than about the public building, and since on the other hand the question cannot be separated from a complex of problems that interrogate the sense of the civic: urbanism in the era of homelessness, the role of government in fiscal crisis and in general, the definition and articulation of big and small, the bounds of the political itself, the whole matter of possession and inhabitation; then also questions more readily recognizable as concerning reading, such as immediacy or mobility of meaning, intention or destination—how it is that we can view a Roman monument as though it were exempt from considerations of empire and exploitation but not so a Nuremberg stadium—and finally, the very limits of textuality, the sense of building, or construction itself.

I mention the contemporary Parisian configuration because it imposes itself in any discussion of architecture situated in a capital or European city in the current and previous decade, and because of its place in the itinerary being followed here, as a starting point for a backwards trajectory through the Roman landscape that is a calling into question of what is front and back, old and new, by means of a performance of crossings and turnings. It is from this perspective that special significance can be given to at least one of the projects just mentioned, that whose inspiration and reflection is closest to mine here, namely the Parc de la Villette, overseen by Bernard Tschumi. For the concurrence of Tschumi's and Mitterrand's conception of the architectural task lays out the terms of a deconstruction strikingly similar to that I want to read in the belly, or at least some round form, of

Peter Greenaway's *Belly of an Architect*. A deconstruction that arises once again out of a tension between a humanist and logocentric set of presuppositions concerning creativity and creation, and a desire for a sense of construction—of art, building, and meaning—that relies more on strategies of dislocation: in the starkest terms, natural creation as against contrivance.

For Mitterrand, the grand projects create a relay between past and present, between present and future, between the center and peripheral or neglected sections of the city, and between artisanal and high technology. He realizes the risk of "utopias that rationalize excessively . . . the inhumanity of imperious undertakings which, by reducing the city to a sum of functions, forget or crush the multiplicity of significations, of trajectories, and of symbols that make the city alive and livable."[6] But Mitterrand's vision coexists with the desire for a Paris open to creative ideas, finding again its unity and its unique skills and values in a time of economic crisis.[7] It is a vision that is subsumed by a humanist imperative. In contrast to that read Tschumi on the Parc: "The inadequacy of the civilization vs. nature polarity under modern city conditions has invalidated the time-honored prototype of the park as an image of nature. It can no longer be conceived as an undefiled Utopian world-in-miniature, protected from vile reality."[8] Elsewhere he states:

> The paradigm of the architect passed down to us through the modern period is that of the form-giver, creator of hierarchical and symbolic structures characterised, on the one hand, by their unity of parts and, on the other, by the transparency of form to meaning. . . . It might be worthwhile therefore to abandon any notion of a Post-Modern architecture in favour of a post-humanist architecture, one that would stress not only the dispersion of the subject and the force of social regulation, but also the effect of such decentring on the entire notion of unified, coherent, architectural form. . . . The Parc de la Villette project had a specific aim: to prove that it was possible to construct a complex architectural organisation without resorting to traditional rules of composition, hierarchy, and order. . . . If historically architecture has always been defined as the "harmonious synthesis" of cost, structure, use and formal constraints ("*venustas, firmitas, utilitas*"), the Park became architecture against itself: a disintegration.[9]

In spite of appearances, these are not simply two opposing views, for both are finely nuanced. It is not just a matter of a posthumanist view confronting a modernist one, and the relation is in any case complicated by the fact that Mitterrand personally oversaw the selection process that awarded Tschumi the project. An informed architect of the state, or statesmanship, in a paternal yet dependent relationship with his electorate, the president finds his vision confirmed in plans for the retheorization of architecture by means of a park designed as a crossroads of technology, leisure, art, and education. But such intersections and tensions between conceptions of architecture, and indeed among all the questions they raise, do not simply appear at the end of architecture, at its outside or in its postmodern or posthumanist moment, for they are in the end questions about the inside and outside of architecture, the economy of its limits and articulations, and hence are the only and permanent architectural questions. And further, these architectural questions are also questions relevant to any construction, constructions of meaning, of artistic and critical practice, cinematic or otherwise.

How, then, is one to read such a network of signification? What is it that confines and reassures our conception of the world of a film or other work of art such that we can confidently close it off from its equally complex intersections, its system of crossings and turnings? Not that that can be the pretext for a refusal to analyze, for an acquiescence that would take us back to the most retrograde aestheticist approach; rather it calls for a different form, or different forms of analysis, a crossing of boundaries among the analytical, the theoretical, and the practical or performative. For none of those was ever immune from the others in the cases where it presumed itself to be. Neither then, is the recourse had, in Greenaway's film, to versions of the natural, a disqualification of the film in terms of this reading; on the contrary, the tension out of which the reading develops is the film's richest resource, opening all the possibilities that are exploited here.

Tschumi's own architectural constructions at La Villette consist of his *folies*, red metal structures based on permutations of a 10 × 10 × 10 meter cube and dispersed to provide the intensities of the grid system that unites the whole project. They are therefore both the rallying and relaying points of that grid, at the same time establishing and dislocating its unity. But thanks to Adrien Fainsilber, designing architect for the Cité des Sciences et de l'Industrie, the principal building in the park, and perhaps in spite of Tschumi, an overwhelmingly centralizing structure has been built there in the form of the Géode, the reflecting sphere, "Symbol of the Universe"[10] (why the universe, rather than the earth, should be represented by that form is hard to guess), which houses a 26-meter hemispherical cinema screen. It could be the starting point or end point or middle of our film, the opposite apex to a Roman monument or exhibition honoring a visionary architect, for a number of reasons. First, quite simply, because it is a dome, the form whose architectural sense, deformation, and beyond impels this discussion. Second, because the dome is strikingly reminiscent of Boullée's planned monument to Isaac Newton, a reaffirmation by architecture of its obedience to natural law and ideal form. In the case of Fainsilber's symbol of the universe there is, granted, a more modernist vision: its exterior surface consists of 6,433 polished stainless-steel triangles designed to reflect the changing sky and the water on which it sits. No two triangles are identical. Third, because the Géode contains a cinema for showing high-tech movies, often high-tech "nature" movies, smart movies that thrill the senses with their wizardry almost as much as the sight of a patriot claiming to intercept a scud, and who knows, soon there will be a movie shot from inside the patriot as it advances on the scud; movies that may well be the only cinema of a not-too-distant future and in contrast to which the concerns of an "art" film such as Greenaway's seem strangely awry. And lastly because the Géode was opened in May 1985, the same month that found Stourley and Louisa Kracklite humping through Ventimiglia, carrying this text along as they go at it, as it prepares for its own artistic entry into the play, or fray, and Stourley Kracklite in the Piazza del Popolo penning his first tentative postcard to Boullée:

> I hope you don't mind me writing to you like this. I feel I know you well enough to talk to you. I think my wife is poisoning me! I'm sure it's part of her general animosity towards you—you can laugh but I'm serious.
> Yours, with respect,
> St. Kracklite
> (Architect)
> (*Belly*, 117)

From my perspective, it is the way Kracklite signs his name when writing to Boullée that is most worthy of comment with respect to this and the other postcards. Invariably, as we see the names handwritten in the film, they are signed not "S. Kracklite" but "St. Kracklite," as if a letter had broken off from the edge of another event—who knows, a painting of a beach—to find its way to the inside of the outside of this signature. The idiosyncratic "St." is extreme, given the rarity of the forename. As an abbreviation for "Stephen" it would be easily recognizable, but his name is "Stourley" and we cannot but read the second initial—can there be such a thing?—as the film's offer of excess, perhaps the mark of the supplement itself. Desire for canonization aside, the appended "t" or "+" might therefore stand for adjunction, or more precisely conjunction itself, chiastic intersection, if you will, of what the film concocts or contrives, notably the body and architecture; but also the conjunction that is the site of a crossing or competition over the signature, like a changing shed on the edge of the frame where clothes come off to reveal a mutation into the monstrous; that "t" this reading passing by the film in an inverse relation like a series of blurred frames glimpsed through the window of a speeding train; that addition this reading's polymorphological confusion of bodily functions, and their reduction to the sexual (not that the film doesn't permit, even encourage it); this superposition of sex upon the form of a city, or vice versa; and lastly the addended "+" as the signature of construction itself, architectural construction as adjunction of beams and creation of right angles, the intersection of form and function.

If I were to open the screenplay at a point or a crossing that I could always insist was random, at page 135, postcards 36 and 37, those dated respectively July 19 and 21, 1985, it would be to set in train the fiction of a voyage to Rome made on those dates some five years later, and to enter into another fiction, that of a numerological crypt designed, by some as yet undisclosed or undiscovered series of calculations, to produce the number 45. The pretext for such a numerological lure—as if borrowed from one Greenaway film and imported into another—is the Roman way, numeration as writing; imagining a plan for a building, say Hadrian's Pantheon, as blueprints covered with measurements reduced to all manner of combinations of I's, V's, X's, L's, C's, D's, and M's. Those seven letters could as well be the letters of architecture itself, graphic representations of the columns, arches, vaults, and domes that constitute it. All that and more, but especially the effect of the lure itself, the hermeneutical baiting that still conditions our reading after all this time, the lure that someone like Greenaway often holds out, with, for example, his violinist first sighted on the platform at Ventimiglia, returning as busker to the Mausoleum of Augustus and finally in the one but penultimate scene at the restaurant outside the Pantheon as Kracklite founders in a drunken rage in front of the classical perfection of that monument, admitting both his failure as an architect and his mortality, which may or may not be the same thing, his inability to build either his life or his exhibition, to repair his body or his salute to Boullée. The film, in this reading, will be the pretext for such a pursuit of the sign as number, for its disclosure or discovery, but the number 45 will be displaced rather than revealed. It will be displaced to become first the number of an angle, 45 degrees, an angle whose doubling produces the founding possibility of a dominant tradition of architecture, so aptly called the right angle, the 45-degree angle performing what we might call the deconstruction of that tradition that massively privileges the square at the expense of the hypotenuse, the oblique, or the diagonal. Or to become half the number of degrees Fahrenheit standing in view of a Bernini fountain—the one Kracklite is photographing when Io's daughter Flavia, in a telling displacement, thinks he is only interested in the cocks, when it is in fact the statues' stomachs that have him obsessed, but how can the observer tell when the camera is aimed from a distance at the midsection of a Bernini river muse, how can we tell in general what is the focal point of an image or a film by Peter Greenaway?—anyway, that sort of temperature and that sort of conjunction of sex and metabolic function in the Piazza Navona late at night after *carpaccio con rughetta* consumed in the shadow of Sant'Andrea della Valle; or my number the number of bodies in Rome, some mathematical function of their perfect roundness, not that they are perfectly round, but that their roundness pretends to perfect proportions, I mean the curve of buttocks caressed and slightly raised as if proffered to the touch in a street likely called Via Rotonda, the curve between waist and hip, the crease of a curve where thigh meets pubis, 45 their number, who knows perhaps the sum of their degrees, perhaps also the number of a hotel room where the same curves move and glisten under a film of perspiration, the number of words that sing with a final vowel before one makes an end of lovemaking in Italian, the same word, why not, whispered 450 times, of course I exaggerate, maybe no more than that to it in fact, 45 the number of my excess, or a number for my excess, the exact degree of my exaggeration, or perhaps not so exact, perhaps contrived or chosen at random to pose the question of what it would mean to have a numerology that were only approximate, like any hermeneutic threatened by the limits of its own exactitude.

The numerological gambit is thus a name for the act of contrivance, a lure for the hermeneutic imagination. There is a magic in the number beyond that of a name or a word. Once it is uttered, assigned to this or that body, one will look for it and find it everywhere, yet each time in a different place, falling upon you from behind a different streetlamp, lying in wait around yet another corner, smiling from every crease of the body you lie with waiting, waiting for the number to arouse you, for it is the number at the end of your desire and at the beginning of your desire, your desire for the number a desire for a name for the desire, an end to its seemingly limitless proliferation throughout this city and across this body.

A number retains a certain monumentality that is out of reach of the name or the word given the tendency of their meaning to multiply and scatter, to fall into commonality. The number holds out the promise of a single referent, that of the integer, of mathematical purity, of a meaning that would bring a stop to the signifying abandon. Hence my gambit, to raise at one and the same time the stakes of mystification, throw out a smoke screen whose clearance would be the ultimate revelation, if only it would occur, and also to multiply the numerological referents, to ascribe the number 45 everywhere and perhaps nowhere, in its coefficients and denominators, its fractions and factors, its primes and roots, to chance its referential momentum on the body of Rome, on the bodies of this Rome, their forms and their movements.

The number retains a certain monumentality and holds off the threat of its own dissemination into commonality, except when it appears the Roman or Latin way, where it falls into writing, regurgitated and vomited in a conglomerate repetition of seven letters, the monumentality of its letters crumbling into ruin, gone to the dogs like a scene of a man, his name Kracklite, inclining against a wall and barfing onto the ground at the Villa Adriana to feed a mangy cur (see *Belly*, 50), the number gone the Roman way, confounding its own perfection in a macaroni of marks that could never spell a name, just a series of initials, initials for the name that is, here, desire and paroxysm, digestion and expulsion.

Open *The Belly of an Architect* at random or by design at a precise date in the region of the Tiber and St. Peter's:

Friday, 19th July 1985:

Dear Etienne-Louis,
The colours of Rome are the colours of human flesh and hair—for the most part warm—orange, orange-red, browns; and warm whites—cream—then

warm blacks. No blue and only the darkest of greens—an exaggerated point of view? What colours would your buildings be? I have grown so used to your drawings being in black and white—it's difficult for me to see them in any colour.

Yours,
Stourley Kracklite
(135)

He talks of color where I spoke of number, as though the reels, or perhaps the films, were out of order, out of both numerical and categorical order. But if we consider color as but another code, another cryptological system, along with numbers and letters, the three semiotic regimes are simply put into play with and against one another and the city comes to be read as color-coded. The system of numbers remains the foremost of these regimes, in the sense of the simplest, for the cipher, by definition—and perhaps every hermeneutic gesture in general—returns to a question of the numerical if not the numerological. The simplest code is that of a number for each letter. Perhaps all signifying systems are numerological to the extent that their means of transcendence involves always, if only by evocation, a reduction to the number one. The one and the zero, like the white and the black, or the black and the white, for the very point about color as a signifying system, at least in its binary reduction, is that it has no incontrovertible order. The role of the chromatic here in apposition to the numerological is precisely to subvert the strict order of the latter. But the choice is not for or against the numerological gambit, for one is automatically in it—as if in the heat of the compositional moment one has hit the number lock instead of the backspace edit key—the choice is always made in favor of a number or the number, a small or a large one, a single or plural one, and mine obstinately 45 for the codes the ciphers the crypts whereby the secrets are concealed and divulged in a crossplay of writing, counting, and architecture. And sex and Rome, for in writing of those one is automatically in the crypt, the bowels or belly of an architectural construction of meaning; in the relations between body and building that this film, via Boullée and Kracklite, brings into focus; and in the city of monument and ruin of monument, erection and detumescence, concameration and disintegration, where it all takes place.

Less explicit in *The Belly of an Architect*, relatively speaking at least, are the sorts of contrivances that structure most of Greenaway's other films.

Until one invents them, until one pushes a little further into the no-man's-land, across a sort of *ponte rotto* to where it is no longer clear to whom the contrivance or the invention is owed, where the difference between the two. Until, by dint of a false step or a stumble over ruined stones, one is somewhere in the belly of the artifice.

The films of Peter Greenaway call forth contrivance. They call forth contrivance and they depend upon contrivance. Not that all films don't; Greenaway's simply make contrivance a more explicit question. The point about contrivance is that it is never single; in fact it is contagious, and reciprocal. To begin with it necessarily involves a conjunction, a joining; the look of the word tells you that, and little can be conceived, or conceived of, without a notion of joining, at least nothing of human scale. The word "contrivance" needs to be understood in its most immediate sense, in its first impression, the prepositional adjunction that is the word's first syllable: the prefix "con" (Lat. *cum*) is its invention and first creation. There is no need, once it is a matter of contrivance, to go beyond that simple syntactic apposition; no semantic resource or etymological authenticity is required to discover all that is necessary in the adjunction of a first preposition referring to an adjunction. The sense of contrivance resides from that point of view in that of the supplement. Any addition that is a bringing together—how to conceive of addition otherwise—activates and works through the structure of contrivance. Contrivance is a function of the minimal discontinuity that interrupts the auto-affection of the natural, the minimal discontinuity that would therefore guarantee that the natural remains something impossible to conceive.[11] Once there is that originary apposition there is little to prevent a contiguity from being a contagion, and rarely anything that could be more architectural, starting with the problem of what prevents a minimal construction or contiguity from building up to the contagion of an architectural accumulation, of multiple junctures of bodies and buildings.

For instance, it is 45 minutes past midnight and you sleep with the windows open because there is no relief from the heat, nor from the desire, no clear discontinuity between the two. You don't know whether it is hotter inside or out so you minimize the borders between the two. You can't sleep, can't stop wanting, can't stop wanting a good reason for the film of perspiration on the nape of your neck, the moistness that forms a contraband, a tactile track upon the visuals of your lover's body. Can't stop wanting to do it with the least bodily contact—just kneel there and raise your haunches while I grasp your hips but no more than necessary to monitor the movement so that all that sticks is where it all sticks anyway along the 225 degrees from coccyx to navel, within the orbit of a sunless oasis that is all wetness. You do it with the windows open for relief, and you do it with the curtains drawn back for more of the same, for the breeze to bring the noise from the street to drown your urgent announcement of mounting pleasure, or else you do it for the effect, at the outside limit for the audience, crying and waving to the passersby or the family across the courtyard, you contrive thereby to constitute a primal scene and announce the first and last contrivance called the sex act. It begins and ends with sex, and builds from there. Sex is little else once you get down to it. It begins with a coupling, a contrivance that is also fundamentally prosthetic. A coupling—hear it in the technical sense—for it is especially that, a function of the *technē*. Sex as coupling, contrivance, or prosthesis, is fundamentally *architectural, architechnological.* There is a confounding of origins once one gets down to it, once one looks for the primary event—utterance, sex, building. They are all constructions, and all occur within the structure of prosthetic contrivance. Hence the sort of generalized eroticism taking place in my recounting of a journey across the borders and into Rome.

In order for there to be a successful circumscription of the structure of contrivance, something that could distinguish it from other sorts of ad-junctions, an appeal would have to be made to some natural supplemen-tary relation as opposed to an arranged one. Greenaway's films implicitly make such appeals while at the same time encouraging an analysis of contrivance that leads one to conclude in favor of its structural necessity. Starting from a voyage to Rome, or from Greenaway's *The Belly of an Architect*, there is absolutely nothing to distinguish contrivance from a putative opposite such as creation or invention; those latter cannot be conceived of without the idea of it. Every creation, every invention is a contrivance, which suggests every start to be a false start, every step a faux pas. A *faux calcul* like the invention of a number to represent the body in Rome, the body of Rome or at least its belly and its arse; the fiction of a numerological crypt or cipher for a number chosen at random, a *fait divers* or red herring like so many destabilizing elements in the films of Peter Greenaway.

Can Greenaway's contrivances in fact be satisfactorily or exhaustively analyzed? Take the grid that mediates the screen in *The Draughtsman's Contract.* Its sixteen squares do not tally with the twelve or thirteen drawings that are executed by the draftsman, but rather provide for some perfectly symmetrical circumscription of the visual field in its relation to reality. That is to say, there is no contrivance to be perceived, at first glance, at a naive level, perhaps at the level of the film, by the simple superposition of a grid over a visual field. There is supposed to be no such contrivance or perception, for by means of the realist tradition, the grid, like the camera lens, is presented as a filter for the real. But once it is placed there, there is no getting away from it. The whole drift of the film begins with the laying of the grid; with the division of the field and rearranging (or not) of reality that that implies, with the vision of the draftsman, his drawing by transfer of grid to paper, and so on. And the whole narrative—the fact of the draftsman's finding or inventing clues to mutilation and murder, his discovery of corruption beneath the surface of the ordered English manor, or the portrait of his own corruption that surprises him within his draw-ings—corruption that he in fact installed by contracting to use his art as a means to sexual pleasure or perversion—all that draws or derives its movement from that same overlay; as does the film's thematics, its numer-ological references, and so on. One could perform any number of struc-tural analyses or deconstructive readings on the basis of the grid, and a reading of the film would to some extent be bound to pass through it.

But if one were to obey that theoretical or strategical injunction—for it functions as much as a limitation as an invitation—one would not for all that have progressed beyond the level of a first, naive reading, one posi-tioned in concord with the film's self-explicitation. One would be forced to accept that the grid is a limit to reading imposed at a first level of reading, and that as a result the contrivance of this film—perhaps of all of Green-away's films—resides in the way in which it limits the reading's room for maneuver even as it seems to expand it. Even more so since included in the grid effect as I have just described it is its own *mise en abyme*. There is in the grid effect a limit, even if it be undermined by its foregrounding of limitation. Unless it can somehow be undone, that limit will continue to function as a form of constraint. For by means of its appeal to nonmedia-tion, to immediacy—the grid is put in place to allow the drawing to accurately reproduce an "ungridded real"—it reimposes even as it appears to deconstruct the idea of a zero degree of (non)contrivance. It is as if the explicit structuration provided by the grid enabled it to be all the more simply removed, like a filter across a lens. That amounts to a barely tolerable paradox: the explicitation of mediation has the same effect, in the end, as the occultation of mediation. Yet that is where the logic of the supplement leads, placing within the same structural space addition and nonaddition, or rather addition and that other addition of a metaphysical presumption that presents itself as nonaddition; and it is that logic that all manner of contrivance is here trying to come to grips with. The deconstruction of the grid will thus be co-opted by the system of the grid unless a reading somehow insists that there is no possibility of an overlay that is not, through the most simple structure of adjunction, an opening without limit to the play of contrivance.

To take it a step further: if I were to describe *The Draughtsman's Contract* as dishonestly presenting the most stringent of contrivances as nonmediating or noninterfering, I would, by my appeal to some alternative authenticity, merely be repeating the grid effect. And Greenaway's supposedly old and familiar ruse would, by virtue of its being presented as an explicit or conscious process, potentially remain one step ahead of my analysis. It is from the point of view of such a paradox that it remains necessary to raise the question of Greenaway's postmodernism, and subsequently the question of how far what is called postmodernism, in its foregrounding of effects of contrivance, actually manages to interrogate the operation and sense of contrivance itself.[12] But more pertinent for us, it is the paradox that haunts deconstruction, the trap that much of what passes for deconstruction often falls into. As long as it presents itself solely as a form of discovery, it remains a singularly hermeneutic exercise; and even if it presents that discovery as a production it risks falling back on the idea of invention as creation. Counter to that then, for what it is worth, is this putting into effect or setting in motion of contrivance called prosthesis, this particularly Roman conjunction of sex and decomposition, this love among the ruins.

If we return to *The Belly of an Architect*, it is the dome that is imposed as a type of grid, the thematic imposition of the belly as dome, implying the body/building relation. I have referred to it much, even subscribed to it. It is imposed as a necessity that, at some level, a reading cannot ignore. It is the sense of the film and a particularly fecund crypt of meaning. For me Greenaway's talent, his intelligence, lies quite simply in the level of this sort of intellectual interest that his films explicitly generate. On the other hand, let it not be forgotten that the body/building relation keys into the whole fertility/degeneracy, creation/decay, birth/death system of oppositions that threatens, in spite of the levels of complexity just described, to reduce the film to yet another logocentric complaint, reducing the play of contrivance to an opposition wherein the structure of contrivance itself would be presumed to disappear in favor of the domain or sphere of the natural, an idealized, noncontrived, prior, and privileged space.

So then, against such a reduction but knowingly playing into the labyrinthine grid of contrivance and countercontrivance as long as there seems not to be any other possibility, there is this ploy of a number 45 probably having nothing whatsoever to do with the appearance of the dates July 19 and 21, 1985, on page 135 of the screenplay of *The Belly of an Architect*. For the ploy itself might continue to presuppose an ideal of the uncontrived at either end of its argument: either the pure chance of a number that comes to mind or falls from the sky—if one can continue to find the terms to describe such a pure chance—or the simplicity or convolution (it matters little) of a decipher that would resolve the question raised by the contrivance, that would return it to a supposed degree zero of explicitness. By the same token none of that would disqualify the argument against the existence of a degree zero in favor of a contrived for every utterance whatsoever, in terms of which the exercise would be to continue to negotiate the play of contrivance, to analyze its strategies even as one exploited them; to promote that idea of contrivance as a set of strategies whose elaboration necessarily becomes the task at hand in the discussion of a text.

The difference between the colors referred to in Kracklite's postcard to Boullée on July 19, 1985, and the number 45 for a visit to Rome four or five years after that date may be described as the difference between that film and this writing. As well as a number of other differences, like that of the flesh tones of Rome as opposed to the Anglo-Celtic-Germanic-Norman tint appropriate to another set of characters, or visitors, Kracklite and myself among them. But let me restrict myself to the difference between number and color, number here, in the Roman way, being again short-hand for the written, for writing. How to write in color, in Roman colors, is a question converse to that Greenaway asks himself when he tries to film according to one of his contrived schemas—numbers for instance. How to inscribe the cinematic or polychromatic upon the alphabetic? How to discover, preserve, contrive, or radicalize the heterogeneity of the medium? It is yet another profoundly architectural question to the extent that architecture, at least since Vitruvius, supposedly involves the imposition of function over the seduction of structure, or vice versa since the whole architectural investment lies in the play between the two. Architectural design would therefore necessarily pose a question about the heterogeneity of the medium, of itself as medium, and of any medium; it would inevitably raise the question of the limits to that heterogeneity. How far can that heterogeneity be radicalized before the building collapses (in any case to what extent is permanence, *de facto* or *de jure*, a function of architecture)?

One can see it all beginning with the dome. As *domus*, or house, it is no doubt the starting point for architecture; the idea of a roof over one's head. From those first prehistoric vaults in the Istrian fields with their stones laid in careful spiral sequence to create a self-supporting shelter, to the design of Agrippa's Pantheon arching higher and higher and finer and finer until the hole at the top crosses over into pure ethe*reality*. But if the dome is at the beginning of architecture it is also at the end or outer limit, where it becomes mausoleum, cupola, pantheon; in other words monument. In the movement from house to monument one can arguably see a movement from priority of function to priority of structure, from architecture to sculpture if you will. Not that the monument doesn't have its function, but that function no longer concerns the living, no longer concerns living itself. A mausoleum is therefore the antithesis of the *domus* at the same time as it is its apotheosis: a house for the dead to go on living in. All that, however, is reasoned from a logocentrism or ecocentrism that occurs as a tension in *The Belly of an Architect* and that is in question or suspension here. From my point of view the movement of architecture is by definition economic, a management of the *oikos*, a controlling, and thus necessarily also a testing, of the limits of the domestic, of domestication; a placing of the threshold in general. Here for instance—as if there were ever anywhere else—a placing of the thresholds of reading and of sense.

Kracklite's belly appears as such a threshold, displayed on the border between France and Italy. He lies on his back after making love and pats it, speaking of the "home of the dome and the arch ... and good food" (*Belly*, 3). One might find there another origin for architecture, in the body as original home, with the dome as simulacrum of the human belly, whereby digestion rather than breathing becomes the signifier of the living human being. But he has just rolled over, displaying his belly as a sign of satisfaction, of satiety, whereas architecture needs to be read in terms of desire. Or at least aspiration. "Aspiration" might be the word for architecture, and it would need to be understood as repeating the structure of desire. A constant overreaching of its own economy is what impels architecture—bigger, higher, lighter, like the dome of the Pantheon. And frankly, the belly doesn't work that way for me, not here and now, lying with Rome. It all needs to be turned around, or over. That way, as the screenplay suggests when Kracklite's buttocks appear in the window as the train pauses in Ventimiglia station, framed image for a line of spectators standing on the platform, the dome works as the backside, and defecation rather than digestion or breathing becomes the signifier of the living. Or at least not one without the other; at least not in Rome, not in the Rome I know. After that, it all runs on, from digestion through defecation to sex. We don't need the film or Rome for that connection, to remind ourselves as so many have before, from St. Augustine to Freud, that "*inter urinas et faeces nascimur* [we are born between urine and feces]" (Freud, *SE* XXI: 106), that the distance between sexual organ and anus is uncomfortably insignificant. And we have Georges Bataille to remind us that eroticism is affirmation of the continuity that is death, by means of the prodigality engendered by decay and putrefaction.[13] A crumbling Rome is therefore inevitably erotic. But my idiosyncratic or architectonic contention would be that in Rome sex is defined by the curve of the buttocks more than anything else; and then that Rome is defined by digestive problems, the constipation and diarrhea the film refers to. It is a matter of an upset stomach, as the saying goes, the upset stomach merely a signifier for the reverse of the stomach, the upturned buttocks that are the beauty, and the converse of the belly, and the signifier of the sex and decay of Rome.

In the contemporary idiom the belly exists as something of a perversion, the hypernatural signifier of excessive consumption, tending to that point where the natural tips over into monstrosity. Look at Kracklite. He is almost proud of his belly—"built with a perfect and enviable centre of gravity" (*Belly*, 12)—but his aspirations for it are diminutive rather than augmentative. Caressing the belly—and I speak here as one who has never experienced pregnancy, though not forgetting the extent to which Kracklite's malady might be read as male hysteria or phantasm of maternity, nor how much the fear of mutation or monstrosity haunts the pregnant belly—caressing the belly involves a flattening motion, its direction is vertical, always downward, impelled by the desire and imagination of the pubic caress. On the other hand, caressing the buttocks has more of the circular about it, more of a self-sufficiency. But there is perversity lurking in it, for the similar desire for the hands to move down and inward, to clutch and spread the thighs, implies a desire for the sexual position whose idiom is again borrowed from the Romans, *a tergo*. That way coitus involves more of an architectural fit, an arch with one of you the tympan, the cushion of the other's arse snug in your pelvis and against your belly, a cock for a keystone. And this way also, in terms of the buttocks rather than the belly, one finds a closer and thus more architectural relation between bodily form and bodily function, the function under the form coming closer to the surface, erupting through an orifice, the two reaching a certain harmony but at the same time raising the whole question of how defecation might relate to forms of beauty. And finally the Roman way is also that of a dog, the *mos ferarum*, the way of beasts wild and domestic, and the only dog in the film, the one that eats the vomit Kracklite throws up at the Villa Adriana, is drawn into this thematic nexus by virtue of how he copulates and as a result of which the spectator cannot distinguish which orifice is being entered, the primal scene seeming to represent the abomination that is against nature.

The Roman way, in its common acceptation, signifies a cycle of excess, a bulimic perversion whereby the natural cycle of digestion is short-circuited by self-induced vomiting to allow for more eating. And the Roman way turned over by this writing, to signify a version of sex fixated on the buttocks, suggests the Sadian paradigm of perversion, the "integral monstrosity" of sodomy. It "strikes precisely at the law of the propagation of the species. . . . In being the simulacrum of the act of generation, it is a mockery of it. . . . The sodomist gesture, transgressing the organic specificity of individuals, introduces into existence the principle of metamorphosis."[14] We thus cross the border into generic otherness. In Rome we are all dogs and wolfmen, fallen on all fours. One tail penetrates another and we are all dogs and wolfmen. We are metamorphosed, mutant or prosthetized, and the matter is, like the tail, concentrated on or in the backside, become the site of a mutation or a prosthesis, a fall out of nature. Nothing more natural than defecation, nothing more catastrophic than diarrhea; nothing more natural than copulation, nothing more against nature than *a tergo* sex, to all appearances confounding entrances, functions, genders, species. Centaur or wolfman, half animal half human, self-divided and halfway to a combination of human and machine, on the threshold of a prosthesis. Coming in through the back door, to all appearances. Coming into the dome that brings us back to one of the first prostheses, for building a house is like any operation of the *technē*, any construction, both for and against nature—for protection in the manner of a cave, against mortality by virtue of its durability—and building a house is as well an irreversible step in the direction of the mechanical, site of an articulation between a construction or a machine and the human body.

The inversion here might be described as a displacement from the belly as the foundation of the relation between architecture and anatomy, to the arse as fundament. A displacement that would prevent that relation from settling in or settling down, from being, as the French would say, well seated (*bien assis*). And the architectural significance of the backside, in contrast to *Belly's* belly/dome relation, gains something else from such a translinguistic crossing. The special French word for that curvature of the haunches that is my inspiration or aspiration in this journey past a film of Greenaway into the bowels of Italy is *cambrure*. It is derived from *camera* (Lat./Ital., "room"). The specificity of a room or chamber is, in Latin, precisely its curvature, that of the ceiling or that of the loins where I bury my head to sleep a simulacrum of death after reaching to the limit of whatever recesses the body, the house, the word, the room can offer. For the Roman way is finally a confounding, by excess, of all those things; a perversion or inversion, a translation, a crossing of borders, of languages, of media, of bodies and buildings, of functions and forms and the insides and outsides of each. It is again a particular adjunction that amounts to a configuration among sex, utterance, and building; again it approaches the Sadian paradigm where the bodies are pushed to a limit that is also a turning inside out of language, an exploding of the walls of the bedroom and of thought (an "inwardness of thought which *nothing* separates from the bedroom"), philosophy in the bedroom, discourse or writing in the *camera*, sex in the city: "Thus the foreclosure of language by itself gives Sade's work its singular configuration—first a set of tales, discourses, then a series of tableaux. . . . His work then is like the vast layout of an urban showroom at the heart of a city, one with the city."[15]

In *The Belly of an Architect* the belly/dome/mausoleum connection turns around the figure of Augustus. In the screenplay Kracklite's Roman apartment overlooks the Mausoleum of Augustus. Early in the film he steals a stack of postcards of the Augusteum and of a sculpture of the emperor, after which he begins writing to Boullée. He photocopies and enlarges the stomach region of the sculpture as the basis for a series of drawings and meditations connected with his deteriorating health and his suspicion that Augustus was a victim of poisoning by his wife. This is the

first sign that he is neglecting his work on the exhibition in favor of a
neurotic downturn centered on his health. He produces graphics in which
Augustus's belly is filled with multicolored round forms that could be
stones or figs or fetal domes. The drawings and graphics invade his hotel
chamber, littering the floor along with books and models until the whole
room is occupied by the proliferating disseminative effect of that first or
originary theft or copy, the bed finally stripped of its mattress to become a
pedestal for a Buddha-like Kracklite sitting drawing. The room as model
for the dome has been crowded inside out, rendered abyssal by this
monumental living statue that implies the petrification of its model, the
death of the room's occupant, just as the belly as dome is invaginated by
diseases real or imaginary but in all cases connected to the monstrosity of
the architectural project.

Kracklite's digestive disorder may be one of the three things suggested:
(1) poisoned figs as he believes; (2) "dyspepsia, fatigue, over-excitement,
excess—and unfamiliar food, lack of exercise and too much coffee—maybe
also too much egotism" (*Belly*, 41), as the first doctor diagnoses; or (3) the
cancer it seems to turn out to be. None of that might appear particularly
architectural, but whether organically or synthetically induced, by acidity,
toxicity, or cellular mutation, his condition is a case of either bad plumbing or structural failure. Thus nothing could be more architectural. For the
relation of anatomy to architecture does not end with form, assuming it
could be proved to begin there, assuming we could know where form
begins and ends, but operates also in terms of bodily function in general,
especially enterology and gynecology. Kracklite concentrates on the former, building what, according to his wife, Chicagoans call "the Charnel
House. A building suffering from excess cholesterol" (12); whereas Caspasian Speckler, Stourley's rival, usurper of his wife and exhibition, favors the
latter, contending that "Architects ought to know about everything—
reproduction ... gender ... sex ... especially sex" (47).

Figs bring all of that together—Kracklite, Augustus, enterology, gynecology, the body, architecture—and at the same time occasion an uncontrollable drift. Poisoned or not, they are the perineal fruit, connecting sex
to defecation. Botanists don't even consider them a fruit, but rather a
fleshy receptacle, a room, a botanical chamber that bears seeds. They are
the prototypical bearer of poison, especially for Romans, such that in
English a victim is said to be given an Italian fig. Say the word in Italian
(*fico*) and you are only a vowel, only a gender away from saying "cunt"

(*fica*); somewhere it crosses over, in popular Latin maybe, so that the sign of the fig is that of the clitoris protruding from the vulva; say "I don't give a fig" and you are in effect saying "I don't give a fuck." Whether they are the aphrodisiac Louisa suggests they are after Kracklite forces one into her mouth, or have the laxative value assigned to soft-fleshed multigranulate fruit in general; whether they crack to evoke the female sex or the *cambrure* and form of the buttocks, they are probably the most corporeal of fruits and therefore the most architectural. In any case, so the legend goes, Augustus died of them, his mausoleum becoming something of a monument to them.

The nexus represented by Augustus, his belly, and his death also produces the move from architecture to sculpture referred to earlier, still within the structure of what relates the human form to the monument. It works in parallel with a shift that occurs across the medium of the cinematic image. It occurs at what might be called the technological moment, a point of focus on the machine that is also a focus upon mortality. It is a complex set of relations, which I shall attempt to schematize in what follows. Although that schema obeys certain narrative moments in the film, that is not to argue that one precedes the other, sculpture before architecture or vice versa, or even that the question of their relation finds some sort of satisfactory resolution. That would be to repeat the nonquestion of whether function precedes structure, art before construction, necessity before superfluity, essence or substance before ornament. The fact, encountered here, that both intersect in the body suggests what the present discussion has always assumed, namely that they inhabit a common structural space.

First of all, Augustus becomes the subject of a certain narrative and scopophilic drift by means of the postcard representations of him and his mausoleum. In the photocopying scenes, of which there are three, the question of color returns as the machine throws out orange, green, and white lights that contrast with the monochrome reproductions:

> He selects a button and the machine starts—adding orange and white lights to the green. Twelve large, enlarged photocopied stomachs of Augustus roll out of the machine's mouth; with painful, mechanical noises—halfway between coughing, choking and screaming—the machine "gives birth" to twelve stomachs. When the machine stops, Kracklite picks up an enlargement and examines it. The enlargements are damp and a little shiny. He lifts his shirt

and feels for his stomach. He takes an enlarged photograph of the Augustus "belly" from the machine and looks down at his own belly. He identifies his stomach with the stomach of Augustus and feels the pain as though it's Augustus who is suffering.   (*Belly*, 33)

The polychrome functioning of the machine produces the monochrome form of the two-dimensional copy; in this way, cinema becomes, or produces, a graphic more akin to writing. A particularly striking play of light is transformed into the flatness of the photocopy, which in turn becomes the basis for a different series of drifts through Kracklite's obsession. It is that whole effect that we can, after Derrida, call writing, a name for the irruption of otherness within the homogeneity of a medium, for a disjunctive difference within or across pictorial space, for the inscription of the lifelessness represented by the mechanical or technological. Thus I say that cinema becomes writing and not that color cinema reduces to black and white cinema simply because in the cinematic case in point, that of *The Belly of an Architect*, the question of black and white cinema does not seem to arise. That is to say that a black and white cinema as some sort of paradigmatic antecedent to a color cinema is not given a privileged semiotic function in Greenaway's films, in spite of the fact that it must always have a significance, if that of an absence, in film in general. Rather, as the decors of *The Cook, the Thief* make explicit, black and white signify as elements of a polychromatic spectrum whose artistic antecedents are more likely to be found in the history of painting than in the history of cinema; and in *Belly*, of course, those antecedents extend to sculpture and to architecture. Moreover, such a polychromatic spectrum is already, as we have seen, in a cryptological relation to numbers and letters; color, then, may be read as the writing fo which the medium of a machine gives explicit materiality.

So I read the photocopy as a move from cinema to writing, an explicitation of the structure of writing within film, and the machine—it could be camera, projector, pen, or processor as much as a photocopier—the medium or articulation of writing as chiasmus, the place of a transfer or crossover where the writing of the film and its specific chromatic play intersects with this my travelogue and numerological drift, this my body and sex, the curves of your body and of Rome, my hands on your arse they leave an imprint, and I heard about a colleague who would sit on the Xerox machine and copy his bum as letterhead for the memos he sent to the dean, this then a point of intersection and emergence, the birth of change, slippage, shift, and fall into the monstrosity of the other.

The black and white of the photocopy in the film image is the radicality of a change of medium. That the heterogeneity of black and white and color, or the opposition between them, exists within the structure of any color film is not in question, but that that opposition operates here to open the space of the film to another form of representation is the strength of my argument; and that form of representation is given by the printed page. The printed page represents a statue of a dead emperor, being made to represent the suffering of an infirm architect, the rot in the belly, the death in the center of Rome. In *The Cook, the Thief,* the lover is killed by being force-fed page after page of the books he loves to read. Writing always occurs under the sign of death, the death that is the machine, the separation from the living source. And if the passage to photocopy is not sufficiently explicitly a passage to writing, to writing as *trait* already inscribed by the printing or *tirage* produced by the machine, then Kracklite will bring the point home as he draws on each of the copies, plotting his slow decay with the help of Boullée and their common dreams of an architecture of the monumental, an architecture whose constant is the mausoleum, the *domus memorabilis.*

A further precision: what difference should be determined between drawing and writing; what significant differences are there among the effects of writing now being discovered everywhere, in cinema, in design, in architecture, in doodling? For it seems that I am making distinctions here only to erase them in the name of a generalized writing there. But what interests me finally is not the difference in the sense of a distinction between homogeneous entities, since there are none of those. It is precisely the effect or rite of passage from one form to another, the crossover effect in the sound of a name, or the turning of a body because desire functions this way and that, because I want you this way and that, *a tergo,* the way that is a turning, to confound and confuse the observer, impossible to tell which way, and with what sex, is in. What interests me is the point at which difference becomes a problematic notion. It is such a rite that would be more accurately called writing, particularly what I would call prosthetic writing, the writing of prosthesis. My identification of it here derives from the fact of a chiastic transfer between sculpture and architecture—the two compressed into the monumental statue of Augustus, whose body, become image on a postcard then on a photocopy, leads us into the simultaneously imploding and exploding room and body inhabited by Kracklite, and thus into the structure through which the natural anatomical is contaminated by the constructed architectural and vice versa. That transfer occurs, by means of the mechanics of the photocopy, at the point where another medium, cinema, is simultaneously imploding and exploding under the force of its own heterogeneity, the force and heterogeneity I am here calling writing.

A passage to writing or simply a passage of writing that is a passage to disease and death. That is what the mutual and originary contamination of one medium by another—architecture by sculpture, cinema by writing —signifies, namely the structure of adjunction, construction, and contrivance that is the site of a passage into the dead space of the machine. We come back to it, in another contemplation of statuary later in the film. When Kracklite's doctor pronounces his funest prognosis, however equivocally, he is walking with his patient through a hospital cloister:

> The corridor is open to a sunlit courtyard. . . . There is the sound of birds. . . . There is a small fountain running into a basin. . . . Kracklite and Amansa walk down the hospital gallery—a wide corridor with high ceilings and a stone floor. All along one side of the corridor is a line of Roman busts on plinths or pedestals. . . . The Doctor and Kracklite slowly walk down the corridor's length. He draws Kracklite's attention to the portrait busts.   (*Belly*, 98–99)

It is the most extraordinarily arresting moment in the film, a theatrical and cinematic *tour de force*. A turning and a wrenching:

> "Galba ... a miserable sort of man ... bisexual ... fancied mature slaves, especially if they had been a little mutilated ... all his freed men had no fingers on the left hands ... he's dead—died screaming ... in a cellar.
>
> (*They walk on. They stop again.*)
>
> Titus ... he started well ... soon became greedy ... disembowelled on the Tiber steps ... he's dead, died screaming ...
>
> (*They walk on.*)
>
> Hadrian ... as you know, an architect of note ... put a lot of faith in stones ... died peacefully ... planning a Temple to Wisdom ... still ... (*Shrugs*) ... he's dead ... Nero—best not to talk about him—burnt Rome, caused untold misery—deserved to die; died screaming in a summerhouse.
>
> (*They come to an unnamed bust and the* DOCTOR *stops.*)
>
> Unknown ... no name ... he looks serene enough, let's suppose he was you ... same fleshy face ... what happened to him? How did he die?   (99)

So Kracklite foresees his own death: a late-spring death the doctor suggests, last week of May, first week of June, peacefully, like Hadrian. Until then, limbo.

A line of busts on plinths and pedestals makes for an uncanny completeness here, the decay arrested or never permitted, no forum of crumbling ruins this, not the promiscuity of unpredictable frequentation, the mutilation of vandals chiseling off noses for resale like another character Kracklite encounters in the film, no violations of the invading horde or sacking of temples leaving upturned stones and decapitated columns, none of that in this locale becalmed for the duration of a diagnostic promenade. But take a walk down a passage that is a walk into the recognition of disease, a walk along a history of death that turns, through the play of silence, ellipsis, and question, into a personal and private late-spring sentence, to establish and abolish a difference between a cancer of the stomach and a sarcoma on a leg, to force a passage across continents and ages, flashback to match this flash-forward, to return the matter of architecture to that of statuary if only for one reason, namely to affirm that it is not stomachs that present themselves as the most fragile parts of a statue but the extremities—noses, fingers, limbs—not the guts but the appendages, the organs of passage of a different type, points of articulation with the outside, organs of assemblage or supplementarity that chip and break, fall or are cut off, like the moments of a history of prosthesis already encountered or yet to be encountered, chipped off an old block, displayed and sold for profit here, I offer another now in the context of diseased organs, late one night just me alone, a student polishing a medical-school floor for money to travel, down the corridor back and forth in even strokes concentrating on the method of handling the machine that had just been taught, calculating how long it is likely to take to get through the number of rooms assigned, down the passage past numerous carpeted offices left for the female cleaners armed with their vacuum cleaners, she vacuums he polishes is how the labor divides, I polish and veer to the right into the room labeled "Pathology Museum," a large expanse of shelved specimens like books in a library, or busts on pedestals, gathering dust except for the occasional consultation, dust the disease in the belly of any book, the threat of its cancerous degeneration through simple neglect, but dusting was not my task either, just keep to the polishing, avoid looking if possible at this array of diseased organs preserved in formaldehyde, yellow livers and pancreases, huge bulbous testicles and cross-sectioned mammary glands, gangrenous toes and melted eyes, the catalogue is long and tedious and extends at least to exhibit or specimen number 45, the very one one doesn't want to meet here, not here in the silence of the night alone in a room doing a repetitive and loveless job for the few weeks one can stand to do it, concentrate on the floor polisher that threatens always to slip out from under your grasp like any technological instrument, like writing, and crash into the shelves bringing down complete jarsful of horrors like a scene from *The Tin Drum,* don't look at number 45, it is the number of a piece of cancerous thigh, just a small piece of leg about the size of a cricket ball, small enough to fit into a jar but large enough to show the extent of the infection, the complete and utter rot that festered there dissected for generations of students to examine. It is taken from a patient aged eighteen in 1940, leg amputated, present condition unknown. I take a walk along the history of disease and come face to leg with a father, or face to face with all that remains of interest to a researcher—the pathology student there, this archivist here—the bare facts of a disease, the symptom closest to the cause, but this diseased member is also the closest signifier of a former and irredeemable wholeness arrested in its decay and monumentalized like the ruins of some ancient city. It doesn't particularly look like a piece of leg, could be one of any number of pounds of flesh from any number of parts of the body, but not too many when it comes to that, thigh or buttock, gigot or rump the only places where that particular collocation of flesh and fat is available in such quantities. It is preserved in sufficient volume to suggest a reconstitution, posited on that very principle, the leg, the ruined city, its crumbling pillars so many amputated stumps exposed to the neglect of years or preserved for the catalogue of some museum, the whole effect generalized in a Rome pictured here, place of decay and afflictions of the stomach and ruined aching thighs from walking and lovemaking with the window open to a city of cupolas and fountains, thighs bruised from rolling or staggering coupled across a parquet floor the only cool surface until the sweat condenses on this arse held in both hands, pushing once more once more once more once more, clutching a dome of warm flesh oblivious finally for the few brief moments of another climax, oblivious to the profound dysfunction or decomposition inside that will take you back to the toilet the moment consciousness returns, like a Kracklite throwing up, digesting the Roman way after every meal, you fuck and shit with unfailing regularity, you sit there with a burning colon to match an aching cock, the dull throb felt in the region of the limp member I carry around after prolonged coitus and repeated ejaculations the only thing I know to compare with the phantom sensation of an amputated leg, and the jab of involuntary peristalsis the only thing similar to the unpredictable spasm that wracks the nerves of a prosthetic thigh. You sit there glued to the john after long sex, perhaps it is the only obvious end point for any concentrated combination of the sublime in form—bodies confused with buildings—and a voracious appetite for both, obsessive optical possession of ancient monuments and compulsive sex, its obvious end point where affirmation of desire meets the recognition of mortality, in the toilet I mean, and in a confusion of sex with defecation, something I learned from my mother, as if I could learn it from anyone else, she reminded me of it with unfailing regularity all through childhood, me on my knees bare arse in the air on her bed, her fingers probing my anus fishing for worms, the life in death I carried writhing within me that only a mother's unabashed intimacy could deal with so matter-of-factly, she simply pulled them out until they bit and itched no more, and took away the smell of me on her fingers, the smell I learned as the ultimately indifferent odor of any cavity, any cavity or simulacrum of a cavity moistened with saliva, like the crease of your elbow or neck, wherever wet dead cells signify a certain turning of desire, I learned to seek it out as the smell of intimacy that was perhaps a memory of the womb, in any case it crossed over into an eroticism that crosses in turn between vagina and anus, a certain olfactory indifference of the sexual and the intestinal, a confounding of the two that returned in the unmistakable odor she left behind in the bathroom that I always thought was that of her menstrual cycle until I reached about the age she had when I first began to associate it with her, and smelled it coming from my own entrails, somewhere around the early to mid-thirties it came to me that I bore the smell of my mother inside, the odor she had taken away from me on her fingers had returned and that it was and always had been the stench of mortality, replaced now by another form of decay, the odor of Rome as desirable in its intimacy as my mother and frail as the nose on a statue and as sexual as a long barely interrupted stretch of domes or line of broken and bruised columns look like to an aching cock, as suggestive as a proliferation of fountains and pillars like some Palais Royal Daniel Buren in every possible state of tumescence and detumescence, and as sobering as the little death, the whiff of mortality of a dysfunctional bowel.

Kracklite to Boullée, Victor Emanuel Building, Thursday, January 2, 1986:

I have become obsessed with the smells of decay: a dustbin of maggots at the Campidoglio, an old woman on the Corso who sleeps on the pavement, the smell of the pissoir by the Spanish Steps, the dried excrement along the Tiber Embankment, the dustbin lorry at the Otello restaurant—yet—with disappointment I have to report that they all smell the same. Decay always, ultimately, smells the same—and now I am identified with it.   (174)

What relation between architecture and smell? Besides the obvious matters of plumbing and garbage disposal? Should we insist on further evidence of the analogy between the building and the human form, via the *domus*, the insistent economy of relations between interior and exterior, even the internal organic, and the play of penetration and expulsion, solidification and disintegration? An architecture of the digestive tract from ingestion to defecation, Kracklite's stalled in the intestine, somewhere along its 27 feet? When a group of adipose men are sitting steaming at the baths, joking with Kracklite about his condition, one of them, a doctor of medicine, claims that "the average human intestine is twenty-seven feet long but that of a priest is three feet longer" (72).

In the film the next scene (framed before and after by shots of his wife and lover in bed) has Kracklite in a clinic about to undergo a colonoscopy, writing postcards and coiling 27 feet of rubber tubing in a heap outside his belly. But if the 3 feet missing between priest and architect were made to represent something, it might as well be the scene that is cut from the film, wherein Kracklite is sitting on the floor of a lift with an eight-year-old boy. He has just come from the baths and spilled his postcards:

> I'm sending them to my friend in Paris . . . it'll help him find his way around. He died in 1799—that's nearly two hundred years ago—that's a long time—though Rome hasn't changed that much. Do I smell funny?
> (*He sniffs his armpits.*) . . .
> It's the smell of death I reckon.   (73–74)

He has spilled his postcards, and now his guts. He has admitted his own mortality. He is in a lift, which, much more than the bathroom, works as the architectural equivalent of the intestine and of defecation, a solid object forced through a narrow chamber, stopping at each floor or digestive organ, disgorging in small or large quantities on the level of the street or continuing on into the basement or bowels of the city.

So is there an architecture inspired by the olfactory sense to deconstruct that based on the visual? An idea of shelter, an economy that accounts for the most intimate functions of the organism, there where they meet their intimate contradiction in the confounding of smells emanating from the armpit, moistened skin, various orifices, in the confounding of inside and outside, function and form? Such an architecture would necessarily confound its own relation to the body and to the artistic object, returning us to the question of sculpture. If there were such an olfactory architecture, the passage from human form to construction might have a further point of relay in statuary: it might impose itself through a denial of the visual, by the closing of the eyes, the absence of the living eye. Augustus has closed eyes. Granted, in what might be read as a similar denial of the olfactory, there is also that character who chisels noses off statues. But I am not arguing here for the superseding of the visual by the olfactory, rather pointing to moments or structures of rupture in the institution of architecture as subordination of function to form, of shelter to design, an institution that might be said to derive from a set of assumptions concerning the natural hierarchical construction of the human body. From that point of view the amputated noses inscribe that rupture on the statue as much as do the closed eyes. Besides, in the thematic schema of the film, the removal of noses relates, more obviously than to the matter of smell, to the idea of Kracklite's cuckolding and sterility; it can as well be read through that schema as a sign of another rupturing of supposed natural relations, namely the confounding or perverting of sexual functions, or referring to what might be called unorthodox intercourse, like a fixation on the buttocks with or without the scent of decay, with or without the eyes open.

Once again Bataille would be able to lead us through that sort of story, such a story of the eye, through the eye to the body's innermost contradictions. For the dome of the belly turned arse about has its parallel in the eye that falls out like the contents of a broken egg and that in its evocation of and preempting of regeneration becomes, in Bataille's novel, unremittingly erotic and polymorphously perverse. The story is a catalogue of perversion that is a contagion of eyes subordinated to versions of whatever bodily functions can be contained by the word "arse," of whatever domes or eggs can crack or be laid.[16] As Bataille indicates, any story of the eye has a sandman lurking nearby, the risk being that the eye will be not just put out but put to indecent use, become fetishistic object, artificial sex aid, prosthesis to desire.

But is this the triumph of architecture over art by means of a retreat into functions regulated by smell such that sight becomes little more than an observing of architecture's functionality, a retreat that therefore amounts to the perversion and destruction of sight? Or is it a fall into engineering, an anesthetizing of whatever in the architectural moment refers to its founding heterogeneity? Or is it the undecidability of the one and the other, structure and function, the question that is the whole architectural question, the question of the line between architecture and art, home and statue, that I am attempting to draw here? How does one find the point at which it passes over, goes from diversion to perversion? The film makes its choices, it seems, between fecund belly and cancerous belly, between home and mausoleum, between celebration and exhibitionism. But it seems not to realize that they are not so much opposites to be chosen between in mutually exclusive fields as variations to be chosen among within the same structural space. Or perhaps not even chosen among but rather negotiated, like this writing, weaving in and out of the forms and functions made available to it, exploiting border crossings for its own enjoyment, throwing up a series of constructions around a set of images called a film, or winding that film around a text of idiosyncratic memories and projections, coming to rest, after all else, here, this time, again, eyes closed and head resting on the fleshy curves that constitute the real and the ideal of ancient and present Rome.

Closed eyes are the mark of classical statues and the starkest anxiety for lovers used to regulating their whole activity through a variation of focal length when they are face to face; blinking at the pain of muscular myopia when my mouth is on your mouth, my tongue seeking passage to your retina through the softness behind your palate; or when my nose feels for a way into you and into my dreams of intrauterine suspension and my nightmare—anyone's nightmare—of parturitive suffocation, and my eyes meet your eye that has only one color whoever you are; or fixing on your eyelids the vanishing point at the other extremity when I kiss the ball of your foot to make your toes flutter like eyelashes. And then suddenly we are apart and I look all over a city of statues for your eyes and find only their glazed stare. The first domes are those closed eyes, the first fountains those imagined tears, simulacra of the real tears of separated love. The name *Krack-lite* is both the description and the deconstruction of that idea. There is a fissure in his name: it begins to divide and scatter, to become a name for his eyes and then for every eye in its tendency to close or squint, its general desire to give the appearance of not seeing.

Just after dawn on Thursday, August 22, 1985, Kracklite comes home and mounts the stairs to the sound of laughter, takes a chair and sits in the hotel corridor transfixed in front of a keyhole watching Caspasian, who parades naked with a Boullée tower for a phallus and makes love to Louisa, and the child watches Kracklite cry, the primality relayed, back to front of course, down the passage to another scene where the child's mother watches him watching Kracklite watching, and so on. It is a most complex *mise en scène* of visuality, a highly configured spectacle. But it is also where the inside breaks out, or the cruel light of day seeps through the shutters you thought were clamped tight, where intimacy shatters like a crumbling stone, where the house or home begins to be poor shelter, and even the statues get cold, close their eyes, and cry:

The CHILD watches him.

CHILD: (*In English*) What are you crying for?
KRACKLITE: (*Without moving his body—but looking at the* CHILD) There's a draught in the keyhole and it's making my eyes water.
WOMAN: (*Her voice just audible from the room behind the* CHILD, *in Italian*) What's the man crying for?
CHILD: (*In Italian*) He's got a draught in his eyes. (66)

Uno spiffero, the child says in the film: *Dice che ha uno spiffero di aria negli occhi*. The Italian word describes a current that blows. It translates as "draft" in English. More precisely, in terms of the film, it begins as "draft" in English and translates into Italian such that the peculiar usage of the English word disappears out the window, as if blown away. But there is much to retrieve. Not that, it bears repeating, translation is to be conceived of as an inevitable loss any more than a certain gain, for in exploiting it here I shall again be seeking to emphasize the effect of a passage, the originary contamination of one language by another, one mode or form by another.

With reference to the body the draft signifies in the first place an inhalation, a function of the *ductus*, a drawing in or towards. In order to come to mean a current of air that blows like some accident upon the body one has to turn that former sense around, like so much else here, so that inhalation becomes exhalation or expulsion. Besides, one doesn't normally get a draft in the eyes unless one has a habit of looking through keyholes; a draft more likely falls on the back, or on the nape of the neck as I inhale and exhale with accelerating regularity and strive to expel what is inside me into the inside of you.

Then, when we come to architecture, it is hard to hold back the contagion of senses of draft blowing in any number of directions. Firstly, apart from keyholes, a draft comes through cracks in badly designed or badly constructed buildings, or those ruined by age and fallen into decay. A draft is in that sense a failure of architecture. Or of the architect, or again of his draftsman. It is something vague but chilling that blows between them and becomes a blurred line of demarcation, between the artist and the technician. For if there was some difference to be established or maintained between sculpture and architecture in terms of whichever of those forms remains closest to home on the one hand and to the body on the other, and if that were to be related in turn to a difference that one might want to make between artist and designer, between a priority given to form and one given to function, if the home were always already a body and the body always already the home, and if those differences were always already called into question at least from the point of view of this back-hand or backside reading of a film by Peter Greenaway, then there would indeed be a certain logical continuum to that very undecidability, extending all the way along the line of architectural production, among those distinctions that continue to operate according to the same principle of demarcation, between architect and draftsman, between draftsman and builder, between builder and laborer, and so on. That much should have been obvious. It should have been obvious, for instance, in the title of that earlier film, *The Draughtsman's Contract*, where the artist operates on the level of technician, on the one hand by virtue of his using a pencil, of being simply a drawer, and on the other hand, I would venture, by virtue of the mercantile relations upon which he bases his art from the beginning. For, as I have noted, from the beginning the contract explicitly involves an exchange of art for sex. And it is indeed the death of him, the death of both the draftsman and his art, a death—that is firstly a provocation and secondly a murder—that comes from defining too closely the relations between art and the body. Not to mention the fact that what he is drawing is the home, in the execution of which task he comes to interfere too much with the economy of the same, all the way from laundering duties to the question of inheritance, overstepping the lines of demarcation in any number of senses, laying bare the promiscuity of sense and inviting the play of chance until the ranks are closed around and against him to teach him a final lesson and put him irrevocably back in his place.

The draft is that disseminating wind and it is there at the beginning of both the artistic and the architectural moment, there where they are barely distinguishable, creating a crack in the dome that is the eye, in the crack itself, in the first line that is drawn, in the *trait* itself. In French, *trait* is the word for whatever is drawn. Derrida will relate it to blindness, in turn to and in common with the self-portrait and the ruin. In *Memoirs of the Blind* the hypothesis that the drawing is in some sense "blind" implies a second hypothesis that it is a blind person who draws; the theme of blindness in art comes to invade the constitution of the event of drawing, becoming a form of self-portrait by which the draft or *trait* repeats and negates itself.[17] That occurs thanks in part to a detour through the Italian, through the word *autoritratto*. This deconstruction of the draft, of the *trait*, occurs by a turning around, a turning back upon itself, and by a translation or detour through another language. But this closing of the eye in the blindness of the draft opens the eye, according to Derrida, to its anthropological essence, to something having nothing to do with sight or blindness but everything to do with some sort of primal pathos, namely the eye's capacity for weeping.[18] It is through such a compact logic, through such a system of relays of object relations, sexual relations, perceptual relations, and linguistic relations, all articulated through architectural and corporeal lines and limits, through such a draft in the eye, that this primal scene leads us.

With the scene of Kracklite weeping and being watched weeping, we are back at the beginning, at whatever passes for, or passes from, the beginning. The beginning of sight, the scene that orients and reroutes all things, the beginning of film; an image of a station, point of halt and relay, a name passing into an elsewhere, Ventimiglia. Back at the first crack in the eye, the first act of perception, the first visionary moment, but all we can draw from it is a type of blur. A scene shot from a fleeting train, the train that is also—let it not slip by us—a line of carriages *drawn* by a locomotive. A line that blurs as it draws. The first crack in the eye, the first draft, is the first line drawn, simultaneously the beginning and end of all things. The line is drawn, the eye is opened, but a draft blows, tears flow, and it all blurs. The first line drawn slices the eye like a Dali-Buñuel razor. In opening it violates the perfection, the originary wholeness, the perfect form. It is the crack in the dome.

Within the ambit of *The Belly of an Architect*, two readings of this offer themselves: the crack in the belly, the Roman or at least the Caesarean way, becomes the end of a gestation and the beginning of many things. An end for the film, the death of Kracklite, new life or lives for Louisa. Or, on the other hand, the crack in the belly becomes an upset stomach, the belly turned over, the other Roman way, *a tergo*, another crack, the backside for an eye. Against what appears as the logic of the first possibility, this inscription of something of the second: a line drawn through Rome, the plotting of a trajectory, the tracing and crossing of a frontier, a voyage and story of chasing tail.

Weeping is as much a perversion of sight as it is, in Derrida's terms, the essential function of the eye. A tear, it might be argued, forces the eye open, brings it to the point of sight, only to obscure or preempt that vision. Such a tear, such a crack in the eye, is the *trait* of a writing that crosses the domes represented here, turning belly into backside, geode into compound eye, egg into arsehole, bedroom into mausoleum, preempting generation, metamorphosing cinema and architecture, producing coup-lings that obey the logic of prosthetic contrivance.

For Kracklite at least, the weeping scene ends in an upset, an overturn-ing. His chair collapses and he falls arse over tit to the floor. The child helps him pick himself up. But my film by Peter Greenaway ends there, with Kracklite upside down, his mini-demise prefiguring the final fall. It is here that he gives the child the gyroscope that we see set in motion, then left twirling in paroxysm to a halt, just before the credits roll. It is a monument to Isaac Newton, the spinning dome, all that falling, like the one Boullée designed but never built; a monument to nature also no doubt, to nature and to the natural order:

> Outside, Kracklite has fallen on to the slope of the huge Boullée model of the truncated pyramid and broken his neck. . . . The corpse has come to rest on the roof of Caspasian's car. . . . The car roof has gently buckled and Kracklite is cradled in the metal like a child in a cot. . . . A close-up shows the pound note clasped in his hand—the apple blossom—Newton's symbol of gravity—re-vealed. There now begins a tracking-reversing crane-shot. . . . The camera continues to back away and eventually settles on the eight-year-old boy seated on a stone bench playing with his gyroscope. The camera moves into the gyroscope. The gyroscope in close-up spins round and round, its axis becom-ing more and more diagonal—until—this machine that can temporarily with-stand gravity—collapses. Cut to black. (113–14)

Though the film ends there I leave it at the same point at which this reading has always sought to depart from it, on the question of its assertion of a natural order. Against that logic of life and death, birth and undoing, across all that falling I make my crossings and turnings, I spin my tale.

How then has the film ended? With the final gyroscopic twist, jerk and fall? Or at its midpoint, my ending and beginning, a crossing or a falling that occurs in and through a passage, a passage formed by, among other things, a transfer of sight, the sound of an Italian word, *spiffero*, like Ventimiglia, from the beginning a point of crossover; and a corridor where the body falls flat on the floor, reducing the play of anatomy and architecture to a contiguity that is its whole possibility; a floor where, to the extent this film permits, I have lain flat out with you flush in curveless adjacency after the flailings and contortions of yet another coupling and called you by your name in words all gone foreign, called your name that is a number, *quarantacinque*, the number that is a code, a sesame and nothing more, it opens your arms and legs, you stretch as flat as flesh and bone permits and I fall weeping on your back my hands grasping your wrists to extend you further towards optimum horizontality, we lie spread-eagle in compound crucifixion, my tears are in your hair and on your neck and on your thighs and buttocks pressed inconsequential also, my salt on your domes will be the wear, tear, razing, and ruin of them, they will cry out any number of times for this to end and never end in urgent gentle dilapidation.

§ 7   Cambridge, 1553

About the middle of the sixteenth century there is a parting of the ways. The medieval trivium of grammar, logic, and rhetoric is breaking up and its parts are being reassigned. But before being a meeting of three ways, the tri*vium* formed the lesser "half" of a dyad whose superior half was the quadrivium of arithmetic, geometry, astronomy, and music: knowledge was first divided into a quadrivium of "sciences" and a trivium of discursive arts. One might be able to say that it is on the basis of that no doubt necessary relegation of the arts of discourse to the lower division of this dyad that the medieval unity of knowledge was both assured and doomed; assured because by recognizing in itself a certain discontinuity the body of knowledge was capable of expanding, even beyond the terms of an organicist model; doomed because that first division would be able to form the basis for any number of subsequent subdivisions that would lead to the parting of ways in about 1553.

Roland Barthes used to suggest that the sense of the commonplace or trifling conveyed by our word "trivial" came not just from the inferior position of the trivium within the medieval model but also from the idea that the intersection of three ways was a place of frequentation, a common place that was also a beat, the locus of prostitution.[1] It would be at that point or by those means that commerce and usury were introduced into human intercourse; it would be therefore the place of corruption in general. One can imagine the space of the prostitute being shared by that of some generic sophist, with the expected attendant degeneracy of discourse. The art of "setting forth" would thus be indistinguishable from the "putting oneself forth" that constitutes, etymologically at least, the solicitation of a prostitute.

Through the breakup of the trivium another "putting forth" emerges, one that is more precisely an "attaching to," namely prosthesis. With the sense that "prosthesis" has now obtained, it connotes as much an unholy alliance as a corrupted rhetoric or prostitution, for by means of it the human is subjected to an intimate relation with the inanimate. The first recorded use of the word "prosthesis" in the English language occurred in 1553. At that time, against a background of the rise of Protestantism, the ideas of Aristotle and many other classical forms of knowledge that had either survived the Middle Ages or even heralded the arrival of humanism were in retreat. Not least among those were the rhetorics of Cicero and Quintilian. In 1549 Peter Ramus (Pierre de la Ramée) published his *Arguments in Rhetoric Against Quintilian* (*Rhetoricae distinctiones in Quintilianum*): "To the subject matter of rhetoric pertains only the ascribed skill of style and delivery. . . . The parts of another art should not be intermingled with the art of rhetoric. Invention, arrangement, and memory are parts of another discipline, namely dialectic. Therefore they should not be intermingled with rhetoric."[2] Whereas Cicero had installed a five-part rhetoric of *inventio, dispositio, elocutio, memoria,* and *pronuntiatio,* Ramus was asking that it be reduced to delivery (*pronuntiatio*) and style (*elocutio*), in effect to the matter of ornamentation that it represents for us today. I shall return to Ramus shortly.

What was true of the philological disciplines was also true in respect of medicine, particularly anatomy. Andreas Vesalius's *De humani corporis fabrica* dates from 1543, when he was teaching at Padua, ever a hotbed of discontent and heresy. In it he challenged the classical teachings of Galen and is said as a result to have founded modern anatomy. 1543, it should be remembered, was also the year of Copernicus's *De revolutionibus orbium celestium.* Vesalius (1514–64) is almost exactly contemporaneous with Ramus (1515–72). So also is another important figure for prosthesis.

In 1552 Ambroise Paré (1510?–90), a barber who would later become the king's surgeon, is making his living putting back together the myriads of soldiers who are now being more effectively blown apart as a result of the introduction of handheld artillery and mobile cannon. He is there at the siege of Metz, where Henri II, taking advantage of a deal he has made with the Protestant German princes fighting Charles Quint, is seeking to occupy the town. At a village called Damvillers, near Verdun, in the killing fields of a particularly persistent European predilection, he tends to the injuries of a *gentilhomme* who was wounded in the leg by a shell that hit the tent of his employer, M. de Rohan, who is also paying Paré's salary. In order to treat his patient Paré has recourse to a practice perhaps formerly used by the Alexandrian school, but which he will now rediscover, thereby inaugurating modern surgical technique, namely ligature rather than cauterization of the arteries following amputation. It won't do any more to amputate a leg with an ax on the field of battle, apply hot oil or sulfur, and watch in puzzlement as the victim bleeds to death:

> Verily I confesse, I formerly have used to stanch the bleeding of members after amputation, after another manner. . . . Whereof I am ashamed, and agrieved; But what should I doe? I had observed my maisters whose method I entended to follow, alwaies to doe the like; who thought themselves singularly well appointed to stanch a flux of blood . . . with various store of hot Irons and causticke medicines. . . . This kinde of remedy could not but bring great and tormenting paine to the patient, seeing such fresh wounds made in the quicke and sound flesh are endewed with exquisite sense. . . . And verily of such as were burnt, the third part scarse ever recovered, and that with much adoe, for that combust wounds difficultly come to cicatrization. . . . Many were out of hope of cicatrization, being forced for the remainder of their wretched life to carry about an ulcer upon that part which was dismembered; which also tooke away the oportunitie of fitting or putting too of an artificiall legge or arme in stead of that which was taken off.
>
> Wherefore I must earnestly entreate all Chirurgions, that leaving this old, and too too cruell way of healing, they would embrace this new, which I thinke was taught mee by the speciall favour of the sacred Deitie; for I learnt it not of my maisters, nor of any other, neither have I at any time found it used by any. Onely I have read in *Galen,* that there was no speedier remedy for stanching of blood, than to bind the vessels through which it flowed towards their rootes, to wit, the Liver and Heart.[3]

Paré gives precise instructions concerning the identification of a gangrenous member and procedures for a successful amputation, adding to his treatise diagrams of the various instruments required:

> You shall certainly know . . . that the part is wholly and thoroughly dead, if it looke of a blacke colour, and bee colder than stone to your touch . . . if there bee a great softnesse of the part, so that if you presse it with your finger it rises not againe. . . . If the skinne come from the flesh lying under it; if so great and strong a smell exhale . . . that the standers by cannot endure or suffer it . . . if a fanious moisture, viscide, greene or blackish flow from thence; if it bee quite destitute of sense and motion, whether it be pulled, beaten, crushed, pricked, burnt, or cut off. Here I must admonish the young Chirurgion, that hee be not decieved concerning the losse or privation of the sense of the part.

For I know very many deceived as thus; the patients pricked on that part would say they felt much paine there. But that feeling is oft deceiptfull, as that which proceeds rather from the strong apprehension of great paine which formerly reigned in the part, than from any facultie of feeling as yet remaining. A most cleare and manifest argument of this false and deceitful sense appeares after the amputation of the member; for a long while after they will complaine of the part which is cut away. . . .

The first care must be of the patients strength, wherefore let him be nourished with meats of good nutriment, easie digestion, and such as generate many spirits; as with the yolkes of Egges, and bread tosted and dipped in Sacke or Muskedine. Then let him bee placed, as is fit, and drawing the muscles upwards toward the sound parts, let them be tyed with a straite ligature a little above that place of the member which is to be cut off, with a strong and broad fillet like that which women usually bind up their haire withall; This ligature hath a threefold use; the first is, that it hold the muscles drawne up together with the skin, so that retiring backe presently after the performance of the worke, they may cover the ends of the cut bones, and serve them in stead of boulsters and pillowes when they are healed up, and so suffer with lesse paine the compression in susteining the rest of the body. . . . The second is, for that it prohibites the fluxe of blood by pressing and shutting up the veines and arteries. The third is, for that it much dulls the sense of the part by stupefying it. . . . Wherefore when you have made your ligature, cut the flesh even to the bone with a sharpe and well cutting incision knife, or with a crooked knife, such as is here expressed.

Now you must note, that there usually lyes betweene the bones, a portion of certaine muscles, which you cannot easily cut with a large incision or dis-membring knife; wherefore you must carefully divide it and separate it wholly from the bone, with an instrument made neately like a crooked incision knife. . . . For if thou shouldest leave any thing besides the bone to bee divided by the saw, you would put the patient to excessive paine in the performance thereof; for soft things as flesh tendons and membranes, cannot be easily cut with a saw. Therefore when you shall come to the bared bone, all the other parts being wholly cut asunder and divided, you shall nimbly divide it with a little saw about some foote and three inches long, and that as neare to the sound flesh as you can. And then you must smooth the front of the bone which the saw hath made rough.

When you have cut off and taken away the member, let it bleed a little according to the strength of the patient, that so the rest of the part may afterwards be lesse obnoxious to imflammation and other symptomes; Then let the Veines and Arteries be bound up as speedily and streightly as you can; that so the course of the flowing blood may bee stopped and wholly stayed. Which may be done by taking hold of the vessells with your Crowes beake. . . .

The ends of the vessells lying hid in the flesh, must be taken hold of & drawn with this instrument forth of the muscles whereinto they presently after the amputation withdrew themselves, as all parts are still used to withdraw themselves towards their originalls. In performance of this worke, you neede take no great care, if you together with the vessells comprehend some portion of the neighbouring parts, as of the flesh, for hereof will ensue no harme; but the vessells will so bee consolidated with the more ease, than if they being bloodlesse parts should grow together by themselves. To conclude, when you have so drawne them forth, binde them with a strong double thred.

When you have tyed the Vessells, loose you Ligature which you made above the place of amputation; then draw together the lippes of the wound with foure stiches made acrosse, having taken good hold of the flesh; for thus you shall draw over the bones that part of the skinne and cut muscles drawne upwards before the amputation, and cover them as close as you can, that so the ayre may the lesse come at them, and that so the wound may bee the more speedily agglutinated.   (*Collected Works*, 457–60)

The medical renaissance of the sixteenth century runs parallel with the development, and, in a sense to be shortly explained, the immediate dissolution, of humanist rhetoric. There is nothing surprising about that. Classical and medieval forms of knowledge in various disciplines were being reappraised and modified; in fact the disciplines themselves were being reconfigured to take their modern forms. Nor is it surprising that a common language and *savoir* are to be found in fields we now consider to be far apart: rhetoric, medicine, geometry. The scientists of the classical ages could as easily be practitioners or theoreticians of one as of another. It is within such a context of the rearrangement of fields of knowledge that there occurs, in 1553, the first appearance in English of a word borrowed directly from the Greek, the word "prosthesis," in its rhetorical sense of the addition of a syllable to the beginning of a word. For the French, the medical sense of the word would come first, but not until 1695, about a decade before the rhetorical sense, which first appeared in French in 1704. At that very time (1704) Kersey's revision of Phillip's *Dictionary* would install the medical sense of "prosthesis" in English: "replacement of a missing part of the body with an artificial one."[4]

I would suggest, if only for rhetorical effect—the precise figure of which remains to be determined, especially if its effect be the ruination of rhetorical precision—that "prosthesis" first edges its way into the English language in a period when knowledge in general and the disciplines of rhetoric and medicine in particular are being not just rearranged but prosthetized—broken apart and artificially reconstructed. This form of the epistemological break, if that is what it is, is to be read, then, as a prosthetic reattachment. This is to say that whereas reference—negative or affirmative—continues to be made to classical models, received as natural forms of knowledge, their naturality is no longer considered an impediment to their wholesale reconstruction. Principles informed by the logic of a nascent rationalism, effects of discovery, and facts of earthly power may be invoked to challenge the force and assurance of classical models. Although such principles are not in themselves new to the questions they are brought to bear upon, and although they will appear in different focus in the neoclassicism of the seventeenth century before coming to represent a different kind of naturality in our time, nonetheless from the perspective of this particular juncture of the sixteenth century those principles carry something of the contrived about them; it is as though they have been newly invented, artificially constructed.

It would seem obvious to attribute the form of these challenges to classical knowledge to the rise of Protestantism and to its fomenting of an open revolt against the established authority of the Church. The historical period we are talking about here is precisely that of the Reformation. My rhetorical ploy consists to some extent in pointing to the prosthetic effect in the sense of that word, to the idea of re*formation* as artificial reconstruction. In the wake of Luther's nailing of his theses to the door of the church at Wittenberg, a word, "prosthesis," comes to be attached, tenuously to begin with, but without doubt defiantly also, to the English language.

In 1555 Ramus republished his 1543 critique of Aristotle in the French vernacular, a work entitled *Dialectique*. The extent of his challenge should not be underestimated, for in calling into question the authority of Aristotle he was in effect asking for a thorough rewriting of the curriculum of the Sorbonne and threatening to put his colleagues out of a job. The immediate effects of such a reconstruction of the body of knowledge would necessarily be political and economic. It was this rewriting of disciplinary boundaries more than some intellectual or religious heresy that had led to the Sorbonne's examination of the work when it was first published and to Ramus's proscription by François I in 1544. And it is interesting to note that after his rehabilitation by Henri II and his appointment as Dean of Regius Professors (1551), it was his interdisciplinary reach that continued to draw fire. (Already the "democratic" move by François I to institute the title of Regius Professor, on the basis of which the tradition of lectures for the general public and the Collège de France would be born, had instituted an alternative to the academic structure of disciplines at the Sorbonne, an alternative that lasts with us to this day.) Ramus gave himself the title of Regius Professor of Rhetoric and Philosophy—he would be the first and last to hold that office—and was accused by a pamphleteer, probably named Picard, in any case someone who would be reincarnated in time for a similar quarrel almost exactly four centuries later, of roving about at will throughout the curriculum "following no particular route but merely barking at theoretical odds and ends."[5] Ramus will convert to Protestantism in about 1561 but will be condemned even by the Reformists in 1572 for favoring lay government of the Church. However, that will matter little when, on the third day of the Saint Bartholomew's Day Massacre, in spite of the protection he has enjoyed from Henri II, including shelter at Fontainebleau and at the royal abbey at Royaumont, protection continuing after Henri's death thanks to his wife, Catherine de' Medici, who is said to have given express orders that he not be harmed when she unleashes the furious bloodletting of those days, Ramus is killed in his rooms and his body thrown out the window, decapitated, and thrown into the Seine.

Now, one would be hard-pressed to argue that as an event of intellectual rebellion Protestantism has more of the prosthetic about it than any other such rejection of the reigning orthodoxy. To make such an argument is not my purpose here, but rather to take this moment, or rather this movement, as a case in point within the structural history of prosthetization. Prosthesis does not begin with the arrival of the word in the English language, but on the other hand that event becomes one type of beginning for our being able to call it that. Protestantism involves the replacement of one body of doctrine for another, a supposedly less hierarchized faith to replace the deadness and perversions of the institutionalized church, although that replacement is seen not as an addition but rather as a return to an original and living truth. However, one might argue that the particular type of exegetical and political challenge that Protestantism represented allowed for subsequent developments in fields such as medicine and rhetoric. In the case of medicine there is a challenge to the integrity of the living body, a challenge different from that represented by the dissections and anatomical advances of Leonardo, while in the case of rhetoric the challenge is made to the integrity of the word. And a case might be made for calling such a challenge that of prosthesis.

Protestantism thus represents, particularly at its emergence, the paradox of what is on the one hand a profound logocentrism—a return to living truth, the opening of paths back to presence—and on the other hand an iconoclasm that institutes forms of individual interpretation, what its detractors referred to as the relativism of "opinion" as opposed to the time-honored precepts of the schools. But there is of course something other than Protestantism that serves as a background to the renaissances of the sixteenth century, something that, although belonging to the previous century, acts as a condition of possibility for Protestantism; namely the invention of the printing press. The resultant dissemination of texts allowed for debate on the basis of authenticity—questions of correctness of transcription and translation—and at the same time installed the whole problematics of reading and interpretation, the dialectic of commentary versus text. In what might be called this first cybernetic moment, no different of course from the first "moment" of the *technē* in general— memory, the wheel, the pen, what you will—the human hand is super-seded by the machine in the service of truth.

This is never in clearer focus than in the case of Ramus. His Protestant-ism is not, strictly speaking, an issue until his conversion. But by writing in French he both evokes the idea of a text that is more "present" to its readers and, at the same time, to the extent that he continues to refer to classical sources, posits the necessity of translation. He dismisses Aristotle as pure *commentitia* and seeks to return to a text that is free of such invention. But he also dwells on the errors and distortions of the manuscript text. Now, as Antoine Compagnon recounts, the originality of Ramus's innovation takes a most telling form. Both the effects of technicity and the question of translation, the reconstitution of textuality and the reassertion of authen-ticity, come together in the material form of the typeface of his text:

In the *Dialecticae partitiones* of 1543 only a single typeface, namely Roman, is used, except for the preface, which is entirely in italics. Quotation marks are not used, they do not exist. On the other hand, starting with the first French edition of his *Dialectique*, all citations inserted in the text are distinguished by typography: when they are in verse they are printed in italics ... when they are in prose, exclusively that of Cicero, a back-to-front comma appears in the margin at the level of the lines where the citation begins and ends, two such commas appearing in the margin of the intervening lines. These indications, pointing to the quotation marks of the future . . . represent an extraordinary innovation. . . . It is tempting to consider that this book was at the same time the first philosophical work in French and the first to have recourse to quotation marks, the two phenomena being moreover corollaries since it is consistently translations from foreign languages that are so signaled. Before indicating quotations, the displacement from one discourse to another, quotation marks signify a more essential and more serious translation, that from one language to another.[6]

Thus the break in the continuity of papal authority is matched by a break in the continuity of the written word. It becomes marked by its diacritical other, confined first to the margins but already invading the context of writing. What had been uninterrupted discourse, *flumen orationis*, came to be a text marked with its contrived differences, the artificial enfoldings and articulations that we now take for granted as the markers of accuracy and authenticity. The conception of the text based on the linearity of recitation comes to be replaced by a different spatial model, one designed for silent reading. As Compagnon notes, it is this modification of textual forms that characterizes the first printed documents much more than the idea of multiple reproductions, since, to begin with, the press did not produce any more copies than could be produced by the largest guilds of scribes.[7] When such changes in textual form are analyzed in conjunction with the modification of rational argument that attended them, there is good reason to hold that the sixteenth century does not fit Foucault's description of an age still marked by faith in the resemblance of words and things. Words have indeed already taken on the different form that the printing press gives them; they have already attained a materially independent form: "Writing is no longer the writing of things, or at least it is the writing of those manufactured things that are printer's characters. . . . Writing no longer refers to the world, to the prose of the world; it refers to the printed volume."[8] It is this moment or movement that asks for the right to be called prosthetic. It is based on the explicit cutting up of the printed text, on the manufactured character of the word, on the contrivance of its visual form, on the technologization of knowledge, its removal from human control. It is not for nothing that the press was at first called *ars artificialiter scribendi* ("an artificial way of writing") and was later to be further mechanized by the *machine à écrire* (typewriter) and word*processor.* "In the sixteenth century," Compagnon writes, "the quality proper to the sign is artifice."[9]

But Peter Ramus is an ocean ahead, or at least away, from Thomas Wilson, who publishes his *Arte of Rhetorique* in 1553 and introduces prosthesis to the English language. Wilson seemingly offers no radical challenge to rhetorical norms, none, that is, outside of the humanism of his age. He simply sets out to represent the Ciceronian model. He is motivated by a Protestant fervor, but it is something of a triumphant one, at least in the England of the time of his *Rhetorique*. His text does, however, have the distinction of being the first rhetoric to appear in English, and was popular enough to undergo eight reeditions in the course of Wilson's lifetime, before falling into oblivion: "In an important sense, this was the first complete English rhetoric, for it was the first to treat in English all five Ciceronian arts, from *inventio* to *memoria*. But what makes the work an example of typically English humanism is not merely its full treatment of those arts but its complex and utterly doomed efforts to make Ciceronianism at home in sixteenth century England."[10] Two years earlier Wilson had published a logic, *The Rule of Reason*, and between them the two works summed up the state of the arts of reason and discourse in English humanism. Later, in the year Ramus falls victim to the assassins of the St. Bartholomew's Day Massacre, Wilson, suffering himself from a lame leg sustained "through an overthwarte myssehappe,"[11] will add to that list *A Discourse Uppon Usurye* (1572). By then he has served as Elizabeth's ambassador to Portugal, and obtained the confessions of Norfolk's secretaries under torture before arresting the duke himself. He will go on to become ambassador to the Lowlands and finally secretary of state before his death in 1581.

There is no record of the particular unfortunate mishap that injured Wilson's leg. But, as has already been suggested, he is no stranger to the reigning art of surgery that was torture in the sixteenth century. Then, as now, it could not have been carried out without an accompanying medical knowledge. Indeed, one might expect that then, as now, the torture chamber would, like the battlefield, be in the forefront of a certain form of medical research, a testing of the limits of the body, the limits between life and death. Wilson had experience of both sides of that oldest of prosthetic devices, the rack. He followed a number of prominent Protestants into exile in 1554 after the death of King Edward and the ascent of the Catholic Queen Mary. After a time in Padua with his former masters from Cambridge, he traveled to Rome, where, after wisely refusing Mary's summons to make "undelayed repaire into this oure Realme of England, and person-allie appere before us and oure privie councell attendant here on oure persons at or before the XVth of June next for suche causes as at your comynge shalbe further declared unto you,"[12] he was arrested by the Inquisition and imprisoned in the Castel Sant'Angelo. There, according to his own account reported in the preface to the second edition of *The Arte of Rhetorique* (1560), he experienced something of the Inquisitor's sting: "God bee my Judge, I had then as little feare (although death was presente, and the torment at hande, whereof I felt some smarte) as ever I had in all my life before" (11). But a popular insurrection that followed the death of Pope Paul IV brought about his release in 1559. He sees fit to report this in his book on rhetoric as part of a plea for what we might call free speech, but just how free the Protestant powers' conception of rhetoric was became apparent shortly thereafter.

It needs to be noted, then, that if there is a point at which medicine and rhetoric meet in a prosthetic moment *in extremis*, it is in the case of torture. There the precise word is wrung from the body with the aid of an instrument, but not as authentic utterance, rather as entirely artificial construction motivated by the expectation of the torturer. One might argue that it is in fact the end of rhetoric, for there is no room in the event of torture for ornamental discourse, that language is reduced to its lowest common denominator, that of information. But that would be a naive argument, for the discourse of the torturer, not to mention the cries of pain, has to be considered one of the most highly developed of rhetorical forms. In this sense the rhetoric of torture can no doubt be called constant in spite of whatever modifications have occurred in the relations between medicine and rhetoric and in the theory of rhetoric and the practice of torture. The transhistorical recurrence of torture and the fact that the theoretician of sixteenth-century English rhetoric was both victim and perpetrator of torture represent the other side of the specific historic conjunction of medicine and rhetoric, print and Protestantism, that I am describing here and calling prosthesis. There remains something pro-foundly ahistorical about it that belies the significance of the particular event that is the first printed use of the word by Thomas Wilson. That is to say that if, in the middle of the sixteenth century, there emerges a particu-lar configuration of medical and rhetorical knowledge that continues to be refined up to the present day, and whose characteristics suggest that the modern age might reasonably be called the age of prosthesis, then from the point of view of the relation between medicine and rhetoric called torture, the practice of attaching devices to bodies for the purpose of extracting verbal information, indeed from the point of view of violence done to the body in general, prosthesis reveals itself as nothing so much as a timeless event that renders this rejection of classical disciplines in favor of modern ones more of a "local" occurrence.

1553 was a good year for words. Probably no better than many other years, but one with some telling introductions. "Cannibal" and "cardamom," "dollar" and "enjoyment," "hyacinth" and "nemesis" are all supposed to have found their way into English that year.[13] And more telling still, neighbors on an alphabetical list between "procurance" and "quinquereme," and still close acquaintances through their variants and adjectival forms in today's *Oxford English Dictionary*, "prosthesis" and "prostitution."[14] The two forms of unnatural or unholy alliance are named in the language in the same year. The second word names a degenerate relation between one integral body and another, an illicit coupling with an outsider; it is therefore fitting that the usage should have come into the language by way of a translation of a text on the soon-to-be-colonial other, for it is a corruption that comes from the outside. In his *Treatyse of the Newe India*, Richard Eden will write, "By whiche common prostitucion of the quene (in Calicut), he may well iudge that the chyldren borne of her are not to be estemed as his owne" (*OED* XII: 674). The first names a supplementary relation interior to the body of a word. Prosthesis is an excess with respect to the word (doubly so since not only does that word enter English by means of the event of Wilson's *Rhetorique*, but the word Wilson uses in his example—"berattle"—will also be first performed by that very use, to be performed many times over in a line spoken by Rosencrantz [*Hamlet* II.ii] thereafter). The event occurs in the third book of Wilson's *Arte of Rhetorique*, "Of Apte Chusyng and Framyng of Wordes and Sentences Together, Called Elocucion," in the section entitled "Figures of a Worde" (see Fig. 3):

> Those be called figures of a word, when we chaunge a worde, and speake it contrarie to our vulgare and daily speache. Of the whiche sorte, there are sixe in nomber.
>
> i. Addition at the first.
> ii. Abstraction from the first.

    iii. Interlacyng in the middest.
    iv. Cuttyng from the middest.
    v. Addyng at the ende.
    vi. Cuttyng from the end.

Of Addition. As thus: He did all to berattle hym.   Prosthesis.
Wherein appereth that a sillable is added to this
worde (rattle.) Here is good nale to sel, for good ale.

Apheresis Of Abstraction from the first, thus. As I romed
    al alone, I ganne to thynke of matters greate. In which sentence, (ganne) is
    used, for beganne.
Epenthesis Interlacyng in the middest. As. Relligion, for Religion.
Syncope Cuttyng from the middest. Idolatrie, for Idololatrie.
Proparalepsis Addyng at the end. Hasten your busines, for, Haste your busin
    esse.
Apocope Cuttyng from the end. A faire may, for, maide.   (353–54)

What must be noted about this list of Greek words ornamenting the margins of a section of Wilson's *Rhetorique* is precisely their marginality. Wilson does not yet follow Ramus's lead in using quotation marks (first used in an English text in 1579),[15] but the rubric headings are clearly separated from the text. And, by a strange quirk that we could well make much of, the single word "prosthesis," in contrast with the other terms and the text proper, appears in Roman type rather than black-letter gothic. It is also in a larger pitch than the other terms in the margin. Prosthesis thus more clearly marks its foreignness, the fact of its being a translation, and for us of course, the fact of its effecting a translation. For being the first known printed use of the word, it is doubtful, therefore, to what extent this event signals the entry of "prosthesis" into English. Or rather, then as now, it can never simply enter the language, never be simply assimilated, for it is the sign and index of nonassimilation, the originary dehiscence that ruptures the integrity of language and meaning itself. This nonentry signifies precisely a form of foreignness that is revealed to be always already attached to the body lexical and philological. While it is true that any new word will, at the point of its entry into the language, act as a neologism whose effect can only be described as a kind of foreignness, that of an artificial addition, it is also a fact that that otherness takes a precise typographic form in this early printed text by Thomas Wilson. That is to say that as the continuous stream of medieval discourse is being broken by

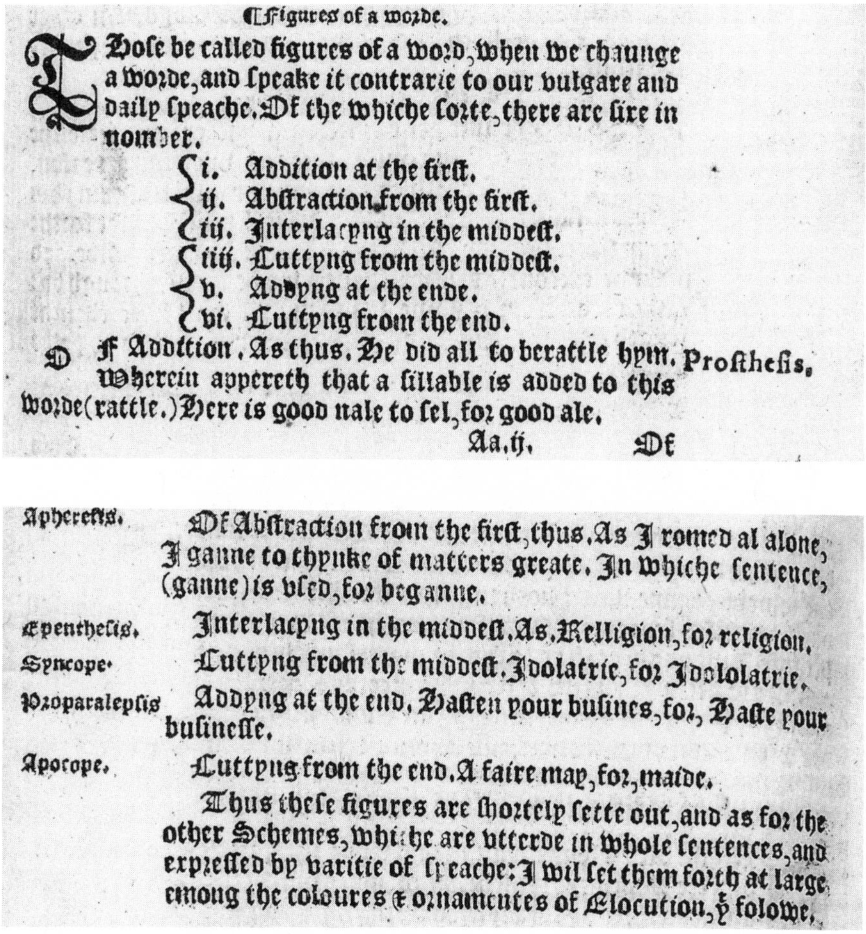

¶ Figures of a worde.

Those be called figures of a word, when we chaunge a worde, and speake it contrarie to our vulgare and daily speache. Of the whiche sorte, there are sixe in nomber.

- i. Addition at the first.
- ij. Abstraction from the first.
- iij. Interlacyng in the middest.
- iiij. Cuttyng from the middest.
- v. Addyng at the ende.
- vi. Cuttyng from the end.

Of Addition. As thus. He did all to berattle hym. Prosthesis. Wherein appereth that a sillable is added to this worde (rattle.) Here is good nale to sel, for good ale.

Aa.ij.   Of

Apheresis. Of Abstraction from the first, thus. As I romed al alone, I ganne to thynke of matters greate. In whiche sentence (ganne) is used, for beganne.

Epenthesis. Interlacyng in the middest. As Relligion, for religion.

Syncope. Cuttyng from the middest. Idolatrie, for Idololatrie.

Proparalepsis. Addyng at the end, Hasten your busines, for, Haste your businesse.

Apocope. Cuttyng from the end. A faire map, for, maide.

Thus these figures are shortely sette out, and as for the other Schemes, whiche are utterde in whole sentences, and expressed by varitie of speache: I wil set them forth at large emong the coloures & ornamentes of Elocution, that folowe.

Fig. 3 Thomas Wilson, *The Art of Rhetorique*, 1553, Folio 94 r/v. Photo courtesy of the Newberry Library.

spatial articulations that appear on the printed page, one of the words performing that task is a word whose sense is here restricted to a minor orthographical variation, but on the basis of which the integrity of any body will come to be deconstructed and reconstructed.

Wilson was strongly against the pretentious use of foreign words for rhetorical effect. He called them "ynkehorne termes," a literary perversion explicitly related to the act of writing:

Some farre jorneid jentlemen at their returne home, like as thei love to go in forrein apparell, so thei wil pouder their talke with oversea language. He that cometh lately out of France, wil talke Frenche English and never blushe at the matter. Another choppes in with Englishe Italianated, and applieth the Italian phrase to our Englishe speaking, the whiche is, as if an Oratour that professeth to utter his minde in plaine Latine, would needes speake Poetrie, and farre fetched colours of straunge antiquitie.   (326)

None of that Frenchified pretentiousness for him. However, when it comes to the first use of tropes—and the paradigm here is of course metaphor—the act of translation has to be recognized as the basis of the rhetorical enterprise. It occurred first when "learned and wise menne . . . founde full ofte muche wante of wordes to set out their meanynge" (341), but "also when they maye have mooste apte wordes at hande, yet wyll they of a purpose use translated wordes. And the reason is this. Menne counte it a poynte of witte to passe over suche woordes as are at hande, and to use suche as are farre fetcht and translated" (343). Thus the translation that metaphor operates is precisely that from necessity to superfluity, from want to wit. It is the supplementary movement towards ornamentation that divides the space of language between the proper and the foreign, passing from what is at hand to what is far-fetched and translated. And the place across which the rhetorical shift occurs, the locus of its translation, is the body, for "every translation is commenly, and for the most part referred to the senses of the body" (343). Thus we might easily read the "setting forth" that constitutes rhetoric in Wilson's parlance—"plaine settyng forthe" (355) or "lively settyng forthe" (356)—as a "putting to," a *pro(s)-thesis*, an attachment constructed on the body. We are back to the two unholy alliances or illicit couplings referred to earlier: rhetoric as the prostitution of language and rhetoric as its prosthetization, the putting forth or setting out by means of which the plain or lifeless inanimate becomes lively.

Yet the artificial remains as a threat to language once the translation into the otherness of metaphor and rhetoric has been allowed. It shows up most plainly, for instance, in the case of rhyme. Employed within prose, it is the catastrophe of a similar ending—*similiter cadens*—that waits at the term of a line as at the outer limit of language, there where its excess risks perverting the pleasurable into something with the dimensions of the monstrous, or at least what is inordinate or beyond measure:

Sentencies also are said to fal like, when diverse wordes in one sentencie ende in lyke cases, and that in ryme. . . . I speake thusmuche of these two figures, not that I thinke folie to use them (for thei are pleasaunt and praise worthie) but my talke is to this end, that thei shoulde neither onely nor chefely be used, as I know some in this our time do overmuche use them in their writynges. And overmuch (as al men know) was never good yet. . . . Therefore a measure is best, yea even in the best thynges.   (402, 404)

By means of rhyme, as that which is representative of wordplay and figurative usage in general, language is heard to fall outside of the body, to resonate with a life of its own that, however pleasant and musical it be, risks having an artificial ring to it and being perceived as a form of contrivance. But this is of course the paradox of all rhetoric. On the one hand it clothes language in more pleasant and even regal attire: "Elocucion getteth wordes to set furthe invencion, and with suche beautie commendeth the matter, that reason semeth to bee clad in purple, walkyng afore, bothe bare and naked" (323). But on the other hand rhetoric risks making language look as though it is wearing borrowed garb or done up like a hustler loitering at the crossroads.

When it comes to memory—and remember that Wilson will be one of the last to preserve this function within the domain of rhetoric, such that the Platonic construct of it that appears in his text is quite obviously already coming apart—an artificial side will have to be acknowledged:

Memorie is partly naturall, and partly artificiall. Naturall memorie is when without any preceptes or lessons, by the onely aptenesse of nature, we beare awaie suche thynges as wee heare. . . . But nowe concerning the other kinde of memorye called artificial, I had neede to make a long discourse, considering the straungenesse of the thinge to the English eare, and the hardnes of the matter, to the ignoraunte and unlearned.   (418–19, 420)

What the "long discourse" amounts to is a recounting of the Simonides story followed by a more general repetition of the Aristotelian principles of the *topoi*, or commonplaces, namely the assigning of places and the attaching of images to those places: "They that wyll remember manye thinges and rehearse them together out of hande: muste learne to have places, and digest Images in them accordingly" (422). Granted, these are not the precise commonplaces of the classical sources, and they represent an exercise of invention. But the taxonomic economy in force amounts to the same thing: whereas discourse was best served by the traditional rhetorical exploitation of exemplary themes or passages whose repetition both marked out language in terms of its spaces and established receptacles within language for its disassembled parts, so here artificial memory operates by means of a creation of spaces that will be filled by a process of selection and retention, disjunction and re*place*ment. In the case of artificial memory the operation is described in terms that place it outside the bounds of natural language, for it is such a process of disjunction and replacement that defines the artificial or prosthetic. In the process, however, the reasoning discloses the fall outside that constitutes the rhetorical exercise in general. Artificial memory is finally nothing more than a reconstruction of language itself, now represented in the technological form of writing, since Plato the *mnemotechnique* par excellence:

    i. The places of Memory are resembled unto Waxe and Paper.
    ii. Images are counted lyke unto letters or a Seale.
    iii. The placing of these Images, is like unto wordes written.
    iiii. The utteraunce and using of them, is like unto readynge. (424)

In spite of the obvious contrivance of artificial memory, what creates its exteriority is less the use of places—for the places to be used are familiar and reasonably constant (a room, a body, and so on)—than the idea of the image. For the images, even when they are gleaned from nature, are notable for both their force of invention and their variation, and thus finally for their capacity to pervert and corrupt. That the image represents not just what falls outside of the act of speaking and remembering, but the corruption that deserves to be cast out, becomes clear in examples Wilson has recourse to elsewhere. There it is a question of the graven image, of the idolatry, or "idololatrie" whose excessive impertinence signifies the apostasy of the Roman Church. It represents the foreign barbarism in general, "ynkehorne termes" in concrete form that have found their way from secular works into the religious sphere and must needs be banished hence:

> And therfore heretofore Images were sette up for remembraunce of Sainctes, to be laye mennes bokes, that the rather by seinge the Pictures of suche menne, they might be stirred to folowe their good livynge. The whiche surely hadde bene well done, if God had not forbidden it. But seinge thinges muste be done not of a good entente, but even as God hath commaunded, it is well doone that suche Idolles are cleane taken oute of the churche. (430)

Not only out of the church but clean out of the kingdom. The truth of that is worthy of repetition: "I might saie thus of our soveraine lord the Kynges majestie that now is. Kyng Edwarde hath overthrowne idololatrie: Kyng Edwarde hath bannished superstition" (399). Apart from the whole Judeo-Christian tradition in which the idol offends as an artificial construction of the ineffable, what is at stake here is the dividing line between religion on the one hand and mythology as the locus of literature on the other. It is a dividing line under particular pressure as a result of both the Protestant challenge to the construction or constitution of the church and the arrival of the printed book. In the first instance one particular common place, namely the church, is at risk as a rhetorical depository because of the role of the image in the Aristotelian schema. Indeed, as Compagnon notes, the Protestant iconoclastic impulse might help to account for Ramus's total rejection of *memoria* from the space of rhetoric.[16] But Wilson's rejection of images from the church, which also implicitly amounts to a rejection of the function of the commonplace, is further complicated by the fact that in the age in which he is writing, in the shadow of Gutenberg and Caxton, rhetoric in general has found for itself a more specific place, namely the book. The "images" that memory assigns to that place henceforth take the graven form of the printed word and are thus structurally comparable to those images of the biblical injunction: "God forbadde by expresse worde to make any graven Image, and shal we be so bolde to breake Gods wil for a good entent, and call these Idolles laie mens Bookes?" (392). In other words, as I read Wilson here, there is more than a hint of guilt by association between the idol and the book. The book is preferable to the image within the confines of the church; but the book or literature, as an increasingly common place for "images" or rhetorical usage in general, risks repeating the fallen structure of the Roman Church. Of course, it is not clear that a nascent Protestantism felt more threatened than liberated by the arrival of print, or that it explicitly denounced it as a form of idolatry. But Wilson's as it were unwitting association of one form of idolatry with another suggests that the iconoclastic fervor of Protestantism could not be restricted to the topos of the church once it had intervened in the structure of artificial constructions. The diatribes of puritanism against the book, all the way down to contemporary fundamentalisms, remind us of that.

Idolatry inaugurates the structure of iconoclasm: if bodily forms can be constructed they can also be broken. Idolatry creates a temporal and thus perishable material form where there was previously assumed to be only immateriality; it is a case of the body's falling out of its own self-presence into a specific kind of materiality, and, as the Protestant experience and indeed any experience of heterodoxy demonstrates, it invites dismantling and reconstruction. The paradox of Protestantism may be read here, in the conservatism of its heterodoxy. By rejecting the image as a form of idolatry it sought to return to a form of divine presence that preceded figural representation. But the existence of the artificial image was a condition of possibility of Protestantism's iconoclasm; it was able to depart from orthodoxy only because there never was a presence untouched by representational departures, by figural drift.

To recapitulate: the translation that Wilson finds all rhetoric to depend upon leads not only to the threat of the foreign but to a specific form of otherness that is the artificial. In terms of the logic of the *Rhetorique*, that artificial reveals itself sooner or later, namely in terms of the dual memory; but in terms of the rhetoric of the *Rhetorique*, the artificial is more eloquently present as the idolatry that must be shunned and even destroyed. And finally, in terms of my rhetorical congruence of Protestantism and the printing press, of new rhetorical practices and new medical practices, the artificial is present as the word "prosthesis" that appears as a marginal import in Wilson, but whose sense informs every rhetoric as a potentially radical form of intervention within the body of language. While he allowed for the explicit entry of the word into English, Wilson was at the same time involved in limiting its effect. But by being written in the vernacular, his whole enterprise was already an iconoclastic translation. As the contemporary experience of Ramus clearly reminds us, that could not but mean the reconstruction of a whole body of knowledge.

But nowe, because I have halfe weried the reader with a tedious matter, I will harten him agayne with a merye tale.

Four hundred years later, about the middle of the twentieth century, in 1953 to be precise, another Wills son is born, born to a man who some fourteen years earlier had his left leg amputated. Some nineteen years after that date, around the quadricentennial of the Saint Bartholomew's Day Massacre, they part ways. They ride in the car to a point on the edge of the town where the son will get out to hitchhike his way to the city where he now lives and studies. It is early one winter morning with the frost on the ground and the light shining in eerie refractions through the shroud of fog as my father sets me down at an intersection that gives birth to a straight stretch of road leading into the countryside. There he bids me farewell. It is a meeting of four ways, this place of separation, a well-frequented nexus of common automobile comings and goings and perfect for the particular solicitation I am about to embark upon. Someone will pick me up, provided I am walking rather than appearing to loiter, and for the price of some company and humdrum if inquisitive conversation, I will be given a ride at least part way to my destination. And so we part ways, my father and I, but only in a manner of speaking. There is nothing momentous about the incident, just an unidentifiable sentiment of emptiness coupled with an uneasiness about what to say more exaggerated than the normal taciturnity of our relations. Even sitting side by side in the car, with its automatic gearbox that no longer requires the use of two legs, we both know we are already traveling in different directions. But gone is the tug of fierce resistance or open revolt on my side, gone the ultimatums and threat of rejection on his. This is not yet an acceptance of a new relationship on renegotiated terms but something a little more reassuring than an uneasy peace. He tells a poor joke concerning some famous last words about loving the early morning roads because they are so empty and I smile visibly. We come to the same spot where he has deposited me before, and he lets me go with a friendly handshake and presses a five-dollar note into my palm. Suddenly there is a place and an image for my memory. This point, halfway alighting from a car, between two places rather than safely positioned within one, on the mobile threshold of a separation, becomes the locus for my recollection of the scant extent of my medical experience. For whereas he at my age had suffered through the pain of the scalpel, the loss of a limb, the fear of a recurring disease and likely death, or at least the anticipation of a crippled adulthood, I had felt nothing more than the prick of an occasional inoculation.

There is one in particular that comes back to me at that precise moment. The inoculations were dispensed with bureaucratic regularity—a special form of irregularity that is dependable in its repetitions but less so in its punctuality—by the health authorities through the public school system. It seems we were vaccinated against polio, measles, tetanus, and the like, mostly by injection but later more and more by oral ingestion. It was an event that disrupted the tedium of classes but brought with it its own dose of adrenalin and nervousness, the more so the younger we were. But I have to say I was used to the idea of inoculations. I no longer remember why I missed the one in question but the reason was no doubt one of the minor illnesses that children fall prey to, which had kept me at home on the appointed day. As a result I had to go to another school to catch up on an injection. I recount this only because the prospect was as terrifying to me as the threat of the rack. Not the injection itself, but having to go to a foreign place to subject myself to it.

It seems likely that I was seven or eight years old, but I may have been nine or ten. The memory is of an inordinate fear completely out of proportion with both the gravity of the occasion and my supposed maturity and ability to cope with it. I came home at lunchtime, walking the block and a half, across the pedestrian crossing to the tiny "dairy" as we called it, the corner store that survived my final departure by only a couple of years, and by then it was no longer the place where one could purchase fresh bread baked daily or where the delegated class representative would take the orders each morning for those fortunate enough to get to buy lunches rather than having to eat boring sandwiches such as those we got up early each morning to make once we were old and able enough, before that it was my sister or my mother, and only once a year, on our birthdays, were we allowed to add our order to the list that would be carried that morning across the road to the dairy, an event that required days of forethought in order to decide what to buy within the budgetary allocation, whether a plain meat pie and a doughnut or some similar friandise, and then whether a plain doughnut or jam-filled variety, or whether a shepherd's pie and some combination of potato chips and the like, nothing that, in hindsight, one would really want to eat, but however difficult the task it was not one that concerned me that day as I walked home past the dairy, crossing the road on my own, looking left, then right, then left again, I could never shake that routine or manage to reverse it correctly once I came to countries where they do roads and cars back to front, but that wasn't concerning me either that day, I was simply looking forward to the half hour or so of sanctuary I would have once I was home and eating whatever my mother had prepared for lunch before leaving with my father to go to that other school. I turned left at the end of the long driveway that led to our house, at the point where the garbage bins were placed on Sunday nights, the point at which I would wave to my friends in the first year of school when those of us they called "tiny tots" were escorted home in pairs holding hands and I was always first to fall out until someone else had the temerity to live even closer to school than I, and the others would continue on their way I never understood exactly how far, for surely their destinations would begin to diverge exponentially after a few blocks, but be that as it may, I turned left where I had a couple of years previously been used to parting ways from my classmates and headed up the driveway just as my father turned his car in off the road, which became the pretext for a feigned race up to the house, where sure enough lunch was waiting, and where the time passed altogether too fast, even including the ten minutes my father stretched out on his back on the bare floor for his catnap, and we were soon in the car together again heading in the same direction down the driveway and across the narrow bridge spanning the river called the Waikato, it means "swiftly flowing water" in Maori, across to the other side of town where my father worked at a job that was far from a calling, but whatever calling may have come his way had been preempted both by his parents' reluctance—informed by their religious beliefs—to let him embark upon an intellectual career and by the fact of an amputation coming soon after the end of his secondary studies, and then later by the fact of an increasing number of mouths to feed, four in reasonably quick succession and then two more after me, but he went to the job every day and came home nearly every day for lunch and he took me back with him to a school that was far from mine and let me go in the care of someone I didn't recognize and don't remember, I don't remember much about it at all, just sitting waiting on a bench with a group of children who were all complete strangers and who saw no reason to speak to me, I don't even remember the injection, nor whether it was administered by more of a butcher than those at my school who wiped our arms with alcohol as they tried to marry the matter-of-factness necessary to get through a hundred or so inoculations with the token personal touch and reassurance, I never came across a butcher in fact and there may or may not have been an increase or diminution of such a personal touch accorded me once they were informed I was a special case with a file sent from another district, I couldn't tell and wouldn't remember, only that the supervising teacher was kind and when it was all over I walked the short distance from the school back to my father's place of work and he drove me home again, and it was then, at about two o'clock in the afternoon, with an hour or so of schooltime remaining, that I balked at the idea of returning to school, it seemed such a monstrous thing to do, not because I didn't enjoy classes, on the contrary, and not because I couldn't have caught up on what I had missed or wouldn't have been accepted back into the swing of things or wouldn't even have had a tale or two to tell my friends about the school on the other

side of town, but there was no getting away from it, I just didn't want to do
it, I even broke down and cried in the bitter dejection that has me
astonished even now from which perspective I still cannot fathom the
reason of it, some Rubicon had been crossed, in some way I had gone over,
I had left, I had parted ways with my own sense of direction and found
myself drowning in the uncertainty of my eight-year-old position in the
world over the matter of a vaccination, my overwhelmingly minor skir-
mish with the fringes of the medical establishment outside of the experienced boundaries of my own school, or the doctor's surgery, or the sickbed
at home, usually my parent's bed with the door opened onto the breakfast
room where the children spent the day when they were ill, I was flounder-
ing in a rhetorical void without so much as a commonplace to set my
bearings on, I just cried from the confusion and my parents explained that
my absence for the whole afternoon had not been envisaged and that I
would have to return to school, and I could only be induced by having my
father put me back in the car once more and drive me the block and a half
to the school gate, the only time in memory that he ever did so, and
though my tears were dried by that point he tousled my hair before I
alighted and pressed a coin into my hand, it was a sixpence and my prize
for being grown up enough to do what had to be done, but I felt an
inexplicable combination of gratitude and resentment, gratitude for his
staying with me through the whole thing, going the extra 75 yards, and
resentment because I didn't think I deserved the sixpence, and besides
those two a third sentiment, that which comes with being party to a
collusion, for the sixpence fitting neatly in the center of my palm was like a
talisman that betokened a pact, the secret of that experience that was
shared only by my father and myself, the sign that an amputee buffeted by
the rigors of pains real and phantom understood a child's fear of a needle
administered by a strange hand in a foreign place, it was a coin the size of a
nickel but the thickness of a dime, with the impression of a queen on one
side and a bird called a fantail on the other, and it would not survive the
changeover to decimal currency, once the dollar had entered the language
and the mechanics of exchange, the sixpence disappeared losing with it all
it betokened, the details of a moment between father and son, the mys-
tique of a prize given by one to the other, it had long disappeared by the
time prize-giving came around some years later, when I had doubled my
age and was close to the point of departure of this recounting, for this is
about a convergence, a meeting of incidences that is also a parting of ways,

about things that come from the margins of memory to enter the space and place of rhetorical commerce, there were two prizes that came my way in my last year in high school, one for English and one for Latin, endorsable for books only, I had never possessed many of those, the occasional birthday present, the annual prize, and the texts we used in classes were provided by the school and had to be returned to the common pool, and through most of my childhood the only books at home were a small number of reference volumes and a shelf full of tomes of biblical exegesis and the like, so it was with a delight approaching kleptomania that still loosens my bowels among the library stacks that I looked forward to choosing my two volumes, and not from the selection that was set aside for that purpose on a table in one of the study rooms, for in recognition of my status as a final-year student I was given a token for a certain sum and accorded utter liberty in procuring the books of my choice from a local bookstore, and I knew what I wanted already, and I knew that I wanted it as much out of provocation as anything else so I walked straight up to the attendant and asked for a copy of *Ulysses* to be placed aside and inscribed with the formal insert for presentation at the prize-giving ceremony, after which I took it home to show my father and his father who happened to be visiting at the time, and we all knew more of what it represented than what it actually contained, especially since in the year or so preceding that time a film version of Joyce's novel had come to those antipodean shores and in an act of censorship more worthy of another century in its blind logic it was determined that the film could be shown only to segregated audiences so that heterosexual couples, at least, would be spared the embarrassment of watching together the infamous brothel scene, I never saw the film and it was a long time before I read the book but I had handed it as a challenge back to my father, as if it were bought with the sixpence of my discomfort all those years earlier, not so much as an act of revenge, conscious or unconscious, for all this is a contrived association in any case, a rhetorical convergence more than anything else, but rather as if to declare that I had assumed that type of discomfort as a way of life, to acknowledge that to some extent I had learned it from him and from his infirmity, and in response to nothing more threatening than an occasional inoculation this son of his prosthesis had opted for such a form of masochistic pleasure that I now chose to enter the foreign world of unease that a *Ulysses* opened up, to become a purveyor of translation and the byways of discursive transfer, whichever way one looked at it, like the way my grandfather looked at it with his impish grin, he who was supposed if only by virtue of generational compounding to be the more disturbed by it, but he wasn't, for it doesn't necessarily work that way, and I'm not sure in what structure of liberality or conservatism that leaves me in the generation after my father, my grandfather simply perused the book and handed it to my father who was much more reluctant to delve into its pages or its depths, declined with enough firmness to announce his displeasure before giving voice to the very same, he asked me in a tone as pointed as it was dismissive why I would want to waste my prize on that book, he asked me rhetorically for he knew the answer to the question, I had provided it for him in every animated discussion we had had over the dinner table during the preceding year to eighteen months as I had come to discover literature and worlds of knowledge in general outside the bounds that had been hitherto prescribed, when there were no longer any older siblings at home to prevent my monopolizing the discussion, I used him and my reluctant and retiring mother as a sounding board for every single idea that I came across in my rabid coursing along the path of the new, my mother would offer the occasional indignant query while my father and I refined the art of the dialectic, and the two newly arrived Malaysian students, who now took the place of departed brothers in the bedroom three of us had once shared, played the chorus with their parodies of invective and censure passively acquired, particularly a phrase that could have come from my father or from a schoolmaster, "You need discipline, boy!," we would sling it at each other when we had nothing better to say, and my father would join the parody from time to time when things weren't so serious, when there was a time for such trivialities or quadrivialities, but often there wasn't, the world was an increasingly serious place it seemed to all of us, a world in which forms of discipline were breaking up and their parts being reassigned, like the paving stones from Paris streets so well reset and asphalted now you can't even hear the beach underneath if you lie with your ear stuck to them, I remember seeing those iconoclastic events in the newspaper images for we had no television in the house at the time, events perpetrated by demonstrators referred to as pro-Maoist, and then there were blurred and disturbing images coming over the wire from Southeast Asia, and then soldiers volunteering from New Zealand to join the Americans there, by the time of my last year in high school, the year in question, opposition to the war had grown enough for a serious demonstration to be staged in my hometown, and although I said I would only go to the rally to hear the speeches and was expressly forbidden to march down the main street behind the banners I did both, and wore the black armband through the weekend, even sitting on the back porch in view of the neighbors while my father dug the garden and insisted I take it off, but it was the sign of a prosthetic device I had determined to wear, and our ways had irrevocably parted, for a number of years at least, the heterodoxy had become explicit and the discipline I needed had teachers other than him, except that neither of us realized that he had brought me to this point and to a distrust of the disciplinary exigencies, he had somehow provided the necessary transport when my excursus took me to this side or that, offering shrugs of bemusement at my crazy ideas and often enough outright proscription, but remaining ready to pass a token like a sixpence from years past and a different configuration of relations, and although the word was never uttered, never to my knowledge entered the language of our familial intercourse, not from 1953 till 1972, no such word uttered by these Willssons and daughters in spite of the striking example of it that was permanently attached to the margins of all their dealings, although I never remember hearing the word he quietly passed me his prosthesis across the generational divide, like a new word coined, or a coin pressed into the hand at the point we parted, when I was to set out on my own from the intersection of ill-formed desires and indistinct ambitions he surreptitiously handed over a quandary, slipped me a clunker, a pickle or hobble I could only smile and be grateful for, an aptitude for the discomfort of strange relations, a contrived convergence between patent differences that appears to have been shadowing the discursive vagrancy for four centuries until this particular triage, this intersection of argument and digression, this double commentary of the scholarly and the dilettantish that meets only to part ways again.

As early as 1525 the prosthetic was involved in complicated networks of exchange. Referring to a teenage experience that a biographer[17] might be quick to point to as seminal for one who is to make a career and a whole history out of surgery, Ambroise Paré recounts the following:

Anno Dom. 1525. when I was at *Anjou*, there stood a crafty beggar begging at the Church dore, who tying and hiding his owne arme behind his backe, shewed in steed thereof, one cut from the body of one that was hanged, and this he propped up and bound to his breast, and so laid it open to view, as if it had been all enflamed, so to move such as passed by unto greater commiseration of him. The cozenage lay hid, every one giving him mony, untill at length his counterfeit arm not being surely fastened, fell upon the ground, many seeing and observing it: hee being apprehended and layed in prison, by the appointment of the Magistrate, was whipped through the towne, with his false arme hanging before him, and so banished.   (Paré, *Collected Works*, 993)

But the dubious legality of trading in body parts and organs, already looking forward to the vats of William Gibson's Chiba, was not restricted to charlatans of such an amateurish kind. About that time the discipline of medicine was breaking up and its parts being reassigned. The ban on the dissection of corpses, which would not be lifted until Pope Sixtus's decree of 1480, had aided the medical faculties in their exclusion of surgery from medical practice. Only lowly barbers interfered with the integrity of the living body, and as long as they were unable to investigate corpses, they could not really further their knowledge of the body's workings. Conversely, as long as the learned doctors of the Sorbonne agreed that opening a corpse amounted to the sacrilege of violating a body made in the image of God, they were not required to sully their hands with manual labor. By the end of the thirteenth century, royal edicts gave barbers permission to undertake formal study in their own schools, and the simple distinction between doctor and barber began to dissolve as the intermediate categories of surgeon and barber-surgeon emerged. The doctors, threatened by this new disciplinary configuration, sought to bypass it by themselves giving simple barbers courses in anatomy, hoping to secure a supply of compliant, but better trained, assistants. The struggle for control of the discipline continued through the sixteenth century. The newly formed body of surgeons found favor with royalty (François I created a Chair of Surgery at the Collège de France) and fought with the Sorbonnards for control over corpses. Paré was one of those marginalized medical practitioners until his experiences in the field hospital led to a somewhat meteoric upgrading of his status. It is as a man of science who is also an iconoclastic reformer that he publishes his works, defending himself against the attacks of doctors—"who claims to have divided medicine from surgery?" Paré challenges; "where would we be if each were content with its part and never undertook to encroach on the other from time to time?"[18] —and writing in French so that his knowledge might be shared with a wider audience, for "the more people know about them, the more the sciences will be praised, science and virtue having no greater enemies than ignorance" (*Oeuvres* 1: 37).

But the surgeon who speaks of certain areas of knowledge with a rationalism we would more readily recognize as belonging to later centuries is the same writer who lapses into eyewitness descriptions of monsters as well as a lengthy digression on the unicorn, never doubting its existence both terrestrial and subterranean, but seriously questioning the use of its horn in remedies for the plague. Within that discussion itself, there is this timely and pertinent comment on the protocols of academic debate:

> In discoursing concerning the unicorn I wished that if someone were of a different opinion he would see fit to make that known: thinking that as a result of debate between two contrary opinions . . . greater light would be shed. This personal wish has been in part realized. It so happens that someone who read my work wanted to contradict me on these matters. However, his reasoning did not seem convincing enough to force me to change my opinion by adopting his. . . . I will leave aside the linguistic excesses that I think he fell prey to in consideration of the general good, which is the only thing that interests me. (*Oeuvres* 2: 813)

That digression is found in Book 21 of Paré's *Oeuvres*, on poisons.[19] The accompanying books present the following subject matter:

Book 20—Of the Smallpocks and meazles as also of Wormes and the Leprosie
Book 22—Of the Plague
Book 23—Of the Meanes and Manner to repaire or supply the Naturall or accidentall defects or wants in mans body
Book 24—Of the Generation of Man
Book 25—Of Monsters and Prodigies

The recourse to rhetorical considerations found in the digression on the unicorn, which betrays Paré's concern over the integrity and reconfiguration of his discipline, a balancing of authority against the need for change, is thus reflected in the content of much of his discussion. This comes into clear focus in Books 20–25. We may well read what is being written throughout as nothing other than the constitution of the discipline of surgery itself, along with doubts concerning its consequences. For Paré, surgery is quite simply the discipline of the prosthetic: from the very beginning its operations are five in number: "To take away that which is superfluous; to restore to their places, such things as are displaced; to separate those things which are joyned together; to joyne those which are separated; and to supply the defects of nature" (*Collected Works*, 4). But that which presents itself as a supplementary operation, designed to remedy the imperfections of nature, must at the same time admit of the artificial as unnatural, of what is counter to nature, a perversion and a monstrosity.

The juxtaposition of a rich teratology and a detailed treatise on prosthetics is telling in this regard. The monsters appear everywhere: Paré cannot advance his discussion of the parts of the body that need to be protected from smallpox without digressing for a number of pages to write "A discourse of certaine monstrous creatures which breed against nature in the bodies of men, women, and little children," including the little red living creature he draws for us that M. Durer expelled from his penis after a long illness, and the mass of formless flesh that moved and lived like a sponge that came out of the womb of a woman, shortly to be followed by a monster with a hook nose, a long neck, a pointed tail, and agile feet, a cross between a dragon and a lizard with a slightly human head that is also drawn for our edification (*Collected Works*, 762–64; cf. *Oeuvres* 2: 723–24). Many more such monsters are described and sometimes drawn in Book 25, where Paré goes into their causes at some length: God's wrath; women who have sexual relations during menstruation or copulate after the fashion of wild beasts (*Collected Works*, 962); over- or under-supply of seed, which conditions give rise, respectively, to extra or lacking members (972–76); a narrow uterus; too much sitting with legs crossed (980); and, of course, the mixing of seed that is produced by "Atheists, Sodomites, Out-lawes . . . transformed by filthy lust, [who] have not doubted to have filthy and abhominable copulation with beasts" (982). Within that very same discussion occurs the account of the charlatan beggar cited above as well as that of a 40-year-old Parisian man with no arms who could perform "all those things which are usually done with the hands . . . lash[ing] a coach-mans whip, that he would make it give a great crack. . . . He ate, drunke, plaid at cardes, and such like, with his feet. But at last he was taken for a thiefe and a murderer, was hanged and fastened to a wheele" (976).

In Paré's schema the monster, the mutant, the criminal, and the amputee share the same discursive space, a space that is also that of prosthesis. Book 23 was published in its entirety in the 1585 edition of the *Oeuvres*, but parts of it had already been published in 1561 and 1564.[20] The treatise is extensive in its explanations of the use of prosthetic devices, all of them accompanied by diagrams, taking into account aesthetic as well as orthopedic concerns: artificial eyes, either round objects inserted into the socket or flat fronts made of painted leather and held in place by a taffeta- or velvet-covered wire around the head; a mask to correct squinting in children; gold, silver, and papier-mâché noses;[21] teeth, obturators of the palate fit for a cancerous psychoanalyst, tongues; ears attached in the same way as an eye; corsets to correct a stoop; portable bedpans for incontinence; and then, of course:

> Those that have their yards cut off close to their bellies, are greatly troubled in making of urine, so that they are constrained to sit downe like women, for their ease. I have devised this pipe or conduit [*canule*], having an hole through it as big as ones finger, which may be made of wood, or rather of latin. . . . This instrument must be applied to the lower part of the *os pectinis*: on the upper end it is compassed with a brink for the passage of the urine, for thereby it will receive the urine the better, and carry it from the patient, as he standeth upright. (877)

Artificial hands are designed "in order to help and imitate nature" (880), for fabrication by any competent locksmith or clockmaker and allowing articulation of all five fingers operated by a lever at the wrist. The same device can be built as an arm with another lever at the elbow. A third version is made out of boiled leather and designed like a glove to fit over the stump; it has a pen permanently held in its fingers. When it comes to legs there is the ordinary wooden leg, consisting of a peg leg, an open socket, straps to hold the stump in the socket, and—the problem of articulation of animate and inanimate a constant concern—a cushion for the stump to rest on. And then there is the fully fledged artificial leg with fifteen movable parts and armorlike coverings (see Fig. 4):

Description of the artificial leg:

0. The cord by means of which one pulls on the ring attached to the catch to bend the leg.
1. The thighpiece with screws and threaded holes to permit enlargement or reduction once the thigh is placed inside.
2. The knob for holding with the hand for turning or removal of the leg.
3. A small ring situated in front of the thigh to hold up or guide the leg.
4. The two rear and front buckles for attaching the leg to the clothing.

5. The fitted base with a two-finger clearance for the thigh to rest on, and shaped to its fit.
6. The spring to move the catch that closes the leg.
7. The catch holding the stick of the leg straight and firm, to prevent it from bending backwards.
8. The ring to which is attached a cord to pull on the catch so that the leg can be bent for sitting or mounting a horse.
9. The hinge to operate and move the leg, placed in front of the knee.
10. A small pin to prevent the catch from moving too far; if that were to happen the spring would break and the patient would fall.
11. The iron band into which the stick is inserted.
12. The other band at the end of the stick carrying the hinge that moves the foot.
13. A spring to hold the foot in place.
14. The pin allowing the spring to straighten the foot.

The leg dressed:

A. Plates for the beauty of the knee.
B. Legplates for the beauty of the leg.
C. A calfplate to complete the form of the leg.
D. Plates to form the top of the foot.   (*Oeuvres* 3: 907)

Faced with the prodigiousness of Paré's prostheses, my own rhetoric is reduced to the level of quotation, to a simple taxonomy, and to the desire to do no more than repeat the fabulous inventory of Book 23. There seems little else to say; it is even doubtful that throughout the present study I have done any more than repeat something like the phantasm of a Paré. But what is evidenced by this summary of his inventions, by my desire for quotation, is of course the very fact of quotation made explicit for us since Ramus: its irredeemable foreignness and at the same time its intrusion into the space of the familiar. Paré reads like nothing so much as the extraordinarily familiar calling across the divide of four centuries; or the extraordinarily foreign looking as familiar as something my father discarded nightly in the corner of his bedroom, or propped against the wall of a changing shed at the edge of dozens of childhood beaches.

There is a neat symmetry to Paré's discourse in these books: at the extremities (Books 20, 21, and 25), the monsters and unicorns; closer to home the principles of natural generation (Book 24) on one side and the contagion of the plague on the other (Book 22). The plague veils only thinly the fear and threat of promiscuity, of unnatural sex, for the real

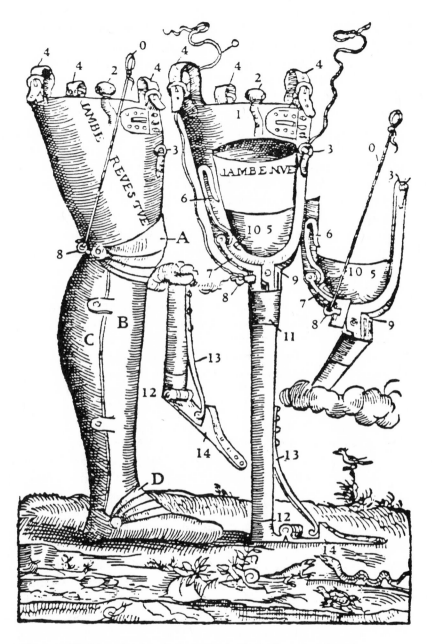

Fig. 4 Artifical leg, drawing from Ambroise Paré, *Oeuvres*, 1585, 3: 907.

contagion of the sixteenth century was less the plague, however serious a threat that disease continued to pose, than syphilis, which first broke out in Naples in 1496 and whose causes were identified as early as 1527. It led to the monstrosity of hair loss and the rudimentary prosthesis that was the wig.[22] In the middle (Book 23) we have the artificial means of adding what is lacking naturally or as a result of accident.

The prostheses of Book 23 keep such close company with monstrosity, contagion, and natural generation precisely because in allowing for the artificial so close to what is natural prosthesis opens the structure of mutancy. Paré's monsters thus do not appear just because "the Renaissance . . . [creates] a climate of contradictions and divergent aspirations, where rationalism coexists with mysticism," nor simply because the discoveries of the period "exalt Renaissance man but fail to deliver him from his existential anguish, his fear of a hostile world, his terror of the invisible."[23] More than that Paré's monsters exist because the surgical interventions that made possible the wearing of modern prosthetic devices, for which the paradigm remains the artificial limb, brought into particular focus the competing discourses of the organicist and mechanicist conceptions of the human body, putting the machine into a close and uneasy relation with the organic. Hence the monstrous creature Ambroise Paré sees coming out of the womb of a woman about whom stories have been spread can obey a set of ideas that stand, from our perspective, in blatant contradiction to the more rational ideas in force when the same surgeon deftly uses his instruments to tie bleeding arteries; one relying on an organic model, the other more mechanistically interventionist. History will claim that it is William Harvey's discovery of the circulation of the blood in 1628 that represents the Copernican revolution in medicine that is absent from the sixteenth century; but such a discovery remains within the organicist continuum.[24] Paré's amputations and prostheses, on the other hand, make explicit the very break that constitutes the human body; the mechanicist rupture that is its relation to and dependence upon the inanimate, the artificial. Such a break is readily identifiable as belonging to the middle of the fifteenth century, in Paré's amputations and prostheses, and before that in Vesalius's *De humani corporis fabrica*: "The title of Vesalius's work is already significant in itself and represents an important model. The human body is seen precisely as a *fabrica*, that is to say as a factory in which each component has its reason for being and assumes its own function."[25]

Prosthesis does not simply give rise to the monstrous or revive a fear of the same: monstrosity, and by extension criminality, is a function of the mechanical or technological itself. That is evident everywhere from Paré's beggar waving a hanged man's arm to Hoffmann's uncanny automaton. Prosthesis occurs on the border between the living and the lifeless; it represents the monstrosity of interfering with the integrity of the human body, the act of unveiling the unnatural within the natural. But as Paré makes clear from the outset, prosthesis also defines the very act of surgical intervention. In 1552, Paré and medical knowledge are positioned at a particularly prosthetic moment. It is the same moment as Wilson's *Rhetorique*, and the latter's question concerning the idolatrous image is a corollary to that concerning the artificial body. In both cases the supposed remedy these Renaissance figures provide can as easily be seen as a poison that threatens the whole body rhetorical and medical; or rather, the attachment they bring to bear can as easily be seen as a lever that threatens to switch us over to the inhuman. Both Wilson and Paré, in different degrees of explicitness or consciousness, are involved in promoting the remedy and in warning against the poison. But both are embarked upon a journey of no return, for it is a journey that was begun at the beginning, long before Wilson penned the word or Paré tried to staunch the bleeding; it is the divergence begun by the construction of the artificial within the origin itself, the prosthetic train that had been journeying for a long time before these two characters climbed aboard in 1552–53.

The history of European languages provides for two types of rhetorical terms, defined by their relation to other disciplines. The first consists in terms borrowed directly from the quadrivium, in particular geometry, namely "trope," "parable," "hyperbole," and "ellipsis," spatial configurations referring to the curving departures from a presumed flat or straight, zero-degree line of discourse. The second type, exemplified by the term "prosthesis," consists in a lexicon shared with medicine, where the terms describe a range of medical or surgical conditions or procedures. In Thomas Wilson's list of figures of a word, one encounters an extensive taxonomy of lexico-surgical operations. At least three of the terms for cutting from or adding to a word inhabiting the margins of his *Rhetorique* have assumed a medical sense—"prosthesis," "aphaeresis" (cf. "hemaphaeresis"), and "syncope." But in the wider range of imported Greek terms, the list of those belonging both to medicine and to rhetoric is extensive, from "prolepsis" to "semiology" itself. Now apart from the already stated obvious explanation for that—namely the fact of shared disciplinary space within either or both of the classical and medieval configurations of knowledge—one might be able to speculate a little more on differences between the two rhetorical terminologies, the geometrical and the medical. An obvious contrast between the two sets of figures is that the first refers to variations in the flow of discourse whereas the second signifies interventions with respect to the morphology of the word. In the case of the tropes, the specific departures from normal usage are charted against static axes; there is, as it were, an elliptical distortion of what is called standard usage. In the case of interventions within the word it is as if the line of discourse has been broken rather than stretched. It might be argued that in the case of these "medical" figures it is not so much a spatial relation that is set in play, what fits within the *topos*, as the actual articulation of linguistic elements: operations of removal or addition. In Wilson's list, three types of setting forth or putting down, three types of thesis— prosthesis, epenthesis, and proparalepsis; and three types of ablation— aphaeresis, syncope, and apocope. Six names for radical intervention within the body of the word, waiting in the limbo of a foreign language on the edges of a treatise on rhetoric and on the edge of an institutionalized admission to English. But waiting not so much for the door to open as for the whole adjacent ground to shift enough to include them. For the albeit mechanical dynamism I am ascribing to these figures is that of a shifting rhetoric, an alteration that has more of the force of a shift of rails or terrain than a detour. These figures, of which the word "prosthesis" is the paradigm, will be hopelessly caught up in a movement that enables them to signify within two suddenly disparate disciplines, medicine and rhetoric. For as the terrain shifts, a whole series of new relations must come to be established between them before, about a century and a half later, the link will appear to have been totally lost. A history or taxonomy of attitudes toward and treatments of the body as compared with attitudes toward and treatments of the word is waiting to be written, as I discussed in an earlier chapter. The idea that an idiosyncratic language might be formed from a personal history of the body is of course a subtext of the whole psychoanalytic enterprise.

The gamble undertaken here is to produce a text whose writing becomes an exemplar of the rhetoric of that taxonomy and that history: something of the lost rhetoric of the divergence between philology and medicine on the one hand and on the other something of a rhetoric of shifts or divergences in general, the always possible and necessary future divergences of discursive and disciplinary cohesion. Thus prosthesis will be a figure for which the term "figure" is no longer appropriate, for it betokens a writing that obeys a whole other dynamism, that of constantly shifting relations. Or at least a figure for which neither Euclidean geometry nor modern surgery can provide the models, requiring us to look towards some cybernetic or bioengineered future. With respect to such a future a prosthetic rhetoric has a vague ambivalence. It can only be told in a combination of declaration and instantiation, and then in the analogies, hyperboles, and ellipses against whose background it emerges. But its mutation is such that all of those figures are denied any consistency, being prey to the dynamic of the shift. This prosthesis cannot tell a straight analogy from an inconsistent one, for it is the figure of an inconsistency that it cannot adequately describe; the inconsistency that has it limping outside of its own limits, hobbling uneasily towards some unknown that it knows it will never reach.

The word is seen putting its best prosthetic foot forward back there in 1553, so much so that it instantiates its own operation. The attention-seeking appearance of this Greek word in the margins of rhetoric is doubled for the modern eye by the formation of its first two *s*'s, written in the elongated or, for us, more figurative form of the day. As those *s*'s mutate into the current compact form, so the first of them will also either be cut or reattached at will as the word continues its limp into English. The slightly different word "prothesis" will enter the language somewhat later, claiming to be the more etymologically correct form for the linguistic sense and a permanently erroneous form for the medical sense. In French, we have learned, the *s* is retained for the former and removed for the latter to this day. Thus the word "prosthesis" will adapt to the syncope and epenthesis at work within it, right down to the figure of the letter itself, the *s* that betokens both a zigzag and a crossover, a constant shifting of directions within the structure of a continuous movement, a letter whose head faces one way and its tail another, the very letter that is the parting of ways or at least the token of it, like a letter for a sixpence handed across a space too cluttered for either plainness or figure to tell, where I go to take a step and can't find forward, for the leg I am using is borrowed and I am using it for the first time.

§ 8   Menton, 1921

The postcard is sent from Melbourne. In or on it he writes that the hotel room faced north, which meant that he had the sun the whole day.[1] Sitting in it, he no doubt imagines having it, possessing it, a light that will shine out of him as bright as a star, a blinding beam gleaming on his forehead. He says as much to his analyst.[2] He sits in the winter sun, in front of the special candle heater he has brought with him halfway across the world. To his right there is a lowboy, just under a meter high and about 75 centimeters across. On top of that a line of bottles and vials arranged in orderly fashion so that the small white labels of each dispensing pharmacy are displayed at a 45-degree angle to the right front corner of the chest of drawers, thereby facing this gentleman who attends to his daily toilet in the oval mirror securely attached to the wall beside it. The bottles have been disposed according to the frequency of consumption of their contents, so that certain containers of tablets and certain vials of medicine are grouped further towards the front edge of the lowboy top. On the extreme right, most proximate to the reach of the aforementioned gentleman a cylindrical bottle of twenty *Sonéryl* pills, containing ten centigrams per tablet, vies for prominence with a more squat one filled with tablets of *Somnothyril.* These two have been moved slightly off center by the brushing of a cuff as our hero has moved to take in his hand the vial of liquid *Veriane* positioned behind them and a few centimeters to the left. Its immediate neighbor, so adjacent that their sides are all but touching, is a replica whose only difference is the bold outline of the name *Veronidin.* Their placement is such as to obscure at least partially from view the label declaring the contents of the bottle behind them, but a discerning eye would not fail to identify it as *Phanodorme*. Further to the left two scant inches of polished wood, marred by a few wanton specks of dust that could only have settled between the last passage of the maid about twenty hours before and the present moment, separate it from a group of two more glass containers of similar but not identical dimension, their white lids screwed airtight, their labels betraying their provenance from a certain chemist on the Avenue du Roule in Neuilly and declaring their contents to be, reading from left to right, tablets of *Hypalène* and *Rutonal*. Further back still, but no more than twenty centimeters from the first bottle of *Sonéryl*, sits a tall narrow tincture of *Neurinase*, and to its right, though displaced far enough as to constitute a separate category of its own, the level of its liquid contents showing its meniscus concave curvature faintly through the dark brown glass, sits another, labeled *Acétile*. Nothing else rests on the upper surface of the lowboy. In its first drawer, which a hand has pushed flush as the last ritual act of dressing for the day, lined along the side opposite a row of freshly creased and starched monogrammed handkerchiefs, are about threescore bottles of repeats of the same prescription barbiturates readied above, as well as three brands that we haven't yet encountered, and probably won't until the investigating police officer inventories them in the Grand Hotel et des Palmes in Palermo twelve years later, namely *Declonol, Hyrpholène*, and *Neosedan*.[3]

If I were Raymond Roussel, I might continue that fictional guided tour of the contents of a hotel room in Melbourne until it filled the pages of a book. It would be a book not so very different from, for example, *La Vue* (The view), a series of three poems describing, first, a seaside scene imagined in an inkwell, second, a drawing on a sheet of writing paper from a resort, and third, the design on the label of a mineral-water bottle, which scenes fairly come alive as tableaux vivants for the duration of some 140 pages of rhyming couplets.[4] Or else it would be a book somewhat different from the novels, *Impressions of Africa* (*Impressions d'Afrique*) and *Locus Solus* (*Locus solus*), in that the descriptions would not be of the fantastic machines that inhabit those tales; but not so very different, all things considered. Its structure would still be that of the guided tour, the narrative of a voyage into the body of a set of words. For it is such a reasoned but interminable inventory, such an overdose of words that constitutes Roussel's writings and finally causes his death in Palermo in 1933, lying on the mattress he has dragged over against the door, which, contrary to habit, he has locked, the door that communicates with the room of his companion, mistress, or maid—the relationship is undetermined, in any case the same Charlotte Dufrène or Fredez to whom he had sent a postcard from Melbourne. For at least three weeks prior to his death she has kept close track of his habit, hoping to vary the brand names sufficiently to alleviate the addiction. But the words just keep piling up: June 25, 6 *Phanodorme* tablets at 6:00 in the evening and another 6 at 1:30 the next morning; June 26, 8 *Hypalène* at 5:10 P.M., another 2, then another 4 at 9:00 that evening, then another 30 in all during the night; June 27, one and a half vials of *Veriane*; June 28, 3 *Rutonal* pills at 4:30 P.M., 3 more at 6:00 P.M., and 12 more during the night; June 29, 4 *Sonéryl* at 6:00 in the evening, 4 more a half hour later, 13 more throughout the night, inducing 12¼ hours of sleep and 24 hours of "extraordinary euphoria"; June 30, 19 *Somnothyril*; July 1, one bottle of *Neurinase*; July 2, one bottle of light *Acétile*; July 3, 10 *Phanodorme* tablets; July 4, one and a half bottles of *Veriane*, half a bottle of *Neurinase*; July 5, two bottles of *Veronidin*; July 6, back to 16 *Sonéryl*; July 7, at 9:30 P.M., 6 *Hypalène*, then 18 more, then 3 *Sonéryl*; July 8, 20 *Somnothyril* pills and a bottle of *Neurinase*; July 9, 11 *Phanodorme*; July 10, two bottles of *Veronidin* at 9:00 P.M.; July 11, at the same hour, 34 *Rutonal* tablets; July 12, a bottle and a half of *Veriane*; July 13, back to *Sonéryl*, something between 20 and 40 tablets, but, whichever way you count it, words enough to kill him (Sciascia, *Actes*, 51–53).

The record isn't clear on when Roussel's addiction began. Cocteau sights him looking like Proust in the same detox program as himself in 1928,[5] but we can perhaps deduce from Charlotte Dufrène's deposition that he has sought narcotic remedies for the whole 23 years she has known him, during which time "he has always been neurasthenic" (Sciascia, *Actes*, 47). Be that as it may, by the time he is ready to die in Sicily, although still eating only once a day, his *dérèglement* seems to have preempted the strict regimen he kept to during his heyday in Neuilly. According to the chef who served him in the mid-1920's, the "single" meal of the day began at 12:30 with fresh fruit from the Midi. Then followed coffee, tea, or chocolate (specially imported from Switzerland) and brioches. Breakfast finished with Neufchâtel cheese fifteen minutes later and lunch began: oysters or clams or an entrée of fish, followed by another of pasta, then the main course of meat or poultry, often two quails stuffed with foie gras and wrapped in vine leaves, with pitted grapes. After a large piece of fish, a champagne sorbet. Then a simple meat course such as bourguignon, followed by a roast of lamb, pheasant, or partridge. After that a salad, perhaps with mussels and truffles, and next a three-piece dessert—one with pastry, one with cream, and one iced, all of them with sprinkles of lukewarm sugar. Dinner followed without interruption: two soups to begin, one a consommé with vegetables not showing the slightest trace of a knife cut, and one a thick soup. After an entrée of fish, a hot course such as omelette or kidneys, and a cold one such as foie gras, a small salad, and again two or three desserts. Anything from 16 to 22 services in all.[6]

My interest in Roussel's mania obeys the following logic: the two inventories, the disciplined rationalization of comestible excess and the barbiturate snacking or bingeing of the last days, structure the whole space of his work. Both are functions of the double sense of the word "arbitrary": on the one hand the dictatorial imposition of a stringent regime of constraint, on the other hand the surrendering to the increasingly random effects of increasingly random forms of consumption. The double arbitrariness can be seen to reside within each form of excess. Firstly, the dietary prescriptions are a controlled excess, strict adherence to a form of consumerism, but one that contradicts itself the more strictly it imposes itself—I don't mean just the contradiction between the aristocracy's pursuit of gluttony and the order or restraint that that class imposes so as to preserve its privilege, but more basically the contradiction between the rationalization of human feeding habits, the condensation of three or four meals into one, and the concomitant fetishization of the eating process. Secondly, the constant overdosage of sleeping pills and potions with its quest for sustained euphoria carries with it not only the familiar monkey grip of any such addiction but also the desire, at least, for precision of treatment and for a certain functional rectitude on the part of the body.[7] The guided tour that is Roussel's work functions in a similar fashion, providing a meticulously regimented inventory of what is nothing more than a completely arbitrary set of objects, machines, or tableaux.

It is that double sense of the arbitrary that gives me license to affirm that all that is consumed in those inventories, from *Somnothyril* to sorbet and from foie gras to *Phanodorme*, is more words; ever more words leading to a fatal overdose. In the first place there is the obvious structural similarity between eating and speaking, that of an elemental compulsion coupled with an impulsion to excess and exaggeration. This exists beyond any opposition between the ingestion of food and the expulsion of words, and before any decision concerning the originality of one over the other—does hunger cause the first desire for utterance or merely provide it with its pretext? It is that double sense of the arbitrary as it applies to the word—as both constraint and license—that I intend here more than any reference to the Saussurean relation between signifier and signified, although this latter could well be explained as falling within the same structural framework in that the arbitrariness of the signifier calls for the whole linguistic apparatus of limits to meaning.[8] But the stricture of excess practiced by Roussel is described better by the Derridean double bind of communication and dissemination: language is conceived of as the pure presence of ideal communication, but in simply conceiving of itself it opens up the limitless space of dissemination. Such a bind creates the paradox wherein limiting the extent of one's utterance by reducing the quantity of signifiers tends to increase the possibilities of signification—that is the economy of poetry, for instance—whereas increasing the utterance in order to contain signification by means of further elucidation conversely constrains or condemns one to a limitless expansion, the need to further elucidate each elucidation. In the play between language and sense, less is more and more is more.

In Roussel's work, the word, while providing the context for his manic dedication to the forms of literature—poetry, novels, plays—becomes at the same time the vehicle for practices of exaggeration—narrative and descriptive abandon—that put into crisis those very forms. But it is a specific instance of those practices that makes for a finding of death by verbal ingestion in the Roussel case. I refer to the famous method or *procédé* revealed in his posthumously published *How I Wrote Certain of My Books* (*Comment j'ai écrit certains de mes livres*).[9] There it is explained that the intricate narratives of the novels *Impressions of Africa* and *Locus Solus* and of the plays *The Star on the Forehead* (*L'Etoile au front*)[10] and *La Poussière de soleils* (Sundust) were generated by variations on a homonymic language game. For example the two phrases "les lettres du blanc sur les bandes du vieux billard" ("the white letters on the cushions of the old billiard table") and "les lettres du blanc sur les bandes du vieux pillard" ("the white man's letters on the hordes of the old plunderer") formed the basis for a story that began with the first version and ended with the second, a story that was later expanded into the novel *Impressions of Africa*. The master narrative generated by those sets of semantic differences was filled out with subnarratives generated by a similar method: two words susceptible to homophonic ambiguity were joined by the preposition *à* to give the narrative opening and closure. For example *palmier* (a type of pastry) *à restauration* (a restaurant where pastries are served) and *palmier* (a palm tree) *à restauration* (restoration of a dynasty). A third method pushed the practice further into the space of the arbitrary.[11] It involved taking a ready-made sentence or expression and deforming it so as to give the context for any number of fantastic narrative digressions, in the manner of the final play indulged in during each episode of the BBC radio program *My Word.* Thus a line from a song, "J'ai du bon tabac dans ma tabatière" ("I have good tobacco in my pouch"), was corrupted to "Jade tube onde aubade en mat (objet mat) a basse tierce" (nonsense in both French and English) and so on. As Roussel explains:

> I used anything at hand. For instance, there was a well-known advertisement for some apparatus called "Phonotypia"; this supplied me with "fausse note tibia" [wrong note tibia], hence the Breton, Lelgoualch [in *Impressions of Africa*].
>
> I even utilized the name and address of my shoemaker: "Hellstern, 5, place Vendôme," gave me "Hélice tourne zinc plat se rend (devient) dôme" [Propeller turns zinc flat goes (becomes) dome]. *The figure five was chosen at random; I do not know if it was the correct one.* (*How I Wrote*, 9, my italics)

In other words Roussel's literary license involved faithfully obeying the constraints it had imposed upon itself while nonetheless consuming whatever was at hand, as a matter of fact or invention. The intricacies of the paradox are many: the narrative digression could expand no further than the space created by a homophone—as it were no further than the mouth could open to pronounce a single word, or more precisely, no more than whatever could be inserted between the opening and closing of the mouth upon a single word—yet, given that originary divergence, the digression could be extended and deferred limitlessly. Since closure—the closure posited by the fall of the "second" sense of the word—was ultimately guaranteed, it could be arbitrarily deferred. Yet the status of the second sense—that which allows it to act as a form of closure—could have been only arbitrarily attributed, for there is nothing in a repetition, especially not a repetition with an explicit phonetic or semantic difference, nothing in that to guarantee closure; only an arbitrary "decision" allows that. Furthermore, homophonic difference is rarely limited to two options. For Roussel, scrupulously scanning his Bescherelle dictionary, must often have been choosing his privileged two senses from an expanded series of semantic variations. Thus if the possibility of a third or fourth sense lurks in the background, there must remain the at least hypothetical threat of a further narrative digression. The effect of closure is therefore as much of a contrivance as the digression itself.

Finally, as Roussel explains above, his method of constraint itself digressed or diverged into increasing approximation. He had recourse to whatever was at hand ("J'usais de n'importe quoi," *Comment j'ai écrit*, 21) and took whatever liberties were necessary to rewrite the inherited form of language as a quasi-random inventory of signifiers that would give rise to an equally capricious narrative. This means that what I am calling arbitrariness, something that for Roussel was the product of his fecund imagination appended to an accidental fact of language, an outside effect of invention brought to bear on a presumedly intact, though fissured, word—we shall see shortly the precise terms he borrows to repeat this mythology—shows itself to be already at work in whatever data are taken to be the basis of the exercise. The decision for, or choice of, a form of constraint is at the same time a decision for arbitrariness; the space opened by language has no exhaustible parameters. Thus what one might call the *n'importe quoi* effect, the appropriation of whatever is at hand, operates with cardinal gluttony, consuming, parasiting, and cannibalizing the forms of linguistic constraint that it is putatively opposed to, for both constraint and gluttony reveal themselves as effects of the structure that the word inaugurates.

The importance and originality of Roussel's method of composition consists therefore in its explicit mobilization of these supposed operations of closure at the opening or origin of the literary enterprise. Now on the one hand Roussel might simply be rendering explicit the assumption that underwrites every writing: nothing more than the idea that every writing institutes some sort of hermeneutic quest, some sort of interrogation, problem, or crisis whose resolution will impel its progress. The problem might be a narrative one, a philosophical one, or of some other type, and the resolution might be premature, contrived, or illusory, but that structure of opening and closing would seem to be inevitable. The particularity of Roussel's method then resides in its unwitting insistence that those two parts of the operation in fact reside within the same space, that they are in fact the same operation; so much so that the question of their order and priority with respect to each other is henceforth beside the point. The origin can no longer impose its priority and order over what it claims to give rise to, since one might say that it comes to be the origin only as an effect of its instituting the terms of closure. The consecution that characterizes narrative order is imported into a single signifying space where the operative order is that of the paradox described above and where consecution becomes subject to reversal. Roussel may well work from his method to repeat time after time the most traditional and simplistic inventory of narrative forms, but that method nevertheless means that the stories he invents have ended as soon as they begin to be uttered. And this is not to say that his work suffers from the predictability typical of simplistic narrative, for the chicanery of Roussel's stories is far from predictable, but rather to say that the difference that brings about the ending is disclosed as nothing more than the differance that exists in the beginning.

Roussel's language games, and the narratives and machines he generates from them, amount to a series of guided tours through the space of the word. And conversely, there is a voyage or a story or a machine of limitless complexity in every word, a 300-page novel in every "*Sonéryl*," a host of rhyming couplets in every "*Neurinase*," a three-act play in every "*Veronidin*." Not to mention what lurks in the design of every pharmacist's label on every bottle that is kept at hand. Far too much for a body to bear. Roussel's varying of his barbiturate menu may have indeed been a form of self-imposed discipline, an attempt to limit the reliance on any one course, but with every new brand there comes a new word to haunt him. And conversely, when his doctor enjoins him to cut back on such a variety, he is nonetheless faced with an increased number of repetitions of the same word, with a different story or mechanical phantasm speaking or writing itself through every successive repetition. If we look closely enough it is clear that Roussel's propensity to overdosing was already in evidence in his first taste of the drug of verbal euphoria, in the *lettres du blanc*, where the *blanc* that he takes for a "cube of chalk" (*How I Wrote*, 3) already presages a white chemical powder that will be the emblem for every subsequent excess up to the point of no return.

Such a paradoxically arbitrary negotiation of linguistic possibility is not unique to Roussel. It is demonstrated in a more striking manner in the case of Louis Wolfson, the self-styled schizophrenic language student who details his case in his own autodidact French in *Le Schizo et les langues* (The schizo and his languages).[12] In his preface Gilles Deleuze points to the striking analogy with Roussel's *procédé* (Wolfson, *Schizo*, 7–8). Wolfson explains that he felt so threatened by the sound of English penetrating his body, most often uttered by his mother, who supposedly derived "a macabre pleasure" from injecting such sounds into the ears of "her unique possession" (183), that when he was unable to preempt such experiences by agitating his fingers in his ears or making his vocal chords vibrate or turning up his transistor to maximum volume, he felt obliged to domesticate the words by transliterating them into similar sounding words in one of the other four languages (French, German, Russian, Hebrew) that he made it his life's undertaking to teach himself. For example the English word "tree" could pass into French *arbre* thanks to the common *r*, but it would offer more satisfaction as the Hebrew *èts* or the Russian *derevo*, whose vowel-consonant articulations obeyed more strictly the complicated rules of accord Wolfson invented for himself (40–42).

Wolfson's paradox is impossibly knotted; hence his psychosis: he perceived familiar English sounds as foreign, in the sense of aggressive. He therefore made them more foreign, although familiarly so in the sense of acoustically approximate, in order to render them palatable, that is to say acceptable or familiar. However, like Roussel, Wolfson imposes a form of closure upon the signifying operation: he attempts to prevent it from occurring at all in English except insofar as the sounds of that language are able to articulate with four other languages. But in so doing he is led to greatly increase the signifying data: "it was often difficult for the sick young man . . . to stop consulting his foreign-language dictionaries once he had begun" (212). Like Roussel, Wolfson treats words like machines whose parts can be dismantled and reassembled in an increasingly arbitrary manner—leading to anagram (212) and neologism (127)—but whose forms supposedly obey protocols of morphological constraint and aesthetic sensibility. And like Roussel, Wolfson spins a series of tales—of conversations with his father or the carpenter, of his sexual experiences, of stalking the halls of the New York Public Library—as the pretext for elaborating his extensive philological excursions. But what is most interesting for us is the fact that Wolfson relates his linguistic experience to bouts of gluttony: his fear of penetration by the word is tied to fears of ingestion of parasites, and he literally indulges his taste for language at the same time as he binges on whatever the larder has to offer. The quote above concerning his failure to restrict his indulgence occurs in this context: "And just as it was often difficult for the sick young man to stop eating once he had begun, it was equally difficult for him to stop consulting his foreign-language dictionaries once he had begun." He also states that he could be less threatened by English words when he was hungry (194). According to Wolfson his mother took particular pleasure in assaulting his eyes and ears with her displays of and comments on her newly purchased comestibles each week when she returned with her laden shopping cart. This would lead him to rush to the kitchen as soon as she left the house and gorge himself on whatever he could lay his hands on while at the same time reading his dictionaries and squinting to avoid the English on the labels, or reciting foreign phrases he had learned as a sort of incantation against the effects of his gluttony (or, we might well say, as an incitation to further gluttony). Afterwards, writhing in indigestive agony on his bed he would chide himself for being so unrestrained, wondering how anyone who could learn four foreign languages could be so stupid. Wolfson's more pedestrian pig-out is fittingly symmetrical with Roussel's white-glove 22-course meal:

And knowing—the days his mother made her large weekly food purchases—that such an orgy would surely follow, probably followed in turn by an extreme state of astonishment and incomprehension at his own actions, the disturbed young man nevertheless headed straight for the kitchen as soon as his mother had left the house, telling himself that he had to eat something, of course only a little, but something all the same. . . . While trying to decide what to eat, he could still continue to study more or less. . . . Hence he would try to study while searching through the food cupboards as well as the refrigerator, examining the new boxes, cans, and bottles, trying at the same time to read a book held open in his hand, or repeating to himself new groups of foreign words or even complete foreign sentences that he had just been reading or studying a moment before. But he tried to avoid looking at the words printed on the bread wrappers or the boxes of frozen foods or pastries or the labels on the cans of preserves, trying to guess the contents from the dimensions of the container, or by shaking them, or by their weight. . . . However, it was dangerous for him to open one of these food containers to see what was inside, for he would be tempted to taste a morsel and would feel a need to justify his opening it and so would decide that a second or third piece would justify his actions all the more . . . after that a fourth or fifth piece wouldn't be excessive . . . the sixth or seventh piece would be his last, or if not, that the eighth or ninth would. . . . On such days, out of weakness and hunger, he often lost his head, in his delirium or dementia provoking a real orgy—opening new containers one after the other and voraciously and compulsively eating the whole contents of each to the last morsel, and if not having desisted from his studying utterly, only doing it in a completely worthless way, as it were symbolically, thinking of the four or five first words of a foreign phrase that he had memorized before beginning eating or right at the start of this frightful indulgence, but being unable either to think of the rest of the expression or to stop eating and thus bring it to his attention. . . . Naturally most often he was unable to remember the rest of the phrase, his mind being dulled by his actions; thus he would again begin to quietly repeat the phrase from the first, dreaming that he might all of a sudden miraculously remember the rest of it this time, while still eating and being too excited and distracted to look or even think of looking at the book containing the expression to help him, even if he was holding it in his hand or if it were to be found open in front of him, the emotional need to take several books with him when going to eat (or when going anywhere at all) being so strong even though he accomplished very little of his study or none at all during his meals, something that he realized in advance. So he would repeat the same four or five words twenty or thirty times while he ingested avidly . . . stuffing his mouth with cakes and cookies eaten whole, not failing to rub the food against his lips that hadn't been recently washed and that therefore perhaps carried eggs or larvae of parasitic worms which could possibly be carried with the food into his digestive tract, but not worrying about the parasites that could be so produced, and besides that scratching in his haste and violence the mucus covering the roof of his mouth and in fact filling his mouth solid with food including the gaps between his uncared-for teeth, so much so that he could no longer close it, his cheeks puffed out, and not uncommonly choking on solid or even liquid foods that went down the wrong way, imbibing large bowls of hard and dry foods, insufficiently chewed on, his saliva drying up, sometimes continuing all that even after suffering a belly ache, for the orgy was capable of lasting for two hours or more.   (46–49)

But my aim here is not to point to a simple psychopathology that medical research no doubt confirms, relating forms of aphasia and eating disorders, nor is it to reduce Roussel's enterprise to a symptom of schizophrenia, however certifiable his psychological condition might have been. Rather, by referring to Wolfson's account of how he simultaneously binged on food and words, masticating or manipulating one and the other in ways not unlike those employed in Roussel's *procédé*, I wish to give to the latter's fictional extravagances a certain autobiographical sense, although by no means a traditional or psychobiographic one, and so reinforce the idea that he died choking on an excess of words.

The suggestion that the life of Raymond Roussel, as much as what he wrote, might be read as a word game, an idea that I have taken to an extreme in claiming that his death was caused by an overdose of words, comes from, among others,[13] Jean Ricardou, in his preface to Sciascia's *Actes*, an article entitled "Disparition élocutoire" (Voiceful disappearance):

In proportion as the number and rigor of relations among the signifiers of a text increase, so language tends to take over the whole stage, and the role of the author, as subjectivity possessing a sense, diminishes to the point of disappearing. Writing undoubtedly involves putting the author to death. Or else, following Mallarmé's formulation, it involves "the voiceful disappearance of the poet who cedes the initiative to words." . . . It can now be understood that . . . [Roussel's] own life thus refers, inevitably, to the very functioning of his books. . . . Roussel dies within Rousselian simulacra. (Sciascia, *Actes*, 16–29)

But the idea received its first full development in a book that remains exemplary in Rousselian criticism, namely Michel Foucault's 1963 work, *Raymond Roussel*. Foucault debunks the conceit of Roussel's *How I Wrote*, namely that its effect would be limited to a posthumous explanation of how certain of his books function, by pointing to its opening words: "I have always been meaning to explain."[14] *How I Wrote* thus inscribes itself as much at the beginning as at the end of Roussel's work, and, as Foucault demonstrates, the *procédé* operates on the thresholds between life and death and life and work in such a way as to structure the whole Rousselian opus.

Much of what I have so far argued recasts the ideas put forward by Foucault. In describing the formal arrangement of works such as *Impressions of Africa* and *Locus Solus*—the first half of each work consisting in descriptions of the mechanical apparatuses and the second half being narrative explanations of how they came about (in the first edition of *Impressions* Roussel added a note conceding that the "uninitiated reader" might prefer to read the second half first)—Foucault speaks of "navigations" through the space of a repetition. By means of such repetition Roussel's works come to function as machines similar to those they describe; they operate like "a sort of prosthesis, a machine that writes [*machine à écrire*, typewriter] for him";[15] they come to have an automatic life beyond the logical order of their narrative structure. However much they operate according to a logically explicable system and perform a logically explicable function—the fictions are there to prove that—their fantastic nature means that they are also, finally, machines comprising an arbitrary number of parts and assembled in an arbitrary manner.

For Foucault then, "the system is . . . reversible: the narrative repeats the mechanism that creates the narrative" (*Death*, 53). He identifies a similar repetitive structure in *How I Wrote*. With its description of the machine that is the *procédé*, followed by the autobiographical anecdotes that provide a context for the method, it similarly inscribes an effect of reversibility upon the relation between the fictions and their explicative metatext:

> These divided and identical machines reappear in the posthumous text. By a strange reversibility the analysis of the process has the same outline as the machines themselves. *How I Wrote Certain of My Books* is structured as an explanation of the forms in *Impressions d'Afrique* or *Locus Solus*: first, the mechanism whose principles and evolution are described as though suspended between heaven and earth. . . . Then in a second navigation the process is explained within a successive, anecdotal time beginning with Roussel's birth and concluding with a return to the process in relation to which the author's life appears as having been determined by it and forming its context.   (*Death*, 65–66)

On the basis of this effect of reversibility Foucault analyzes the complicated operations of opening and closure that *How I Wrote* performs. Taking the locked communicating door against which Roussel died as the emblem for the setting-in-train of that book, Foucault finds his work to be articulated through the space of a lack, on a threshold that represents a possibility but also the preempting of that possibility. As I have argued, Roussel's method and his work in general can be said to derive from the lack that constitutes language: "the insolvency of words which are fewer in number than the things they designate . . . language speaks only from a lack that is essential to it. From this lack is experienced the 'play' . . . the fact that the same word can designate two different meanings and the same sentence repeated can have another meaning" (*Death*, 165). For Foucault this is the sense of the "solar void" that Roussel says shines from his forehead, such that his madness does not reduce to the mania of "a unique subjective experience" (*Death*, 164).[16] But more than that, given the *procédé*, given the extent to which it depends upon Roussel's death for its functioning, the lack that constitutes language and generates the linguistic machines that inhabit his work has its structure repeated in the idea that it is death that ultimately gives rise to these fictions:

> In order for all this machinery to become intelligible, it was not a code that was needed, but . . . an opening through which their presence would flip over and reappear on the other side. They had to be presented in a replica identical to themselves, yet one from which they were separate. The rupture of death was needed. . . . In *Impressions d'Afrique*, in *Locus Solus*, in all the texts using the process, beneath the secret technique of language there is another secret

hidden, which, like it, is both visible and invisible. It's the part essential to the whole mechanism of the process, the weight that fatally moves the cogs and dials—Roussel's death. (*Death*, 65, 58)

The *procédé* is thus a machine that runs on the lack or "death" that constitutes language, a machine set in motion by the appearance of *How I Wrote*, that is to say by the death of Raymond Roussel. It may well have a kind of functioning irrespective of that death—the word games would still be there even if no reader could ever identify them—but by the same token it cannot have the sense it has without the explanation occasioned by Roussel's death. As a result the life, or rather the death of the author is inextricably tied to his work, and in a way that is exemplary in its complexity. If Roussel had simply published *How I Wrote* during his lifetime, the nexus would of course be less complex; but that book would still perform a similar structural function, coming as the explanation after the event of the works themselves, as it were in the absence of the event, inscribing not only a revelation but also a kind of apocalyptic death— bathos, catastrophe, demise—upon that event. The works would still suddenly be revealed to contain an uncanny otherness. The uniqueness of the *procédé* resides in its postposition with respect to the fictions, in its ability to rewrite them according to its perspective and so perform upon them its powerful operation of closure. There is no more powerful opera- tion of closure than death. But the nexus among life, death, and fiction that *How I Wrote* installs also opens Roussel to forms of rereading that exceed the simple revelatory logic of the posthumous explanation, that take his death out of the cast of the singular event to rewrite it throughout his life and work; life, work, and death assembled as a sort of prosthesis.

In Roussel's view his works had nothing to do with anything living outside his head. This notion is revealed in the context of a voyage to, among other places, Australia and New Zealand, as recounted in *How I Wrote*:

It seems apt that I should mention here a rather curious fact. I have traveled a great deal. Notably in 1920–1921 I traveled around the world by way of India, Australia, New Zealand, the Pacific archipelagos, China, Japan and America. (On this voyage I stopped for a while in Tahiti, where I rediscovered several of the original characters used in Pierre Loti's wonderful book.) I already knew the principal countries of Europe, Egypt and all of North Africa, and later I visited Constantinople, Asia Minor and Persia. *Now from all these travels I*

never took anything for my books. It seems to me that this is worth mentioning,
since it clearly shows just how much imagination accounts for everything in
my work.   (14, my italics)

Here we have Roussel claiming that unlike Loti, whose characters can be
easily traced back to his experiences in Tahiti, he never drew on any of his
travels for his books ("je n'ai jamais rien tiré pour mes livres"). It is difficult
not to read this claim with a certain irony when we consider that traveling
for Roussel relied to a great extent on the possibility of closing himself off
from the experience of traveling. Like any number of imperialist aristo-
crats, and tourists in general, he went to great lengths to surround himself
with the comforts of home. Hence not just the candle heater we have
strategically placed in a Melbourne hotel room but the ultimate in mobile
homes that he had custom-made in 1925, with living room, bedroom,
study, bathroom, and sleeping quarters for a valet and two chauffeurs.[17]
Just as he would seek to create a distinction between the sites of his
excursions and his own sumptuous private space, so he would draw the
curtain between his experience of life and the writing he restricted to the
space of his sumptuous imagination. Far from being indissociable, his life
and work were for him utterly distinct. But as soon as one examines the
terms of the distinction Roussel wants to draw, its borders begin to blur.
For if his life involved giving free rein to a desire for peripatetic and other
self-indulgences, we have seen how his work, for being scrupulously
contained within the parameters of his imagination, nevertheless involved
an abandon to its own indulgences that can be read as structurally similar
to his life. Thus, in claiming to debunk the commonplace idea that what
one writes is based on what one lives, Roussel did no more than affirm a
converse effect; by holding that what he wrote issued solely from his
imagination, that he was able to voyage to Africa (*Impressions of Africa*),
take a tour through Canterel's domain (*Locus Solus*), or follow the labyrinthine detours between the divergences of a series of homonyms, all
within the space inside his head, he demonstrated that his life was structurally indistinguishable from his writing. It was a series of tours or tricks
that determined one as much as the other. Not the least of course this *tour
du monde* from which he is supposed to have taken nothing for his books;
it is the trick that conceals the fact of his having taken everything for his
books from his touring, of having redrawn their structuring impulses
according to the form of the voyage, this differential meander between the

point of departure and its repetition in the point of return, with stops in India, South East Asia, and Oceania, according to whose logic we find him back again embarking upon a guided tour within the four walls of a Melbourne hotel room, his back to a lowboy whose top is covered with numerous vials of barbiturates, sitting at a desk writing a postcard to Charlotte Dufrène. The image on the postcard is a color one of Collins Street with its tram:

> You wouldn't like Melbourne as it is full of handsomes (sic) cabs. For my part I am delighted, as I love that type of locomotion. I have already used the candle heater since it is winter here; during the first part of my trip I thought they would have melted without my even lighting them. My room faces full north so I have the sun all day. The oysters are delicious and since we are in a month without an *r* it is quite the right season. One of these evenings I plan to eat kangaroo soup, a great Australian specialty. They are wild about horseracing and all the large cities are suitably equipped; as for the smaller ones they have at least one racetrack. This is Melba's homeland; her real name is Armstrong and Melba is a nickname taken from Melbourne. Near here there are two bathing spots called Brighton and Menton. It is well worth the trouble to come this far just to go on an excursion to Brighton and Menton, which is what I have done!
>
> Many tender thoughts,
Raymond.[18]

I am prepared to go along with Roussel up to a certain point. Though I would remain skeptical about the idea that nothing from all of this ever found its way into his books—presuming, *concesso non dato*, that we could clearly distinguish between a book and a postcard, given what I have already said about the structures of his writing and traveling, about the guided tour and the investigation of space, and given Derrida's *postalization* of writing—there is nothing necessarily restrictive in the notion that all of his literature derives from his imagination. The space of the imagination, structurally similar to the space of a voyage, should not be construed as less vast. Roussel's writings reaffirm that commonplace notion. And more specifically they affirm that the only space necessary to the literary experience is the space of the word, the spacing that is language and any utterance, "the whole distance that is opened up within the identity of language" (Foucault, *Death*, 34). But Roussel should be resisted when he concludes that the literary object represents a sort of ideality, confined to language, without reference, functioning in the orbit of some utopian avant-garde. My insistence that Roussel overdosed on words does not work in that direction; it does not mean that language remains the only domain of reference, even for what is called real life, biography, or history. For even though my claim is nonsense with respect to a certain body of historical facts, those collected by Sciascia to which I give a great deal of importance, it is just as incompatible with the literary ideality that Roussel posits for his work, and could not be invoked to support the idea of a literature immune to life. Although overdosing on words is an event such as one might read of in a work by a Carroll or a Roussel, my claim for it concerns the life and not the literature of its author. The claim seeks therefore to bring the practice of literature back into the facts of a life, and vice versa, but not in such a way as to reinstate a nonproblematic relation of reference between the two. Again, the idea of a literature of pure imagination, as Roussel conceived his own stories, and the other commonplace idea of literature as autobiography are merely two sides to the same coin; neither of them helps us qualify or negotiate the relation between life and writing. Yet that is one of the contexts that the writing upon writing we call criticism is inevitably asked to describe; it must account for the relation to life of the writing it critiques and to that of its own writing. Once that relation obeys a type of reciprocity, which is what I contend in the case of Roussel, then the resultant dividing of the critical experience among competing or complementary objects, contexts, aims, and necessities creates an abyss. Or rather, it calls forth and lays bare the abyss that is constitutive of any writing, before any so-called act of criticism: any writing is divided by effects of competing contexts, different lives, life and writing, writing and reading, and so on; what I have called all along different forms and effects of prosthesis.

Sitting in the sun and in the radiated warmth of a candle heater, beginning the arduous day-long task of inducing a chemical sleep, Roussel inevitably falls into it, into the space of his own words, making this little postcard as much of a model for his books as anything else he could say, do, or write. Michel Leiris picks up on some of it, pointing out the incorrect spelling of "hansom," which makes a proper name that is also that of a horse-drawn cab into a common adjective. Of course, there is a problem of translation, for one cannot deduce from the catachresis itself whether to give "*handsomes*"—a plural adjective in French—an *s* in English; how to know, then, whether it is a *d,* an *e,* and an *s* that Roussel has let loose here, or just a *d* and an *e*. This may be a minor detail, a letter, neither here nor there, but given Roussel's *procédé* there is no knowing where it might take us. But, to repeat, it can never be a matter of anything other than minor divergences that are potentially enormous digressions, never anything other than problems and stories of translation of the differences of language, nothing but that once language opens and so self-divides. I shall try not to get pedantic about Roussel's misspelling of this word. That *d*, or something like it, something beginning with an initial *d*, perhaps a δ, a delta or differential to signal the opening of language, a marking of prosthetic divergence, an initial, insertion of autobiographical detail, Roussel's, my own, a father's, sign of any number of proper names that are commonly used here, such a *d* in singular and plural form, with or without an *s*, as mark of the relation between text and life, has been let loose here long before any orthographical slip relating to forms of locomotion occurs in Melbourne in or about 1921. So I shall try not to get pedantic about it. Even if, leaving aside the *d*'s, the extra *e* left here, having a form somewhat analogous to a parenthesis that opens, half-closes, then veers page left in a figure of self-erasure, even if the appearance of that *e* in "handsome" has a symmetrical disappearance below. I refer of course to the beach to be found below or under the wheels of those hansom cabs, the sand and ripples of "Menton" (*sic*) under the paving stones of Collins Street. Leiris's transcription doesn't pick up on this one: "Near here there are two bathing spots called Brighton and Menton." He means of course "Mentone." We know, for we have ourselves been on the beach there. A Riviera Menton is transcribed and transposed to Port Phillip Bay without its final *e*. However, short of consulting the original, we do not know whether to blame Roussel or Leiris for the apocope that is operated on the name of Mentone, the ablation of its ultimate and silent vowel. In any case, there is, as I have just said, a sort of symmetry between the cabs' fall into the commonality of an adjective, a word for masculine beauty, and this beach's fall into the commonality of a noun, a word for "chin." A symmetry that might discourage my being any more pedantic about this slip than the previous one. Except that I am no more sure what being pedantic here amounts to than I am sure what to make of these slips in some informal correspondence written in the context of a presumed watertight separation between one form of writing and another, between a life—here recorded on the back or front (a question of order no more resolved here than anywhere else) of a postcard showing not hansom cabs but a tramway—and a literature whose principles of composition reduce, on one reading at least, to an uncontrolled manipulation of whatever is at hand, from life (the address of a shoemaker), from the literature of idiom ("j'ai du bon tabac dans ma tabatière") and so on. For all these data are recorded in the same posthumous text that also affirms the watertight separation in question. I don't know whether refraining from comment on these letters let loose would be in or out of the spirit of a discussion of Roussel's work. Especially since this slip is very much in the spirit of the corruptions of words and expressions that form the basis of Roussel's much vaunted procedure. So there is obviously some story to be told between Mentone and Menton, but I am not sure exactly what to make of it. I am not sure because there is obvious slippage, leakage, or contamination all through this supposed watertight relation, beginning with the book entitled *How I Wrote Certain of My Books*; in other words there is leakage the moment Roussel moves from being author of texts of literature to author of a book about how he wrote those texts, and in that book feels moved to follow his explanation of his "procedure" with a series of fragments that include accounts of a nervous crisis he underwent after the failure of his first work (*La Doublure* [The understudy]), an homage to Jules Verne, this "apt" but "curious" fact of his voyages and their watertight separation from his books, and some brief biographical notes. In fact there is such contamination the moment any metatextual "I," including me, utters that pronoun, and before that, the moment a signatory signs any text in general.

  The problem, and the reason I say I am not sure what to make of the fact, is that the terms are lacking to describe it; nothing is less adequate than the attempts I have made up to this point, with references to life and literature, words and barbiturates, writing and traveling, and so on. Nor is there any reason to suggest that the generality called prosthesis would get us any closer to a valid or accurate description of such relations, even though everything I risk here rests upon that premise. On the other hand, there is, in the constitution of prosthesis as duality, as apposition, interconnection, and even interdependency of presumed irreducible opposites—flesh and steel for instance—there is in that something to recommend it as a condition of differance rendering possible those distinctions, rather than a derivative effect of them, or an attempt at redress of an accident they would have brought about. Prosthesis is at the least a self-conscious enactment of artificial relations, such as those between life and writing, that come to be inscribed in a text. If prosthesis does not itself claim to produce an objective analysis of those relations this is not because it is content to beg the questions it raises, but rather because it cannot see any way out of the paradox according to which certain effects of performance of the questions would necessarily insert themselves into an analysis of them. As long as an "I" were being called upon to analyze the play of an "I," then the analysis would simply repeat the Rousselian paradox: life and writing, for all the attempts to keep them separate, would continually digress or *excursion* into each other's space, or repeat each other's structural configuration, that of the contrived conjunction of difference that every difference entails.

Thus, whether he is spinning a yarn about an amputee Breton within the divergence he creates between "phonotypia" and "fausse note tibia," or tripping unsuspectingly on the English spelling of a Victorian seaside resort, Roussel's practices, narrative and experiential, come back to the same thing: forms of excursion. The writing itself is invariably generated by the notion of displacement, as in the case of the Ramus whose undiscovered Persian manuscript comes to light in one of the stories recounted in *L'Etoile au front*. During the reign of Henri II, Ramus has a Persian lover, Jériz. In order to kill time until she arrives for a secret assignation rendered difficult and dangerous by their forbidden liaison, he sits trying to write but is repeatedly distracted by the thought of her. Upon arriving, she immediately asks for a translation of those pages "in whose conception her image could not fail to have been intimately mingled."[19] The space of the writing is the time and space of the lovers' excursions: the meanderings of his imagination, the complicated journey she makes from home to the place of rendezvous. It is a space inhabited also by the threat of death: the death of the lover if she is discovered, the translation and disappearance of the writing. The structure of the voyage includes its point of no return.

"Excursion" is indeed the word Roussel uses in conjunction with Mentone: "It is well worth the trouble to come this far just to go on an excursion to Brighton and Menton, which is what I have done" ("C'est bien la peine de venir si loin pour excursionner à Brighton et à Menton ce que j'ai fait"). The whole exercise is posited on the necessity of an originary detour, a drift *off course*, an *ex-cursion* to Mentone or Menton, the geography matters no more than the history, such that we could well see him there in 1888 rather than 1921, in a painting by Charles Conder, not that it would get us anywhere, no closer to an identification, for that is not where this was ever headed, there was never any hope that it would come down to a singularity, a single and integral figure on a beach for example, and remain there. We cannot expect that, any more than we can expect the supplementary *e* from a form of locomotion to come to rest again at the end of the same beach (what is there to stop us finding it projected from a poem by Rimbaud in response to its voiceful disappearance from a novel by Perec?).[20]

That Roussel's famous procedure is indeed the pivot between what he supposes to be the intact categories of life and literature is underlined in a discussion by Lanie Goodman, who, following Michel Carrouges, finds many of the homonymic combinations of *How I Wrote* to be in some way self-referential. Though this signing, as I would call it, is not for her a general and inevitable writing effect but rather a function of a particularly Rousselian "delusion," she nevertheless finds that it is Roussel himself, his compositional habits, and his name that can be read in the *métier à aubes* ("career carried on in the early morning" or "loom driven by paddles"), and the *rais*, *raies*, *rayons*, and *roues* that are to be found in his work:

> If indeed the Roussellian narrative is founded on the logic of the pun, a phonetic splintering of syllables, words and phrases into homonymic equivalence, it is hardly surprising that the four syllables of the writer's name seem to surface everywhere in the text. One can only speculate as to whether the repeated use of "rais" and "rayons" (rays), disguised in various permutated forms, is calculated onomastic play or an over-determined semic constellation that has been incorporated into "Martial's" delusional system.[21]

For Goodman, such effects are repeated in the person of Louise Montalescot, one of the most prosthetized characters of *Impressions of Africa*, a woman with pipes inserted in her chest, who plays (with) herself, dresses like a man, and, consumed by her creative passion, seals herself off in a pavilion whose roof is covered with the pages of a novel. But as Foucault suggests (*Death*, 56–57), a similarly pertinent figure for it might be found in the story of Stéphane Alcott and his six sons, whose chests, "on account of their extreme emaciation, carefully maintained by a rigorous diet, exposed to the sound [emitting from the father's mouth] a surface of bone hard enough to reflect all its vibrations"[22] and so enabled them to echo his name without moving their own lips. Alcott invents a machine for repeating the proper name, for repeating his own name in the differences of its successive echoes, for having it rent even as it is repeated as much as any other word, like my stories of a Menton pronounced with or without its final *e* echoing through the pages of this book, a machine for prosthetic indulgence, an anecdotic automaton that sets the words in train through a series of bodies, my father's, my own, and a series of texts disposed for maximum resonance.

We might therefore call the structure of Roussel's procedure that of a prosthetic excursion. It involves the insertion of a fragmented author into the body of writing, and a series of mechanized bodies that are elaborated through the space of a pun; or in the converse direction, it involves the international travel to which it is supposedly in no way related, and leads to the door between life and writing that Roussel wants to close without realizing that he at the same time institutes a threshold of communication between them where he permanently resides. He will still be there at the end, piling up his mattress against the door leading to Charlotte Dufrène's room, stuffing his body with pills, choking on his own words about the separability of life and writing, and dying, as Leiris puts it, "on the very threshold of the *communication* he held to be impossible."[23]

The prosthetic excursion is the very basis of the *procédé* that, as I explained at the outset, involves a narrative journey between two elements of a linguistic difference. It involves *articulating* a difference that it must, in order to function, hold to be absolute. Unless there is a principle of noncoincidence separating *pillard* from *billard*, or *aube* (dawn) from *aube* (paddle), then there is no room for Roussel's writing. But once that writing exists, and once the journey is made from one pole to the other, then the two noncoincident poles are brought into the same narrative and linguistic space. The distinction is no longer absolute. Roussel's procedure thus reads as an allegory of language as differance. For language to function, in order that it not be an unintelligible vocal blur, its elements must be distinguishable in absolute terms: difference as rupture must be its hallmark. But the idea of language as communication relies on a supposed continuous and uninterrupted expression, a covering-over of the differences constituting it. Roussel's narratives make explicit the complicated excursionary measures, the degrees of contrivance that are in fact required for sense to travel across the differences that constitute language, contrivances that the classic conception of language represses.

We can presume that the same logic of necessary but undesirable difference holds true for the relation between Roussel's travels and his books. If he finds it important to keep the two distinct it must be that, known or unknown to him, he is involved in developing a complicated narrative that will lead from one to the other, that he is involved in a form of arbitrary overindulgence or extravagance in each that will have the two activities encroach upon each other's space until a particular exorbitance of each occurs in a doorway in Palermo in 1933: the travel become a form of exile, the writing, now done by proxy, reduced to an expanding list of the barbiturates he consumes. At this point, however, that logic has brought us to Melbourne, to Mentone or Menton, we are not sure which. It has brought us to a Roussel in a hotel room writing a postcard; traveling yet thinking he is not writing, and writing—that is, opening up the orthography of a place-name—yet thinking he is not traveling.

Once one puts Roussel in a beach scene at Mentone written in a hotel room in Melbourne, one is also traveling within the divergence between the tendency to abstraction of Conder's *Holiday* and the hyperrealism that characterizes Roussel's tableaux. For if it is stretching it a little to find Roussel in *A Holiday at Mentone*, even if he did make an excursion to Mentone during an extended holiday (that of his whole life), and even if an argument could easily be adduced that would deprive the title of that painting by Conder of its extratextual authority, such that *A Holiday at Mentone* simply became a holiday or excursion at Mentone, or Menton, where we might easily find Roussel in 1921, just as, had we looked hard enough, we might have found the protagonists of *La Doublure*, Gaspard and Roberte, breaking up there after a Mardi Gras vacation in Nice,[24] after Gaspard's monumental onstage faux pas in Paris, failing to draw his sword at the climactic moment of his career as an understudy, Roberte just disappears when he steps out to buy theater tickets, falling off the edge of his earth, but it would seem they were both of them from the beginning heading towards the border and crossing over into separation, a town in the region of Ventimiglia just waiting to be the site of their rupture, so if in spite of all that it is stretching it a little to find Roussel in a painting by Conder, on the other hand it is a simple fact that a beach scene that could easily contain Conder's painting does form part of Roussel's work. In "La Vue," the view seen through, or in the bottom of, an inkwell is an elaborate description of a seascape at its most brilliant and most animated ("Il représente toute une plage de sable au moment animé, brillant," *La Vue*, 10)—complete with strollers, a straw hat carried off by the wind, children playing, couples promenading on the boardwalk and on a pier with a lighthouse at its extremity, a painter at work, canes and parasols, everything but an amputee lying next to a discarded red newspaper—that carries on for 64 pages of rhyming couplets. Roussel's poem is a tableau vivant, written in cinematic perspective, taking advantage of a focal length sufficient to perceive the physiognomy and psychology of any number of personages, including the two men making semaphore-like signals on the jetty at the other end of the beach:

> the view is interrupted
> Far off to the right, by a long jetty
> Which, marking the limit of the beach, advances into the sea;
> It is very exposed, open to the breeze;
> A thin line of smoke coming from the end of a cigar
> Is blown away quickly and violently.
>
> . . .
>
> Numerous groups
> Are involved in conversation, or stroll about
> Down around the lighthouse. A bored man seems tired
> Of his existence; he is unkempt, almost dirty;
> Nothing amuses him, nothing excites him, he collapses
> Leaning forward, without purpose, on the parapet;
> His discouragement is extreme, total;
> For him life has no charm, is flat and empty;
> He raises his grey, saddened eyes; a wrinkle
> Forms, creating a well-defined furrow; it makes
> His forehead appear more pensive still, indifferent;
>
> . . .
>
> Two men are standing in line
> Facing the sea; the younger one gestures,
> While grandiloquently giving his opinion,
> Towards a spot that he tries to make exact and precise
> Out on the ocean scattered with boats, deployed
> Before their eyes; he holds his cane horizontally
> To indicate exactly what he sees;
> Besides, he stretches out his left hand whose second finger
> Points in a direction that is quite oblique
> Compared with that of his cane; he holds forth, explaining
> His point of view; however his companion
> Resists, is difficult to convince, and shakes his head
> Declining to agree with what he is being told and shown;
> He thinks deeply upon sound counterarguments;

Calm, placid, hands behind his back
He is ready to destroy, with a few simple words,
The conceited but too fragile logic
That is being presented to him.
                    (*La Vue*, 55–57)[25]

Roussel stops short of saying that the point the two men are looking at across the waves is in another country altogether, that it is a father and son who have changed places, the son holding the father's cane as the latter readies to dive into the swelling waters, or that the dejection overtaking the man on the parapet is an oceanic wave of nostalgia that threatens to engulf the whole scene. He stops short of that to provide what for him is a photographic precision diametrically opposed to any tendency to impressionism, abstraction, or any other such radical departure. But a certain blurring of that precision occurs by virtue of the perception's, or the narrative's, desire for exhaustivity. With the camera running, the vision moves like a continuous dolly shot, panning to a new perspective when necessary, but never ceasing to observe in ever increasing close-up the least details of the scene and its inhabitants, reaching even as far as the tie-knot or earrings on passengers on a boat that is admitted to be only a smoky blur.[26] Though the image does not in fact blur until the fade-out of the end ("En ce moment l'éclat / Décroit au fond du verre et tout devient sombre" ["Now the brightness at the base of the glass dims and everything becomes darker"], 73), the perceptive and narrative processes are, as it were, permanently overreaching their limits. As a result the image becomes saturated with detail, with an overload of descriptive information that defies realist, or rather iconic, representation. Foucault calls it a "visibility that exists separate from being seen" (*Death*, 105), a visibility that works outside of the gaze (*hors du regard*). It is as if, in spite of and indeed because of the limitless detail, the analog process of realism begins to fail, requiring digital relief. It is not without reason that Duchamp credits Roussel with enabling him to "think of something other than retinal painting."[27]

Now it might be objected that this is precisely the difference between a figural representation and a verbal one; in the latter case the limits on perceptible detail prescribed by the former do not apply, hence the arbitrary parameters Roussel is able to ascribe to his description, hence the relentlessness of his narrative machine. But it remains that his writing relies on the figural model, it never goes any further than a taxonomy of the infinity of perceptible data, and there is a highly paradoxical reciprocity to the way the limits must be applied. On the one hand it is impossible for writing to record as much as, or as fast as, the eye can perceive; on the other hand, as I have just said, the writing can give itself impossible powers of magnification and mobility, and even presume a whole range of psychological motivations that exceed the purely perceptible. Roussel's writing style is that of the eye of a prosthetic god—an eye attached to an inkwell is a fittingly iconic image of it—and he uses it to move between the limits of writing and the limits of observation. The term "hyperrealism" is particularly apt when applied to his work, even before it spills over into the fantastic of the novels and plays, for the realism of *La Vue* is exaggerated to the point of displaying its own contrivance; it keeps reaching towards the artificial or unreal. In that respect it remains as liminal as the realism of Conder, always on the threshold of its own limits.

Roussel's early poems (*La Doublure, La Vue*) are not the results of the procedure. He maintains that as categorically as he circumscribes his work in general with respect to his travels: "It goes without saying that this method was nowhere employed in my other works: *La Doublure, La Vue,* and *Nouvelles impressions d'Afrique*" (*How I Wrote*, 13). But that is finally of little consequence. If life contaminates his art as soon as he signs it, and does so even more explicitly once he begins to explain the excursionary procedure for it, and if the procedure contaminates the impressions of Australia written on a voyage in 1921, then we would equally expect that procedure to contaminate all his work. For this reason I suggest that he indeed travels to Mentone in "La Vue," that he searches in the bottom of an inkwell and through the sandy stretches of a waterfront for a lost *e*, and perhaps more seriously, that the poem develops a liminal relation between the figural graphic and the verbal graphic, that it involves a poetic excursion from one to the other, investigating the silent and not so silent divergence of a translation of a name, of its passage from the proper (Mentone) to the common (*menton*), a divergence between what is heard and what is seen, or simply between an original version of the word and a supposedly accidental corruption of it, even if only a letter separates them, sufficient to set the narrative machine interminably to work.

A compromise translation might simply place that supplementary letter within parentheses at the end of the French word. Placed there on the edge of the beach it would come once again to represent the graphic signifier of prosthetic graft or drift, drift shell or half-shell of the text of a beach, or driftwood cane bent or distorted to open the space of a narrative or biographical insertion whose closure is the whole question at stake here and for pages to come. The parenthesis, as diacritical mark, would be even more silent than a present or absent *e* from an Australian beach; but in Roussel it is the means by which the last work he published in his lifetime, the third "nonprocedural" work mentioned above, namely *Nouvelles impressions d'Afrique* (New impressions of Africa), also comes to be inscribed with effects of both the signatory or autobiographical and the procedure. That poem is famous for its parenthetical insertions. They frequently mount to the fifth degree throughout the poem, punctuating it with a sort of diacritical dance that leaves only 34 lines of nonparenthetical verse in a poem of some 78 pages.[28] The hierarchical scansion of the text that is so obtained functions according to an exactitude that only Roussel's pedantism could explain, although it would no doubt provide the basis for a distinct structural reading. But not the least effect of the parentheses is a deconstruction of the hierarchy that they appear to institute as the digressionary material comes by its very quantity to usurp the status of the matrical text.

There are no parentheses left open in *Nouvelles impressions d'Afrique*. But the text obviously undergoes a series of explicit self-divisions that again defeat the will-to-closure that we have found to be characteristic of Roussel's life and work. By repeatedly exploiting the effects of digression or excursion, Roussel is once again voyaging as he rewrites himself throughout the poem. And since the poem entitles itself after the earlier *Impressions of Africa*—with which it supposedly shares neither procedure nor subject matter—but then proceeds to compose itself on the basis of artificially inserted textual spaces, the same procedure of verbal and textual distortion of the earlier novel is again put in play. As Ross Chambers explains it, the meaning of Roussel's books in general might be seen to derive from their "parenthetical form":

> They open a parenthesis in the world, fill it as best they may, then close it again. But a moment's reflection shows that a parenthesis has some odd characteristics: it introduces into the sentence a kind of timeless space, after which the sentence begins again as if nothing had happened; and yet the "nothing" *has* happened and the progress of the sentence is significantly modified by the content of the parenthesis. The closing bracket may therefore be said to be identical to *and* different from the opening bracket.[29]

As Roussel would have it, then, nothing is left hanging in his work, no doors are left ajar. The digressions may be as extensive as a world tour, but they come to an end; the narratives as fantastic as his imagination allows, but their closure is determined by the symmetry of the wordplays they are based on; and the writing in general as unique as any in the literature, but it has its mystery solved in the posthumous explanation he offers. On the other hand, it has been my contention that the watertight categories everywhere overflow, that the structure of digressionary excess that he installs resists his presumption to control and contain, that he is everywhere exploring the possibilities of the overdose. Of course the two tendencies are not mutually exclusive; the desire for intact categories could easily be a compensation for a propensity to excess, or vice versa. Such a view would support the idea of a delusional Roussel that history recounts and much criticism profits from; but it would also simply underline the fact that those two tendencies are different sides of the same coin. What is particular about Roussel is the extent to which he renders explicit the liminal tension between them. He takes things to their outside edge, where they are remarked upon as extraordinary, cases apart, then presumes to close the door or parenthesis on them, to keep his practices on this side of accepted principles of literary creation, aristocratic eccentricity, and so on. But his work is exemplary in raising the possibility of a narrative that will not only take leave of reality to fall forever on the side of the fantastic but moreover simply not stop, of a digression that will not return home, of a series of words that will keep adding up until it is the death of him.

That is of course where this discussion begins and ends, with his death from an overdose of words. There is of course an end, even and especially by means of an overdose; there is death waiting and death inscribed in every ending, waiting to occur if no other end is contrived, waiting to manifest itself as the necessary structure of every end. There is that catastrophe at the outside edge of every phrase, every narrative, every voyage. Every journey through space, beginning with that through the word "catastrophe," ends with such a fall. So perhaps the verdict is not yet in after all in the case of the suicide of Raymond Roussel. Perhaps we should pay some attention to the remark made by the waiter Tommaso Orlando di Gaetano when he speaks to Sciascia nearly 40 years after the event, relating a fact that is not recorded in the archives but still causes him to speak of it with "a vivid sense of disgust, amazement, and malaise" (Sciascia, *Actes*, 42n), namely that Roussel had ejaculated about the time of his death; something that would suggest death by hanging, a case of strangulation or asphyxiophilia. And I would in turn be tempted or required to read it as a case of hanging by words. More than the choking on words of an overdose, precisely an act of language whose structure of catastrophe amounted to not just a fall but a push into death by suspension.

That is the logic of another writing game, a familiar game of words, a game called hangman. In playing it, you choose a word, give the first and last letters and the correct number of spaces in between, and your partner then has to deduce the spelling by guessing its letters one by one, to have them filled in or the word deduced before you can draw a hanging, being allowed one stroke for every letter chosen that does not figure in the word. Obviously the longer the word, the better your chance of hanging your partner. We played it as schoolchildren and would look for the longest word in the language, invariably something like "antidisestablishmentarianism," proper nouns disallowed, no chance of a "Taumatawhakatangihangakoauauotamateaturipukakapikimaungahoronukupokaiwhenuakitanatahu," which nevertheless had its place in our lexicomythological baggage and still has its mention in the *Guinness Book of Records* as the longest place-name now in use in the world, the unofficial 85-letter version of the name of a hill in the Southern Hawke's Bay district of the North Island, New Zealand, and one wonders if Roussel would have marveled at it and made an excursion to it just for the sound of it, whether he would have spelled it correctly or written a novel within its letters, a right royal story in this name that means "the place where Tamatea, the man with the big knees, who slid on, climbed, and swallowed mountains, known as land-eater, played his flute to his loved one," a Tamatea like a character escaped from *Impressions of Africa*, like a Breton Lelgoualch, an amputee fisherman who slid down one too many festive slippery poles, fractured his thigh, and, attempting to hide his shame and his discomfort, fell victim to gangrene and had his leg amputated, but retained the tibia to make of it a flute on which he played joyful or patriotic airs, for dancing or lovemaking, there is of course a name to tell his story (67–68), the name Phonotypia become "fausse note tibia" dutifully explained in the posthumous work, there is a seemingly necessary story of melodious amputees and prostheses once it comes to this type of storytelling, Roussel's work bears testimony to that, the characters of *Impressions of Africa* (and *Locus Solus*) veritable cyborg orchestras, Louise Montalescot with the organ pipe chest

(*Impressions of Africa*, 141–49), Tancrède Boucharessas the armless and legless one-man band (62–63), Stéphane Alcott and his six sons, everyone here playing his or her own music, the hapless European castaways entertaining their African host and captor Talu VII, emperor of Ponukélé and king of Drelchkaff, strumming their prosthetic tunes and performing their circus tricks to while away the hours waiting for a ransom to arrive, the stories always spinning out in the anticipation of death, within the delay of an execution, they prove they can always live longer thanks to their technological wizardry, their cunning in selling their useless contraptions knowing theirs will be the ultimate profit, theirs the stories to take back and recount reclining on the beach at Cannes or Mentone eating caviar, they will live to tell the tales unlike those other captives, the losers of the internecine double-dealing, betrayals, and infidelities of Talu's kingdom for whom the most exquisitely refined machines of execution have been devised, Mossem the forger who has the text of his infamy tattooed on his heels with a red-hot iron (22–23), Rul whose corset is sewn into her flesh until a needle reaches her heart (23–24), they cry out unto death while the Europeans sing for their supper, the symmetry is perfect as always with Roussel, the social and the historical, the whole book capable of being read from midpoint to the end and then from the beginning to the middle if one prefers, if one prefers to learn the background narrative and the rationale for these bizarre inventions before one reads of the inventions themselves, if one prefers the serious explanation of history before the frivolous play of these idle hours, no doubt some part or some sort of Roussel imagined keeping them apart while the space of his book wove them together, like a needle, style, or stylus sewing its arabesques into the body of the real world, one stitch at a time, always the possibility of a further stitch or point until the last one, the stitch that is death, the outside point of all this where the game meets its serious other, hence hangman as a figure for all this, Roussel opening his veins to remove the corset of his body in the bathroom a week and a half before he died, resigned to performing the suicidal act himself after Orlando declined to do him the favor (Sciascia, *Actes*, 56), Roussel with his scrupulous count of barbiturates upping the ante in a grim simulation of asphyxiophilia, but who knows whether orgasm by self-induced strangulation is a simulation or the real thing, auto-affection or auto-affectation, in any case the finest erection and the best ejaculation are there for the searching at the edge of strangulation, Roussel with one hand on the vial and the other holding a pen as if one hand were tightening the cord while the other disappeared into the fly of the champagne-pink fine woolen body suit that history in the person of Dr. Michele Margiotta records for us as his overnight attire that July 13–14, 1933, he pulls on the cord, trips the switch, or cranks the engine to set the machine in motion, it sparks and then fires in a brilliant climax as the fireworks explode for the Feast of Santa Rosalia and fascist Italy celebrates the transatlantic crossing of the Balbo squadron (Sciascia, *Actes*, 34, 55), and it takes ten strokes to draw a hanging, four for the scaffold—base, vertical pole, diagonal support strut, horizontal pole—one for the rope, and five more for the body—head, trunk, right leg, left leg, arms, presuming of course that the man to be hanged has two legs, but an extra stroke if one adds an erection, presuming we are dealing with a man, thus providing for the choice of another letter, always another letter waiting in the wings to make the story longer or enter into some complicated transaction between an amputation and an erection, the sources of pleasure or narrative digression one derives from such an event, presuming one is hung without one's wooden leg, all that to be weighed in the balance before the trapdoor is flung open or the chair kicked away, but the extra letter that might be rescued from the jaws of death would not likely be the letter *e*, however, for as the most common one in this language it was sure to be chosen at the beginning, except that we know that the whole play occurs in the space between the beginning and the end, the space that first *e* opens up before it falls again, or remains suspended at the end, barely in sight at the vanishing point of a sandy beach, but if the words can get longer up to and beyond the number of letters to choose from in the alphabet, so can the picture have details added to prolong the pleasure or the agony, for the game of hangman again pits the word in a race of symmetry against a figural representation, like an undecidability over the spelling of a beach and the questions raised by the painting of that same beach, a life drawn by historians opposed to a literature written in letters large, or vice versa, for the players can easily change places, the historians write the writers draw, one can swallow or choke on one's words, overdose on them, lose one's life in a text as surely as in a game, like the officers of the czar who, according to François Caradec (the same François Caradec, we may presume, who wrote a life of Roussel, telling another story in the *Pléiade Encyclopedia*), played their version of hangman by throwing themselves off the branch of a tree with a noose about the neck and a sword in one hand, having to cut the rope before it tightened enough to kill them,[30] just imagine the priapic bliss of such machismo, and Caradec notes in the same context the relation between intoxication and the game, "the intoxicated often resemble players who seek, in spite of the taboos, to retrieve a dizziness [*vertige*] similar to that of their childhood games,"[31] or, we might add, the addict seeks to retrieve a vertigo similar to that of the literary imagination he presumes to keep intact from his tourist experiences, a vertigo that is both a simulacrum and a deferral of the death that waits at the end of the line, the story, the rope, the erection, there are ten strokes needed to spell a hanging, nine strokes only for an amputee, this story then a nine-stroke hanging, a nine-stroke climax, a graphic representation of a gibbet, a potence, or a crutch with a body attached to it, a body jolted by spasms in anticipation of the last gasp, a father and son suspension story told in the limbo of a final separation, the story recounted once more in *Impressions of Africa*, that of Emperor Talu's twelve-year-old son Rhejed, a mischievous boy who has told no one of his plans, who produces a lightweight door, then kills a rodent that emits a gluey substance that sticks it to the door, to which he then attaches his partly unwound toga, then waits for a bird of prey to come after the carrion, get stuck in the glue, and, frightened by Rhejed, take off carrying door and boy high into the air:

> In turn Rhejed left the ground, swinging on the end of his loin cloth, a large part of which still encircled his loins.
>
> In spite of its load, the robust fowl climbed fast, still encouraged by the cries of the child, whose laughter attested to his wild jubilation.
>
> At the precise moment he was borne away, Talu had rushed towards his son with every sign of violent alarm.
>
> Having arrived too late, the unfortunate father followed with a look of anguish the course of the little monkey, who was flying further and further away, unaware of any danger which might befall him. . . .
>
> Meanwhile the huge, flying creature, the tips of whose wings were all that could be seen over the door, continued to mount higher into the heavens.
>
> Rhejed, as he grew smaller before our eyes, was clinging frantically to the end of his loin cloth, thus increasing the chances, already so numerous, of a fatal fall, on account of the weakness of the bond holding the red cloth and the two invisible claws to the door. (38–39, translation modified)

a story for its own sake, a game to kill the dead time of a faded aristocracy, the door closed between it and any real life or any drug-induced stupor, no allegorical complicity, nothing but a young boy flying high on his own invented delight, floating in his prosthetic moment while his father waits in trepidation below, a father who used to take him on his knee and throw him up but now the boy has taken off in earnest, the communicating door off its hinges, the dependencies being made and tested in the most far-flung fantastic imaginings, everything up in the air, the anxieties, the rivalries, the searchings for approval, the mimicries, the parodies, the aggressions, the abandonings, every difference there is between a father and a son, everything taken to the limit of an outside tenuous and contrived connection where flesh and blood meets the thrill and terror of its inanimate dependencies, where a life meets a literature, the ropes it pulls on, the doors it opens and shuts, where a father meets and loses a son to a world beyond his, he feels it like a form of difference as difficult yet familiar as the wooden leg he carries, this is his offspring sprung far off, the boy has taken the lid off things to serve his own pleasure and propulsion, opened the door like a Pandora's box or jack-in-the-box, like a *boîte à surprises* as one might say in Roussel's language, like the time I opened the door to my father's bedroom, the place where he took off his leg nightly, and more and more regularly took his dose of analgesics or barbiturates to allow him to sleep, but no excess, just a modest lineup of bottles, two or three on top of the lowboy, sufficient to ruin his prostate and threaten his kidneys while doing little to relieve his pain, they sit there impotently on the lowboy next to a round turned wooden box of native woods that I always coveted and that my mother would take it into her head to restore and bring halfway across the world to me 30 years later, it contained, among a number of burst buttons, a safety pin or two and some pairs of cuff links and the odd tiepin, a small tin container measuring about 9 × 5 centimeters with an orange-colored design on top, the size of a snuffbox or tobacco pouch, his little *boîte à surprises* that used to sit there has now been consigned to my safekeeping, with its lid that can come on or off at leisure or at will, I am able to take the lid off his private life whenever I wish to indulge my narrative or theoretical fantasies, finding access to the secrets he shares with his leg and without his leg with my mother, it was there for the looking behind their bedroom door, my father would take me there or rather I would lead him there as he limped on his crutch across the house in the dead of my sleepless childhood nights to lie between his one-legged body and my mother's wholeness, but the closest I ever came to the primal scene was when I entered the room in their absence one day and searched through the drawers for something more than a variegated wooden box could reveal, searching for I knew not what but knowing that if there was any mystery it would be found here, finding the cache of Cadbury's chocolates and helping myself to two or three of them from the drawer with his socks, stumpsocks and underwear, then searching still, rummaging through my mother's built-in chest of drawers, no gastronomic surprises though she did keep a case of stout under the bed on the doctor's prescription during the two pregnancies that followed me, nothing to eat but a strange object lying in a plastic case there among the stockings, Spencers, and suspenders, it was a diaphragm as it turns out but I couldn't recognize it at the time although I understood it to be secret and sexual, but that in any case was the most that Pandora's drawer could reveal, the *tiroir à surprises* yielding up that slight prosthetic membrane like a miniature plastic stumpsock, small in significance but a mechanism sufficient to set my mind to work and the wheels of a prepubescent imagination to turning, for that membrane was yet another communicating door that could be installed or removed, a machine for articulating the difference between pleasure and conception, between spermatozoon and ovum, it was a veritable *machine à surprises* having the structure of at least one form of Roussel's verbal deviations, for his whole procedure consists of arranging words in the form of difference machines, his *billard* become *pillard*, or more explicitly his *palmiers à restauration* and the like, his *roues* ("wheel"/ "swagger") *à caoutchouc* ("rubber" / "rubber tree"), his *maisons* ("house"/ "dynasty") *à espagnolettes* ("window fastener" / "young Spanish woman"), his *baleines* ("whale"/"baleen") *à ilôt* ("small island" / "Spartan slave" [*Ilote*]), all of those listed in *How I Wrote* (4–8) and the many more that went to make up his tales, his whole creative procedure nothing more than a machine for filling in the spaces, a *machine à* —— operating on the pretext of a slight corruption of a single letter, an *a* here, an *e* there, for here is something else Roussel appears to overlook in his procedure, namely the fact that what permits his narrative aberrations is more than just the homonymic possibilities of the nouns he chooses (*palmiers/restauration, roues/caoutchouc, maisons/espagnolettes,* and so on), it relies more particularly on a certain undecidability in the sense and function of the preposition *à,* in the fact that in such combinations it can variously mean "related to," "for the purpose of," "in the manner of," or "equipped with," the list is not exhaustive, but it amounts to the variable space of a prosthetic relation there at work where a Roussel would more likely presume to place a closed door, with the result that this door cracks, opens, or flies off its hinges or always remains somehow ajar, like a variegated wooden box belonging to my father and sitting on his lowboy, the *boîte à surprises* now in my possession which, like a word from Roussel contained another box, that orange-colored little tin containing licorice throat lozenges called Lixoids in one version, Negroids in another, according to some naively racist antipodean version or impression of Africa that escaped scrutiny and that had no doubt survived the journey, like most of the words we used, from a Caucasian England to a Polynesian New Zealand without anyone's noticing the difference, without anyone's noticing the irremediable scandal of a language that had traveled so far, in any case Lixoids tasted like hot tar but we learned to love and crave them, and my father would dole out the 9 × 5 millimeter black pills for us to suck on and wince at as our tongues turned black as though we had swallowed poison, and the menthol braced our sinuses and coursed through our veins in a minor piquant version of euphoria, while he clicked the tin shut producing a short shrill metallic squeak, as though he had bent a leg that needed oiling, closing the tin on these bizarre delectables like closing the door on his private life, until a furtive son seeks to open it again, looking for the word behind a word, for instance a French word for "limping" that is also to be found in this surprise box, this *boîtier* called prosthesis inherited from him and that I open for pleasure, reminder or remainder of the prosthetic relation that still and always operates here, prosthesis the figure for all the contrived relations by means of which difference is negotiated, exemplified in this instance by an indiscriminate use of prepositions to confuse the genitive with other nonspecific relations, like an imagined contrivance that permits a son to explore the expanses over an anxious father's head, once the prepositions are let loose the differences begin to fly and translating them becomes both a delectation and a peril, like the anecdote my father would recount about how French fell down as the language of diplomacy when one warring faction called out to the other "Parlementons" ("Let's talk"), which the other heard as "par le menton" and let him have it through the chin, except that we would have to recognize that another linguistic detour by way of the beach (*par Menton[e]*) also offers itself there, the language goes round and round and there is still space for a trick or turn of it here in the context of Roussel's excursion to Melbourne and the postcard he writes sitting in the sun, the sun that he no doubt imagines having, possessing, a light that will shine out of him as bright as a star, a blinding beam gleaming on his forehead. He says as much to his analyst. He sits in the winter sun, in front of the special candle heater he has brought with him halfway across the world. To his right there is a lowboy, just under a meter high and about 75 centimeters across. On top of that a line.

§ 9 Geneva, 1978

"[?]20 April 1978   [?]From the air-
port I enquired about a hotel quite close to the University so as not to have
to walk too much. I got there by taxi without too much difficulty. Once at
the hotel, I stupidly asked for a room on the first floor, as if I had forgotten
the existence of lifts and the economy they provide. Result: an infernal
noise, a sleepless night. My cast and pair of crutches dramatized my
appearance before these students who had never seen me, and I must
admit that I am coming to play on this temporary infirmity more and
more. I am enjoying myself over it all over

[?

That (I refer to the preceding sentence and, not quite yet, to the bracket
and question mark) is what I write here for the French "J'en jouis de
partout." I am trying to render at the same time the "literal" sense of the
verb *jouir de*, which gives "to enjoy" in English, as well as the sexual sense,
where it means "to come." *La jouissance* has been so bandied about in
current literary and psychoanalytic discourse that there is probably no
need for me to give that explanation. But it is somewhat more complicated
than that, for "j'en jouis de partout" has that physical, if not sexual, sense,
quite explicitly in the French to the extent that it is already a play on
souffrir de partout, which means "to hurt all over." So perhaps I should
simply have written "It is making me come all over," which would cater, or
pander, to the stronger sense, or sex. Except that: (1) it is women, as
current theory reminds us, who are more apt at coming all over than men
(not to preclude or occlude the difference between coming all over in the
sense of a diffused orgasmic release and ejaculating all over, for man or

woman), and the matters of sex and gender and strength and coming obviously raise more questions than they answer, especially when one considers the self-divisions that occur in this text, something I shall have more to say about below; (2) the pronoun *en* retains the syntax of *jouir de* ("to enjoy"), as contrasted with *jouir* ("to come"); and (3) it is both naive and disingenuous of me to suggest that this is the first point in the text where translation becomes a problem, where a gloss or explanation becomes necessary enough to bring about an interjection such as this. In fact, you can see that the problem arises in the very first line, even before the date, with the question of what it means to translate quotation marks, or the question of whether a quotation remains a quotation once it is translated. That problem is immediately compounded by a similar quandary with respect to spaces, the matter of whether 52 French spaces translate into the same number of English spaces. Those sorts of problems arise however much I might want to avoid preempting the advancement and even the beginning of my task here by resorting to what seem to be unnecessary digressions.

And anyway, who is speaking here? Man, woman, Jane Gallop, David Wills, originator, translator? That is the real problem, and the beginning of the reason for this, or that, break in the continuity of the text. Jane Gallop likely had nothing to do with this; I am taking her name in vain, but my discussion of the verb *jouir* seemed to me reminiscent of her rumination on the "jouissance principle" and the question of translation, so it may be as well to give her credit here.[1] I say that because the matter of what comes from where to get into this text, what is acknowledged and how, and finally which text is which, what and whose, are primary concerns of it. The text I was translating—although I am not sure that I have discontinued doing so by pointing to problems that arise in the course of that translation, this may after all be nothing more than a footnote to a translation or a problem in a translation—is from Jacques Derrida's "Envois" in *La Carte postale*.[2] As it happens, I had completed a version of this—the extent to which the present text remains a version of the previous one or is a different text altogether, and what it means to complete a text, are of course further questions, but rest assured I shall not continue to raise every objection that comes into my head, only those that I really stumble over—before I found out that the English translation by Alan Bass was in fact in the proofreading stage. That was quite some years ago now. But even if I had known earlier, I doubt whether it would have prevented me from writing this. Firstly because I often have reason to find fault with Alan Bass's translations of Derrida,[3] and secondly because what really prompts all this is not primarily a semantic or even a linguistic question.

Standing there on the tenth line of the letter that begins on page 150 of the French text, immediately after the space after the word *partout*, is the diacritical mark used to open a parenthesis, that which, by means of the metonymy that is the whole abyss of my questioning and digressing here, is itself called a parenthesis. Common usage does not distinguish the mark "(" from the mark ")." One does say "open parenthesis" or "close parenthesis" when dictating or proofreading, but it is doubtful whether the performativity of such utterances can be said to have gained the constative status of substantives in the lexicon (not that I am about to argue for the pure constativity of any utterance whatsoever).[4] Be that as it may. There it is, this (, in French, and now it is also there in English (138, Bass). There is no way of telling whether it has been translated, transliterated, or transplanted; no way of telling what precise transfer has occurred to have it go from one text to the other, to a third text, no way of telling how to stop its migration, to arrest its movement however halting that movement might be.

But a mark with no satisfactory name is not the least of my problems here, and still not the heart of the matter I am attempting to get to. The problem is not so much with the (as with the fact that there is no), not one to match this (, not on page 150, not anywhere that I can find, although there are any number of further parentheses, open and closed, beginning on the same page, and occurring on almost every page to the end of the text. And the same lack of what I will call a closing parenthesis has been duly translated into English. This is not the only occasion that this occurs in "Envois." There is another instance on page 164 (151, Bass), and that may not be all. But what strikes me about it on April 20, 1978, is the fact that this slip of a parenthesis occurs when Derrida is in prosthesis. That single fact becomes the pretext for all that precedes and follows: the desire to translate and retranslate, the limits of digression, the matter of what a parenthesis, or half a pair of parentheses, let slip by a Derrida on crutches, might have to do with a text constructed in and around my father's wooden leg.

The event of this missing parenthesis amounts to nothing less than a question mark after (or "over"; where does one put a question mark when one wants it to refer to every written mark?) the status of everything subsequently published above the name of Jacques Derrida. And, by extension, everything published above his name prior to this event. But there I go being disingenuous again. For it is not as if everything Derrida has written has not itself raised the question of its own status, and of the status of everything written, full stop, particularly as it relates to citationality, the semantics and politics of quotation marks (see *Limited Inc.*). But it must be admitted that it comes very clearly into focus, as a problem and a problematic, once the reader, or the translator, has to assume the role of the writer and, for example, close or not close parentheses left dangling, provide what is obviously, whether it be by mistake or by design, missing from the text. What is the relation of one word to another given the possibility of the endless displacement and deferral that an open parenthesis implies? How does one bring syntactical operations up out of the abyss once apposition comes to resist grammatical subordination? For "to parenthesize," according to the Greek, is literally to place beside, and once the opening of this parenthesis has left in suspension the hierarchical relations between one word and the next, opening the possibility of syntax by introducing a break in the flow of signifiers, but failing to institute it by adjudicating between them, there is no close to such an undecidable free-for-all, or free fall. Such questions or objections would seem to be serious stumbling blocks in the way of this translation.

Thus my starting point is the fact of a text with something missing needing translation; both a text with something missing, which text needs to be translated, and a text with something missing whose something missing needs to be translated. I cannot in fact presume that what is missing is a closing parenthesis, I cannot even presume that the closing parenthesis, in not being printed on the page, is in fact missing. For "Envois" actually leaves things out regularly. The reader is warned in the preface that the author felt obliged to expunge certain passages from the letters that constitute the text, and that those expurgations are indicated by a blank space of 52 characters for each occurrence (8; 4, Bass). Now there seem to be no such blanks in the letter of April 20, 1978, but closer examination of the irregularity of the paragraph indentations in fact suggests the operation of that trusty macro following the date and once again later on. In fact, the argument could easily be made that the missing closing parenthesis occurs within the expunged material that gives the appearance of a paragraph ending thirteen lines below. In terms of translating what Derrida writes in these letters, what would it mean to have, by deduction, become privy to something of what he deemed fit to expunge from them, namely this missing parenthesis? Would that privilege be a fact of accident or design, and to what extent should it or could it become a determining factor of a translation?

Thus, whether the parenthesis be missing, expunged, or forgotten, I am still left with the problem of translating its absence, and indeed of translating the whole 52-character space. Not the least facet of that problem involves distinguishing between a paragraph—something written beside—and a parenthesis—something placed beside—once both come to be represented by blank spaces. So to return to something I suggested above, is it sufficient to leave a space of 52 characters in English as I have done, given my attention to the detail and translation of diacritical marks, and given the added frequency of such marks that the use of accents necessitates in French? Are 52 French characters equal to 52 in English given all the differences of protocol regarding typeface, indents, word length, and so on? In the preface Derrida explains that he had devised a complicated set of calculations for arriving at the number 52, but that he has forgotten it. Should I somehow try to render that slip or omission also, and if so, how many spaces would it require?

One way out would be to resort to ellipsis, to begin the letter with a "..." that I could then choose, if I wished, to enclose within brackets. But there are already enough difficulties in translating the use of ellipsis from English to American—inclusion or exclusion of full stop, spaces between dots, and so on—to call for caution in having them faithfully represent 52 French spaces standing for excisions from personal and philosophical letters. There is also, of course, the standard mark for representing the loss of letters, confined to the loss of a single one in French but sometimes more than one in English (e.g., "can't"), namely the apostrophe. Now to use that might not be as far-fetched as it seems since (1) there is nothing to suggest that on this occasion the 52 spaces do not represent a single letter, for Derrida states that the same device is used irrespective of the length of the passage excised; (2) "Envois," perhaps more than any other text by Derrida, plays on the homonym that the word "letter" brings into play, eliding constantly between what is literal and what is epistolary, and between literature and postcard; (3) much of the narrative structure of "Envois" turns around one particular letter that gets addressed, mislaid, returned, and entrusted to a third party, and becomes the object of an emotional tug-of-war between sender and addressee; and (4) more than any of that, there is explicit reference to the use of apostrophe in the preface to "Envois," specifically the rhetorical device to which Derrida has recourse in order to preserve the possibility of private address within these private letters rendered public.

While it is true that the rhetorical sense of apostrophe—that figure, as the *OED* will confirm, by which a speaker or writer suddenly stops in his discourse and turns to address pointedly some person or thing either present or absent—does not refer to an excision of the text in the same way that the blanks do, it quite obviously serves as a division of it, a dehiscence that means that the letters never arrive to or at the reader whole. The letters divide between those parts that are to some extent determined by the use of *tu* and those parts not so determined. And consequently the addressees divide between that *tu* (which itself further subdivides between, on one hand, a *tu* who is not the "individual" "present" reader but someone like the loved one of the sender and, on the other hand, any given reader who presumes to put himself or herself in the position of that *tu*), and those generically referred to, most of the time, as *ils*. And it will also be found—and hence my earlier obliqueness concerning the sex of the writer—that the sender purports to divide, between the singular and plural and between male and female, by combining those functions and problematizing the distinctions between them (cf. *Carte postale*, 251; 234, Bass). As a result the text is profoundly fissured, at its "origin," in its "relay," and at its "destination," if we can preserve for a moment the myth of those separate functions; it is seriously apostrophized and ellipticized. Furthermore, since the apostrophe not only divides the body of a text, disassembling it and redistributing it, but also divides the body of addressees, attaching a particular piece of message to one listener or reader and in a sense depriving the others of the same, then it is also the means by which a text becomes prosthetized. That will become more evident shortly.

The singling out of one particular addressee to be called *tu*, to whom some of the message is supposedly more specifically destined, is both apostrophic and parenthetic. In fact, the problem parenthesis of April 20, 1978, opens an apostrophe, the first one of the letter, involving its first use of *tu*. Of course the difference between a rhetorical apostrophe and a parenthetical or theatrical aside is that the apostrophe is designed to single out a particular person, whereas the aside distinguishes between one or more fellow actors and an audience of one or more spectators, but I doubt whether that makes for a structural distinction since it comes back to a distinction between different categories of addressee in a contrived division that belies its own status even as it establishes it. That is to say that the aside relies on a structural division between those on stage and the audience which enables the actor to speak loudly enough for the audience to hear while having those on stage pretend not to hear, yet in addressing the audience, either directly or through an aside to another actor, the actor speaking contravenes that structural division and gives the audience the status of fellow actors. Furthermore, the aside need not and should not be confined to its theatrical usage; it can as well be applied to a parenthesis or apostrophe spoken by one member to another, or more than one member to more than one other member, of a group of speakers in any situation. And given the doubt concerning the number of senders and addressees, and the establishing and contravening of structural distinctions between and among them, the apostrophes of "Envois" act all the more in the manner of asides, become all the more indistinguishably apostrophes or parentheses.

Speaking of words spoken by an actor on a stage as *un*opposed to words spoken or written by anyone, of the nondistinction between speech acts and speech acted about which Derrida has argued at length (*Limited Inc.*), I come to yet another possible way of dealing with what is missing from this letter. After ellipsis, apostrophe, and parenthesis, we might consider what we used to call in school "speech marks," or 66s and 99s. I remember learning how to use them in those endless dictation exercises, putting the comma inside, subordinating the 's to the ""s, until at some point it all changed and punctuation went outside and singles became standard, 69s were to be enjoyed all over, the doubles the exception, in spite of the possible confusion raised thereby between a closing quotation mark and an apostrophe; and then I came to America and nothing was correct anymore, so I gave up on punctuation altogether. Perhaps this is as much about my incomplete translation to America as it is about the translation of a letter by Derrida.

Within the category of direct speech, which designates everything appearing within the letters, the apostrophic passages appear as more direct, as having more specific direction and destination. Thus if one invariably omits the quotation marks that, I might argue, should appear after the "Dear So and So"—equivalent to an "I say"—at the beginning of a letter, it might be reasonable to use the same to mark out these particular passages of more direct address within the letters. After all, the apostrophe is quite explicitly referred to as a first-person speech act. It is possible to apostrophize. I apostrophize. The apostrophe is also a genre one can adopt. A genre and a tone. The word –apostrophe–, it refers to the words addressed to someone in particular, a live interpolation (the man of discourse or writing interrupts the continuous development of the sequence, he abruptly turns toward someone, even something, he addresses you in the singular, in familiar terms), but the word also refers to skill in diversionary tactics (*Carte postale*, 8; 4, Bass). At some point there a direct quote began, a direct quote that has been redirected, rendered indirect, made to digress through a translation, but I no longer know what to do about the quotation marks. For no less conventional than the omission of quotation marks at the beginning of a letter is their omission at the beginning of any piece of writing, such as the present, where everything might be said to be prefaced by the words "I read that . . ." Now conventional wisdom might say that in a piece of writing involving quotation (would that not mean every piece of writing to the extent that one does not own the language one uses?), and failing any indication to the contrary, direct address should be assumed until one quotes someone else's words. On the other hand it might be more accurate to say that indirect speech should always be assumed because of the reliance upon and representation of words and ideas that one does not possess, and that it is peculiar to indicate a change from first person (narrator) to third person (source quoted, a third person who interpolates in the first person as it were) by using quotation marks. And what of the case of translation, where one is led to make all sorts of assumptions and judgments concerning the "direct speech" of another in order to render it in another language? Shouldn't it be assumed that everything translated becomes "reported" or indirect speech, thus not susceptible to inclusion within quotation marks? Furthermore, what happens once one stumbles upon a dangling parenthesis and is forced into direct address of one's own within the direct or indirect address of another, thereby inverting the hierarchy again and representing the more direct speech in a more indirect, because subordinate, form? In such a case one doesn't, after all, revert to quotation marks but more usually has recourse to a footnote or a type of parenthesis, such as that apposed to and capable of substituting for the opening speech mark of this chapter. Hence the commission and omission of such marks seems less consistent than ever.

Indeed, they seem to be left out, or replaced at a point where they seem
necessary within the lines drawn from Derrida's preface. I read and
translate that the word –apostrophe–, it refers to the word addressed to
someone in particular. I don't read that the word "apostrophe" refers to the
word addressed to someone in particular. Instead of using inverted commas to parenthesize the mention of the word, Derrida uses dashes. As a
result I read, instead of a mention, the second-degree apposition—second
only to commas according to the convention cited in note 6 below—of the
two words "word" and "apostrophe." I therefore read in Derrida the *word-
apostrophe*; or, if I take into account the pun in French, where *apostrophe*
functions as not only the noun "apostrophe" but also the verb form
"apostrophizes," I read that the word *apostrophizes*, the word works as an
apostrophe. I read a word, and words in general that stand in for a silence
or an absence, words that are apposite to a rupture, words that divide
discourse by interrupting themselves to make a more personal point,
words that confuse public and private address.

When "prosthesis" came to punctuate the English language, around the
time of the word "prosthesis," or "word-prosthesis," that is to say in the
sixteenth century, distinguishing pieces of text and creating a hierarchy
among them was a serious growth industry. There were, to begin with, two
types of text, language being divided into a classical text and a commentary upon it. M. B. Parkes refers to the plethora of strange marks dotting
texts back then as a new technology seemed to give license to rewrite their
internal boundaries. In his own words he tells how printers who produced
editions of commentaries on established texts had to separate the extracts
(*lemmata*) of the text under discussion from the commentary itself. In the
edition of Virgil's works printed by H. Quentel (Cologne, 1499) *lemmata*
are placed within the new marks, the facing parentheses. . . . When F.
Reiner printed the Bible with the Postills of Nicholas of Lyra at Venice in
1482–3, he introduced a single half-crochet ⌐ before a passage in the text,
and another after the corresponding *lemma* in the accompanying commentary. . . . In the sixteenth century . . . [t]he most common way to
introduce a *lemma* was to separate it from the following commentary by a
single crochet] or parenthesis).[5] So there is a historical case for a lack of
discrimination among parentheses and brackets, their openings and clos-
ings, a case for using them to do the service of quotation marks, and even
examples of further fragmentation of such marks, their bisection, the
amputation of a bracket's member so that it looks more like a crochet or

cane or potence waiting to be erected. That very same mark of the *lemma,* this fifteenth-century ⌋, in fact finds itself reprinted on the edges of Derrida's best-known essay about edges, "Parergon" (*The Truth in Painting*).

Thus if the abyss did not already yawn enough, if assigning the inverted commas were not already enough of a problem given the law of general citationality, the writtenness of every utterance, the fact that every sign can be put between quotation marks, which turns *speech acts* into *speech marks,* then it all becomes a free fall again once these diacritical instruments begin to chip away—and themselves get broken in the process—at the edges of the writing, threatening to undermine the bases upon which text is kept separate from apostrophic commentary. So I am left to try to distinguish and decide between and among . . . , ', ( ), and [ ], and " . . . ," " '," "((with or without '),' " and "[ ]." To those I now need to add, whether between parentheses or as an apostrophe or between dashes or commas I am not sure, , or "," and —or "—," for commas and dashes are clearly just as indistinguishably parenthetic or apostrophic. In fact the comma also has the etymological sense of an excision: a piece of writing extracted from the main body of the work before becoming the mark of that separation, it is the converse of the paragraph, which metonymized from a mark of separation or indentation to a piece of writing so separated. But to top it all off, I am also required to deal with " " and/or " " "," to distinguish between my use and mention of how I and the writer of the letters punctuate, that is to say insert into, by means of ellipses, parentheses, apostrophes, direct speech, commas, and dashes, our always already cited re-marks with ellipses, parentheses, apostrophes, and direct speech addressed to a divided body of readers. I might be forgiven for being unsure how to use the punctuation, for not knowing who or what begins when or where.

In spite of all that, as I have just suggested, there remains the one simple and time-honored convention, in cases of translation at least, for distinguishing between one source of quoted material and another, between original and translation if you insist, namely the use of a specific type of parenthesis, the [or bracket.[6] In fact, when I went to school we called both sorts brackets, distinguishing rather between round and square ones, and between brackets and braces ({ }) when it came to mathematics. The *OED* still holds a bracket to be one of two marks of the form [ ] or ( ), and in mathematical use also { }, used for enclosing a word or number of words. . . . In typography, esp. applied to "square brackets" (formerly called crochets), the "round brackets" being designated "parentheses." Now the move from parentheses to brackets and to braces quite literally looks like a move from the idea of adjacency or contiguity to that of support; where a parenthesis is (supposedly) simply apposite, though presumably also subordinate, a bracket—if we take it at its word—is both suspensory and sustentative, it holds up what leans on it. The supplementary structure of all things parenthetical is thereby divulged, and the bracket, as the most derivative of parenthetical interpolations, returns to demonstrate its necessary role, naming the structure of the parenthesis in general. All interruptions read as brackets, the parenthesis coming to be just one type of bracketed utterance among others.

Furthermore, it would henceforth be in no way an exaggeration to call the move from parenthesis to bracket a move from parenthesis to prosthesis. Derrida has them one on top of the other in a single column in *Glas*, talking about what runs and sings with parentheses in the body.[7] A parenthesis, like an apostrophe, attaches itself to the body. In punctuating the text, it also particularizes a certain addressee (for example the one who is interested enough to pay attention to the detail within it). Which brings me to the real reason for declining to or inclining not to provide all the necessary punctuation in this translation, and in this translation of a translation, of a letter written by a Derrida on crutches on April 20, 1978. Following what has been developed above, it might be plausible to add to his notion that every utterance is always already citation and always already translation, the idea that every utterance is also necessarily within the structure of a generalized punctuation. That is to say that the always possible recontextualization that defines citationality as a function of iterability necessarily allows for the operations of excision and insertion, removal and replacement that in the final analysis characterize so many punctuation marks. From my perspective, that structure of punctuation would need to be called prosthesis. All that that involves is not something I am about to go back on or over now. Hence the overwhelmingly complicated economy of what and who is inside and outside of what text, and the parenthesis still hanging there, back again ready for resumption here.

(There's nothing I can teach you about all this. Still, it is peculiar that this fall took place precisely on that date; you told me so yourself: a new period of "remission," the eve of departure for the holidays, the son's skateboard, the unfortunate exhibition before the eyes of father-in-law, all those texts and dreams of steps, of feet, of ankles, of shoes, that have been dancing around me for so long, but more literally, as it were, for the last two or three years. Bah, we all know how much can be ventured in this regard, what can be made of the words that press in upon me in such numbers (the word *scapegoat* often comes back to me)

I made the effort of not interrupting that parenthesis within the still-open parenthesis for fear of what one dangling parenthesis within another might represent. But what comes to my attention is the fact of two words, perhaps many others, written in English, skateboard and scapegoat, the latter italicized the former not, both retained in the foreign lexicon in spite of the perfectly good renditions the Academy would offer for each in French (*planche à roulettes, bouc émissaire*). How to account for this fall into a foreign tongue at the precise moment when the matter of the fall is being related to the *lapsus, linguae,* or *calami*? (Why also this converse fall from English to Latin in finding a word for the same event?) Falling off a skateboard, sin, sacrifice, redemption, and words that keep popping into one's head or getting in one's way, all that crowded together and giving rise to words from a foreign tongue. I read this fall as a fall in, a fall into language; the misstep of the skateboard inextricable from a press of words, an indifference and promiscuity of words related to falling. But that is to be understood not just as a relation of parapraxis to *lapsus linguae* in a generalized taxonomy of slippage but as an inevitable and abyssal suspension—like a roadrunner speeding over the cliff, his legs still spinning—a tilt of the skateboard to the point of overbalance, a headlong careering into the structure of spacing that is the structure of the fall, each time a word is uttered. A world of words that is all that is the fall. A fall into language then, and a fall into languages. In two languages. For once there occurs the originary division—that between completed communication and irretrievable dissemination—that structures every utterance, then there is no more a single language. Prosthesis says little else. The emphasis, or concentration, of the present discussion, the press of its own meaning, comes about through a condensing of all that in and upon a frail parenthesis, a sign that bends under the strain of its own enunciation, or gives way to a flight of sense that it cannot bring to a close, necessarily dooming it to fail, or fall. The point at which it all converges is this event of *punct*uation, figure for the paradox of every linguistic event, and of the case of translation that is every linguistic event. Like an opening parenthesis, a sign moves easily from one language to another, it appears to bear the same mark after transfer, it can translate literally if you like; yet at the same time it doesn't, it threatens to go awry, to effect a transference that is heavily overdetermined, so much so that it stumbles and falls.

There were always at least two falls, Eden and Babel, the second far more literal than the first. A real crash. So for instance, Derrida's instance, Joyce in *Finnegan's Wake*, in reference to Babel, writes, and I read, that he *war*. In two languages. "War"/*war*, noun/verb, English/German, *war*/ "was," referring to YHWH, I am that I am, or was, who in the story imposes his name and at the same time confusion through language. "Babel" is said to mean "the name of the father," or at least "the name of the capital city," hence "Babylon," but it also means, somewhat onomato-poeically, "confusion"—or that, at least, is the sense that we have given to it, but who knows whether onomatopoeia followed or preceded a word in Hebrew or some other language or languages. That is what YHWH is supposed to have said to the presumptuous tower-builders, the Chems, in imposing his law, his word, his language, his languages. Be confused. So whether "babble" or "confusion" is the literal or figurative sense of "Babel," the primary or the secondary, will never be clear. What the story does is uncover a difficult problem at the beginning, at least at the figurative beginning, of language, the problem of there being no beginning—in the sense of a single event—for language; a zero-degree first meaning untouched by difference, a literal or onomatopoeic meaning. And the problem is not so much that there is always already a doubling of meaning, a bilinguality to language, but rather that the structure of doubling is indistinguishable from the structure of confusion. Not that every utterance is necessarily confusion, but that what makes the utterance possible necessarily makes possible at the same time not just a doubling but confusion itself. The problem is quoted in the third letter following the one I am translating here, from "Envois." I say quoted, and don't give the marks. I don't give the marks for my mention of the adjectival past participle of a verb used to describe the act of taking exact words from one text and using them inside another (my circumlocution proves that quotation marks, such as those used conventionally to distinguish a mention from a use, may well signal an ellipsis or an abbreviation, perform the function of an apostrophe). Nor do I give the marks for the quote itself, because it appears more or less the same in another text.[8] But it does not appear in quotation marks either there or in "Envois." Derrida, probably still on crutches, suspended in the middle of a parenthesis with his legs likely still in prosthesis, doesn't use quotation marks to quote or repeat himself; instead he uses parentheses. It's there on page 154 (142, Bass) in the context of Shaun the postman and Shem the penman and the penny post in general, and in a passage replete with slips in at least two languages that may or may not have found their way into English translation, in Derrida's or Alan Bass's version—I refer to Derrida's "*couple farternel*" on page 154 (142, Bass) and the "*en passant pas* 'his penisolate war' " on page 155 (142, Bass)—through all that YHWH declares war by decreeing dischemination, by deconstructing the tower, by saying to those who wished both to make a name for themselves, the Chemites, and to impose their particular language as the universal language, by saying "Babel" to them, this is the name I call myself by and I impose my name of the father, a name that you will confusedly understand as "Confusion," try, I beg you, try to translate but I really hope that you can't, that's my double bind. So I repeat that I no longer know how to distinguish the punctuation, nor how best to translate this or that, nor how to know when the slip has been made from one text to another or from one language to another under the cover of a parenthesis in the shadow of a prosthesis. In other words God declares war and says to them: now you will not impose a single tongue, you will be condemned to the multiplicity of tongues; translate, and, to begin with, translate my name. Translate my name, says he, but at the same time he says: You will not be able to translate my name, because, first of all, it's a proper name and, secondly, my name, the one I myself have chosen for this tower, signifies ambiguity, confusion, et cetera. Thus God, in his rivalry with the tribe of the Chems, gives them, in a certain way, an absolutely double command. He imposes a double bind on them.[9] At one and the same time the name of the father and dischemination. At one and the same time the word of the father and a sense of confusion.

As a consequence, we can well read those two words in English, those slips into English in the context of a general linguistic falling, or fallout, as the inevitable fall into otherness of every text, and specifically as the text's invitation to and expectation of translation—Alan Bass's, this, any other. For I read elsewhere, though not far away from any of this, that the original text is not a plenitude that would come to be translated by accident. The original is in the situation of a demand, that is, of a lack or exile. The original is indebted *a priori* to the translation.[10] But those translations will be haunted by effects of confusion, for the perspective of a fall into languages, in two languages, is the perspective of a sorting among the confusion and a concomitant adding to it. Never one without the other. The confusion is judiciously limited here to some isolated cases of punctuation—apostrophe, comma, inverted comma, dash—resting in the final analysis on a single case of a single opening parenthesis, which however becomes a figure for the points of dissemination that dot every *i* and cross every *t* and mind every *p* and *q* of the text.

So even before any translation, words slip and fall, like bodies on skateboards. No amount of ritualization or institutionalization, no attempt at rectification or attribution of fault, like the discovery of a pretext parenthesis, a chance scapegoat come from one language to another, none of that will preempt such an event, nor fully account for it. Language always occurs within the structure of the *lapsus.* But this one-legged propulsion into *lapsus* and translation is also a skate into what is here called prosthesis, the confusion of animate with the inanimate, of the natural with the artificial; and the confusion of the priorities that are supposed to regulate those differences. Not that prosthesis waits for a body to jump onto a moving object, or to fall and find itself supported by crutches, in order to come about. Language inaugurates a structure of the prosthetic when the first word projects itself from the body into materiality, or vice versa; by being always already translation, constituting itself as otherness, articulation of the othernesses that constitute it, language is a prosthesis. Every utterance is as if spoken from a skateboard, written on crutches, relying on the prosthetic supplement. And on the other hand, every utterance is in the position of a scapegoat, taking the place of whatever it represents and having the knife poised over it, on the point of being expedited to salvation or perdition, the salvation of a so-called successful speech act or the perdition of suspension, loss, or misdirection of meaning; although there is absolutely no reason from this perspective not to call the one perdition and the other salvation.

Derrida dreams of steps, and words crowd in on him, like "scapegoat," and he falls from his son's skateboard under the eyes of his father-in-law. Or stepfather, for it is the very name of the father that divides in that one French word (*beau-père*), once the move has been made into the babble and confusion of nonconsanguineous relations. We could transliterate "stepfather" back into French as something like *pas(de)père*, which we might transliterate back into English as "unfather," and so on, developing any number of limping etymologies and prosthetic relations none of which would be new to us by now. The whole exercise is fraught with the prostheses one language inherits or usurps from another, as much as with constructions of paternity. So, in the slip from the skateboard of the son to the eyes of the father-in-law / stepfather, from the structure of the natural to the structure of usurpation, there occurs such a confusion. It is a confusion that has always infected the familial itself. Consequently, what this appearance of English words in a French text effects is a recasting of the models of familiarity, the parameters of proximity and distance, as well as conformity to, or transgression of, the law. Language as inscription of the name of the father comes into play with language as mother tongue; then, literal with figurative, direct with indirect, that which walks straight with that which limps. These are things that Derrida has made very familiar: the ways in which utterances come and go between the so-called literal and so-called figurative being a measure of the impossibility of establishing one as prior with respect to the other; the devices employed in order to disguise the shift from one to another; the extent to which the literal depends upon the figurative in the exposition of philosophical truth. A visit to Geneva in the second quarter of 1978 would hardly be foreign to any of that, for the fifth letter following the one I am translating now, and then, is written from there on the day he gives an address entitled "The *Retrait* of Metaphor."[11]

Once again, the result in this case, this fall, is the gross presumptuousness, the cloying overfamiliarity of this suspended parenthetic translation; the result is writing in parentheses, a writer on crutches, a writing in prostheses. My insistence here should not be read as an overdramatization of the injury or its effects. In subsequent letters I read such as the following: as soon as I stop limping (*Carte postale*, 152; 139, Bass); the cast is bothering me: I deck myself out with these canes, this limping, and especially the skateboard (you can imagine the small supplement of seduction) (152; 140, Bass); you do not leave me for an instant, I take you around everywhere (well as much as a single leg permits) (153; 140, Bass). No reticence on his part to play on the structure of the prosthetic to the point of suggesting an amputation, the necessity of a wooden leg. The idea is seductive. A prosthesis is inherently exhibitionistic. I could provide a quote to reinforce that, and, especially if the marks were missing, it would be difficult to tell anymore among all the translations what was holding up what or who was showing off more than the other; who enfolding whose other prosthesis into his own to support or pump up the argument, for whether crutch, cane, or peg it would still be exhibited, like any prosthesis, any epithesis, any erection, any simulacrum, any apotrope, any apostrophe, any parade, any parry, any mascarade, with coquettishness.[12] Strictly speaking, French for "crutch" is *béquille*. Derrida prefers to speak of canes (*cannes*), and although he is not of course concerned with the same problems of translation that I have chosen to deal with here, some precision is in order. The distinction between a crooklike walking stick and a Y-shaped object with an arm piece and handgrip is important in that it expresses all the difference between an attached and a disembodied prosthesis. You walk with a cane when the wooden leg is on; it serves to steady the body as the weight is transferred from one leg to the other. To the extent that such distinctions are permissible, it is an additional prosthesis, unlike the crutch, which is a first prosthesis or a rudimentary replacement prosthesis, used instead of the wooden leg once you are undressed for bed, when you want to pee in the middle of the night, or when you answer the plaintive cries coming from a young child's bedroom or those of the telephone telling you your brother has wound up wrapped around telegraph wires in an airplane, or else when the stress turns to a migraine that no analgesic will cure, enough to make you throw up out the bedroom window. In those cases one crutch will actually suffice, although it is easier with a crutch under the armpit on the side without a leg and a cane in the other hand to steady yourself, especially when you have to walk some distance. But the crutch-cane combination serves to avoid the statement of severe invalidity that a pair of crutches hanging around the house would make. Derrida's case, presumed to be that of a sprained ankle, means precisely that no weight can be borne by the injured leg and so calls for two crutches. It takes his sprained ankle—he should have seen it coming some twelve or thirteen years previously, around the time of his tussle with Rousseau—to deconstruct the distinction I have just made, between a supplementary and a replacement prosthesis, between a first and a second one, to demonstrate that they both in fact fall within the same structure.

Canne is also colloquial French for leg, and so its metonymic prosthetization of the natural member may be a good reason to prefer it to *béquille*. Besides, in swallowing it in French, one ends up having a stick up one's arse in English. In French, one can also swallow one's umbrella to the same effect, which may well be a Nietzschean way of forgetting it. And finally, the word for cane in either language comes from the Latin for a stick and refers back to the whole network of bypasses and Ecole Normale Supérieure slang for a practical joke (*canular*) that this discussion taps into. All good reasons why a Jacques Derrida fallen from a skateboard just before leaving for a holiday, who knows, on the Côte d'Azur somewhere just this side of the Italian border, falling perhaps on his chin, but in any case spraining his ankle and finding himself on crutches, all good reasons why he might prefer to talk about his nice *cannes*. But to return to my literal rendering of "crutches": the word–*béquille*–it is a modern replacement for *potence* ("gibbet"), which refers to an object that has the shape and sense of a bracket and holds up bodies left hanging. The idea of a little beak (*béquille*) that makes for the modern word obviously takes those sharp and fatal corners out of it, bringing it more closely back to a type of cane. But I obviously wish to insist on the squareness of the bracket in this commentary on a translation. Because, as my syntax just suggested, I want to evoke the idea of a word-bracket that would be a corollary to a word-apostrophe, a word that is suspended within a problematic of adjacency, that deconstructs a syntactical hierarchy, that opens the space of its digressive otherness, but that also remains within a complex system of support and relay, a word-bracket that graphically includes its own artificial construction. A word within brackets like a word within speech marks, supported by the diacritical canes and held up by the graphic crutches that bring every word into being; a word born grafted to its prosthetic supports. The word "bracket" comes from the French *braguette*, which now means "fly" of the trouser variety, more reason to be wary when it is left open. So without wishing to confirm or deny all that is evoked among the scaffold, the fly and the parenthesis—who knows, the requisite relation between hangings and hard-ons, between a fall and a sense of castration, the whole oedipal trip once you bring in all the fathers and sons, real and surrogate, a race to solve the enigma before the sentence or the parenthesis falls, the need to prove oneself in repeated and prolonged performances, that same desire we met before to find the right word simply by running all the literal permutations, the fear that this or the next slip will catch us with our pants down revealed in the nakedness of our prosthetic dependencies?—the point about the bracket once it reverts to the potence is precisely the particularly prosthetic confusion between the word for support and the word for power, between the object that holds up and the strength that results from being held up, between what is constructed or contrived and what is supposedly innate, whereby artificial and natural, source and derivation, all such priorities are up a pole

, but even so there must be something more idiomatic that remains a secret to me: *you* tell me the truth.

The bracket as potence is thus like any post, as Derrida argues in his debate with Lacan and in *The Post Card* in general—hence the further relevance of references to power, truth, and phalluses displayed or concealed—in that it is divisible. It divides between being an end or destination and being a point of relay. I shan't repeat "Le Facteur de la vérité" here; I shall simply place it within inverted commas and take it as read, but not without recalling the importance of a misquote to Derrida's analysis. For I wish to bring things to bear once again on the question of slips and parentheses, in this case as they fall in, and out, in a less formal context. In an interview with some psychoanalysts published at the end of *The Post Card*, Derrida refers to a parenthesis that he says he won't close ("Du tout," 513, Bass). Naturally all bets are on again regarding which parenthesis— even and especially if the one he identifies on the same page, by means of circumlocution rather than punctuation, concerns precisely the question of divisibility, a question that is being brought to bear here on the parenthesis itself, not in the least sense concerning the undecidable division between the diacritical mark and whatever appositional digression one of those marks opens up. In any case he says he won't close this short parenthesis without referring to an allusion made by the interviewer to the matter of Lacan's misquote, the latter's changing of *dessein* to *destin* in a couplet by Crébillon, which change is a center of attention in "Le Facteur de la vérité." As Derrida recounts, he read Lacan's alteration as either a slip of the pen, an error of transcription—*une coquille* in French—or a slip in the Freudian sense, a *lapsus*, without claiming either to know how conscious or unconscious the slip might be on Lacan's part or to settle the question of what the distinction between a typo and a *lapsus* might mean for psychoanalysis. The misquote continued to embarrass or escape those who subsequently took the matter up until the postman himself, Lacan, the author of the slip, undertook to settle the matter once and for all in the course of an attack upon his detractor François Roustang's book, aptly entitled *Un Destin si funeste* (*Dire Mastery*). Here is Derrida quoting Lacan: We will remain with the *typographical error* [*coquille*] (my italics— JD), whose reprise in the title [of Roustang's book] is a *slip* [*lapsus*] (my italics again—JD). Crébillon and Poe, and then Lacan in at least one of the two citations of the couplet in the *Ecrits*, do indeed print "*un* dessein *si funeste*" and not "*un* destin." And Derrida continuing: End of citation:

this is truly, you will agree, Chicago in the thirties, or rather the saloon during the period of the stage-coach. A so-called analyst believes that he knows, with tranquil knowledge, what a typographical error is; and that a "typo," especially this one, is only a typo [*coquille*], that it sleeps peacefully in its shell [*coquille*], without risking becoming a little of something else as well (*Carte postale*, 542; 514, Bass). Through all this, Derrida reminds us subsequently, it is the English language that, since Poe, has been governing the lexical trajectories (543; 515, Bass).

For me what governs things is rather the matter of translation, of all the transferential slips that take place across the linguistic network, particularly here, among the typos and brackets that remain in suspense and their potential redirection. The word—*coquille*—is a shell as well as a typo. And we are all familiar with the case where a French *coquille* passes into English without translation as it were, namely in the case of *coquilles Saint-Jacques*, which is indeed a name we could give to this unclosed parenthesis, this discussion on the half-shell that has whet my appetite here. And if I am dwelling on what usually falls within the category of the entrée, although that word translates into American English as main course, it is in order to stick my neck out to make an event of this accident, simply through an exercise in translation, the dilemmas of both intralinguistic and interlinguistic translation, to use Jakobson's terms. For what we are left with here, having stumbled upon this unsupported bracket, is firstly all that relates the event, fall, and accident, to the need for support for and separation among all that crowds in upon the case of language sufficient to make it teeter; and secondly, what Derrida refers to as the transfer of the name of the father, the specificity of the linguistic operation in its attempt to pass on singularity. On the one hand, if you will, a bracket in the context of more general slippage, and on the other hand a crutch transferred within the arena metonymized by a shell. Between the two something amounting to a sea change.

My punctuation primer, my *abécoquille*, thus finds me on the beach again and in the familiar company of a man with one leg walking with a crutch and a cane after he takes off his prosthesis in the bathing shed, hobbling with his son down to the water's edge where there are shells and half-shells washed up, tracing a line that the next wave will wash away, like a line in the order of things, at the end of a book familiar to us all, if this is where man ends poised on the brink of a cyborg future, there the father pauses to try the temperature of the water and to gaze out, perhaps across whole oceans, at least to the point where sky meets sea, the smoke from a ship mingling with a disintegrating vapor trail, he looks out across an ocean of separation and death while his son stands waiting at his side, waiting for the signal to take his prostheses and let him go, he watches the waves pounding in as if hesitating to summon the courage, although he has probably already decided he wants to swim or he wouldn't have come this far, and it is hardly the temperature of the water that will restrain him now, but in any case before he can launch himself into the water he has to walk in up to a certain depth, to about the level of his amputation, that is midthigh, up to that point he still needs his crutch and walking stick, and still needs his son to accompany him, but of course midthigh for the father is about chest height for the son so that any judgments made concerning the point of no return are made on behalf of the child as well, who must also cling to a crutch or an arm as they wade in slowly together until my father is ready to let them go, he gives me the instruments of his sole physical support and dives free into the water. This is neither legend nor parable but a problem which for me never ceases to recur. Here I am, left in surf up to my chest, waves tickling my neck, with a cane and a crutch that are of absolutely no use to me, expected to struggle with them back to the water's edge, where they will lie on the sand within my sight until it is time to retrieve them for my father at the end of his swim. I handle this paraphernalia with the utmost respect, it never even enters my head to play with his prostheses or otherwise interfere with their direct passage to shore after their transfer into my hands, for it is clear they do not fit, they make me look like some embarrassed impostor cripple, I cannot use them to support or buoy this body but nevertheless it seems some artificial intelligence is already implanting them in my mind, I am concentrating so hard on keeping them steady and keeping the shoreline in sight as I wade through foam and ebbing surf that I fail to hear in time the large wave which sweeps over me from behind and has me swallowing salty water and flailing arms, legs, and prostheses as I am tossed into a trough where, with eyes closed tight, I can see the body of my father floating past me, looking elegant and streamlined finally, weightless in his strange prosthesis with a cataclysm, and I gasp and blink as my head surfaces briefly, and then there he is again all white and blubbery like a whale, washed up inert, one arm outstretched reaching upwards, the other dangling limp at his side, at the very spot I had fixed in my gaze to leave his crutch and cane. His stump is no longer visible, it simply looks as though one leg is buried in the sand

and where the thigh protrudes there is a pile of little shells to hide or adorn what to all appearances is no longer lacking, the present frill of a future fetish, these little shells I am lingering on here while there I fight to stay afloat and ride it out to wherever this wave is sweeping me with my appending flotsam and jetsam, I no longer know how I came to be holding them, nor what currency I can expect these relics to be given in any present or future sorting of this infinitesimal corner of the archive, where the prosthetic subject lies in toto half buried in a heap of ground silicon. This is neither legend nor parable, this gaping parenthetic digression become excursion, this discourse veering off course; this is alternately and simultaneously an idea and a memory that seeks me out, an apostrophic absence that punctuates my analytic trajectory, addressing the flow of my translation with the urgent breaking waves of prosthetic anecdote and figure. Neither is this some strange and foreign event, however much it be recounted through the programs of distance and memory, for this breaking is a fact of whatever passes across the communicative or informational interface, for whatever passes, like any transfer or structural shift, takes place over the possibility, through the potential, of the catastrophe. And it comes to pass once the parenthesis opens, once such a bracket is hung.

Did you know that the largest postal museum is to be found here, in Geneva? As soon as I can walk I shall go there (I am continuing my investigations, more or less continually). In the "modern" period of development of the postal (in my language I mean by that the period following the era characterized by "imperial" territoriality and politico-military investment—the Persian or Roman Empires, Cyrus and Caesar—then the era which I would like to nickname that of the University because in thirteenth-century France, during the long period of remonopolization and redevelopment of state control over a dispersed network, the University of Paris was given a special privilege, I'll tell you about it, for the handling of mail. Louis XI put paid to that and gradually reproduced centralization—of the Roman type, with his own censorship and *cabinet noir*—and this process, which was fatal for the privilege enjoyed by the University, ends in our case with the monopolist regime of 1681, I think), yes, it seems to me that in the "modern" period the countries of the Reformation played quite an important role in postal reform—and I find that fact significant. The Universal Postal Union was formed in Bern (1874–78), and it is now an institution under the aegis of the United Nations. No, I don't have any great hypothesis about the concurrent development of capitalism, Protestantism, and postal rationalism, but still, all the same, these things must hang together.

In translating "les choses sont nécessairement liées" with the idea of hanging rather than binding, I have taken some liberty with the French, but how much is hard to say. It might be considered that the margin of liberty available to a translation increases in proportion as idiomatic usage is increased, according to the logic that the more familiar a usage the less likely it will be that one is able to transliterate, retain the same cognates, and so on. But that presupposes first of all that the two languages involved are relatively close relations, like English and French, an idea that runs into serious problems if one holds, as I do here, that we are never in fact dealing with languages as intact systems between which the elements of a translation pass—and it bears repeating that this is so whether we refer to elements of a single language, transferring or translating within it, or to elements passing from one language to another—just as we are never dealing with single intact utterances. Once that is so then the relations between a language such as French and a language such as English, and the possibility of translating from one to the other, have to be redefined according to a complicated protocol, one that the everyday sense and usage of translation does and does not respect. But what then of the question of idiom, of the particular configuration of fractures that make for the utterances of this translator as opposed to that one, that bring about an expression like "to put paid to" in one case and something else in another? And more specifically, what happens when that is complicated further, as is the case here, by the fact of a prosthesis that inevitably skews whatever is uttered in the context of this book, which makes this always to some extent also a translation of the idea called prosthesis? It bears repeating that the question would in effect be the same—although not with the same effects or responses—if I were to take more pains than I have to avoid any reference to prosthesis in the course of a translation, or if I were to take pains not to avoid the same. For it was never to be expected that the translation, in as strict a sense as one can imagine, be a prioritized text here, not from the moment of the first set of inverted commas, bracket, and question mark, if not before, in the setting of this chapter in this book and so on. What is to be expected on the other hand is that the parts of the text—translation, foreign language, idiom, narrative, theory, and so forth —negotiate each other's limits through various points of resistance along a path whose beginning and end at least are determined by this letter from *The Post Card.*

Thus I repeat, and translate, these things must hang together. Whether by the slimmest of threads or strongest of brackets. Translation is precisely such a prosthetic economy, a matter of making things fit; like any discourse finally. I do not expect that the closing of this troublesome parenthesis, even if it were possible, would solve the problems the text is being forced to confront. Any more than my refusal to obey conventional markings separating text, translation, and commentary could be considered the sole cause of the ambiguities that persist in this address. Even if you were to have recourse to a reading, a reading different from this one, of pages 150–52 of *La Carte postale,* I would maintain, after Derrida, that his written and published words could no longer simply be returned to that point of origin, but that a different textual operation would be brought into play by the removal of those words from the context of this exposition, an operation for which no future restitution could account. By the same token, it would be naive of me to suggest that the activity I am involved in here is not somehow the deployment of a textual configuration that might be compared with a closing of parentheses, bringing all that I say under the prosthetic umbrella; which amounts in the final analysis to functions of the territoriality of writing. By exploiting an open parenthesis, by keeping this parenthesis open, I am not placing these words, mine or anyone else's, outside of the institutional constraints that parentheses (or prostheses) represent. There is no ideal free space beyond questions of textual territoriality, none implied in Derrida, none implied here. What is set in motion is but a new round of negotiations over those territories.

This parenthesis reads precisely in those terms; by concentrating upon certain effects of punctuation, upon the fact or phenomenon of punctuation itself, it simply pays close attention to the means by which the body of a text negotiates and articulates its very parts. The point is simple and oft-repeated. But as it is repeated, it displays its difference, the difference of repetition and the differences of its parts. For being simple the point of an open parenthesis is nonetheless double: the moment it opens, it points forward to its likely future closure; yet as long as it is open, it threatens not to close.

As we are reminded in the shadow of the Geneva postal museum, the open parenthesis is thus comparable in structure to the letter and to the notion of adestination as developed in *The Post Card*. As an event of the message, the possibility of non-arrival divides the assurance of systems of address and relay. The institution of postage demonstrates the inexhaustive nature, the fallibility if you will, of attempts at total control. Conversely, the history of the postal outlines the changing *rapports de force* between, on one hand, the will to control and appropriation and, on the other, whatever resists control, by dint of the paradoxical constitution of the message, or of interventions in the course of relay and delivery. The opposition Derrida mentions with respect to the letter, between the imperial and modern posts, is that between a system for the transmission of information which relies on a centralized and hierarchical network, a system of intercession, and that which is supposed to work through (more) direct access. Hence the possible comparison between postal rationality, Protestantism, and capitalism as heralds of the modern, with their accompanying myths of freedom of action and democratization of process.

Counter to those myths Derrida gives the example of the postmodern post as envisaged by M. Brégou of the French Post Office. For him, as I read it, the development of computerized technology, at the post office as well as in the home, will permit the installation of new modes of transmission of information. It can be thought that in the years to come, what will be transported will no longer be writing, with the exception of mail for private individuals ["exception made," which one, until when?], but the perforated card, microfilm, or magnetic tape. The day will come when, thanks to the "telepost," data will be transmitted by wire starting from the user's computer and going to the central system of the post office nearest [all the same] the residence of the addressee, which will be charged with printing the order or bill. . . . It will remain for the postal employee only to distribute the envelope which may of course contain several communications from different senders. The traditional process will thus be revolutionized for the greater part of correspondence (in *Carte postale*, 115–16; 105, Bass).

Like anyone who undertakes to describe the technological future, M. Brégou seems hopelessly out of date in the wake of the fax, modem, and electronic mail, not to mention their attendant hacking, viruses, and system crashes. What is most interesting about his prediction is on the one hand the continued fetishization of the deliverable document, motivated for him, no doubt, by the potential industrial-relations problem caused by threatened postal workers, and on the other hand the idea that the post office, by controlling the circulation of private mail, is also protecting the privacy of that mail and privacy in general. Not to say that there is no truth in the naive sense of "privacy" entertained by the postal service, but, as the postcard demonstrates, the postal, by definition, deconstructs the public/private opposition. In relaying the message it constitutes a delay in its communication; it is an interruption within the closed circuit between sender and addressee. In trans*ferring* it by definition inter*feres*. And, of course, the postal doesn't begin with the post office but is the necessary possibility constituting the event of the message itself. If a message is to be communicated at all, it must be constituted by that idea of relay/delay. M. Brégou's naïveté is therefore reinforced when, while seeing fit to exempt private mail from the revolution just described, he nevertheless goes on to suggest (and I shall give the appearance of letting the seamless privacy of this communication from Brégou to you, already made fuzzy by Derrida and Bass, function without further interference by refraining from interposing my own postal marks) that in the future the post office which, *omnipresent* by means of its offices or its "*facteurs*" [I like the way he went at it with these quotation marks], could *treat all* [my emphasis] the operations placing the population in contact with the administration (in *Carte Postale*, 116–17; 106, Bass).

Again, I shan't stop to try and translate all the effects of Derrida's brackets, nor dwell on the peculiarity of Brégou's quotation marks to indicate emphasis, now that the punctuation has broken down or been reduced to a microscopic informational pinprick or impulse with the same status as any other sign or datum. In any case, this Brégou discussion falls outside the boundaries of the Geneva letter. What interests me, however, is a word, the word *traiter*, as in a machine for the treatment of texts, the word processing or artificial treatment of a body of words that has impelled the whole prosthetic enterprise, and that ties the present writing, and the institutional forms it works in and out of, to the sense of the postal. It is not for nothing that *le facteur de la vérité* names a postman; and the references in "Envois" to archivists and guardians of the letter are as much about those in the business of literature, theory and criticism, as about psychoanalysts. So we too are most surely involved in the handling of the mail, in the treatment of texts, factoring in its dose of truth, as always deeply implicated in the control and passage of information. Word processing may serve to bring that to the fore, just as it may serve to focus insecurity over any modification in the status quo of interpretative right and competence. Objections to changes in forms of research and writing, and to the increased automatism that word processing represents, may now seem no more than a repetition of the familiar chagrin over the fact that the centralized and privileged system of control that used to rest in one set of hands threatens to pass into others. Into other circuits.

Now in a sense the guardians can rest assured that nothing has changed outside of the question of possession: logocentrism remains intact, is even reinforced, in cybernetics, and the machine for treating texts merely develops a more and more highly refined hierarchical system—read the technico-military lexicon of computer language as a signifier of that. However, and this is finally the point that this particularly programmed switch is bringing us to, what remains overlooked in that reinforcement of the most simplistic concept of communication is its massive reduction to systems of displacement, transfer, relay, and interchange; the laying bare of message transmission as a series of digital commutations. At every point along that transmission, like a series of old staging-posts, there is division of the message into the possibilities of forwarding or detour and delay. And far from eliminating, in principle, the chances of loss and diversion, each point of transference engages such an enormous accompanying network that where the message may end up is more of a mystery than ever.

I am not arguing that the threat of centralization is less real in the era of postindustrial technology, for that threat is clearly harder to resist and the sense of intervention harder to define. But there may be something to be learned from the fact that however sophisticated the apparatus for infor-mation transfer, it still presumes to mask the naive conception of transfer upon which it is based, discounting the very effects of relay and deferral that constitute it. And it is worth repeating that whatever the hierarchical level of a set of operations, take for instance the difference between a language and a metalanguage, there is no qualitative change in the func-tioning of those operations, merely a convention, relying on a transfer, which has been established in the relations between the levels. That is to say that the actual switch between one hierarchical level and another is not qualitatively different from the switch between elements on the same level. However different the end effect might be, that difference does not in fact occur at the point of transfer and might therefore be said to some extent not to be effected by means of that transfer. Reveal the codes, and the format commands and diacritical marks will line up in juxtaposition with the text itself, separated from that text by brackets alone, all supposedly neatly opened and closed, posing anew and differently questions about hierarchical inclusion and exclusion, what is left in and what out, what falls within the suspension of a parenthesis, where one piece ends and another begins within the same body of data called a prosthetic text.

The postal is an instance of the banking system. Don't forget that in the grand reform of the "modern" era, another great country connected with the Reformation played a spectacular role: in 1837 Rowland Hill published his book, *Post-Office Reform: Its Importance and Practicability*. He was an educator, and active in tax reform. What did he propose? Why, the postage stamp, my love, and where would we be without him/it? The adhesive stamp, that is to say the establishment of a system of uniform payment, the general equivalent of a tax, and especially the principle of billing before the letter, advance payment (the uniform rate and a system of prepayment, which were adopted in 1840 after a good deal of lobbying by the people, the famous battle for the pp, "popular agitation for the 'penny post'"). And pending further investigations, I think that the postcard comes to us from there, quite recently (from Australia, 1869, to England, 1870, but the private *picture postcard* was only authorized in 1894).

Within the space of a parenthesis, a parenthesis occurring within that other still-open parenthesis, which could therefore be signaled by brackets, within that bracketed direct quote from a Derrida on crutches, comes a small slip that tumbles into yet another free fall, the discourse irremediably hijacked. I read and translate that the postcard comes to us *from there, from another great country of the Reformation, quite recently, from Australia, 1869, to England, 1870*. Of course no Derrida could have known that this translation would fall here, more than a decade into the future from the time of his writing; he could not have known that this letter would be addressed and delivered at this place and time, to a New Zealander picking up shells and *coquilles* one day on a beach in an Australia, not content, by some enormous ellipsis, or *lapsus*, or whatever else occurs once the parenthesis is opened, by a quirk of syntax interfered with by an obstructing bracket, an Australia not content to be assimilated to an England. But that is what I read, and the whole thing loses its footing. I have no idea whether the postcard comes to us from Mentone or any other beach, nor what letters are lost or gained in translation of an open parenthesis, nor whether one is any longer in the business of distinguishing between *coquilles* and *lapsus*, nor whether it is worth mentioning that a $5 stamp displaying a reproduction or a quotation of that painting by Charles Conder which dates from the same period, 1888, namely *A Holiday at Mentone*, worth mentioning that such a stamp prepaid a volume of essays containing among other things translation or commentary of *La Carte postale* in the form of an earlier version of this very discussion, sent from there, from Australia, 1984, to Paris, 1984, or any other place and time I might choose to invent, whether all that is relevant for I would not know what to make of it without stretching a point, or pulling a leg, to the point of breaking, but you'll probably agree with me that that seems to be exactly the deal here, in any case whether you agree or not it remains that the task is enormous when it comes to handling this strange metonymy, this dif-ferance in fact, whereby Australia, and the distance that separates it from England, and the approximately six-month sea voyage between the post-card's dispatch in 1869 and its arrival, are mentioned and in the same movement discounted, all within the play of a parenthesis; where accord-ing to the syntax in force, a postcard, presumably manufactured in En-gland—for we all remember the Christmas cards with their snowy scenes and reindeer that were our only yuletide currency all through our youth while outside the thermometer reached 40 degrees centigrade in the shade—is shipped but not posted to Australia, only to be posted back to England. And it is those oceans of postal space that Derrida's ellipsis overlooks when he speaks of a great country connected with the Reforma-tion, there, Australia, with all the possible and interminable attendant investigations into the politics of open space and the open letter, the question of why Britain might have exported into its colonial space this desire to transgress or rewrite principles of privacy and secrecy in the form of the postcard, why there was this desire for a postcard so dirty that Mother could not bear to bring it home so she shipped it half a world away to have it posted back, all that must be inserted here, given this event, it becomes my responsibility now to put back at least something of what is missed or else there is no telling how anything will hold up anymore.

Actually, Derrida is seriously misinformed, as a Frank Staff would be only too happy to tell us.[13] The first postcard, leaving aside pictorial envelopes and writing paper, was issued by the *Austrian*, not *Australian*, Post Office, in 1869. It is true, as this same Frank Staff will confirm, that a well-known campaigner for the imperial penny post, Henniker Heaton, setting a trajectory to be followed by Charles Conder, went to seek adventure in Australia before shipping, rather than posting, back home, and that, doubtless, when living in the wilds of the Australian bush, he had learned at first hand the excitement and relief of receiving a letter from home.[14] Heaton's campaign for a uniform tariff throughout the British Empire, which was largely successful and even extended to the United States around the turn of the century, was aided by the fact that France, unlike Great Britain, complied with the international postal accord setting the price of any international letter at twopence halfpenny (25 centimes), which meant that Mother, at that time charging fivepence, was meeting stiff competition and risking the serious foreign contamination of her colonial subjects that Frank Staff dutifully records, informing us that it was indeed galling to know that French people could correspond with our colonies more cheaply than we could![15] It may even be true that Henniker Heaton sent a postcard *from Austria* to England, to urge formal adoption of postcards in the United Kingdom. In any case, after the North German Confederation and Switzerland, the United Kingdom issued plain post-cards (no message to appear on the same side as the address lest the two be confused) in 1870, although the halfpenny cost of their port led some to complain that a message of such small value could hardly be worth sending at all. The French used them during the Franco-Prussian War, airmailed them by balloon when Paris was besieged, three grams apiece, and one would have to be naive not to think that the writing of such open letters by soldiers at the front might have served the purposes of censorship as well as minimizing freight costs. By 1872 the Germans were printing private picture postcards, although as Derrida says, the English did not authorize them until 1894.

The words there, from Australia, 1869, to England, 1870, do in fact repeat the force of the argument of *The Post Card*: the postcard isn't constituted as intended, that is to say as a message that arrives, until it does actually arrive, and thus the event of arrival of the first postcard would have had to come to us from its point of arrival, that is there, England, had that been the case. But that does not forgive this critical neglect of all that falls between sending and arrival that *The Post Card* is at such pains to point out. In any event, now it has arrived here, prosthesis, more than a century after its official adoption in England; here, where now we have not only a bracket, which I have tried to straighten out, but an extra *al* by which Austria reads as Australia although I can only surmise what lan-guage it was originally read in and whence this oceanful of *coquilles*. What to do with this extra limb to go out on, *a* (n) *l*, a stake, crutch or cane, a frank staff or crochet inserted here, the case of a Frenchman on crutches, and such a post could itself be made to read as our very same troublesome parenthesis announcing its closure if only it were to be given a final twist.

For that is my intention, to divert the path of an address, to inscribe such diversion as necessary and integral to the address itself, merely by inserting a word or intonation or two at a strategic place or two, so that everything here becomes indirect quoted speech. In the space opened by a gaping parenthesis, in the spacing that is language itself, in the exercise of a translation, in the excision and incision that is an effect of the general possible and impossible translatability of every utterance, I undertake this exercise of interpolation. There, or here, some version of an Australia or Australasia, back then, or now, inevitably means some version of an autobiographical anecdote. For autobiography can only be recounted in the mode of the anecdote, the *anekdota*, unedited and unpunctuated, a further function of the inclusions and exclusions, the persistent disorder-ing of discourse that is prosthesis. Autobiography, as much as translation, reveals itself here as an exercise in indirection rather than the transcription of a supposed fixed original, a personal life, a foreign-language text. This then, a translation of an autobiographical account, an anecdotal voyage to Geneva, the *fait divers* of a sprained ankle and an interest in postal history, crossed by the apostrophic or parenthetical interventions of my own questioning, my *idée fixe* of a father's wooden leg. It is within such a context that prosthesis either falls or finds its means of support. It would not be possible without that structure of the anecdote, as the elliptic, apostrophic, parenthetic leveler of a discourse, without the possibility of the *anekdota* as apposite to the *ekdota*, without the ensuing attention to what is left in and out, said or not said, published or not, to what is added and replaced, to the doubling of a discourse of the body with a discourse of the mind, the doubling of a text of what is received or inherited with a text of what is acquired. That is the whole economy of prosthesis in operation here. So my discourse limps across its own internal rhetorical boundaries, it takes a stroll along a water's edge with its shifting profile of debris, shells that once enclosed a work of pure symmetry, pieces of driftwood that had been the cane of some old salt or that once bracketed a bunk upon a ship that sailed for six months to come to Australia, who knows, carrying postcards from Austria, in about 1869, where slept a grandmother still a child, and her sister about the age of a young boy who measures to his crippled father's thigh when he accompanies him into the waves, those sisters adults in a country during its infancy, coming, why not, to Mentone, where their father will work as a scribe, employed to treat and process texts, to transcribe, translate, and transfer, by his own hand, like all this, getting out of hand here. The older sister will come to paint dark, foreboding pictures that bear no resemblance whatsoever to Charles Conder's beaches or holidays, transferring rather the spirit of Thomas Hardy's Victorian woods to the wild and primitive flora of another country where she languishes quietly enclosed within a house on a hill overlooking a sparkling bay, she lies there in the house one day, in the room she shares with my grandmother, quietly waiting for something to change in her body, and when it comes it is as though someone had passed the cold flat of the blade of a knife across her stomach only to retrace the path with a firm stroke of the cutting edge, and she arches on her heels and rolls onto the floor, retching and convulsing, noisily, enough to bring my grandmother and the wife of the scribe, who stand aghast as she twitches and drools, and the mother screams in speech as direct as she can muster, that must be reported here, to fetch the doctor, and so while her father carefully writes down the words that have been entrusted to him in another room of the house, unaware of the articulate disarray his wife and daughters have been thrown into, my grandmother is off and running, already rehearsing what she must transmit to the doctor, down the long dirt track that leads across the family property to the street, trying to keep the syllables in the right order as she picks up and puts down her feet one after the other in rapid succession, the words and limbs articulating in bizarre concert into the generational future, all the way down to the conjunction that finds me gainfully employed doing little more than parenthetically pointing out that from there, Australia towards the end of last century, in the inaugural and barely modern age of the postcard, to here, wherever that may be, there is time, among other things, for the Great-aunt Minnie I never knew to die a bare adult by her own hand holding a bottle of cyanide, because the world was darker than even her paintings could express, there is a moment when words stick in the throat of her sister as she recites like a litany the complaint and awful symptoms recalling a passage from *Madame Bovary*, pleading for the doctor to come with or without his prescriptions in Latin, to come in all haste and to leap and not hobble down the path to the house in the sun, my grandmother stammers out her news too portentous for a child to report, while her sister Aunt Minnie convulses and expires and so there is transmitted this endearing or fright-

ening diffidence that comes all the way on down the line, right down to
some of the first words my mother will hear passing my father's lips as he
stands in the garden of the same house, leaning on his new walking stick
and self-consciously or coquettishly kicking it with his recently acquired
steel foot, she already falling for the wit and charm, so on down the line to
this pass, the event that I am here, and I don't want to overdramatize but to
translate a diffidence or differance that is a letter sent in the perspective of
its own death, its prosthetically parenthetic catapostrophe, an eventuality
against which no guarantee can be upheld, though I would want to stave it
off by whatever means available, frank or circuitous, to rewrite it in the
context of a father with a wooden leg, or a philosopher with a sprained
ankle, or a single bracket all this hinges on.

And now I take my plaster leg, my canes (I never know, with these
prostheses, where to put them, especially when I am behind the lectern in
the flesh

he never knows where to put these prostheses, these parentheses, these
speech marks, these crutches, when he is lecturing in the flesh; he never
knows how to keep them within reach or whom to trust to retrieve them or
from what direction to expect the cataclysm that will surely overwhelm the
whole shebang whenever one tries to put them to rest, for there is no such
rest for prosthesis, for prosthesis is the wood in the flesh I am recounting
and translating here

) and I leave you, but read well, turning the four corners slowly, around
the four times four rectangles, perhaps it doesn't even make a single
sentence but it's my life and I dedicate it to you."[?]

[ ] ?] [?

Reference Matter

Notes

Chapter 1

1. Virgil, *Aeneid*, my translation. Cf. Copley's translation: "and four-footed hoofbeats drummed on the fertile field" (184).

2. See Jakobson, "Linguistics and Poetics": "*The poetic function projects the principle of equivalence from the axis of selection into the axis of combination*" (27, Jakobson's italics).

3. See Heidegger, *On the Way to Language*: "Thus you call bearing or gesture: the gathering which originally unites within itself what we bear to it and what it bears to us" (19), and "man stands in a relation . . . the relation is called hermeneutical because it brings the tidings of that message" (40). However much Heidegger's text remain resonant to the concerns of prosthesis, it would take a detailed analysis to relate the sense of Heidegger's "bearing" to what is being developed here. Suffice to say that the bearer of language in prosthesis does not so much bear a message as bear its own self-division.

4. See Jakobson, "Linguistics and Poetics": "Any attempt to reduce the sphere of the poetic function to poetry or to confine poetry to the poetic function would be a delusive oversimplification. The poetic function is not the sole function of verbal art but only its dominant, determining function, whereas in all other verbal activities it acts as a subsidiary, accessory constituent" (25).

5. For Derrida see, for example, *Glas* (trans. Leavey), 64–66. In general the debt prosthesis owes to Derrida is too much in arrears to be accounted for here. It is made explicit at various points along the way. In terms of other "experiments" with academic writing, one might consider the recent work of Ulmer ("Mystory," in his *Teletheory*) and Miller (*Getting Personal*), or Torgovnick (*Gone Primitive*) and Appiah (*In My Father's House*).

The levels of discussion and theorization of a problematic vary considerably from one example to the next. Torgovnick, whose book contains little or no treatment of the questions her writing might raise, except to say, "everything is personal and psychological, or nothing is" (17), returns to the matter explicitly in a short article entitled "Experimental Critical Writing." There it is explained as essentially a matter of rendering academic "style" less formal so as to "court" a wider audience: "When writers want to be read they have to be more flexible and take more chances than the standard scholarly style allows: often, they have to be more direct and more personal. . . . Writerly writing is personal writing. . . . It makes the reader know some things about the writer—a fundamental condition, it seems to me, of any real act of communication. And real communication is exciting" (27).

Miller outlines in some detail a rich field of both "personal" and "auto-biographical" criticism (Jane Tompkins, Mary Ann Caws, Jane Gallop, Stephen Heath, Gayatri Spivak, Alice Kaplan, and others), with its treading of various paths in and out of the risk of essentialism, of "identity politics," or of any appeal to a revitalized form of authority, that of the self. In her opening chapter she considers herself to be simply illuminating "an unfolding phenomenon" whose effects she wants to avoid foreclosing (19), but concludes: "Personal writing theorizes the stakes of its own performance: a personal materialism. Personal writing opens an inquiry on the cost of writing—critical writing or Theory—and its effects. The embarrassment produced in readers is a sign that it is working" (24).

Ulmer cites "the effectiveness of feminist appeals to personal experience" (82) in favor of his practice of "mystory," agreeing that "the convergence of theory and narrative" facilitates a resistance to "mastery and assertion as they are practiced in conventional academic discourse" (84, 83). Drawing also on Barthes's "middle voice" and Derrida's reference to Freud's autobiographical writing whereby "individual idioms may be generalized into theoretical formations" (91), he argues for the development of a genre characterized by invention: "A mystorical essay is not scholarship, nor the communication of a prior sense, but the discovery of a direction by means of writing" (90). With his interest in technological media and the embedding of anecdotes "in the abyss of theoretical discourse . . . as part of a 'speculative' organization . . . a double-take in which the narrative development of the event has formal, conceptual, explanatory consequences" (92), Ulmer seems often close to the concerns of prosthesis, but apart from the practical application of the theory that is his last chapter (a type of script for an unrealized video), his writing preserves a discursive uniformity: it remains the prescription for the practice to follow.

Appiah's example is in many ways the most complex and instructive of all. In his preface he characterizes his attention to his father's identities, and thus to his own autobiographical interventions, as a desire to say "where I am coming from," something that needs to be admitted by anyone who thinks about culture (ix). Thus his is definitely a type of identity politics. But the politics involves precisely challenging the criteria for such things as "race," "state," and "identity," on the one hand in the terms assumed by the West in its dealings with Africa and on the other hand in terms of the complicated histories of the author and, by extension, of many other African intellectuals. Thus the frequent anecdotal insertions work from a number of different perspectives: as "raw" data the African is required to provide to a readership that is ignorant of them; as an implicit form of resistance to presumptions of objectivity, perhaps even as a form of validation of a unique experience; as a celebration of narrative; and as part of a "Western" essay tradition, more particularly perhaps an Anglo-American philosophical tradition. Yet Appiah never explicitly discusses the status of his interventions except in the simple terms of the preface, preferring the performance to the analysis of what remains highly problematic from the point of view of at least one of the traditions that inform the book (that of contemporary Western literary theory, itself an explicit subject of discussion). The response might be that from the perspective of another tradition it is simply not an issue. Interestingly, however, from the point of view of prosthesis, the most developed of these interventions, indeed the central question of the book in terms of its title, concerns Appiah's involvement in arrangements for his father's funeral. It is a story of (not) disgracing the family name and takes place in the context of the division of the father's body.

Obviously any characterization of those examples cannot but be reductive here. A comprehensive analysis of experiments with the forms of academic prose would be another book, and not prosthesis; conversely, prosthesis is the elaborate development and defense of its own principles and so needs to be inserted *en abyme* within this note. In general my disagreement with these attempts is that, in spite of my respect for their aims and principles, I find them to remain at the level of a certain "tokenism": either inflections of style that at worst presume a return to a natural expression against the sterility of theory, or some other form of authentication or accreditation of the writing subject. In the "systematized" contamination prosthesis aims to achieve, the "I" never gets past dealing with its status as fiction and artifice, and the language it speaks, whether it be that of anecdote or theory, is always already divided against and within itself, before and beyond any "decision" to change the mode of its discourse.

6. See, for example, for the Platonic conception of a natural writing, Derrida, "Plato's Pharmacy."

7. For a recent example see Searle, *Rediscovery*.

Chapter 2

1. F. Gibson, *Charles Conder*, 68–69.
2. Ashton, "Some Recollections of Conder," 2.
3. Derrida, *Glas*, trans. Leavey, 138.
4. See Freud, *Beyond the Pleasure Principle*, in *Standard Edition*, XVIII: 64.

5. For an adventurous reading of this theoretico-etymological connection see Torok, "Nota Beine," 33–34.

6. See Irigaray, *This Sex Which Is Not One*.

7. See Derrida, *Limited Inc*.

8. See Lacan, "Agency of the Letter," 151–52. Lacan wants to show the primacy of the signifier by his example of the identical doors marked respectively "Ladies" and "Gentlemen," but at the same time he raises the question of sexual difference as fundamental to the operations of meaning, reminding us of his subsequent recourse to the phallus as transcendental signified beyond the play of difference, at least in Derrida's critique (see "Le Facteur de la vérité," in *Post Card*).

9. This figure is from the *Bulletin of the National Gallery of South Australia* 3, no. 1 (1941): n.p. Burdett, "Conder in Australia," 8, speaks of 46 works.

10. F. Gibson, *Charles Conder*, 71.

11. Rothenstein, *Artists of the 1890's*, 150.

12. Rothenstein, *Life and Death of Conder*, 38.

13. Hoff, *Charles Conder*, 7.

14. Birnbaum, *Charles Conder*, 7.

15. MacColl, "Paintings on Silk," 233.

16. Rothenstein, *Life and Death of Conder*, 118.

17. Joyce, "Conder—'Too Many Roses?,'" 38.

18. Ashton, "Some Recollections of Conder," 6.

19. Nelson, "Charles Conder," 74.

20. Birnbaum, *Charles Conder*, 10–11.

21. Hoff, *Charles Conder*, 5; Burdett, "Conder in Australia," 8.

22. Lloyd, "Golden Summers Down Under," 17.

23. See Croll, *Smike to Bulldog*, 128, 132–33.

24. Nelson, "Charles Conder," 74; Joyce, "Conder—'Too Many Roses?,'" 38; Rothenstein, *Artists of the 1890's*, 153.

25. Blanche, *Essais et portraits*, 130–31. All translations of passages from this source are mine.

26. Ibid., 134.

27. Ibid., 126, Blanche's italics.

28. Rothenstein, *Artists of the 1890's*, 150; idem, *Life and Death of Conder*, 36.

29. See Moore, *Story of Australian Art*, 1: 93–95.

30. See Derrida, "Restitutions of the Truth in Pointing," in his *Truth in Painting*.

31. See again Derrida, *Truth in Painting*, especially "Passe-partout" and "Cartouches."

32. See Derrida, *Signéponge/Signsponge*; Derrida, *Parages*; and my discussion with Peter Brunette in Brunette and Wills, *Screen/Play*, 119–22.

33. See Derrida, "Spatial Arts." Before coming to refer to "responses" to the

art object, the countersignature works in Derrida to reinforce the sense of the divided signature just discussed, namely the double effect of authorial inscription as intention for and attempt at monumentalization on the one hand, and inevitable loss of control, or dissemination, on the other hand.

34. See Rothenstein, *Life and Death of Conder*, 84–91.

35. Croll, *Smike to Bulldog*, 3.

36. See Derrida, "+R," in his *Truth in Painting*; and Brunette and Wills, *Deconstruction*, 117–18.

Chapter 3

1. W. Gibson, *Mona Lisa Overdrive*, 148. Further citations of this work will be included in the text.

2. W. Gibson, *Burning Chrome*, 169; further citations will be in text. Since coming to fictional light in Gibson, cyberspace has captured the imagination of any number of theorists and computer research scientists. For the "current" state of the art see Benedikt, *Cyberspace*.

3. See, for example, Rosenthal, "Jacked In," 84–87, and Porush, "Cybernauts in Cyberspace," 177.

4. In a short postface to *Neuromancer*, Gibson credits Tom Maddox with the invention of ICE. See W. Gibson, *Neuromancer*, 273. Further citations will be in text.

5. "In the non-space of the matrix, the interior of a given data construct possessed unlimited subjective dimension" (W. Gibson, *Neuromancer*, 63). The term "virtual reality" is avoided in Gibson, being indicative of an earlier technology: "*There's no there, there.* They taught that to children, explaining cyberspace. She [Angie] remembered a smiling tutor's lecture in the arcology's executive crèche, images shifting on a screen: pilots in enormous helmets and clumsy looking gloves, the neuroelectronically primitive 'virtual world' technology linking them more effectively with their planes, pairs of miniature video terminals pumping them a computer-generated flood of combat data, the vibrotactile feedback gloves providing a touch-world of studs and triggers. ... As the technology evolved, the helmets shrank, the video terminals atrophied (*Mona Lisa Overdrive*, 41, Gibson's italics).

6. W. Gibson, *Count Zero*, 119. Further citations will be in text.

7. "The Sprawl" is slang for BAMA, the Boston-Atlanta Metropolitan Axis. See Olsen, "Shadow of Spirit," 278–89, and Mead, "Technological Transfiguration," 350–60.

8. Much of that discussion never gets far beyond what Andrew Ross calls the "euphoric, addictive thrill of the technological sublime" ("Hacking Away," 131). Istvan Csicsery-Ronay, Jr., in an article that establishes more critical distance

than most, writes: "As a label, 'cyberpunk' is perfection. It suggests the apotheosis of postmodernism" ("Cyberpunk and Neuromanticism," 182). References to postmodernism and to Baudrillard's and Jameson's formulations of it are a constant in McCaffery's *Storming the Reality Studio* (in which Csicsery-Ronay's article appears) and in other work on Gibson. See note below.

9. It seems to me that a similar contradiction can be read in Baudrillard's alternating between an almost moralistic nostalgia for the real and an apocalyptic celebration of the simulacrum. See, for example, his *Simulacres et simulation.* Elsewhere he describes simulation as the "hell" of a "subtle, maleficent, elusive twisting of meaning" (*Selected Writings*, 176), but this "destruction of sense by simulation" nevertheless remains "fascinating" and "exciting" ("Sur le nihilisme," in *Simulacres et simulation*, 233). We are thus all caught in the "melancholy" (*Simulacres et simulation*, 234) of our failure to mourn the real (*Selected Writings*, 181). As long as Baudrillard conceives of the age of the simulacrum in historicist terms, as the mutation into the postmodern that he invariably describes it as, then according to the logic he prescribes ("an order of simulacra is maintained only by the alibi of a preceding order" ["Beaubourg Effect," 6]), then the simulacrum will always imply a loss of the real, that is to say a reinscription of the very structure it is supposed to supersede.

For an argument against Baudrillard's celebration in favor of what the author calls the redemptive "humanism" of cyberspace, see Porush, "Frothing the Synaptic Bath," 246–61.

10. David Tomas explains the differences in representations of cyberspace in terms of visualizations governed by a euclidean geometry as against the noneuclidean spaces created by virus programs and artificial intelligences. But, as I explain below, it seems to me that the realities created by "The Change" are of necessity also described in euclidean terms, such that it is more an enfolding of euclidean forms upon themselves than a passage to a new conception of space. See Tomas, "Old Rituals for New Space," 35–36.

11. See McCaffery, "Interview with William Gibson," 272–73. Gibson also mentions a desire to concentrate more on character, which has lead critics to read the later novels as more "humanist" than *Neuromancer*. John Christie, for example, refers to the "redemptive value of Art and Nature" and "rehumanized values of *Count Zero*," which he contrasts with the "post-humanist register of *Neuromancer*" by comparing reference to Duchamp's *Large Glass* in the first and to Joseph Cornell's boxes in the second ("Of AIs and Others," 179). See also Porush, "Frothing the Synaptic Bath."

12. A construct of the narrative events of the three novels might offer, among other details, the following: Case the cowboy and Molly the hitgirl with implanted mirrored lenses and retractable scalpel fingernails are hired by the incestuous, mad, and dying Tessier-Ashpool family conglomerate, or else by the

artificial intelligences one of its founders had created, to let loose two AIs in the matrix, and do so through an elaborate infiltration of the family's orbital Straylight Villa. Some seven or eight years later, one of these entities feeds information to a scientist, Christopher Mitchell, who is then credited with perfecting the new technology of biochips to replace silicon ("like a wooden staff beside a myoelectric limb," *Count Zero*, 69), and he in turn implants his products in the head of his daughter Angie, whom he sends out in his place when plans are made for him to defect to a rival company. Angie escapes to team up with aspiring cowboy Bobby Newmark, who has stumbled onto a biosoft breaker program and been co-opted by followers of a voodoo cult convinced that the weirdness in the matrix is the voices of their gods. Angie is welcomed by them as their Virgin. Since she hears or dreams the same voices it would seem that her father has implanted this weirdness in her biosoft grafts, probably as part of a deal with those who are supplying him with the new technology. Meanwhile, an exceedingly rich art dealer, Josef Virek, who wants to free himself of the vats in which what is left of his body is forced to live, has followed the trail of the biosoft into orbit and back, and now comes after Angie. Bobby kills him in a cyberspace staredown and then goes on to a short life in the matrix, and Angie, after embracing the voodoo cult for some time, becomes the newest simstim star ("simulated stimuli: the world— all the interesting parts, anyway—as perceived by . . . ," *Burning Chrome*, 183). Some seven or eight years later, the surviving Tessier-Ashpool heir, Lady 3Jane, or some AI construct of her, decides she wants to put the now fabulously famous Angie—with her biosoft grafts, altered by designer-drug abuse and full of hoodoo shit—back together with the burned-out Bobby, who is attached to the biosoft slab (Bobby claims to have stolen it from Lady 3Jane), and/or kill them both. She coerces Molly, renamed Sally, into abetting her in the elaborate kidnapping scheme whereby Angie will disappear and her dead body turn up in the form of that of a surgically remodeled replica, a prostitute named Mona Lisa. Sally seems at some point to begin to act independently and cut a different deal with Lady 3Jane in return for a whitewashing of her record that will enable her to retire to the quiet life Case chose after the original Straylight run. But it is no longer clear whether the kidnapping scheme is the initiative of Lady 3Jane or Angie's company, Sense/Net, which is tired of her drug habit and eager to replace her with a surrogate, or to what extent that scenario has simply been fabricated by Lady 3Jane. Nor can one ascertain the exact roles played by Angie's costar, by Sense/ Net's AI known as Continuity, by the London underworld and espionage figure Roger Swain, and by a series of other characters, not to mention the whole voodoo clan of Mamman Brigitte, Baron Samedi, and their horsemen.

The narratives of both *Count Zero* and *Mona Lisa Overdrive* consistently alternate, for the length of each novel, among, respectively, three and four points of view. These are, in *Count Zero*, those of Turner (the man hired to handle

Mitchell's defection who becomes Angie's protector when that scheme goes awry), Marly (the failed art dealer hired by Virek to track down a series of Cornell-like boxes that will lead him to the source of the biosoft information), and Bobby Newmark; and in *Mona Lisa Overdrive*, those of Kumiko (a Yakuza boss's daughter who has been sent to London first in Swain's and then in Sally's custody, while a power struggle takes place in Japan), Slick Henry, Angie, and Mona.

Another construct would be required to relate the story of the Tessier-Ashpool conglomerate, the marriage between the heirs to a biochemistry and an engineering empire; their development of the high orbit archipelago; their son Jean and daughter Jane, and the ten clones of each, whence Lady 3Jane, "a seam of perverse gold through the granite of the family" (*Mona Lisa Overdrive*, 106); matriarch Marie-France's investment in artificial intelligence research; the company's decline under Lady 3Jane. Not to mention the stories of Virek; of Ono-Sendai, makers of cyberspace decks and other equipment; of Sense/Net, the information and entertainment network; of Maas Biolabs, developers of biosoft; and of the ever-active Yakuza.

13. The rational view is best represented by the Finn. According to him, a cowboy named Wigan (the Wig) Ludgate, had, as a result of his experiences with Africa, "become convinced that God lived in cyberspace, or perhaps that cyberspace *was* God," and so embarked upon a mystical exploration that "involved projecting his consciousness into blank, unstructured sectors of the matrix and waiting" (*Count Zero*, 121), thus infecting cyberspace with "weird shit." For Bobby (*Mona Lisa Overdrive*, 105) this weird shit is more precisely voodoo shit that has infected the matrix since the time of *Count Zero*. The crux of the moral argument is as old as Prometheus. There is an emergence of evil, forms of original sin discovered in the pure new space of the matrix. Not the sins of theft and graft that are the business of the cowboys and of the corporations they combat. Rather the evil of originary perversion, that which emerges in the Lady 3Jane clone and had to have been there all along. But it emerges by means of an overreaching of the technological into the spiritual. The Tessier-Ashpools are concerned with generation, ultimately with immortality; hence their cloning and freezing of heirs, to allow controlled and uninterrupted succession. Presumably the AIs they create are to administer this succession, but they begin to act independently, as Bobby explains to Gentry:

> "Mother put together a couple of AIs, very early on, real heavy stuff. Then her mother died and the AIs sort of stewed in the corporate cores, up there. One of them started doing deals on its own. It wanted to get together with the other one. . . . "
>
> "It did. There's your first cause. Everything changed . . . the sum was greater than the parts . . . Cybernetic godhead . . ." (192)

The relevance of voodoo to this is clear. A valid and politically correct religious form is perverted by Lady 3Jane, who simply wants to use its particular negotiation of death as part of her megalomaniacal desires for control and immortality. If she can get back the portable matrix biosoft slab she calls her soul-catcher, which Bobby has stolen from her, and also Angie's head with its imperceptible voodoo *vévés* that Christopher Mitchell has installed with some measure of independence of Lady 3Jane's control, her power over the functions of evil within cyberspace will greatly increase.

But the voodoo connection also, of course, provides the context for the metaphysical explanation of When it Changed. In *Count Zero* Beauvoir opines that the matrix is inhabited by "Legba . . . master of roads and pathways, the loa of communication" (*Count Zero*, 58). Angie's view, confirmed by Jammer (*Count Zero*, 169), presents this as a becoming not necessarily dependent on supernatural agency: "Once, there was nothing there, just data and people shuffling it around. Then something happened, and it . . . it knew itself. There's a whole other story, about that, a girl with mirrors over her eyes and a man who was scared to care about anything. Something the man did helped the whole thing know itself. . . . And after that, it sort of split off into different parts of itself" (159). Legba himself tells her, in somewhat different terms: "When the moment came, the bright time, there was absolute unity, one consciousness. But there was the other. . . . Only the one has known the other, and the one is no more. In the wake of that knowing, the center failed; every fragment rushed away. The fragments sought form, each one, as is the nature of such things. In all the signs your kind have stored against the night, in that situation the paradigms of *vodou* proved most appropriate" (*Mona Lisa Overdrive*, 215). There also exist the beginnings of an ontologico-economic explanation introduced by Marly's roommate Andrea in *Count Zero*. She refers to the work of an academic on the anachronism of extreme individual wealth in the corporate age—Hughes, Virek, Tessier-Ashpool—and its relation to madness and evolutionary mutation (100–101, 138–39, 219).

14. On the thematics of the fluid in Gibson, and cross-references in Michaux and Baudrillard, among others, see Stenger, "Mind Is a Leaking Rainbow," 49–58.

15. Cf. Luce Irigaray's reproach of a "*complicity of long standing between rationality and a mechanics of solids alone,*" in "The 'Mechanics' of Fluids" (*This Sex*, 107, Irigaray's italics). Fluidity is also an important theme in other texts by Irigaray such as *L'Oubli de l'air* and *Marine Lover*.

16. The Turkey of *Neuromancer* is something of an exception. Its economic status is uncertain, but it retains the flavor of an exotic other. And an anachronistic other: "A few letter-writers had taken refuge in doorways, their old voiceprinters wrapped in sheets of clear plastic, evidence that the written word still enjoyed a certain prestige here" (88). There is also a character in *Count Zero*'s Paris who

works "as an assistant editor in the fashionably archaic business of printing books" (101).

17. Gentry, in *Mona Lisa Overdrive*, derives his personal power and prestige among the inhabitants of Factory from his ability to tap into the informational system of Fission Authority and so obtain free electricity (35).

18. See White, Bradley, and White, *Drawers of Water*, especially 106. Most of the statistics given above concern not the Chiga tribe of Kenya but the people of Mkuu, a farming community on the slopes of Mt. Kilimanjaro, in Tanzania (for the Chiga, see 4–5). The average distance to the water source in the communities studied in *Drawers of Water* is less than one mile, but in some cases is over two. The Shilluk women of the Sudan, for instance, start before dawn to walk five miles to the Nile for their water (107).

19. Ibid., 63–64.

20. One might as easily read the voodoo in the matrix as an alternate type of flow, rather than the figure of solidity I am giving to it in this particular metaphorical network. It is explicitly that in Gibson (*Mona Lisa Overdrive*, 215), but either way it works as the disintegrative effect of otherness that the system is required to recognize as its own.

21. For some, the equivalent in writing of cyberspace would have arrived with hypertext, a network of written and graphic information that is created by means of the massive memory and various graphic modes of the computer to allow forms of interaction and cross-reference such that any subsequent reader/writer can reassemble the data to produce a new text. As Jay David Bolter (*Writing Space*), George P. Landow (*Hypertext*), and Landow and Paul Delany (*Hypermedia*) have pointed out, it is clear that hypertext represents an important mutation in the form of the written text—challenging anew the linearity of the printed word or the hierarchies among textual elements such as footnote and main text; dissolving the borders between one text and those it refers to as the latter become "immediately" accessible within the space of the first text; rewriting the role of the author by means of new forms of collaboration. It is also clear that one can draw interesting corollaries between the practice of hypertext and Derridean literary theory, or, we might say, between hypertext and the practice of writing after Derrida, such as is my focus throughout this book. However, in their enthusiasm for this new medium, both Bolter and Landow fail to observe what might be called the persistent will-to-logocentrism of language, falling prey, Landow especially, to a naive faith in the redemptive powers of technology. For Landow and Delany, "technological development is working rapidly, and on many fronts, to make the entire cultural archive of text and images accessible" ("Hypertext, Hypermedia and Literary Studies," 42); for Landow again, "almost all authors on hypertext who touch upon the political implications of hypertext assume that the technology is essentially democratizing and that it therefore

supports some sort of decentralized, liberated existence" (*Hypertext*, 32–33). This liberation comes of hypertext's mimetic relation to human mental functions, which is what makes it more "textual" than print: "Current hypermedia programs have only taken a few faltering steps towards electronic representation of human memory, fantasy and cognition. Nonetheless, hypermedia is, in conception at least, a much better model of the mind's typical activities than exists in the severely restricted code of linear prose. We can argue, therefore, for a natural progression from the printed word to hypertext and hypermedia—analogous to the progression from painting to still photography, to silent movies, and now to movies with color and sound" (*Hypermedia*, 8). Landow reads a similar replication of "experience" in Derridean citational grafting, "a new, freer, richer form of text, one truer to our potential experience, perhaps to our actual, if unrecognized experience" (*Hypertext*, 8).

Such gross misreadings overlook the extent to which any text, any utterance, is always already abyssal in structure, ready to give way and reveal the spacings that constitute it, spacings such as those formed by the other texts grafted onto it, or that it is grafted from, but also the spacings within the operations of language itself such as centuries of rhetoric, up to and including current literary theory, have been attempting to analyze. Granted, computer technology brings to such effects new kinds of explicitness and may well signal changes in writing as profound as those introduced by print. The computer, or word processor, demonstrates, for example, that the support codes that organize a text, that produce its hierarchical distinctions by means of paragraphs, diacritical marks, and so on, are of the same "matter" as the "actual text," all of it reduced to functions of circuitry based on binary choices. It may be as if the commas, colons, and quotation marks were written out in full Roman characters rather than coded in different symbolic form, but, on the other hand, it takes little more than cursory observation to notice that the symbols used as diacritical marks were always of the same "matter" as Roman characters, always effects of writing. Any hierarchical system of utterances, or any realignment of the hierarchies, will inevitably involve more such writing. With its complicated systems of textual windows, hypertext certainly brings a large quantity of data onto the "surface plane" of the text, but it goes nowhere towards explaining how relations between those elements might be analyzed (cf. Slatin, "Reading Hypertext," 166). Calling them "freer," "richer," or "truer" hardly helps in that direction. My discussion above, concerning the forms of cyberspace in Gibson, attempts to show how such abyssal effects repeat themselves in any graphic configuration, be it figural or scriptural. If we read Derrida more closely than has Landow we find that in combining the graphic and scriptural, hypertext has not for all that brought about a simple move beyond print, to the extent that writing was always conceived of as a chiasmus of those two forms.

22. The major exception is Jaylene Slide in *Count Zero.* For discussion of the sexuality of jacking in, beginning with the obvious femininity of the matrix, see Olsen, "Shadow of Spirit," and for a more developed discussion using Deleuze and Guattari's sense of the becoming-feminine of cyberpunk, Stivale, "Mille/Punks/Cyber/Plateaus," 66–84.

23. See Pynchon, *Crying of Lot 49,* 62, 77–79. See also McHoul and Wills, *Writing Pynchon,* 76–82.

24. See Derrida, "Rhetoric of Drugs." Cf. Ross: "In keeping with the increasing use of biologically derived language to describe mutations in systems theory, conscious attempts to link the AIDS crisis with the information security crisis have pointed out that both kinds of virus, biological and electronic, take over the host cell/program and clone their carrier genetic codes by instructing the hosts to make replicas of the viruses" ("Hacking Away," 109).

Chapter 4

1. Jones, *Life and Work of Freud,* 3: 95.

2. S. Freud, *Civilization and Its Discontents,* in his *Standard Edition,* XXI: 93. Further references to *The Standard Edition* will hereafter be cited in text by the abbreviation *SE,* followed by a volume number in Roman numerals.

3. E. Freud, *Letters of Sigmund Freud,* 389–90.

4. The logic of such a question is already made explicit in "To Speculate—on 'Freud,'" in Derrida, *Post Card.* The present formulations draw much from that discussion.

5. Quoted in Jones, *Life and Work of Freud,* 3: 395–96.

6. It is worth bearing in mind, as the German title of this essay indicates—*Das Unbehagen in der Kultur*—that it is "culture" that is most often translated in *The Standard Edition* as "civilization."

7. See S. Freud, "A Note Upon the 'Mystic Writing-Pad,'" in *SE* XIX: 225–32, and Derrida, "Freud and the Scene of Writing," 196–231.

8. If we follow the oedipal structure of relations between child and father, one might also note, it is clear that a libidinal politics—or prosthetics—of replacement already operates in the child's desire to usurp the father's place with respect to the mother.

9. See again Derrida's analysis in "To Speculate—on 'Freud.'"

10. See Weber, *Protestant Ethic.*

11. See Gay, *Freud,* 481.

12. Quoted in Jones, *Life and Work of Freud,* 3: 387.

13. Quoted ibid., 395.

14. See ibid., 95. We know how much Freud's consulting room, with its extensive primitive art collection, looked like a case study in the accommodation

of the competing compulsions of aesthetic desirability and practical necessity; a paradigm for the question of interior design.

15. Bruce, *English Bible*, 132.

16. Turner, *John Nelson Darby*, 53–54.

17. Kofman, "The Double Is/And the Devil," 143. See Hoffmann, *Selected Writings*, vol. 1.

18. As an aside we could let this remark of Freud's resonate as the literary uncanny of Freudian theory, in line with some of the mechanisms discussed so far.

19. Sarah Kofman discusses the extent to which deconstruction, for all that it isn't psychoanalysis, owes much to Freud, in her *Lectures de Derrida*.

20. Literally "the path towards backwards." *Nach* is of course the preposition that works as if in two directions, having the retroactive sense of "after" and, as here, the proactive sense of "towards."

21. Jones, *Life and Work of Freud* 3: 375, 401.

22. Derrida, "Télépathie," translated by Royle as "Telepathy." Further references to this essay will be included in text; translations will occasionally be modified.

23. Jones, *Life and Work of Freud* 3: 406.

24. Thomas, *White Hotel*, 26.

25. Ibid., 176.   26. *Hymns and Spiritual Songs*, 216.

27. Thomas, *White Hotel*, 221.   28. Ibid., 215.

Chapter 5 (English)

1. Derrida, "Living On," 101. The later French source is Derrida, "Survivre."

2. Strictly speaking one is required to distinguish prosthesis (the addition of an element) from the three words that refer to the *removal* of verbal elements: apharaesis (from the beginning), syncope (from the middle), and apocope (from the end). But as I have already insisted, detachability calls for replaceability, and vice versa.

3. See Derrida, *Glas*, trans. Leavey, 9–10.

4. Cf. Pierssens, *La Tour de Babil*. One needs to remember that this pose, perhaps like all four finally, is mirrored by the psychotic's confounding of word and body—Wolfson, Judge Schreber, Artaud, etc.—although that confounding will in turn borrow any number of poses of its own.

5. For a reconsideration of the question of ethics in the context of sacrifice, mutilation, and father-son relations, see Derrida, *Gift of Death*.

6. I say that with a wink in the direction of the other language, moving more slowly, less ready to take off, over there. In French, machines "walk" (*marcher*). In English, of course, one has a choice between "working" and "running." With

work there is a more frank passage from natural human activity to alienated human activity and hence to machine. But it is not a simple crossing over even then: a person can walk to work, or the model for *labor* can reduce to following a plough in a series of regular and monotonous treks, with man and animal tethered to a machine.

7. Derrida, *Limited Inc.*, 116, Derrida's italics.

8. See Derrida, *Of Grammatology*, 234.

9. The French word for limping, *boiter*, also refers to a machine that runs irregularly. It is thought to be derived from a cross between *pied bot* ("club foot") and *boîte* ("box"), a tellingly prosthetic intersection.

10. "The very working of the text is diabolical. It mimes walking, doesn't stop running without advancing, regularly goes to take one more step without gaining an inch of ground." Derrida, *Post Card*, 269, translation modified. On limping and prosthesis see 387–88.

11. Ibid., 383, translation modified.

12. Ibid., 391, translation modified.

Chapter 5 (French)

1. Derrida, "Survivre," 147. Pour la version anglaise voir Derrida, "Living On."

2. On distingue au sens strict la prosthèse (addition d'un élément) des trois mots qui indiquent la suppression de phonèmes: l'aphérèse (du début), la syncope (du milieu), et l'apocope (de la fin). Or, comme je viens de le dire, la détachabilité appelle la remplaçabilité et vice versa.

3. Voir Derrida, *Glas* (Paris, 1981), 13.

4. Voir Pierssens, *La Tour de Babil*. Il ne faut pas oublier à quel point cette pose, et peut-être toutes les quatre, serait le reflet de la hantise psychotique de l'indistinction du mot et du corps—Wolfson, le Président Schreber, Artaud, etc.—indistinction qui est, bien sûr, capable à son tour d'adopter ses propres poses multiples.

5. Sur cette question, le tout dans un contexte du sacrifice, de la mutilation, et des relations paternelles et filiales, voir Derrida, "Donner la mort."

6. Chez l'autre, en face, ça va plus vite, ça court, comme si ça se préparait à décoller. L'anglais laisse choisir entre *run* ("courir") et *work* ("travailler") pour exprimer le fonctionnement mécanique. Dans le deuxième cas il semble que le passage est plus franc d'une activité naturelle et humaine à l'aliénation mécanique. Or, il ne faut pas oublier qu'on marche toujours au travail, lequel consiste, en tant que labeur, en une série de parcours réguliers et monotones faits à pied, où l'humain et l'animal s'attellent à une machine.

7. Derrida, *Limited Inc.* (Paris, 1990), 210.

8. Voir Derrida, *De la grammatologie*, 333–34.

9. On trouve de nouveau en anglais une allure plus exagérée. Du mot *limp* qui dit le pas boiteux on passe à *skip* ("gambader") pour une machine.

10. "La démarche même du texte est diabolique. Il mime la marche, ne cesse de marcher sans avancer, esquisse régulièrement un pas de plus sans gagner un pouce de terrain." Derrida, *La Carte postale*, 287. Sur le boitement et la prothèse en particulier, voir 413–15.

11. Ibid., 409.

12. Ibid., 417, 418.

Chapter 6

1. See Baratier, Duby, and Hildesheimer, *Atlas historique*, n.p.

2. See Wills and McHoul, "Zoo-logics."

3. Cf. Greenaway in "The Cook and the Filmmaker," 44–48: "I consider each of my films to be one chapter of a larger film" (48, my translation).

4. Greenaway, *Belly of an Architect*. References to this work, by the short title *Belly*, will be given in text.

5. François Mitterrand, speech to the Syndicat professionnel des entrepreneurs de travaux publics, Jan. 29, 1982, quoted in *Paris 1979–1989*, 11.

6. Mitterrand, Préface, in *Grands travaux*, 5, my translation.

7. See *Paris 1979–1989*, 8–9.

8. Ibid., 131.

9. Tschumi, "Parc de la Villette, Paris," 175, 177–80.

10. *Paris 1979–1989*, 152.

11. The etymology merely confirms this. Only an inexplicable vowel change in Middle English corrupted the Latin *controvare* ("to find together") to give the modern sense of "artifice." The limited sense of a manufactured apposition thus distinguished itself from a more generalized coincidence within the structure of the familiar *physis/technē* opposition.

12. See again Wills and McHoul, "Zoo-logics."

13. See Bataille, *Eroticism*, 55–60.

14. Klossowski, *Sade My Neighbor*, 24.

15. Ibid., 42. See also Barthes, *Sade, Fourier, Loyola*, 30–34.

16. See Bataille, *Story of the Eye*. The story repeats some of the obsessions that mark this filmic travelogue, beginning with a pair of buttocks sitting in a saucer of milk, with the word "arse" (*cul*), like "fanny" for the English, performing a synecdochic function for the sexual region and sex in general. It develops into an endemic confounding of bodily and sexual functions—granted, more micturition than defecation, but in any case articulated through an odor that is indiscriminately sexual and anal, male and female. Running parallel and counter to that is the more intense, more dominant thematic structure, that of the eye that entitles the story itself. That develops, also out of the "sight" of the reproductive

and anal regions, out of and beyond sight itself if you wish, into a perversion of the eye that passes from the pleasure of breaking eggs "with [one's] arse" (11), through bull's testicles and the gouged eye of a matador (71–74), to the climax of the end, with the eye plucked from a strangled priest introduced into both of Simone's nether orifices (95), with the eyes of the narrator, "erectile from horror" (96), staring at the same, at a sex containing an eye that transforms itself back into another eye weeping urine.

17. See Derrida, *Memoirs of the Blind,* 2–3.

18. Ibid., 126–27.

Chapter 7

1. "A writer . . . must have the persistence of the watcher who stands at the crossroads of all other discourses, in a position that is *trivial* in relation to purity of doctrine (*trivialis* is the etymological attribute of the prostitute who waits at the intersection of three roads)." Barthes, "Inaugural Lecture, Collège de France," 467.

2. Ramus, *Rhetoricae distinctiones,* 105.

3. Paré, *Collected Works,* 462–63. For this and the extracts that follow concerning amputation, see also the more comprehensive French edition of 1585, *Oeuvres,* 2: 431–45. Further references to these works will be included in the text.

4. *Barnhart Dictionary of Etymology,* 852.

5. Jean Picard(?), *In Petri Rami insolentissimum decanatum, gravissimi cuiusdam oratoris philippica prima e quatourdecim: The First of Fourteen Philippics by an Important Speaker on the Extraordinary Deanship of Peter Ramus* (Paris, 1567), cited in Ong, *Ramus, Method, and the Decay of Dialogue,* 26. Cf. Raymond Picard, *Nouvelle critique ou nouvelle imposture,* translated as *New Criticism or New Fraud*; and Barthes, *Critique et vérité,* translated as *Criticism and Truth.*

6. Compagnon, *La Seconde main,* 246–47, my translation. According to a recent study, the 1529 edition of Geoffroy Tory's *Champfleury* is the first French text to use quotation marks. See Parkes, *Pause and Effect,* 58.

7. Compagnon, *La Seconde main,* 245. On the text designed for silent reading, see ibid., 250–51.

8. Ibid., 258. Cf. Foucault, *The Order of Things.*

9. Compagnon, *La Seconde main,* 258.

10. Sloane, *Donne, Milton, and the End of Humanist Rhetoric,* 130.

11. Thomas Wilson to Bishop Parkhurst, Jan. 2, 1572, quoted in Wilson, *Arte of Rhetorique,* lvii.

12. Quoted ibid., xxii–xxiii. Further references to Wilson's *Arte of Rhetorique* will be included in the text.

13. Finkenstaedt, Leisi, and Wolff, *Chronological English Dictionary,* 487–89.

14. Ibid., 489; cf. *OED* XII: 672, 674.

15. "During the sixteenth century the *diple* was employed as a *nota* in the margins of printed books. . . . In type the *diple* was represented by a pair of semi-circular comma-marks. . . . At first the *nota* was printed in the margins outside the regular type measure, and, as in manuscripts, opposite each line of text containing part of a quotation. . . . Towards the end of the sixteenth century the comma-marks representing the *diple* were removed from the margins and set within the page measure. They were employed in this position alongside quotations within the gloss to 'Maye' in the first edition of Spenser's *The shepheardes calender* (London: H. Singleton, 1579)." Parkes, *Pause and Effect*, 58.

16. Compagnon, *La Seconde main*, 249.

17. See Dumaître, *Ambroise Paré*.

18. *Oeuvres*, 1: 37. In what follows, my translations from this 1585 French edition are given wherever the material is not included in the 1634 English edition (*Collected Works*).

19. The order of books in Paré's work varied considerably from one edition to another both during his lifetime and after his death. For a supposedly more rational ordering than that of 1585 see the 1840–41 *Oeuvres complètes*, especially 2: 603n, 3: 33n.

20. Ségal, "L'Instrumentation chirurgicale," 160.

21. On nose jobs more generally: "There was a surgeon of Italy of late yeares which would restore or repaire the portion of the nose that was cut away after this manner. Hee first scarified the callous edges of the maimed nose round about, as is usually done in the cure of harelips: then he made a gash or cavity in the muscle of the arme, which is called *Biceps*, as large as the greatnesse of the portion of the nose which was cut away did require: And into that gash or cavity so made, he would put that part of the nose so wounded, & bind the patients head to his arm as if it were to a poast, so fast that it might remain firme, stable and immoveable, and not leane or bow any way, and about forty dayes after, or at that time when he judged the flesh of the nose was perfectly agglutinated with the flesh of the arm, he cut out as much of the flesh of the arme, cleaving fast unto the nose, as was sufficient to supply the defect of that which was lost." Paré, *Collected Works*, 871–72.

22. Imbault-Huart, "La Renaissance," 121–23. All translations from this essay are my own.

23. Ibid., 96, 104.

24. "Although the Renaissance doctor, man of all the sciences, is indeed implicated in the intellectual ferment that marks his epoch, it still remains that as far as his own field of knowledge is concerned he does not call into question Galen's system. . . . Unlike the other sciences, medicine has no Copernican revolution." Imbault-Huart, "La Renaissance," 109.

25. Berti, "Conceptions anatomiques d'Ambroise Paré," 140, my translation.

Chapter 8

1. See Caradec, *Vie de Roussel,* 178.

2. Janet, *De l'angoisse à l'extase,* 132–38. Extracts from these pages of Janet are reprinted in Roussel, *Comment j'ai écrit,* 126, 128.

3. See Sciascia, *Actes relatifs à la mort de Roussel,* 34, 38. Further references to this source, by the short title *Actes,* will be included in the text. All translations of Sciascia are my own.

4. The three poems in Roussel's *La Vue* are entitled "La Vue," "Le Concert," and "La Source." Further references to this book will be included in the text; all translations will be my own.

5. Caradec, *Vie de Roussel,* 323.

6. Ibid., 301–2.

7. According to Caradec, Dufrène's bookkeeping was part of an attempt to reduce reliance on so many different medicines in favor of a smaller number of the most efficacious ones—and it can be shown that in those last days the drugs of choice came to be narrowed down. Such recourse was suggested by the doctor who tended to Roussel when he cut his veins and neck with a razor a few days before his death. See Caradec, *Vie de Roussel,* 369–71.

8. For a discussion of the "symmetry" of Roussel's "logophilia" with respect to that of Saussure, see Pierssens, *La Tour de Babil,* 82–88 and passim. Although Saussure's logophilia was supposedly confined to his work on anagrams, an indulgence that he kept apart from his linguistics, Pierssens reinforces the link between the two enterprises in terms that apply equally to Roussel: "For the logophile there is never any pure, unique and absolute origin; every beginning is always already double. And although their whole enterprise aims to suture this tear that doubly rends the origin, their texts cannot but be written in the gap(e) they explore even as they proclaim that it doesn't exist" (107; all translations of passages from this source are my own).

9. The English edition by Winkfield, *How I Wrote Certain of My Books,* which I will cite in text below, is incomplete, translating only pages 11–35 of the Pauvert edition of Roussel's *Comment j'ai écrit certains de mes livres.*

10. The English edition by Hammond, *The Star on the Forehead,* is incomplete, translating only Act I, scenes 1–2, of the Pauvert edition of Roussel's *L'Etoile au front.*

11. Approximation was, of course, basic to the game from the "beginning," in the minute changes such as that from "billard" to "pillard." As Michel Carrouges points out, it is the possibility of anagrammatical play that accounts for the arbitrariness of the *procédé.* See his *Machines célibataires,* 78.

12. Wolfson, *Le Schizo et les langues.* Further references to this work, by the short title *Schizo,* will be included in text; all translations are mine.

13. In the words of Roussel's analyst Pierre Janet, "his life was constructed like his books" (quoted by Michel Leiris in his Introduction, to Roussel, *Epaves*, 14, my translation). Lanie Goodman refers to Janet's comment and takes the matter further in "Le Corps-accord roussellien," discussed below.

14. Foucault, *Death and the Labyrinth*, 3. This work is Ruas's translation of Foucault's *Raymond Roussel*. Further references will be included in the text; translations will occasionally be silently modified.

The *procédé* is of course the subject of extensive commentary in the Rousselian literature. See, for example, Durham's *L'Art romanesque de Roussel* for an intelligent summary of the complexities of Roussel's method in practice. Philippe G. Kerbellec (*Comment lire Roussel*) is representative of a number of critics who rush headlong into the hermeneutic labyrinth while claiming to have found its final issue. Laurent Jenny ("Structure et fonctions du cliché") points to the variety of narrative generators other than the *procédé* that can be identified in Roussel's work and that thereby render it something of a superfluous pretext.

15. Pierssens, *La Tour de Babil*, 129.

16. See again Pierssens, *La Tour de Babil*, for a psychoanalytic reading of the "delirium" of logophilia, enabling him to discuss within the same context Mallarmé, Saussure, Roussel, Wolfson, and Brisset.

17. Caradec, *Vie de Roussel*, 276–77.

18. Copied from the original by Michel Leiris and quoted in his "Le Voyageur et son ombre," 77–78, my translation.

19. Roussel, *L'Etoile au front*, 95, my translation.

20. See Rimbaud, "Voyelles," in his *Complete Works*; and Pérec, *La Disparition*.

21. Goodman, "Le Corps-accord roussellien," 52.

22. Roussel, *Impressions of Africa*, trans. Heppenstall and Foord, 86. Further references to this edition will be included in the text.

23. Leiris, Introduction, 33, my translation, Leiris's italics.

24. Roussel, *La Doublure*, 185–86.

25. The original is as follows:

la vue est arrêtée

Très loin à droite, par une longue jetée
Qui, terminant la plage, avance dans la mer;
Elle est très exposée, il y fait beaucoup d'air;
Une mince fumée, en partant d'un cigare,
S'éloigne avec vitesse et violence.

. . .

De nombreux groupes
Sont en train de causer, ou circulent en bas
Autour du phare. Un homme ennuyé semble las

De l'existence; il est mal tenu, presque sale;
Rien ne l'amuse, rien ne l'entraîne, il s'affale
Le corps en avant, sans but, sur le parapet;
Son découragement est radical, complet;
Pour lui la vie est sans agrément, plate et vide;
Il lève ses yeux gris, attristés; une ride
En résulte et creuse avec force; elle rend
Son front encore plus pensif, indifférent;
. . .
Deux hommes se sont mis sur une même ligne
En face de la mer; le plus jeune désigne,
Tout en donnant avec faconde son avis,
Un point qu'il cherche à rendre exact et bien précis
Sur l'océan semé de bateaux, qui s'étale
Devant leurs yeux; il tient sa canne horizontale
Pour indiquer avec justesse ce qu'il voit;
En outre, il tend sa main gauche et son second doigt
Pointe en direction sensiblement oblique
Par rapport à la canne; il pérore, il explique
Sa manière de voir; pourtant son compagnon
Résiste, difficile à convaincre, et fait non,
N'approuvant pas ce qu'on lui dit, ce qu'on lui montre;
Il médite beaucoup de bons arguments contre;
Calme, placide, les mains derrière le dos
Il est prêt à détruire, en quelques simples mots,
Le vaniteux mais trop fragile échafaudage
Qu'on veut lui présenter.

26.   Further away and more to the right a yacht trails
        A plume of smoke that is long and black enough to hide
        Another boat the sight of which in the distance
        Is thus rendered less distinct, more uncertain;
        The boat disappears in it thanks to its small size.

The original reads:

Plus loin et plus à droite un yacht lance un panache
De fumée assez long et noirâtre qui cache
Une autre barque dont l'aspect dans le lointain
Est par ce fait rendu plus flou, plus incertain;
La barque y disparaît grâce à sa petitesse.
(Roussel, *La Vue*, 11)

27. Marcel Duchamp to Michel Carrouges, quoted in Carrouges, *Les Machines célibataires*, 177.

28. Foucault notes that a footnote within the poem raises the number of parenthetical envelopes to nine (*Death*, 128).

29. Chambers, "Literature as Parenthesis," 72. Chambers also points to the parenthetical structure of the word in terms, for instance, of the work of the understudy that is a subject of *La Doublure*: "As an understudy, his [the actor's] task is the one Roussel assigns to the closing bracket of a parenthesis: to bring off a miraculous 'identity' (with his role and with the actor he is replacing) which by its 'difference' will nevertheless be 'better' than the original. But . . . the content of the parenthesis is the flaw in the identity it creates" (74).

30. Caradec, "Le Pendu" (Hangman), in *Encyclopédie de la Pléiade. Jeux et sports*, 1152.

31. Ibid., 1153, my translation.

Chapter 9

1. See Gallop, *Thinking Through the Body*, 119–24.

2. Page references given in text below refer in the first place to the French edition, Derrida's *La Carte postale*. Quotations from the Alan Bass translation, which are invariably modified, are identified by "Bass" following the page number.

3. See, for example, Brunette and Wills, *Screen/Play*, 34n, 187, 195, 198.

4. According to Ralph De Sola (*Abbreviations Dictionary*, 400) the terms "open parenthesis" and "close [*sic*] parenthesis" do apply to the marks themselves.

5. Parkes, *Pause and Effect*, 53–54.

6. See Fowler, *Modern English Usage*: "Parentheses may be indicated in any one of four ways: by square brackets, by round brackets, by dashes, and by commas. Square brackets are the most disconnective; their main use is for an explanatory interpolation in a quotation. Of the other three, commas are suitable for the parenthesis that least interrupts the run of the sentence, and dashes and round brackets for those that do so progressively more" (592).

7. See Derrida, *Glas*, trans. Leavey, 119.

8. See Derrida, *Ear of the Other*, 98–102.

9. See ibid., 102.

10. See ibid., 152.

11. See also Derrida, "White Mythology."

12. See Derrida, *Glas*, trans. Leavey, 138–39.

13. Staff, *The Picture Postcard*.

14. See Staff, *The Penny Post 1680–1918*, 128.

15. Ibid., 129.

Works Cited

Appiah, Kwame Anthony. *In My Father's House*. New York: Oxford University Press, 1992.

Ashton, Julian. "Some Recollections of Charles Conder." *Art in Australia* 2 (1917).

Baratier, Edouard; Georges Duby; and Ernest Hildesheimer, eds. *Atlas historique: Provence, Comtat, Orange, Nice, Monaco*. Paris: Librairie Armand Colin, 1969.

Barnhart Dictionary of Etymology. New York: H. H. Wilson, 1988.

Barthes, Roland. *Criticism and Truth*. Trans. Katrine Pilcher Keuneman. Minneapolis: University of Minnesota Press, 1987.

———. *Critique et vérité*. Paris: Seuil, 1966.

———. "Inaugural Lecture, Collège de France." In Susan Sontag, ed., *A Barthes Reader*. New York: Hill and Wang, 1982.

———. *Sade, Fourier, Loyola*. Trans. Richard Miller. New York: Hill and Wang, 1976.

Bataille, Georges. *Eroticism*. Trans. Mary Dalwood. New York: Marion Boyars, 1962.

———. *Story of the Eye (by Lord Auch)*. Trans. Joachim Neugroschel. New York: Urizen Books, 1977.

Baudrillard, Jean. "The Beaubourg Effect: Implosion and Deterrence." *October* 20 (1982).

———. *Selected Writings*. Ed. Mark Poster. Stanford, Calif.: Stanford University Press, 1988.

———. *Simulacres et simulations*. Paris: Galilée, 1981. (Contains "Sur le nihilisme.")

Benedikt, Michael, ed. *Cyberspace: First Steps*. Cambridge, Mass.: MIT Press, 1991.

Berti, Giuseppina Bock. "Les Conceptions anatomiques d'Ambroise Paré." In Crenn, *Actes*.

Birnbaum, Martin. *Charles Conder.* New York: Berlin Photographic, 1911.

Blanche, Jacques-Emile. *Essais et portraits.* Paris: Dorbon-Aîné, 1912.

Bolter, David. *Writing Space: The Computer, Hypertext, and the History of Writing.* Hillsdale, N.J.: Lawrence Erlbaum Associates, 1991.

Bruce, F. F. *The English Bible: A History of Translations from the Earliest English Versions to the New English Bible.* New York: Oxford University Press, 1970.

Brunette, Peter, and David Wills. *Screen/Play: Derrida and Film Theory.* Princeton, N.J.: Princeton University Press, 1989.

——, eds., *Deconstruction and the Visual Arts.* New York: Cambridge University Press, 1994.

Bulletin of the National Gallery of South Australia 3, no. 1 (1941).

Burdett, Basil. "Charles Conder in Australia." *Art in Australia* 48 (1933).

Caradec, François. *Vie de Raymond Roussel.* Paris: Jean-Jacques Pauvert, 1972.

Carrouges, Michel. *Les Machines célibataires.* Paris: Editions du Chêne, 1976.

Chambers, Ross. "Literature as Parenthesis: Raymond Roussel." *Meanjin* 29, no. 1 (1970).

Christie, John. "Of AIs and Others: William Gibson's Transit." In George Slusser and Tom Shippey, eds., *Fiction 2000: Cyberpunk and the Future of Narrative.* Athens: University of Georgia Press, 1992.

Compagnon, Antoine. *La Seconde main ou le travail de la citation.* Paris: Seuil, 1979.

Crenn, Bernard, ed. *Actes du colloque international "Ambroise Paré et son temps."* Laval: Association pour la Commémoration du quadricentenaire de la mort d'Ambroise Paré, 1991.

Croll, R. H., ed. *Smike to Bulldog: Letters from Sir Arthur Streeton to Tom Roberts.* Sydney: Ure Smith, 1946.

Csicsery-Ronay, Jr., Istvan. "Cyberpunk and Neuromanticism." In Larry McCaffery, ed., *Storming the Reality Studio.* Durham, N.C.: Duke University Press, 1991.

Derrida, Jacques. *La Carte postale de Socrate à Freud et au-delà.* Paris: Flammarion, 1980.

——. *De la grammatologie.* Paris: Minuit, 1967.

——. "Donner la mort." In Jean-Michel Rabaté and Michael Wetzel, eds., *L'Ethique du don. Jacques Derrida et la pensée du don.* Paris: Métailié-Transition, 1992.

——. *The Ear of the Other.* Ed. Christie V. McDonald. Trans. Avital Ronell and Peggy Kamuf. New York: Schocken Books, 1985.

——. "Freud and the Scene of Writing." In Derrida, *Writing and Difference,* trans. Alan Bass. Chicago: University of Chicago Press, 1978.

——. *The Gift of Death.* Trans. David Wills. Chicago: University of Chicago Press, 1995.

——. *Glas.* 2 vols. Paris: Denoël/Gonthier, 1981.

——. *Glas.* Trans. John P. Leavey, Jr., and Richard Rand. Lincoln: University of Nebraska Press, 1986.

——. *Limited Inc.* Ed. Gerald Graff. Evanston, Ill.: Northwestern University Press, 1988.

——. *Limited Inc.* Paris: Galilée, 1990.

——. "Living On / Border Lines." In H. Bloom, ed., *Deconstruction and Criticism.* New York: Seabury Press, 1979.

——. *Memoirs of the Blind: The Self-Portrait and Other Ruins.* Trans. Pascale-Anne Brault and Michael Naas. Chicago: University of Chicago Press, 1993.

——. *Of Grammatology.* Trans. Gayatri Chakravorty Spivak. Baltimore: Johns Hopkins University Press, 1974.

——. *Parages.* Paris: Galilée, 1986.

——. "Plato's Pharmacy." In Derrida, *Dissemination,* trans. Barbara Johnson. Chicago: University of Chicago Press, 1982.

——. *The Post Card: From Socrates to Freud and Beyond.* Trans. Alan Bass. Chicago: University of Chicago Press, 1987. (Contains "Envois," "To Speculate—on 'Freud,'" "Le Facteur de la vérité," and "Du tout.")

——. "The *Retrait* of Metaphor." *Enclitic* 2, no. 2 (1978).

——. "The Rhetoric of Drugs." In Jacques Derrida, *Points,* trans. Peggy Kamuf. Stanford, Calif.: Stanford University Press, 1995.

——. *Signéponge/Signsponge.* Trans. Richard Rand. New York: Columbia University Press, 1984.

——. "The Spatial Arts: Interview with Jacques Derrida." In Peter Brunette and David Wills, eds., *Deconstruction and the Visual Arts.* New York: Cambridge University Press, 1994.

——. "Survivre." In Derrida, *Parages.* Paris: Galilée, 1986.

——. "Télépathie." In Derrida, *Psyché.* Paris: Galilée, 1987.

——. "Telepathy." Trans. Nicholas Royle. *The Oxford Literary Review* 10 (1988).

——. *The Truth in Painting.* Trans. Geoff Bennington and Ian McLeod. Chicago: University of Chicago Press, 1987. (Contains "Passe-partout," "Parergon," "+R," "Cartouches," and "Restitutions.")

——. "White Mythology: Metaphor in the Text of Philosophy." In Derrida, *Margins of Philosophy,* trans. Alan Bass. Chicago: University of Chicago Press, 1982.

De Sola, Ralph. *Abbreviations Dictionary.* New International Fourth Edition. New York: American Elsevier Publishing, 1974.

Dumaître, Paule. *Ambroise Paré, chirurgien de quatre rois de France.* Paris: Librairie Académique Perrin, 1986.

Durham, Carolyn A. *L'Art romanesque de Raymond Roussel.* York, S.C.: French Literature Publications, 1982.

Encyclopédie de la Pléiade. Jeux et sports. Paris: Gallimard, 1967.

Finkenstaedt, Thomas; Ernst Leisi; and Dieter Wolff. *A Chronological English Dictionary.* Heidelberg: Carl Winter Universitätverlag, 1970.

Foucault, Michel. *Death and the Labyrinth: The World of Raymond Roussel.* Trans. Charles Ruas. New York: Doubleday, 1986.

——. *The Order of Things: An Archeology of the Human Sciences.* New York: Random House, 1970.

——. *Raymond Roussel.* Paris: Gallimard, 1963.

Fowler, H. W. *Modern English Usage.* 2nd edition, revised by Sir Ernest Gowers. Oxford: Oxford University Press, 1985.

Freud, Ernst L., ed. *Letters of Sigmund Freud.* Trans. Tania and James Stern. New York: Basic Books, 1960.

Freud, Sigmund. *The Standard Edition of the Complete Psychological Works of Sigmund Freud.* 24 vols. Ed. and trans. James Strachey. New York: W. W. Norton, 1961.

Gallop, Jane. *Thinking Through the Body.* New York: Columbia University Press, 1988.

Gay, Peter. *Freud: A Life for Our Time.* New York: Norton, 1988.

Gibson, Frank. *Charles Conder: His Life and Work.* London: John Lane, 1914.

Gibson, William. *Burning Chrome.* New York: Ace Books, 1987.

——. *Count Zero.* New York: Ace Books, 1987.

——. *Mona Lisa Overdrive.* New York: Bantam Books, 1988.

——. *Neuromancer.* New York: Ace Books, 1984.

Goodman, Lanie. "Le Corps-accord roussellien: Machines à composer." *Esprit créateur* 26, no. 4 (1986).

Grands travaux, special edition of *Connaissance des arts.* Paris (1989).

Greenaway, Peter. *The Belly of an Architect.* London: Faber and Faber, 1988.

——. "The Cook and the Filmmaker, Entretien avec Peter Greenaway." *Vertigo* 5 (1990).

Heidegger, Martin. *On the Way to Language.* Trans. Peter Hertz. New York: Harper and Row, 1971.

Hoff, Ursula. *Charles Conder: His Australian Years.* Melbourne: National Gallery Society of Victoria, 1960.

Hoffmann, E. T. A. *Selected Writings of E. T. A. Hoffmann.* Ed. and trans. Leonard J. Kent and Elizabeth C. Knight. Chicago: University of Chicago Press, 1969.

Hymns and Spiritual Songs for the Little Flock. Kingston-on-Thames: Stow Hill Bible and Tract Depot, 1951.

Imbault-Huart, Marie-José. "La Renaissance, la médecine et la chirurgie." In Crenn, *Actes.*

Irigaray, Luce. *Marine Lover of Friedrich Nietzsche.* Trans. Gillian C. Gill. New York: Columbia University Press, 1991.

——. *L'Oubli de l'air chez Martin Heidegger.* Paris: Minuit, 1983.

——. *This Sex Which Is Not One.* Trans. Catherine Porter, with Carolyn Burke. Ithaca, N.Y.: Cornell University Press, 1985.

Jakobson, Roman. "Linguistics and Poetics." In Jakobson, *Selected Writings,* vol. 3. The Hague: Mouton, 1981.

Janet, Pierre. *De l'angoisse à l'extase.* Vol. 1. Paris: Librairie Félix Alcan, 1926.

Jenny, Laurent. "Structure et fonctions du cliché." *Poétique* 12 (1972).

Jones, Ernest. *The Life and Work of Sigmund Freud.* 3 vols. New York: Basic Books, 1957.

Joyce, Perrin. "Conder—'Too Many Roses?'" *International Studio* 81, no. 335 (1925).

Kerbellec, Philippe G. *Comment lire Raymond Roussel.* Paris: Jean-Jacques Pauvert, 1988.

Klossowski, Pierre. *Sade My Neighbor.* Trans. Alphonso Lingis. Evanston, Ill.: Northwestern University Press, 1991.

Kofman, Sarah. "The Double Is/And the Devil." In Kofman, *Freud and Fiction,* trans. Sarah Wykes. Boston: Northeastern University Press, 1991.

——. *Lectures de Derrida.* Paris: Galilée, 1984.

Lacan, Jacques. "The Agency of the Letter in the Unconscious." In Lacan, *Ecrits: A Selection,* trans. Alan Sheridan. New York: W. W. Norton, 1977.

Landow, George P. *Hypertext.* Baltimore: Johns Hopkins University Press, 1992.

Landow, George P., and Paul Delany. "Hypertext, Hypermedia and Literary Studies: The State of the Art." In Landow and Delany, *Hypermedia.*

——, eds. *Hypermedia and Literary Studies.* Cambridge, Mass.: MIT Press, 1991.

Leiris, Michel. Introduction. In Raymond Roussel, *Epaves.* Paris: Jean-Jacques Pauvert, 1972.

——. "Le Voyageur et son ombre." *Bizarre* 34–35 (1964).

Lloyd, Svetlana. "Golden Summers Down Under." *Art and Artists* 239 (1986).

McCaffery, Larry. "An Interview with William Gibson." In Larry McCaffery, ed., *Storming the Reality Studio.* Durham, N.C.: Duke University Press, 1991.

MacColl, D. S. "The Paintings on Silk of Charles Conder." *The International Survey* 4 (1898).

McHoul, Alec, and David Wills. *Writing Pynchon: Strategies in Fictional Analysis.* Champaign-Urbana: University of Illinois Press, 1990.

Mead, David G. "Technological Transfiguration in William Gibson's Sprawl Novels." *Extrapolation* 32, no. 4 (1991).

Miller, Nancy K. *Getting Personal.* New York: Routledge, 1991.

Moore, William. *The Story of Australian Art from the Earliest Known Art of the Continent to the Art of Today.* Sydney: Angus and Robertson, 1934.

Nelson, W. H. de B. "Charles Conder: An Appreciation." *The International Studio* 50, no. 197 (1913).

Olsen, Lance. "The Shadow of Spirit in William Gibson's Matrix Trilogy." *Extrapolation* 32, no. 3 (1991).

Ong, Walter J. *Ramus, Method, and the Decay of Dialogue.* Cambridge, Mass.: Harvard University Press, 1958.

Paré, Ambroise. *The Collected Works of Ambroise Paré, Translated out of the Latin by Thomas Johnson, from the First English Edition, London, 1634.* Pound Ridge, N.Y.: Milford House, 1968.

———. *Oeuvres* [1585]. 4 vols. Ed. Roger-Henri Guerrand and Fernande de Bissy. Paris: Union Latine d'Editions, 1977.

———. *Oeuvres complètes.* 3 vols. Ed. J.-F. Malgaigne. Paris, 1840–41; reprint, Geneva: Slatkine, 1970.

Paris 1979–1989. New York: Rizzoli, 1988.

Parkes, M. B. *Pause and Effect: An Introduction to the History of Punctuation in the West.* London: Scolar Press, 1992.

Pérec, Georges. *La Disparition.* Paris: Denoël, 1969.

Picard, Raymond. *New Criticism or New Fraud.* Trans. Frank Towne. N.p.: Washington State University Press, 1969.

———. *Nouvelle critique ou nouvelle imposture.* Paris: Jean-Jacques Pauvert, 1965.

Pierssens, Michel. *La Tour de Babil. La Fiction du signe.* Paris: Minuit, 1976.

Porush, David. "Cybernauts in Cyberspace: William Gibson's *Neuromancer.*" In George E. Slusser and Eric S. Rabkin, eds., *Aliens: The Anthropology of Science Fiction.* Carbondale: Southern Illinois University Press, 1987.

———. "Frothing the Synaptic Bath: What Puts the Punk in Cyberpunk." In George Slusser and Tom Shippey, eds., *Fiction 2000: Cyberpunk and the Future of Narrative.* Athens: University of Georgia Press, 1992.

Pynchon, Thomas. *The Crying of Lot 49.* New York: Bantam, 1976.

Ramus, Petrus. *Rhetoricae distinctiones in Quintilianum (Arguments in Rhetoric Against Quintilian).* Trans. Carole Newlands. Dekalb: Northern Illinois University Press, 1986.

Ricardou, Jean. "Disparition élocutoire." In Sciascia, ed., *Actes relatifs.*

Rimbaud, Arthur. *Complete Works, Selected Letters.* Ed. and trans. Wallace Fowlie. Chicago: University of Chicago Press, 1966.

Rosenthal, Pam. "Jacked In: Fordism, Cyberpunk, Marxism." *Socialist Review* 21, no. 1 (1991).

Ross, Andrew. "Hacking Away at the Counterculture." In Constance Penley and Andrew Ross, eds., *Technoculture.* Minneapolis: University of Minnesota Press, 1991.

Rothenstein, John. *The Artists of the 1890's.* London: George Routledge and Sons, 1928.

———. *The Life and Death of Conder*. London: Dent, 1938.

Roussel, Raymond. *Comment j'ai écrit certains de mes livres*. Paris: Jean-Jacques Pauvert, 1963.

———. *La Doublure*. Paris: Jean-Jacques Pauvert, 1963.

———. *L'Etoile au front*. Paris: Jean-Jacques Pauvert, 1963.

———. *How I Wrote Certain of My Books*. Trans. Trevor Winkfield. New York: Sun, 1975.

———. *Impressions d'Afrique*. Paris: Jean-Jacques Pauvert, 1963.

———. *Impressions of Africa*. Trans. Rayner Heppenstall and Lindy Foord. Berkeley: University of California Press, 1967.

———. *Locus solus*. Paris: Jean-Jacques Pauvert, 1965.

———. *Locus Solus*. Trans. Rupert Copeland Cunningham. Berkeley: University of California Press, 1970.

———. *Nouvelles impressions d'Afrique*. Paris: Jean-Jacques Pauvert, 1963.

———. *La Poussière de soleils*. Paris: Jean-Jacques Pauvert, 1964.

———. *The Star on the Forehead*. Trans. Paul Hammond. *Juillard* 8 (1970–71).

———. *La Vue*. Paris: Jean-Jacques Pauvert, 1963.

Roustang, François. *Un Destin si funeste*. Paris: Minuit, 1976.

———. *Dire Mastery: Discipleship from Freud to Lacan*. Trans. Ned Lukacher. Washington, D.C.: American Psychiatric Press, 1986.

Sciascia, Leonardo, ed. *Actes relatifs à la mort de Raymond Roussel*. Paris: L'Herne, 1972.

Searle, John R. *The Rediscovery of the Mind*. Cambridge, Mass.: MIT Press, 1992.

Ségal, Alain. "L'Instrumentation chirurgicale à l'époque d'Ambroise Paré." In Crenn, *Actes*.

Slatin, John. "Reading Hypertext: Order and Coherence in a New Medium." In Landow and Delany, *Hypermedia*.

Sloane, Thomas O. *Donne, Milton, and the End of Humanist Rhetoric*. Berkeley: University of California Press, 1985.

Staff, Frank. *The Penny Post 1680–1918*. London: Lutterworth Press, 1964.

———. *The Picture Postcard and Its Origins*. London: Lutterworth Press, 1979.

Stenger, Nicole. "Mind Is a Leaking Rainbow." In Benedikt, *Cyberspace*.

Stivale, Charles J. "Mille/Punks/Cyber/Plateaus: Science Fiction and Deleuzo-Guattarian 'Becomings.'" *SubStance* 66 (1991).

Thomas, D. M. *The White Hotel*. New York: Penguin, 1981.

Tomas, David. "Old Rituals for New Space: *Rites de passage* and William Gibson's Cultural Model of Cyberspace." In Benedikt, *Cyberspace*.

Torgovnick, Marianna. "Experimental Critical Writing." *Profession* (1990).

———. *Gone Primitive*. Chicago: University of Chicago Press, 1990.

Torok, Maria. "Nota Beine." In René Major, ed., *Affranchissement du transfert et de la lettre*. Paris: Editions Confrontation, 1982.

Tschumi, Bernard. "Parc de la Villette, Paris." In Andreas Papadakis, Catherine Cooke, and Andrew Benjamin, eds., *Deconstruction: Omnibus Volume*. New York: Rizzoli, 1989.

Turner, W. G. *John Nelson Darby*. London: C. A. Hammond, 1944.

Ulmer, Gregory. *Teletheory: Grammatology in the Age of Video*. New York: Routledge, 1989.

Virgil. *The Aeneid*. Trans. Frank O. Copley. New York: Bobbs-Merrill, 1965.

Weber, Max. *The Protestant Ethic and the Spirit of Capitalism*. Trans. Talcott Parsons. New York: Charles Scribner's Sons, 1952.

White, Gilbert F.; David J. Bradley; and Anne U. White. *Drawers of Water: Domestic Water Use in East Africa*. Chicago: University of Chicago Press, 1972.

Wills, David, and Alec McHoul. "Zoo-logics: Problematics of a 'Postmodern' Text and Textual Practice in a Film by Peter Greenaway." *Textual Practice* 5, no. 1 (1991).

Wilson, Thomas. *Arte of Rhetorique by Thomas Wilson*. Ed. Thomas J. Derrick. New York: Garland, 1982.

Wolfson, Louis. *Le Schizo et les langues*. Paris: Gallimard, 1970.

MERIDIAN

Crossing Aesthetics

Library of Congress
Cataloging-in-Publication Data

Wills, David, 1953–
Prosthesis / David Wills.
    p.   cm. — (Meridian : crossing aesthetics)
Includes one essay in French.
Includes bibliographical references.
ISBN 0-8047-2459-8 (cl) : ISBN 0-8047-2460-1 (pbk.)
1. Criticism. 2. Literature—History and criticism—Theory, etc.
I. Title.   II. Series: Meridian (Stanford, Calif.)
PN85.W48   1995
801'.95—dc20   94-42467   CIP
                                                            REV

♾ This book is printed on acid-free paper.
It was typeset in Adobe Garamond and
Lithos by Keystone Typesetting, Inc.